D0790719

Romance on a Global Stage

Romance on a Global Stage

Pen Pals, Virtual Ethnography,
and "Mail-Order" Marriages

NICOLE CONSTABLE

University of California Press

BERKELEY   LOS ANGELES   LONDON

"Filipino Baby"
Words and Music by Clarke Van Hess and Billy Cox
Copyright © 1940, 1968 Shapiro, Bernstein & Co., Inc., New York
Copyright renewed.
International Copyright secured. All rights reserved.
Used by permission.

"Merchant of Love" by Joan Armatrading
Copyright © 1995 Universal-Polygram International Publishing Inc.
on behalf of Giftwend Ltd. (ASCAP)
All rights reserved. Used by permission.

University of California Press
Berkeley and Los Angeles, California
University of California Press, Ltd.
London, England
© 2003 by the Regents of the University of California

Library of Congress Cataloging-in-Publication Data

Constable, Nicole.
    Romance on a global stage : pen pals, virtual ethnography, and
"mail-order" marriages / Nicole Constable.
        p.   cm.
    Includes bibliographical references and index.
    ISBN 978-0-520-23870-1 (pbk. : alk. paper)

    1. Intercountry marriage—United States.   2. Marriage
brokerage—United States.   3. Mail order brides—United States.
4. Asians—United States.   5. International correspondence—Social
aspects.   I. Title.
HQ1032.C65 2003
306.84′5—dc21   2002152989

Manufactured in the United States of America

12   11   10   09   08
10   9   8   7   6   5   4

The paper used in this publication is both acid-free and totally chlorine-
free (TCF). It meets the minimum requirements of ANSI/NISO z39.48–
1992 (R 1997) ♾

For Joe

Contents

Acknowledgments

In the course of researching, incubating, and writing this project, I have been the beneficiary of criticism, encouragement, inspiration, and support from a wide array of sources.

The University of Pittsburgh provided material support without which this project would not have been possible. This included grants for preliminary Internet research from the Faculty of Arts and Sciences and from the Asian Studies Program in 1998. Travel to the People's Republic of China and the Philippines in 1999 and 2000 was funded by the Asian Studies Program Small Grants, Chinese Studies Faculty Travel Grants, Hewlett International Small Grants Program, and the Chancellor's Distinguished Research Award. A University Center for International Studies Faculty Fellowship allowed me the luxury of writing during Fall 2001.

Numerous individuals have been tremendously helpful in facilitating my research in China and the Philippines. My friend and colleague Wenfang Tang encouraged me to add a China component to the research, helped arrange my stay in Beijing, and provided food for thought throughout the project. Shen Mingming, director of the Research Center on Contemporary China, kindly facilitated my visits to Beijing. Bell Yung generously provided me with housing in Hong Kong, and Elizabeth Sinn, deputy director of the Centre of Asian Studies, arranged for me to have access to University of Hong Kong computer and library resources. Meisheng Wu and Catherine Hu are among many women who helped make the China phase of research especially fruitful and enjoyable.

During the Philippine segments of the project, I benefitted greatly from the hospitality, assistance, and introductions of Josephine and Kenneth Meissner, Mark and Marissa Stankowitz, Joy Cobar, Ching Villamor, Corazon and Jun Canete, and the staff at the Commission on Filipinos Overseas

(CFO). Nathan Watts and the moderators and members of several Internet lists of Asian-U.S. couples were invaluable for introducing me to women and men involved in correspondence relationships, sharing information about the immigration process, introducing me to different points of view, and directing me to sources of information about correspondence on and off the Internet.

There are hundreds of Chinese women, Filipinas, and U.S. men (on and off the Internet) who shared views, stories, and opinions that are woven into the tapestry of this book. Although I do not thank them by name out of respect for their privacy, some will recognize themselves in the pages that follow, despite my use of pseudonyms. To those whose words and lives have contributed in one way or another to this book, I offer both thanks and apologies; thanks for the trust and willingness to "be studied" and to allow me to know enough to read against the grain of many common misassumptions, and apologies to those who will disagree with my representations and interpretations of their lives.

During the thinking and writing stages of this project, sections of this book were presented at the Asian American Body Workshop at the University of Illinois, Urbana-Champaign (2000); the Women's Studies Faculty Seminar at the University of Pittsburgh (2000); the "Migration and the 'Asian Family' in a Globalizing World" conference at the National University of Singapore (2001); the Anthropology Department Seminar (2001); the Association for Asian Studies Meeting, Chicago, Illinois (2001); the American Anthropological Association Meeting, Washington, D.C. (2001); the American Ethnological Society Meeting, Montreal, Canada (2001). To the organizers, discussants, and participants at these forums, I am especially grateful. In particular, I wish to thank Kathleen Erwin, Martin Manalansan, Jane Margold, Kathryn Robinson, Nobue Suzuki, James Tyner, S. Carole Vance, and Brenda Yeoh; and Kathleen Allen, Kathleen Blee, L. Keith Brown, Maureen Greenwald, Marianne Novy, Frayda Cohen, Abby Margolis, Kevin Ming, Connie Oxford, Amy Speier, Leah Voors, and Nell Zhang at the University of Pittsburgh. I am grateful to Naomi Schneider and Sheila Levine, editors at the University of California Press, and the anonymous reviewers. Nancy Abelmann has been a constant source of inspiration and intellectual sustenance. Antoinette Constable, Marianne Constable, and the late William A. Shack each contributed in obvious and subtle ways.

I thank Nathaniel and Peter Constable Alter for the welcome (and not so welcome) distractions from my computer, and for lessons they have taught me that go far beyond the pages of any book. Finally, this book is dedicated with love to Joseph S. Alter, who has lived with a western feminist for almost two decades, in peace, harmony, and with very little complaint.

Introduction

This project was conceived during a period of post-tenure freedom and mid-life academic and personal questioning. I had recently finished a book about Filipina domestic workers in Hong Kong and was looking for a new project, one that would allow me to follow up on intellectual issues that were not fully explored in my earlier work and that fit with my practical concerns. I was interested in globalization and transnationalism—as opposed to unidirectional approaches to migration—and in ideas about the intersections of political economy with everyday lives. My interest in gender, sexuality, love, and romance in cross-cultural perspective joined with a newfound interest in marriage, kinship, and the family. As an academic, I had come to question the place of anthropology in a postcolonial world, and I was increasingly attracted to what anthropologists have called "feminist ethnography."

On a practical level, I was at a stage of my life when it was not feasible to undertake prolonged stints of field research that would interrupt my children's schooling, nor did I desire to spend long periods of time away from home. A project with a "local" component would suit both my pragmatic and my intellectual concerns. As an anthropologist, I wanted a project that would lend itself to an analysis of transnational flows and exchanges of people and ideas, one that would allow for a critique of binary constructions of "them" and "us," allowing me to contribute to a critique of anthropological representations of our subjects as ethnographic or cultural others. As a feminist of sorts, with certain leanings toward postmodernism as well as a critical appreciation of political economy, I sought a project that would allow me to question the limits of my commitment to feminism, to further explore relations of gender and power within a context of migration and shifting global boundaries. Unwilling to give up ethnographic research, a

1

cornerstone of anthropology with certain advantages over more purely discursive cultural studies, I aimed to design a project through which I could explore gender, transnationalism, and globalization, and also raise issues of epistemology, methodology, and ethnographic writing.

When I began this project, I was not fully aware of the problems inherent in the terms "mail-order brides" or "mail-order marriages," and I was unaware that many people who are—or whose marriages are—labeled as such take offense at the terms (often for good reason). In the course of my research on domestic workers, I was struck by the number of Filipina overseas contract workers (OCWs) I met in Hong Kong who wrote to pen pals abroad. Most of them had met their pen pals through magazines and agencies, or through friends who passed on the names and addresses of men whose letters they had received, but most had yet to meet their pen pals in person. They harbored hopes of meeting face-to-face and, if all went well, imagined marrying and going to live abroad. At the time, I took note of this phenomenon but paid little close attention. In 1998, my interest took a more serious turn. I had agreed to talk about *Maid to Order in Hong Kong* at a local Borders bookstore, and at the end of the talk I met "Ben."

A tall man with blue jeans and long hair, in his early fifties, Ben would not have been out of place at a Berkeley bookstore, but he stood out in the suburbs of Pittsburgh. A law professor with a remarkably open attitude toward anthropological research, he introduced himself as someone who had just become engaged to a Filipina whom he had met by way of a pen pal introduction service. After a brief conversation, Ben readily agreed to be interviewed. Like many anthropological "key informants," he became an important entrée for me into the community of Filipino-American couples and into both the real and the virtual communities of men and women who have met and courted via correspondence.

In some ways Ben fit the popular stereotype of men who pursue relationships with women abroad: he had been married and divorced twice, he was middle-aged, and although outgoing, he did not feel comfortable meeting women at bars and parties. In other ways, he did not fit the image of "losers and sociopaths" who are rumored to pursue this route to finding a wife. He was a highly articulate and insightful, educated professional; his politics were in many ways left-leaning; he considered himself a feminist of sorts or was at least sympathetic to certain feminist concerns, and he was not unattractive. Why would Ben (and tens of thousands of U.S. men), I wondered, decide to subscribe to a magazine or an Internet agency and write to women thousands of miles away in the hopes of finding a spouse? Were there reasons—besides the stereotypical issues of poverty and desperation—why a young, attractive woman like Rosie would write to Ben, a man twenty-five years her senior, and in the course of their first face-to-face meeting, agree to marry him? The answers I found, in their case as in others, were not always—or not simply—the expected ones.

Throughout the 1990s, the number of Filipinas listed by recruitment agencies has continued to grow, despite passage of Republic Act 6955 in the Philippines in 1990, which prohibits recruitment of Filipinas for marriage to foreign nationals. Filipinas, followed by Eastern European women and women from the former Soviet Union, are the most numerous nationalities listed by introduction agencies. By the 1990s, Chinese women from the People's Republic of China (PRC) were also drawing the attention of pen pal services and U.S. men in search of foreign marriage partners, and their numbers continue to increase. I thus began to design a multisited research project that focused on the experiences and perspectives of Chinese and Filipino women and men from the United States. The research included more conventional anthropological interviews, participant observation, and face-to-face encounters in China, the Philippines, and the United States, and also a less conventional component of virtual ethnography—fieldwork from my computer—in the electronic, mass-mediated community of those involved in global correspondence relationships.

For about three years, beginning in 1998, from my home or university computer in Pittsburgh, as well as from the University of Hong Kong library and at cyber-cafés in Hong Kong, Beijing, Manila, Cebu, and Butuan, I communicated via the Internet with several hundred men and women who were involved in correspondence relationships. I initially contacted about forty women from China and forty from the Philippines through one of over 350 marriage-oriented introduction agencies listed on the Internet. Many of these women I met and got to know in person in 1999 and 2000. Others were introduced to me by their friends or partners. I was granted permission as a researcher to join four private lists whose members were mainly men with Filipina or Chinese wives, fiancées, or girlfriends. As a subscriber to these lists, I met several hundred men. I got to know about thirty men through repeated communications, including private e-mails; about twenty others, like Ben, I met and got to know in person. In the course of my research I followed private chats and news groups, studied online introduction services, examined personal web pages and photographs, and communicated through the Internet. At the peak of the research, I received over a hundred e-mail messages a day and communicated with men and women from all over the United States and from different regions of China and the Philippines.

Although meeting marriage partners from abroad is not new, the Internet has fueled a global imagination and created a time-space compression that has greatly increased the scope and efficiency of introductions and communication between men and women from different parts of the world. As such, it is integrally associated with transnationalism and globalization, and presents many new challenges for ethnographic research. One problem I faced, for example, was knowing when to stop. In contrast to anthropological field research in a faraway place that is bounded in time and space and has a more definite beginning (when one steps off the plane) and end (when one says good-bye and returns home), virtual ethnography enters one's home and office, blurs the boundaries between here and there, and threatens to draw in the researcher in such a way that she risks going native in virtual space, neglecting the ultimate task of writing.

The topic of correspondence courtship and marriage between U.S. men and Filipinas or Chinese women has allowed me to address questions about gender and power in ways that my prior research on domestic workers did not. Although most reviewers recognized my work on Filipina domestic workers as a feminist study—one that deals with the subtle articulations of gender, class, nationality, and power—one reviewer suggested that I had not fully utilized feminist theory. Another commented that I had focused almost exclusively on the perspectives of the workers, but had (admittedly) not represented employers in such a comprehensive manner. In formulating this study, I could not ignore feminism for two main reasons. First, any analysis of correspondence courtship involving western men and foreign women would require that I grapple with feminist and popular ideas about universal gender inequality, the "traffic in women," and marriage as an oppressive patriarchal institution. Among the most common, yet problematic, of various feminist perspectives on the issue of correspondence marriages are those that assume "mail-order brides" to be a singularly oppressed category of victimized women who are "trafficked" and in need of rescue. Second, to many men "the western feminist" (often characterized as a singular type with a single perspective) represented the antithesis of the Asian women they are courting. Western feminists—and the putative damage they have done to the western family and gender roles—were often cited by men as one of the factors that motivated them to look for a foreign spouse. Thus I analyze both men's critical, often hostile, views of feminists and feminism, and also feminists' critiques of correspondence relationships.

Contemporary feminist theories provided tools with which to understand international correspondence relationships. Rather than focus on women and universal female subordination, contemporary feminist concerns lie in understanding gendered heterogeneity and differences that are complicated by class, nationality, race, and so on. Rather than view women as simply dominated by men, attention is paid to more complex and subtle articulations of power, as well as to the way in which institutions and processes (such as immigration and citizenship) may be engendered. Power, in other words, is not something men "have" and women do not. The more I learned about correspondence relationships, the more inadequate binary notions of "women's oppression" or "male domination" seemed, and the more important contemporary feminist concerns with power, ideology, representation, and positionality became.

As with my focus on domestic workers, in which I justified my relative omission of employers' perspectives on the basis that domestic workers were the ones whose voices were often unheard, I was tempted to focus exclusively on the views of Filipinas and Chinese women and to ignore the men except as they were represented by women. Women who are labeled "mail-order brides" appeared to me to be less fairly represented, less well understood, and at a disadvantage in having their voices and their perspectives heard compared to the men. Often women are spoken for or about, but their own perspectives are difficult to discern. ABS-CBN News, a Filipino online news web site discussed in chapter 2, describes "the typical Filipina mail order bride" as one who "believes that marrying a foreigner is her ticket out of poverty." Such marriages may "lead to a descending hell of spousal abuse or white slavery. Yet still the march goes on—of young Filipinas eager to sell body and soul for a way out of the country. As one Filipina succinctly says, better to be a foreigner's whore than a pauper's wife."[1] The "mail order bride industry" is often depicted as "a microcosm of the larger international sex industry."[2] Women are often portrayed (in contrast to the ABS-CBN quotation above) not as making an active choice, but as passive pawns in a larger game that denies them agency. Women are said to have no choice but to "sell themselves" as brides: "Amidst poverty and oppression, the promise of the good life as touted by the matchmakers and reports of 'success' by friends who opted for life outside the Philippines have influenced, even forced, women to seek future mates through the mail. They see Americans as their 'knights in shining armor' who will snatch them away from their life of poverty and oppression."[3] Given such simplistic depictions of women and their motivations, it was tempting to focus solely on their side of the picture. I thought it would be easier to empathize with them, and render them more understandable and sympathetic, than with the men. One of my main objectives was to explore ways in which women made informed, logical choices from an array of available yet structurally limited options.

It would have been easier to avoid the men, except as seen through the eyes of women. One could argue that there is less need to present the men's side of the picture, and that it would be difficult to maintain sufficient objectivity in representing them. Yet this is not the case. Men and their perspectives, I learned, are—like the women—often misunderstood or glossed in stark and stereotypical terms. Men are depicted, for example, as "buying" brides, as wanting women they can control and exert power over; they are said to want women who are subservient, submissive combinations of sex slave and domestic servant.[4] Among the best known images of men who met their spouses through correspondence are those who have received significant media coverage, for example Terry Nichols (convicted in the Oklahoma City bombing) and Timothy Blackwell (who shot and killed his estranged Filipina wife and two of her friends in a Seattle courtroom). Yet these cases, as well as less famous ones designed to shock and titillate on the talk show circuits, are far from representative. Heeding the old but important critique that gender studies should not focus exclusively on women, and that gender involves ideologies, roles, and relations, I decided to include men as an integral and necessary part of this study.

To try to understand and be fair to the men and their perspectives posed at times a serious challenge. The suspicion and overt hostility that some men directed toward me and my research, their derogatory views of western women, their demeaning images of foreign women, and the occasional cases that seemed to fit the worst stereotypes were sometimes difficult to stomach. Some men I met in person were not, to my mind, at all likable. Yet there were also many pleasant surprises. Some men welcomed an effort to "set the balance straight" about them and their relationships and were extremely open and helpful. Many put aside their preconceptions about me, overlooked my intrusions into their lives, introduced me to their wives, told me their life stories, and shared personal details about their relationships. The questions they posed about my research and my accountability were more challenging than any academic audience or professional review process I have ever faced.

I have come to see the men involved in correspondence relationships as a very diverse group of people; many are decent and well-intentioned human beings who have learned a great deal in the process of their relationships. Many men, for example, experienced a brief but significant sense of helplessness, loss of independence, and often dependency on their girlfriends or fiancées as they traveled outside the United States (often for the first time) to meet their pen pals. On Internet discussion groups, such men reminded each other that their own disorientation abroad is just a fraction of what their wives are likely to encounter in the United States. When one man expressed relief upon returning to the United States, another urged him to remember these feelings when his "loved one" is lonely or home-sick in America. Some men demonstrated strong interest in learning about their partner's culture; a few explored possibilities of settling abroad. Many went to great lengths to ensure their partner's comfort and happiness in the United States. Some went so far as to move to a different city or state so that their wives would feel less isolated and would have the support of a lo-cal Chinese or Filipino community. As the mostly non-Asian partners of Asian women, some men reflected on their first encounters with racism in the United States and abroad, and many came to question their presump-tions about the privileges of race, nationality, and gender in relation to the immigration process. For some, the experience of meeting a foreign part-ner was accompanied by a greater awareness of and sensitivity to differ-ences and dislocations of various sorts. Others, it seemed, were far more callous or naive in their expectations, and their desires for and presump-tions about masculine power and authority remained intact.

One problem with including men's perspectives is that they risk becom-ing dominant, taking over the text. When men spoke about their experi-ences and those of their partners, they often did so in authoritative voices. Many claimed to speak for the women they knew. Men often signed their e-mail messages to me and to the list as a couple, although the messages were often just from the men. Aware of this risk, I have struggled to bal-ance it in the research by addressing women in private, away from their partners as much as possible, and in my writing by treating men's and women's voices as multiple. Just as there is no one woman's experience, men's perspectives and experiences are also varied.

Although I aim to be fair to people in this study, certain biases are in-evitable. I have chosen to focus mainly on the less-known, more common, yet less sensationalist side of correspondence marriages. What many peo-ple "know" about "mail-order marriages" are the stories—such as those of Timothy and Susana Blackwell—that are publicized because they involve murder, violence, or domestic abuse, or the sensationalist cases of teenage women who speak no English and serve as maids and sexual partners for elderly men who end up on the popular talk show circuit, or wives who are suspected of marrying their husbands to acquire a green card.[5] Such stories are well-known, important, and sometimes heart-breaking, but they are hardly representative, nor are they unbiased in their presentation.[6]

There is another, little-known but much more common, side of the picture. It involves less intrigue, and less sex and violence. It involves more of the everyday challenges that take on new meaning when lives are transplanted to another part of the world; more of the challenges of dealing with the Immigration and Naturalization Service (INS) and its masses of paperwork and bureaucratic red tape; more of the challenges of getting to know someone at a distance and learning to deal with his or her flaws and imperfections face-to-face; and more of the challenges of waiting for months, sometimes years, before a fiancée can come to the United States or a married couple can live together. Once in the United States, for women, it involves adjustments to things that appear minor to many Americans, yet are in fact highly significant, such as where to buy the "right" kind of rice or fresh fish, streets and neighborhoods that seem abnormally quiet and unfriendly, a new schedule that may include remaining at home alone for most of the day. A woman's sense of loneliness and dependency on her husband may last for varying periods of time, depending on a wide array of factors. The frustrations, necessary patience, and high degree of commitment that is necessary to see this process through are among the issues that these couples face. It is this less-known, more mundane side of the phenomenon that I aim to convey. As one U.S. man married to a Filipina wrote on an online news chat forum, "We only read about the abusive situations and the men who take advantage of their foreign wives because stories like Nathan's and mine . . . and the Fil-Am couples that I know in the United States who have loving relationships *don't* *sell* *newspapers*!!! How about this for a headline: 'MAN LOVES WIFE HE MET THROUGH A PEN-PAL AGENCY, TRIES HARD TO TREAT HER RIGHT.' Yawn."[7] It is my hope that, in contrast to the popular media, scholarly books are of interest despite a lack of sensationalism. As I explained to members of an Internet chat group, scholarly studies have less pressure to sensationalize and can therefore potentially reveal the problems and inaccuracies of popular representations.

Besides looking at the wider historical and political-economic context in which such relationships are imagined and experienced, I stress that this study focuses primarily on the views and experiences of Chinese and Filipino women and U.S. men who are contemplating correspondence, in the process of correspondence, recently married, or about to be reunited. I do not examine marriages in the United States in any detail. This book ends where the stories of these couples' marriages begin.[8]

There are some costs to my approach, and I anticipate criticisms from different sides. I have no doubt that whatever I write, some of the men will feel seriously maligned. For some of them, this book will represent yet another feminist study by a researcher who has betrayed their trust by not painting them all in glowing colors. Others may be disappointed that this is not a quantitative, empirical study that scientifically "proves" that their motives are good and their marriages more likely to succeed, or that provides them with a list of useful tips on how to make their marriages work. Some participants in this research had an exaggerated notion of the power of one ethnographer. As one man wrote (I paraphrase): "I hope your work will help convince the world that we are not a bunch of weirdos and losers and that these marriages are happier and more successful than others." Aside from his distorted impression of the audience for an academic monograph, happiness and success are difficult to measure.

From a very different vantage point, others have questioned the need to speak for the men involved in these relationships, since they are commonly assumed to have the power to speak for themselves. As mentioned above, however, that is not entirely true. Were it true, I would not continue to encounter the same tired stereotypes of men (and women) in feminist, scholarly, and popular work. Although men may indeed—largely by virtue of education and class privilege—have greater opportunities to air their views, especially on the Internet, their opinions do not circulate far into the larger public, and they are left, as one man put it, "preaching to the church choir." Just as women I met do not fit the image of "mail-order brides," the men do not fit the image of all-powerful, dominant white males. If this study succeeds in its humanistic project of depicting women as something other than mail-order brides, desperate victims, or hyperagents, motivated solely by economic hardship and desperation and willing to marry any western man who approaches them, and if the men (many of them, anyway) can be seen as something other than simply consumers of women as commodities, then this work will have succeeded, at least in part. My aim is to allow the men and women to emerge as a diverse group, with different opinions, experiences, and motivations, and yet to also see them within a particular historical and global context as people who both exert power and are subject to it.

Another criticism I anticipate is that I have elided the more urgent issue of domestic abuse. Immigrant women can be, for very specific reasons, more vulnerable to abuse by their husbands than women who are citizens.[9] By focusing mainly on other issues here, I do not intend to deny the existence of such serious problems. However, a better understanding of the diversity of these relationships should ultimately help to produce more realistic views and legislation and support the creation of fewer bureaucratic stumbling blocks for U.S.-foreign marriages, fewer obstacles to U.S. immigration, and looser restrictions on citizenship requirements. As Uma Narayan has argued, greater policing of marriages and more bureaucratic red tape for these couples may prevent such marriages, but they will not prevent domestic abuse.[10]

Images of "mail-order brides" as docile victims, reproduced in feminist writing and in the popular media, may inadvertently perpetuate the very images that appeal to men who are more inclined to control or abuse women. If images of Asian women as active agents who will not submit to or tolerate violence were more prevalent, perhaps men who aim to control and abuse women might not so readily look to Asia for spouses. As one man told me, "If other Chinese women are anything like my wife, some of these men who expect Chinese women to be meek and obedient are in for a very rude awakening!" Deconstructing hegemonic images of "mail-order brides" or of men and women who meet through correspondence may not provide a solution to the problem of domestic abuse, but it may constitute one step in that direction.

The persistent negative stereotypes of "mail-order marriages" that have taken root and are perpetuated in many corners of society provide an opportunity for reflection and critique. Why has this topic captured the U.S. popular imagination? What do correspondence relationships say about gender relations in the United States? How is the treatment of this topic symbolic of other societal fears and concerns about race, sexuality, nation, and gender? What are the wider implications of feminist writings that traffic in the same negative images of submissive Asian women that they criticize as demeaning when espoused by introduction services? What is, and what should be, the role of the state in policing transnational marriages and determining their legitimacy? Why are the laws and policies governing immigration and citizenship of foreign children adopted by U.S. citizens so different from those governing foreign spouses of U.S. nationals? How are these relationships indicative of the power relations and disciplinary regimes of transnationalism and globalization? How is political economy linked to the cultural logics of desire?

· · ·

Chapter 1 begins with stories of Moira, Netty, Faith, and Bob. Their stories contrast sharply with many popular ideas about "mail-order brides" and with many scholarly studies of "mail-order catalogs." These sketches begin to illustrate the complex motivations and experiences of "real people" behind the popular stereotypes and (mis)representations of "mail-order brides." Chapter 2 describes various Internet dimensions of my research and the rich ethnographic potential of virtual ethnography. This chapter also shows how men and women involved in correspondence relationships form an imagined global community that builds on commonalities of gender and nationality, yet also crosses national, ethnic, racial, and class boundaries. In contrast to Arjun Appadurai, who views electronic media as a means of creating imagined communities that stand largely in opposition to nation-states, this chapter considers how the Internet community both traverses and reinforces state boundaries and definitions of citizenship.[11]

Chapter 3 examines and criticizes popular images of "mail-order brides" as "trafficked women" and victims. Such representations present a skewed and partial picture that is grounded in older assumptions about gender inequality and marriage that reinforce orientalist stereotypes of Asian women and reduce "mail-order marriages" to a form of capitalist market exchange. Inspired by contemporary feminist ethnography and by feminist writings on sex work and prostitution that are particularly attentive to issues of agency, I propose a critical rethinking of such images alongside other forms of marriage and introduction.

By examining the stories of two Filipino-American couples, chapter 4 draws on, yet further critiques, feminist and cultural studies analyses of "mail-order brides" and catalogs. Two arguments run through this chapter: one is that ethnographic field research can serve as a critique of textual and discursive approaches that overemphasize the sexual dimensions of correspondence courtship and overlook women's agency; another is that the recurring fairy tale motif of a young woman who is rescued by a prince reveals tensions regarding gender, class, and marriage. Overall, I argue that these marriages paradoxically support conservative notions of gender and "family values" while simultaneously opposing conservative views about interracial relationships.

Chapter 5 turns to political economy and cultural logics of love and desire. I argue against a dichotomous or discontinuous view of love and opportunism that treats pragmatic concerns as incompatible with emotional ones. I argue that political economy is not simply a backdrop to such a study, nor is it the determining force in creating correspondence marriages, but that cultural notions of love and desire are shaped by political economy.

Chapter 6 grapples further with the issue of women's agency and the expressions of, and also limits to, women's power in relation to concerns about sex and money. This chapter also considers global hypergamy—the assumption that Asian women marry "up"—and asks, "up" in what ways and according to whom? Chinese and U.S. ideas about marriage help to explain the asymmetry of gendered geography of global hypergamy, and the "humor" surrounding the topic of relationships between Asian men and western women.

Chapter 7 places contemporary Chinese and Filipina brides and correspondence relationships within the wider context of the history of Asian immigration to the United States. Tales of waiting—poignant stories about the trials and tribulations of the immigration process—reflect the inequities of race, nationality, class, and gender in relation to migration and show how U.S. immigration policies police borders and marriages.

The concluding chapter reconsiders the advantages of the concept of transnationalism over the ideas of "trafficking," migration, and "mail-order marriages," which imply a unidirectional flow of bodies and ideas across borders. I point to different attitudes and policies regarding the immigration and citizenship of Asian adoptees and Asian brides. Such differences illustrate inequalities in the immigration process, and also the complex and contradictory ways in which migration is linked to ideas about sexuality, marriage, and family.

1 Making Introductions

> I'd travel miles and miles and miles to find the place, with
> treasures much more rich than gold.
> I just want a heart that captures my soul . . .
> I'm willing to wait for lasting treasure, with promises that
> won't ever break.
> Someone help me find the merchant of love, with a full
> guarantee.
>
> JOAN ARMATRADING, "Merchant of Love,"
> from *What's Inside*, 1995

POPULAR IMAGES

In newspapers, magazines, talk shows, and among the general public in the United States, images of so-called "mail-order brides" tend to echo two different but interconnected stereotypes of Asian women. One is the sweet and innocent, sexual-romantic "oriental doll" or "lotus blossom"; the other is the conniving, devious, and shrewd "dragon lady." These two images did not originate with contemporary Asian brides, but rather are deeply rooted in much older popular stereotypes of Asian women. Such images have long been reproduced and popularized in what Renee Tajima describes as simplistic, inaccurate, persistent, and unchanging images of Asian women over time in Hollywood films.[1] As lotus blossoms, Asian women are seen as an "utterly feminine, delicate, and welcome respites from their often loud, independent American counterparts."[2] As dragon ladies, prostitutes, and devious aggressors, they represent the threat of foreign women's hyperagency. These images underlie the simplistic, dualistic images of mail-order brides as either willing and helpless victims of controlling western men, or alternatively as shrewd foreigners out for a green card and a free meal ticket through marriage fraud and immigration scams that dupe innocent U.S. men.[3] Inaccurate though they are, such popular images of Asians and Asian-Americans are rarely far from the surface of representations of so-called mail-order brides.

A large body of scholarly work focuses on mail-order bride catalogs and the images they portray. In one of the earliest articles, Ara Wilson observes that catalogs "encourage a voyeuristic objectification of Oriental women as 'other'" in contrast to liberated western feminists.[4] Venny Villapando describes the catalogs as part of the mail-order bride business that involves "an Asian woman" who "dreams she will meet and marry someone rich and powerful, someone to rescue her and free her from poverty-stricken bondage" and "an American man" who "dreams he will meet and marry someone passive, obedient, nonthreatening, and virginal, someone to devote her entire life to him, serving him and making no demands."[5] Rona Halualani argues that mail-order bride catalogs diminish women's attempts to assert agency, and create a "collage of economic, sexual, and racial hegemonic discourses [that] celebrate dominant Anglo patriarchal capitalist ideology by fashioning an ideal product—the colonized Pilipina 'Oriental Butterfly' doll."[6] Kathryn Robinson points to the way in which catalogs present Asia as "a site of fantasy for men in an era when they feel that 'traditional' values of male pre-eminence in the family are being undermined," and Roland Tolentino considers how "the discourse of mail-order brides is situated in the historical positioning of Filipina bodies into a transnational space inscribed in colonial, militarist, and capitalist histories."[7]

Many of these authors acknowledge the limitations of studies based exclusively or primarily on catalogs. Wilson concludes with a recommendation that "the anthropological gaze must look up from the pages of the mail-order marriage catalogue to encounter the American men and Southeast Asian women beyond the representations."[8] Similarly, in an excellent critique of the market metaphor in relation to so-called "mail-order brides," Robinson recognizes that "there have been few studies that focus on the women themselves: their motivations and aspirations, how they come to advertise on the web sites, or what their experiences are once marriages have been contracted."[9] In her analysis of the Australian discourse on Filipino brides, Elizabeth Holt also points to the absence of women's voices and to the discursive absence of men and women as anything other than common stereotypes. Anna Tsing reminds us that "there is another way to read these catalogues," and Wilson and Robinson both observe that analyses of catalogs and texts leave us wondering about the "real people" behind the listings.[10]

In contrast to studies that focus more narrowly on catalogs and thus risk reducing men and women to a single voice and a single depersonalized image, this book takes a closer ethnographic look at the lives behind the catalog listings and questions simplistic images of controlling men and powerless women that are often simultaneously criticized by and reinscribed in such studies. Moira, Netty, Faith, and Bob's stories—and the stories that follow in later chapters—suggest the variety of aspirations, motivations, and experiences of women and men involved in correspondence relationships.

At various stages of the process of correspondence and courtship, women and men express initiative, make choices, and exert control. To say that they are active agents in the process of correspondence, however, is not to say that women and men are not influenced by ideologies of gender, race, and nationality, that their actions are not limited by social, structural and cultural factors. Nor is it my intent to romanticize or idealize the courtships or the marriages. The women, I hope to show, are far more than the products—or the two-dimensional reflections—of an orientalist gaze, and the men are more than consumers of—or adherents to—an orientalist fantasy.

The main purpose of this chapter is to introduce Moira, Netty, Faith, and Bob. Based on interviews, face-to-face encounters, and Internet communications that span two years or more, their stories, presented in my words, contrast sharply with many popular and scholarly ideas about mail-order brides and women in catalogs. While analyses of catalogs provide insightful critiques of gender ideologies and of the objectification and commodification of Asian women, they also reveal an important gap between scholarly interpretations of catalogs and actual lived experiences as expressed by women and men.[11] This gap provides an opening through which to begin to critically rethink and reconceptualize correspondence relationships and the notion of mail-order brides. In the course of introducing these individuals, I also provide a preliminary sense of my research methods, the interface between my face-to-face field research and my textual and Internet research, and the ways in which I was drawn into people's lives as researcher, sometimes as confidant, advisor, and friend, topics that I expand on in chapter 2. These sketches contribute to my wider argument that ethnographic research can differ in important ways from analyses that are based solely or primarily on textual sources.

MOIRA

Moira is from Beijing and is one of about forty women from China and the Philippines whom I first contacted via an Internet introduction agency in 1999 and then later met in person. As I got to know her over the course of two years, I learned why she wanted to meet an American man, her experiences with the men she had written to, her near decision to "give up" on meeting men via the Internet, and then in late summer of 2000, her correspondence with a U.S. man she thought might be "the one." Like those of many others in this book, Moira's experiences should be considered neither typical nor entirely unique.

Moira is one of many urban Chinese professionals who experienced the post-Mao reforms up close. With the PRC's "opening up" to the West and to the United States beginning in the late 1970s, economic and social relations have developed in ways that were unheard of during the Maoist era.[12] Moira knew several women who—as a result of this new openness—had met foreign men and gone to live abroad. Twenty-five years ago, due to frosty relations between communist China and the capitalist West, such relationships would not have been permissible or possible, and would not likely have been so appealing to either party. It was in this context of greater sociocultural openness and radical change that Moira wondered, when I first met her, whether she might be fortunate enough to meet the right man and share the fate of several of her friends and co-workers who now live abroad.

Like most of the women I initially met over the Internet, Moira's name was listed with a large agency aimed at introducing women of different nationalities to western men. Her listing included the following information:

Age: 45; Country: China; City: Beijing; Height: 5'5" (165 cm.); Weight: 120 lbs. (54 kg.); Smokes: no; Drinks: no; Religion: unspecified; Children: yes; Education: university; Profession: engineer; Marital status: divorced; Contact by: e-mail.

In her mid-forties, she was older than many Chinese women listed by the agency, the majority of whom were in their thirties, and she was considerably older than most Filipinas, most of whom were in their twenties or early thirties. Like many Chinese women I encountered, she was divorced and had one child. In contrast, the vast majority of Filipinas listed are single, and a few are widowed (divorce is illegal in the Philippines).

When I first saw Moira's listing, it did not include her photograph, but rather the agency's standard tiny, black-outline silhouette of a shapely woman in a short skirt and high heels, with wavy shoulder-length hair, hand on her hip, and a caption reading "sorry no picture." Moira's self-description (which she later explained had been copied almost verbatim by a number of colleagues who later submitted their own names to the agency) stated: "I am a warm-hearted, easy-going, tender, sincere, caring, educated, Chinese woman, 1.65 cm tall, 54 kg in weight, black hair. I am divorced and have a 17 years daughter. Honest, reliable, faithful, intelligent with a good sense of humor. [Looking for] a soulmate" [sic]." She listed her work unit (a state-run engineering firm), her e-mail address, and telephone numbers.

The first e-mail message I sent to Moira explained that I was a woman researcher who hoped to meet and interview Filipina and Chinese women who were in the process of writing to or trying to meet foreign pen pals. Her first response reflected confusion about who I was:

"From your letter, I wonder if you want to seek a pen pal or not? . . . My description says . . . I want to share my life with someone who appreciates being loved and wanted. My major goal in life is to make a home, have a family and fulfillment of a happy marriage. I love all the things in the family that is possible under my power. Because I enjoy the house very clean and tidy. I enjoy weaving, sewing and cooking but they are all Chinese tastes. I'm fond of flowers, green grass, sunny days, warm beaches, holding hands, slow walks, lyrics of music, slow swimming and so on. My dislike: rude people, unwashed people, liars, frivolous people, unreliable people. . . . Once again, I really want to meet a man to love and to be loved in return. If you were that man please tell me more about yourself. I am looking forward to hearing from you soon. Sincerely, Moira"

My response began: "Dear Moira, Thank you for writing back. I am sorry that my message was not clear. I am not looking for a marriage partner. I am a woman (lady) professor who is doing research about correspondence marriage." She answered promptly and apologized for her mistake. "I am already making you as my friend, although we haven't seen each other. I hope you do too," she wrote, "Hope to see you soon." We corresponded several times and she expressed interest in helping with my research. We met at her workplace in Beijing in the summer of 1999 and numerous times in 2000, and kept in touch via e-mail while I was in the United States. During my visits we spent many hours together and I had the opportunity to get to know her, her co-worker Lu, and other women she knew who were writing to pen pals abroad.

On a July morning in 1999, in the middle of a severe heat wave, Moira met me at the gate of her work unit. The large enclosed compound housed residences, office buildings, dining halls, and large grassy areas. Moira showed me where I could park my bicycle and accompanied me to her office in a spacious, air-conditioned, multistory brick building. She offered me tea and showed me her desk, her computer, and photographs of herself and her co-workers. She gave me a glossy brochure that described her work unit, and showed me around the neatly manicured grounds, which included a huge statue of Chairman Mao. With a very pale, wide face, Moira was stylish but conservatively dressed by contemporary Chinese standards, and wore only a touch of makeup. She seemed very organized, with a cheerful and outgoing personality. Her spoken English was better than her written English. Although her occupation was listed by the agency as "engineer," her job actually entailed making arrangements for foreign engineers (often

Russians), coordinating their meetings with their Chinese counterparts, helping them to communicate, and making sure they knew their way around the institute's guest house and facilities. She was sometimes extremely busy at work; other times she had time to chat with co-workers, write to pen pals, or meet with visitors.

Our visit, the first of many, lasted several hours. Moira agreed to be interviewed, and I jotted down notes as she spoke. Later we had many less structured conversations over meals, on outings, or in her office, about pen pals, her life, and her friends. She introduced me to several colleagues: a woman who had lived in Texas with her Chinese husband for several years; Lu, who was listed with the same introduction agency and was corresponding with many of the same men as Moira, and toward whom Moira felt quite competitive; and another—a man—who had listed his wife with the agency using a description very much like Moira's, in the hopes that she would meet someone else, divorce him, and leave. Moira confirmed that his wife was not a pleasant person and she spoke little English, so he wrote to pen pals on her behalf and with her full knowledge. Puzzled by this story, I wondered whether he planned to use his wife as a way to get to the United States himself. Moira doubted it, and simply thought that his wife had agreed to leave him on condition that she find a foreign husband.

Like many Chinese women I met, Moira was divorced, and her parents had suffered during the turmoil and tragedy of the Cultural Revolution (1966–76). As engineers, intellectuals, and experts, Moira's parents were criticized and sent to work in labor camps in the northern oil fields, where they underwent political reeducation. Moira and her elder sister went to work in the countryside, where they remained for several years. In the 1960s, as a teenager, Moira went to work in a rural factory for five years, followed by two and a half years in the army, and then in the mid-1970s, when the worst of the Cultural Revolution was over, she attended a year and a half of college, mainly studying English. In 1979 she went to work in a Beijing factory. There she met her husband, a co-worker at the factory, and they were married in 1980.

Moira described her marriage and divorce in sad, hushed tones. She had been married for thirteen years when she learned of her husband's infidelity. Deeply hurt and unable to trust him, she filed for divorce in 1993, a time when the divorce rate in China was beginning to rise and divorce was no longer quite as shameful and humiliating as it had been before. As she recalled, "maybe it was a mistake to divorce him" since he never remarried, but she "didn't love him anymore, couldn't trust him, and felt deeply hurt."

Her parents urged her to meet other men, but it was "difficult to open my heart to someone else."

Like many other divorced Chinese women in their thirties and forties, Moira commented on the difficulty of meeting suitable local men. Many single men her age or a bit older are interested in much younger women or have little interest in remarrying. Jen, manager of a pen pal agency in Beijing, echoed similar sentiments. As she explained, "The women who are in the most difficult situation in China are those who are educated, professional women in their mid-thirties and forties or older who are divorced. Local men want younger women and often are not comfortable with a woman who is successful or who earns more money than they do." From her experience working at the agency, Jen found western men to be less interested in very young women than Chinese men were.

Moira did not trust local men and thought foreign men might be different. She reasoned that since Americans are often well off, they would not be interested in her for her money or her flat, and since divorce is common in the United States, they would not look down on her for being divorced. Thus, when Lu suggested she write to foreign men to "help her to forget the past," she gave it a try. When I first spoke to her, Moira was optimistic. This would help her "change my life, find a good man, leave this place, and forget."

In the summer of 2000, she spoke of giving up her comfortable white-collar job and the small but newly remodeled apartment she owned. As we sat in her air-conditioned living room, sheltered from the Beijing heat, her miniature Pekinese dog scratched at our legs, and I stared at the newly papered, wall-to-wall image of what appeared to be a scene from the Swiss Alps. Moira said she would be happy to work very hard in the United States if she met the right person. She dreamed of opening a small restaurant, even just a small food truck at first, if she met a man who was supportive of this plan. But she would be willing to stay at home and cook and clean if her husband preferred. To my initial surprise, yet like many Chinese women who prefer not to work, Moira seemed quite willing to quit her job and commit herself to a husband.[13] Having her own business, no matter how small, or becoming a housewife was to her—under the right circumstances—preferable to her current situation, in which she was reasonably well paid and comfortable, but stuck in a job that seemed to hold little opportunity or chance of advancement. Her lack of work satisfaction and her status as a divorced woman were key factors in her desire to meet a foreign man and go abroad. She imagined America as a more "modern" place with more open-minded people, where she could escape her past and begin anew.

Moira and Lu knew four women who were engaged or married to their pen pals. One was living with her husband in Germany and seemed very happy. A second, whom I had the chance to meet in 2000, was married to a Chinese-American man but remained in China for the time being. She was ambivalent about leaving Beijing, and it was unclear whether he felt any urgency about bringing her to the United States. A third woman was awaiting her fiancée visa. Although she was not certain that she would marry her fiancé, she had agreed to visit him in the United States and to decide whether or not to marry him when she was there.[14] The fourth woman—whom Lu and Moira worried about—had left for New Jersey on a fiancée visa two years earlier. She did not write often, but her communications expressed dissatisfaction. Her husband was an automobile mechanic who was not highly motivated. His wife was frustrated by his lack of diligence and frugality. She had begun to work part-time as a clerk, to save money, but he spent what money she earned and she was concerned about their future.

The men Moira had written to in 1999 and early 2000 were disappointing. When she wrote and asked, "Am I the only one?" they either stopped writing or she stopped writing to them. Meanwhile, Lu (who received letters from some of the same pen pals) received three male visitors from the United States. The first had written to Moira for a while, and she was unimpressed by him in person. The other flirted with Moira although he had come to visit Lu; this bothered Moira, it seemed, more than it bothered Lu. Lu was not interested in him and she encouraged Moira to write to him, but she had no desire to do so. The third was an ex-convict whom Lu liked but considered too risky.

Moira and Lu described various men, asking my reaction and trying not to give away their opinions. One U.S. man had sent Lu photographs of his family, his home, and of his Chinese ex- fiancée at their engagement party in the United States before she had called off the engagement and returned to China. What did I think of that? Another sent Lu photographs and magazine clippings of women dressed in the style he preferred. As he explained to Lu, in his role as company manager he attended many formal functions, and required a partner who was stylish and elegant to help entertain his clients. He asked for Lu's dress size and measurements. As we spoke, I noticed Lu had lost some weight since the year before, and she wore a loose, dark brown, polyester pant suit, and a touch of makeup. I asked how she felt about him wanting to dress her in a certain way. Both she and Moira rolled their eyes, grimaced, and burst out giggling. They agreed that none of these men seemed worth the trouble.

Lu was a few years older than Moira, was also divorced, and had a son in his early twenties. She had been married for ten years. Her ex-husband had a violent temper and was verbally and physically abusive. After her divorce, she was involved with a Chinese man for almost nine years; two years earlier he had left her for a much younger woman with whom he now lived, unmarried. I had originally contacted Lu at the same time I had written to Moira, but she did not respond. Only later and coincidentally did I meet her.

I clearly remembered Lu's photograph because I had been surprised to learn that she was in her late forties. The photograph was, as Moira put it (with some resentment), "a glamour shot" or an "art photo" that made Lu look twenty years younger and bore little resemblance to her in person. While sending this photograph could be interpreted as simply an attempt to attract greater male attention, there is a cultural side to the story that may not be so obvious. Chinese studio shots—which I was told spread to China from Hong Kong and Taiwan—have gained great popularity in recent years. These photographs have different implications than professional photographs in the United States. In a Chinese studio shot, a woman or man might look radically different from her or his everyday self. The subjects of these photographs often resemble models or movie stars, an image that is enhanced with make-up, costumes, props, air brushing, and photo enhancement. Such photographs are expensive and often prominently displayed (sometimes poster size) as status symbols in homes. To look "one's best" even if it does not look "like you," is not considered wrong or dishonest. While in the West the aim of a professional photograph is to make the person look as attractive as possible, it is also expected to capture a "likeness" of the person and to remain inherently recognizable. This photograph made Lu look like a dashing rock star in her twenties, not a woman approaching fifty. As such it portrayed an imaginary self.

As a result of the stunning studio photograph, Lu received several dozen letters. She answered seven, but her English was not as good as Moira's, and after a few communications, men complained that she did not write often enough. Only later—when men expressed interest in her appearance and asked for more photographs—did Lu begin to realize that they seemed to lack an understanding of the likely distance between her everyday appearance and the glamour shot. She became concerned about attracting a man for superficial reasons, and once asked me point-blank, "Do American men care much about women's bodies?" Eventually she sent her pen pals some more "natural" shots, at which point several seemed to lose interest. Indeed, many men sought "attractive" women and were wary of being duped by a photograph. Moira told me a cautionary tale she had heard from a friend about a foreign man who had sent a picture of a handsome model cut out from a magazine. When his pen pal met him in person he turned out to be ugly, old, and bald. His pen pal walked right out of the airport lobby and refused to speak to him. I heard similar tales from men as well.

Moira and Lu contrast with many common stereotypes of mail-order brides. They submitted their names and information to the agency on their own initiative, without familial or economic pressure, after learning about the procedure from friends and colleagues. They selected which information and which photographs to list, and the information was not edited or changed. Tsing argues that "the catalogues, like much scholarship, create a gaze in which we victimize and homogenize," and she urges us to see that "the photographs and letters that American men interpret as signs of sexy selflessness are, for the women who chose to send them in, features of a search for self-actualization."[15] As I argue later, all men do not read these images in the same way, yet I agree with Tsing that women's listings and their own intentions often resist common assumptions of "sexy selflessness" or that they are "exotic, docile and poor."[16]

Moira and Lu had good jobs, reasonable salaries by local standards, and comfortable lifestyles. Both thought going abroad would be a good opportunity for their children, but in neither case was this their main motivation. Their children's fathers were in Beijing and both hoped, but neither took for granted, that their children would go abroad. Both were motivated in part by dissatisfaction with romantic relationships in China and with their limited romantic possibilities as middle-aged, divorced women, and they hoped to find more suitable men abroad. Unlike many other Chinese women I spoke to, neither Moira nor Lu expressed a preference for men in white-collar positions. They preferred men who posted clean-cut looking photographs of themselves in a suit and tie, and balked at pictures of men in muscle shirts or tank tops showing off tattoos. They claimed that hardworking, honest men in any occupation would be okay.[17]

In the late summer of 2000, shortly after I received Moira's e-mail saying she was giving up on pen pals, she began writing to Pat, a fifty-five-year-old businessman from South Carolina. She wrote to say that she had finally met a very nice man and that she had given him my telephone number, so that I could tell him more about her. He phoned my office. At first it was reminiscent of giving a job recommendation for a student, but soon he seemed more eager to impress me with *his* qualifications, government connections, finances, and his suitability for Moira. He said he was very well off, and the person he married would not need to work, but could if she wanted to. He described himself as physically fit, and a "Southern gentleman" who held women in very high regard, put them on a pedestal, considered them equals. He was a "kind and romantic man" who would "always do right by her." He liked Moira and hoped to arrange for her to visit. When he learned that it would be extremely difficult for her, as a PRC citizen, to get a tourist visa to come to the United States, he went to visit her instead.

NETTY

Like Moira, Netty is a professional Chinese woman; she owns her own flat and listed her name with several introduction agencies. The differences between Moira and Netty, however, are greater than their similarities. Netty is an extremely fashionable and stylish Cantonese woman who works as an office manager in a small firm in Hong Kong's Central District. She was born and raised in the (then) British colony. When I met her she was forty, but she had listed her age as thirty-four because, in her words, "people always think I'm much younger than I look." She received about fifteen or twenty messages a day, most of them from men in Hong Kong. Most were not from the agency through which I had contacted her and Moira but through a less marriage-oriented and more dating-type list.[18] Netty said she deleted the majority of the messages she received, especially those from Chinese men, any men with "dark skin," or any men whom she considered unattractive.[19] She did not automatically delete messages from older men, as long as they were attractive, or from men who were married or divorced, although as far as she knew, she had not arranged to meet any married men in person. So far, she had agreed to meet in person ten men she had corresponded with through the Internet. Several were expatriates who lived and worked in Hong Kong; the rest were in Hong Kong for conferences or business.

Netty's friends describe her as "formidable," and she is indeed stylish and self-assured. She suggested we meet for a drink at an upscale bar in the Central District. The clientele was largely non-Chinese professionals. She knew the waiters by name and ordered her usual nonalcoholic mixed drink. I ordered the same and was shocked to find that our two drinks cost well over US$25. She answered my interview questions and described one man who wanted her to come to the United States and marry him. When she asked him flippantly, "How do you expect me to do that?" he answered, "It's simple. One, put all your stuff in storage; two, say good-bye to your family and friends and have a big party; three, come and join me." She laughed and shrugged him off. "He wouldn't even come and see me first!" She was appalled that he imagined she would drop her job, her friends, her career, her dog, and even her hamsters. She imagined such women might exist, but she was not one of them. She hoped to meet a different sort of man: one who was romantic and gentlemanly, one who might fit into her life in Hong Kong on a short-term basis.

Netty was unique among the women I encountered because she claimed she was not looking for a "lifetime partner." Her goal, she said, was to have fun, not to marry. Although she later backtracked on this point and expressed some ambivalence, she was not optimistic about meeting a marriage partner and she doubted that she was the marrying type. She wanted to have a good time, and if she happened to meet the "one," so be it. She was not attracted to Chinese men and preferred westerners or Europeans of any nationality. Living in Hong Kong, she had many opportunities to meet foreign and expatriate men. She found them "more handsome, more romantic, and more chivalrous" than local men. She pointed to a group of Cantonese businessmen who had entered the bar. "See how unattractive they are?" she said. "Western men open doors for you, compliment you, and take care of you. Local men only do this until they get you into bed."

While I was in Hong Kong, Netty was looking forward to meeting Len, an Australian banker who was in town for a week on business. By e-mail, he seemed interesting, but as she explained, "you never know how it will be in person," so she always leaves herself an "out." Netty agreed to meet him at his room in an upscale Tsimshatsui hotel where he drank a beer and she drank mango juice as they watched *You've Got Mail* on the pay-per-view television. After about an hour Len whispered in her ear and tried to kiss her. She became annoyed and told him it was difficult to watch the movie, but his advances continued. Shortly afterwards her cell phone rang; she answered it, abruptly made her apologies, and left. The first time she meets a man she always arranges for a friend to call her about an hour into the date. If she likes him, she lets the call go. If not, she tells her date that her father has just been admitted into the hospital for heart surgery. She told Len she had to rush to the hospital and assured him that if her father pulled through she would be in touch in a few days and would try to meet him for dinner before he left town.

Netty urged me to accompany her on her second and final date with Len.

As she explained, she couldn't stand to be alone with him, but he had offered to buy us dinner, and it would be good for my research. She had told him I was a friend whom she wanted to spend time with before I left town, and under pressure, Len had invited me along. Each time Len stepped outside for a cigarette (she insisted he not smoke in the restaurant), Netty talked about a Danish man whom she had recently met from the Internet. Originally she had told him she couldn't see him because a friend had come to visit for the week, but after her first date with Len, she called him back to say that her "girlfriend" from Australia had changed a lot, had kids now, and that they had grown apart. His response was, "It's so sad when that happens, but now you'll have time to see me." Of all the men she had met so far, she liked him best and looked forward to meeting him again.

BOB AND FAITH

Faith and Bob are a Filipino-American couple who had been married fifteen years when I met them in the Philippines in August 1999. At that time, Bob was close to eighty and Faith was in her early forties. They had two preteen children, and they lived in an upscale housing development outside of Cebu City. Although Faith wanted a part-time job, she agreed to stay at home because Bob preferred it that way. Bob was retired but active in the local Rotary Club and a number of other local philanthropic and business organizations. As he explained, he far preferred the local Filipino community to the "scruffy" expatriate Americans. The decor of their home included a life-size sculpture of an American eagle, a prominently displayed American flag, and a carved elephant. "I like eagles and elephants," Bob laughed, "because I'm American and Republican."

Bob was a retired professional who had, until he met Faith, spent most of his life in the United States. He had served in the U.S. military, had been a prisoner of war of the Japanese, and had been the mayor of a small eastern U.S. city for six years. He began his story of how he and Faith met and married with his first conscious memory of meeting Filipinos in the United States just before his first wife died. He had been briefly hospitalized for minor surgery. When he awoke from the anesthetic, the Filipino doctor was holding his hand, and the Filipina nurse took very good care of him. After his first wife—to whom he had been happily married for several decades—died in the early 1980s, he was miserable. He described the year following her death as the worst time of his life, even worse than the time he spent as a POW. After she died, he returned to the hospital for a checkup. Learning of his bereavement, the Filipina nurse gave him the names and addresses of several women friends in the Philippines, urging him to write to them. He wrote to three women. One thought him too old and passed his letter on to Faith, who was twenty-four at the time. As Faith explained, her friend had many pen pals, so she had asked if she might have Bob's letter. She promptly wrote, gave her mother her letter to mail, and began to count the days until his reply. After two weeks she was devastated to learn that her mother had not mailed the letter. Despite the initial delay, she and Bob began corresponding regularly. Meanwhile, Faith had received a visa to emigrate to Canada, but she decided not to go despite her parents' mild objections. Instead she chose to wait in Cebu to meet Bob.

Initially devastated by the loss of his wife, Bob decided to travel to Europe and Asia. He continued to write to Faith, looked forward to her letters, and then went to meet her in person. Faith had not received the telegram he had sent to inform her of his arrival, so when he appeared at her doorstep, Faith's clothes were dripping wet from the laundry she had been doing. Faith's father was so embarrassed at the sight of an unexpected foreigner arriving in a chauffeur-driven car that he fled to Faith's sister's house. Bob invited Faith to dinner at the Cebu Plaza Hotel, where her married sister accompanied them as a chaperone.[20] He proposed, and then asked her parents for their permission. Bob and Faith's original plan was to secure a fiancée visa so that they could get married in the United States in the presence of some of Faith's relatives. Like many Filipino families who know of women who have been "taken advantage of" but never married, Faith's parents and her brother vehemently objected to the plan of her marriage abroad. They preferred that Faith and Bob be married in the Catholic church *before* leaving the country, as it would be more honorable and respectable. More than half the couples I met ultimately chose to marry in the United States because the visa process is frequently considerably shorter for a foreign fiancée than for a foreign spouse, but this is often a sensitive issue for Filipinas and their families who consider the church marriage in the Philippines an important means of assuring the sanctity of the marriage.[21] Succumbing to family pressure, Bob and Faith were married in Cebu. Two weeks later Bob returned to the United States. He was told by the INS that it could take up to a year for Faith to receive a visa and join him.

Spending time in politics and in the military had taught Bob to "start at the top." So he wrote letters to then-president Ronald Reagan, Nancy Reagan, his congressman, and his state representative, explaining the situation and his position as an "upstanding citizen." After only three months, thanks to a letter of support from Nancy Reagan, Faith's visa was granted and she joined Bob in the United States. At the time of my research (1998–2001), many couples complained that the spousal visa for women from the Philippines often takes over a year, and many criticized those who exert political influence to expedite their cases at the expense of other who were ahead of them in line.

Within five years of her arrival in the United States, Faith became a U.S. citizen, and in the next several years she and Bob had two children. Despite relatives and a few good friends, Faith was not happy in the United States. She was concerned about their finances because Bob's retirement income was limited and he did not want her to work. Thus, after a few years, at her prompting, they returned to the Philippines to be near her family, and where their income would stretch much further. Their children attended a good private school; they had a nice house, a household helper, and a cook, and they saved for their children's college education.[22] One major concern was medical care, but Bob traveled to Manila for regular checkups.

As the three of us sat in their spacious living room, Faith described the joy she felt upon meeting Bob. She had never had a boyfriend and she thought very highly of Americans; several of her relatives had moved to the United States. She was attracted to older men, she explained, because they could provide "the love of a husband, a father, and a grandfather all in one." At first Bob's adult children from his first marriage strongly opposed their relationship. Faith was not put off. She thought it "only natural" that they be protective of their father. Bob was less patient with their criticism. He drew the line when his daughter-in-law referred to Faith as a "prostitute" and his son urged him to have her sign a prenuptial agreement. Other men often reported similar experiences with the hostility, mistrust, and prejudice expressed by U.S. family members and friends toward their foreign partners. Despite his children's objections, Bob refused a prenuptial agreement. Eventually his children came to like and trust Faith. As Bob explained, when his first wife died, he longed for a family again. Like many other men who initially wrote to several women, Bob knew "from the day he first met her" that Faith was "the one." He had been writing to two other women at the time, but after he met Faith in person, he went to see them to explain that he had met the woman he would marry.

DISRUPTING THE HOMOGENIZING GAZE

Moira, Netty, and Faith are very different from one another, and they bear little resemblance to the images of women in catalogs, or of notions about mail-order brides in the U.S. popular media. These women were not desperate, economically or otherwise. They did not write to just anyone. They were not pressured by families, brokers, or economic circumstances to form relationships with foreigners, and none of them were eager to leave their local communities. Of the three, Faith had the most difficult economic situation, but she had already obtained a visa to go to Canada when she met Bob, and she chose to forego that opportunity and remain in the Philippines to pursue their relationship. Later, rather than settle permanently in the United States, she convinced Bob to settle near her natal family in the Philippines.

As I argue in the chapters that follow, political economy—global and local patterns of power—plays a role in these relationships and in the gender ideologies that promote a perception of the attractiveness and desirability of western (usually white) men and Asian women. As Margaret Jolly and Lenore Manderson have argued, "'Sites of desire' are formed by confluences of culture" and involve border crossings and "fluid terrain in the exchange of desires" rather than simple unidirectional flows of power or desire.[23] Yet I also ask how personal circumstances, personality, imagination, serendipity, and other imponderables also factor in. Social inequalities that are tied to political economy, class, imperialism, race, gender, and mobility do not mean that Moira, Netty, Faith, and others cannot imagine various options, choose from among them, and react in different ways. Nor does it mean that love or emotional ties are absent or unimportant. Moira, Netty, and Faith made informed decisions about whether and with whom to correspond, and whether or not to meet in person. None of them hinted at desperation or a sense that they were "forced" to accept a foreign man's proposal. None of them wanted to marry just any foreign man. The "right man" meant something different to each of them, yet also reflected contemporary "cartographies of desire," or cultural mappings of imaginable relationships.[24]

Moira, Netty, Faith and Bob's stories, and those of many others, form the core of this book, and it is from such stories that my analyses are spun. These narratives, fragments of conversations, and excerpts from e-mail messages have undergone various forms of editing. They have been edited for the benefit of a researcher who is sometimes viewed as a friend, and some stories, such as those of Faith and Bob, have been shaped by repeated telling, refining, and romanticizing with the passage of time. I have selected which fragments to present and how to weave them together in an effort to illustrate the humanity and the texture of lives rather than as hard and fast facts or data.

At the turn of the twenty-first century, ethnographers continue to struggle with questions of representation, about ethnographers' ability to "give voice" to our subjects or to distort their voices, and the risks and possible benefits of speaking for them and about them in our texts.[25] Contemporary feminists have shared this concern, but are torn between a more practical and political stance that aims to advance women's rights and a need to acknowledge women's different voices and experiences, concerns that are at the forefront of the "feminist ethnographies" of the 1990s.[26]

Although feminist anthropologists have long criticized the notion of a "universal woman"—with singular interests and a shared identity—there still exist many contexts in which nonwestern women are measured by the yardstick of western middle-class feminists.[27] Despite recognition that women's needs and interests may be as diverse and heterogeneous as the social and cultural groups from which they come, some scholars and activists still adhere to a rescue narrative in which "other"—especially nonwestern—women are viewed as helpless, powerless victims in need of protection by others who are more educated, outspoken, powerful, and assumed to be more enlightened.[28] As Chandra Mohanty has so eloquently written, viewing Third World women primarily as victims of local men, local religions, and local family structures creates a pattern of domination—a form of discursive colonization—whereby western women are the yardstick by which progress is measured.[29] The term "mail-order brides" discursively colonizes Third World women. The term evokes a homogenous image of foreign women who are helpless, oppressed, "trafficked," and thus in need of rescue. The mail-order bride is a ready symbol of female subordination, male power, and gendered and racialized images of Asian women. The problem with this symbol is that it predefines women as victims and prematurely forecloses on the possibility of their being otherwise.

This is not to say that foreign brides cannot become victims; such cases are well known and popularized by the news media.[30] Yet the image is flawed and misleading because it defines a woman solely as a victim and conflates all foreign brides as such. Most significantly, this image neglects the local voices and the insider's perspective long called for by ethnographers and feminists. Moira, Netty, Faith, Bob, Ben, and others who met and pursued a relationship by correspondence do not fit (or identify with) the notions of "trafficking" or mail-order brides. The views and experiences of characters in this book are meant to resist reduction to simplistic stereotypes and to resist the homogenizing gaze of popular images that blur the differences between those who actively pursue this method of meeting a spouse and those who are somehow "forced" or manipulated into a marriage under false pretenses. To say that women express agency—they make choices and negotiate their situations—is not to romanticize or to ignore the structural and ideological factors that constrain their choices.

Troubling to some critics is that many women who opt to marry U.S. men—like Moira—express a preference to remain at home and not to work if there is no financial need to do so, and a willingness to define themselves primarily as wives and mothers. Should we assume that they are acting out of a gendered false consciousness?[31] To argue that some men prefer wives whom they imagine they can "control" and that some women willingly devote themselves to the roles of wife and mother begs the question of what we mean by power and control.

A common assumption is that the men "have power" in these relationships and women do not. Following Michel Foucault, I argue that power is best understood in terms of location and circumstances, rather than merely assuming that power is something that some have and others do not.[32] As Judith Butler explains, also drawing on Foucault, a subject may simultaneously "resist" and "recuperate" power, thus forming what she calls a "bind of agency."[33] Women may resist certain forms of gender inequality, but in so doing they can simultaneously reproduce these structures. Despite their national, class, and educational backgrounds (which vary greatly), and despite the wider global political economic power structures in which these relationships take place, women such as Moira, Netty, and Faith nonetheless demonstrate a degree of power, creativity, and initiative in their choices regarding correspondence, and in their relationships as well. They exert some control over the process of courtship and the conditions under which a marriage takes place, even as they simultaneously reinscribe certain conditions of gender inequality and subordination. Their partners, we should remember, are also subject to power even while they resist the gender dislocations they encounter in the United States and look for partners abroad. Men and women are both subject to bureaucratic and state forms of power which they simultaneously resist and reinscribe through their encounters.

This book is meant to contribute to a growing literature on the engendering of transnational processes. Overall I argue that women involved in correspondence relationships are not merely pawns of global political economy or the victims of sexual exploitation, nor are men simply the agents of western sexual imperialism. In the pages that follow, I aim to convey some of the complex and subtle ways in which personal experiences and life trajectories articulate with historical factors, political economy, and global imaginaries to produce (and sometimes deter) relationships between Chinese women, Filipinas, and U.S. men.

2 Ethnography in Imagined Virtual Communities

Mick wrote at 10:15 A.M:

>Hi Nicole,
> . . . I ordered the book [Maid to Order in Hong Kong] on line
from Barnes & Noble. . . . My sister noticed there were some
pages missing. I'm embarrassed to say I never even noticed!
Probably just a few pages missing of references, statistics and
mind numbingly dull academic trivia anyway. :-) (I'm glad you
have a sense of humor about all this ribbing!) Mick

Nicole answered at 11:35 A.M.:

>Hi Mick,
>Just wait until I describe you in the next book!!! (I'm glad you
have a sense of humor too! ;-))

>Nicole

Daniel wrote at 1:39 P.M.:

>Hi Mick
>I can just see what Nicole is going to say about [you]. Lets see,
a paranoid dirty old man who has a wife half his age and was
very afraid the government was not going to allow [her] into
the states. . . . Plus I forgot to mention his slave labor in his
basement writing his letters and answering his e-mails. Daniel

Nicole answered at 4:13 P.M.:

>Daniel, That about sums it up! Can I quote you?!! Nicole

Daniel answered at 5:35 P.M.:

>Hi Nicole,
>I do not mind at all. But you might want to check with Mick.
Daniel

IMAGINED COMMUNITIES

In his watershed study of the rise of nationalism, Benedict Anderson described how the development of printed media in the eighteenth century allowed for growth of the "imagined community" of the nation.[1] Print media promoted the articulation of nationalism among individuals who would never meet face-to-face and whose identities and interests otherwise varied greatly. Arjun Appadurai extends Anderson's ideas to twentieth- and twenty-first-century electronic mass media that serve as resources to create new "imagined selves and imagined worlds." These imaginaries are neither "purely emancipatory nor entirely disciplined," yet they have the potential to create "communities of sentiment" or sodalities that are transnational and "frequently operate beyond the boundaries of the nation."[2]

This chapter describes a global community of men and women who are involved in correspondence courtship and marriage, and takes up the question of how the development of the Internet and related electronic forms of communication have allowed the emergence of new types of imagined communities and how anthropologists might go about studying them. Pen pals and arranged marriages involving correspondence are not a new phenomenon. European women who married men in the U.S. western frontier during the nineteenth century and Japanese and Korean "picture brides" who immigrated to the United States in the early twentieth century to marry Japanese and Korean men in the United States are cases in point. But there is something qualitatively different about how the Internet has turned correspondence into more than a method of introduction and into a community in a larger sense.

In contrast to Appadurai, and more in keeping with Aihwa Ong, I argue that although these imagined communities of men and women are in a sense outside and beyond the state, and thus serve as a "space of contestation," men and women who ultimately marry across state boundaries nonetheless depend on the state, reify the state, and reinforce its boundaries while also crossing them.[3] As Ong has written, "Appadurai's formulation begs the question of whether imagination can be so independent of national, transnational, and political-economic structures that enable, channel, and control the flows of people, things, and ideas."[4] The Internet allows for the articulation of preexisting group identities, while it simultaneously creates opportunities for the breakdown, violation, or calling into question of more narrowly conceived boundaries of local groups, local communities, and nations, which are replaced in turn by new expressions and imaginings of global and transnational identities. As such, the Internet provides phenomenal opportunities and challenges for ethnographic study.

The Internet is especially pertinent to my research on correspondence courtship, since many of the men and women among whom I conducted research had met and corresponded through the Internet. My initial contacts with men and women (like theirs with one another) were over the Internet. My pattern of "knowing" people through the Internet and then later meeting face-to-face also echoed the pattern of many correspondence courtships. In this chapter I describe the role of the Internet in my research, especially among several groups of men who corresponded with other men with Chinese or Filipina partners. I explore the ethical and practical dilemmas as well as the benefits and the limitations of this type of research. I also consider how the Internet serves as more than a tool for introduction and correspondence between individual men and women. The clusters of people who interact by way of the Internet, I argue, constitute new global communities, virtual communities that overlap and intertwine with those that are more face-to-face, supposedly more "real" or more territorialized. These communities are global and transnational in scope, yet remain imagined communities in the same sense as the nations that Anderson described. Like global ethnoscapes, they are "landscapes of group activity" that are "no longer familiar anthropological objects, insofar as groups are no longer tightly territorialized, spatially bounded, historically unselfconscious, or culturally homogenous."[5]

Traditionally oriented ethnographers may be surprised (perhaps appalled) at the notion of conducting ethnographic research in virtual communities in cyberspace. Yet many scholars have shown that these communities are complex, organized, and worthy of study.[6] Methodological concerns and questions of representation—"Who are these people? Who or what do they represent? How do you know they are who they say they are?"—are important to all ethnographic studies, and the process of discovering the answers to such questions is not so different among localized and virtual communities.

Virtual communities may spring from localized ones or, as in this case, may precede or help to create communities of people (for example, those who share the experience of a relationship with a foreign fiancée or spouse abroad) who would otherwise have little chance of meeting in person or communicating with one another since they are geographically highly dispersed and they come from vastly different sociocultural backgrounds. The virtual communities I encountered, in particular the communities represented by private lists of U.S.-Chinese or U.S.-Philippine couples, had leaders, organizers, marginal members, and active participants. Members shared certain interests with one another and lent practical and moral support. They circulated highly specialized knowledge and experience. Some members were more vocal and popular than others; many communicated regularly, sometimes exchanging several messages a day. These Internet communities at times actively recruited new members from bulletin boards and other chat rooms or through personal networks, and other times experienced retrenchment as they attempted to screen and restrict participants or to break off and form smaller groups. Such lists provided a context in which friendships and animosities developed. Some online or "virtual friendships" among men or among couples became "real" when they arranged face-to-face meetings, regional gatherings, or group reunions that might be shared online, with photographs and captions for the rest of the group.[7] A few members knew one another in person before becoming list members, but most became acquainted through the Internet. Some men regularly communicated with list members whose immigration timetables or visits overlapped in time and space. For the first year and a half of my membership on the lists, the vast majority of members and participants were men. Sometimes Chinese women or Filipinas "lurked" (or observed the list without participating), and they sometimes filtered information back through their partners, but few participated themselves. By the second year, as more wives and fiancées arrived in the United States, women often complained about the amount of time their husbands spent on the Internet. In some cases this led to men's withdrawal from the list; in others it meant that women began to participate more actively. This marked a striking evolution of the lists in which women began offering men advice and suggestions. As we shall see, the participants in different Internet groups — news chats, bulletin boards, lists, and so on — often overlap with one another and form an array of social networks and alliances.

WRITTEN CONVERSATIONS

Research on the Internet allows one to observe individuals, converse with them, and, to a far greater degree than non-Internet research, have an opportunity to lurk or to "listen in" unobserved and without people's awareness. As scholars have observed, this raises ethical and scholarly questions concerning copyright, privacy, and the protection of human subjects.[8] Who "owns" the material on the Internet? Should the researcher cite the source or protect the writer's anonymity? Can a researcher who is a member of a private discussion group freely quote materials from the site? Should materials on private lists be cited like published material, personal letters, archival materials, or a private interview? Many of these questions are important to raise, but the answers remain complicated and contested.[9]

Despite the similarities between oral, face-to-face conversations and Internet ones — in which individuals can discuss topics and reply to one another — several striking features distinguish most Internet written "conversations" from oral ones. First, Internet conversations are relatively fixed and are more readily recorded on computer disks or saved in archives. Four of the groups I belonged to maintained a message archive that began with the group's founding. All messages were accessible to members, with the exception of one list where the moderator deleted messages he deemed unimportant, redundant, or off topic, and was accused of "rewriting history." Although I saved and filed certain messages, I could look up others in the archives by tracing subjects, key words, senders, or approximate dates.

Second, Internet conversations often (but not always) entail a longer period of time between the utterance of a statement and its reply than spoken conversations. This is not the case with ICQ ("I seek you"), Internet Relay Chat, or software that allows for oral conversations or immediate responses. By the late 1990s, such methods were just beginning to gain popularity among the couples I knew.[10] Several Chinese women described painstaking methods of receiving an e-mail message at work, translating it into Chinese, then writing out a paragraph-long response in Chinese at home in the evening, and then finally translating it into English with the help of a dictionary, a process that could take several hours just to write seven or eight lines of text. Some women wrote well but had difficulty expressing themselves in spoken English, so they preferred e-mail communication to immediate chats such as ICQ because of the delay.[11]

Third, people are sometimes less reserved over the Internet than they might be in a face-to-face conversation. A friend of Ping's, a Chinese woman in her forties, for example, responded by e-mail to a "sex man" who wrote "about all his sexual desires in the first letter." Although appalled at the idea of engaging in such a conversation face-to-face, she wrote to "tell him off" and engaged in an e-mail dialogue with him for several days because of the safety she believed the Internet provided. Some individuals seem more aggressive, rude, or verbally abusive than in face-to-face public space, and lists sometimes experienced "flame wars" or "flaming."[12] Although it is possible that unpleasant people are attracted to the medium, it is more likely that people feel fewer constraints and more safety and anonymity with this medium.

I was often struck by men's and women's ability to open up over the Internet, not only in group communications, but also in private messages. Many researchers and visitors to China have commented that Chinese are more reserved about their private lives than their western counterparts. Yet several women seemed especially trusting and open over the Internet. I was especially surprised that women I had met only once or twice were willing to tell me about their failed marriages, previous romantic involvements, parental conflicts, and sexual experiences or concerns. When I men-

tioned this to Hong, she explained that we were "old friends from the Internet" who were "reunited" in the real world, and that this contributed to
the intimacy of my interactions with her and our mutual friends Anna and
Meili. I was also struck by the emotional intensity and honesty of some
men on the lists discussed below. Although openness about personal matters is sometimes thought of as an "American" tendency, it is not often associated with men—especially not on a "public" forum "in front of" many
other men. Yet on one of the lists I belonged to, discussions of love and of
intimate personal feelings and experiences were not uncommon.

Fourth, like telephone conversations, Internet conversations lack the fa-
cial cues and body language that accompany most face-to-face conversations. Internet conversations lack aural clues as well, so conversations often
seem more direct, blunt, and rude than might be the case in a face-to-face
interaction. New forms of communication such as emoticons— :o) ;-< —
have thus developed to supplement written punctuation, to convey a better sense of the writer's attitude, and to "lighten" the tone.[13] As in the epi-
graph to this chapter, criticisms of *Maid to Order in Hong Kong* became the
topic of friendly banter and gentle ribbing. The friendliness was often
highlighted by emoticons that smiled :-), grinned, winked ;-), or stuck out
their tongues :-P.

One example helps to illustrate this point. In 1999, at a time when one
list was in the process of voting whether or not to allow me (a researcher)
to join, a member sent a message asking whether anyone had an e-mail address for the immigration department at the U.S. Embassy in Hong Kong.
Thinking I might be helpful, and since the moderator had encouraged me
to participate while the vote was being tallied, I responded by providing the
e-mail address of an INS officer who had helped me in Hong Kong the previous year and had given me his business card. In response to my message,
one member of the list proclaimed that he would certainly not vote for my
admission to the group. Giving out someone's e-mail address without their
permission demonstrated (to him) my lack of trustworthiness, and my
problem with "confidentiality."[14] The awkwardness and rapid escalation of
this situation might have been avoided in a face-to-face situation.

E-mail falls somewhere between letter writing and conversation. Internet conversations are not quite like oral conversations, yet they are not
quite like printed media either. In contrast to fixed forms of printed media,
the books, newspapers, magazines, and printed sources to which Anderson
refers, the Internet allows for a more rapid rate of response and a higher
degree of interaction from a greater variety of people. The Internet is in this
sense a more democratic medium. Although a reader might respond to a

published text with a review, or a letter to the editor, such reviews are most often produced by experts and often subject to strict editorial processes. Responses to published work, moreover, are relatively slow. On the Internet, however, the author of a statement and the author of a response to the statement often have equal authority, at least insofar as each is able to have his or her say, often without the interference of any editorial process.[15] The rate of response to an Internet statement is relatively fast; it can be posted and read by others within seconds or minutes, and within a day many readers can respond to the same source, as in the newsgroup described below. Although there are innumerable public spaces on the Internet, even the more restricted ones are not impermeable. Individuals who are deemed "unwelcome troublemakers" on private lists may be "unsubscribed" by the list's moderators, only to reappear again in a new guise with a different user name and e-mail address. Thus "troublemakers" participate in conversations, as do "outsiders" whose viewpoints may be welcomed. These transgressions are particularly important because regardless of the controversy that different viewpoints and opinions produce, they have the overall effect of challenging boundaries and forcing their way beyond narrower conceptions of shared cultural values and shared local identities. In extreme cases, often stemming from disagreements with the moderator's policy on the scope of the group's membership or on the definition of appropriate or off topics, divisions ultimately cause the group to fission and new ones to emerge with different rules and objectives.

INTERNET RESEARCH

The Internet aspect of my research involved several different but overlapping parts: research among Internet introduction agencies, research in or around Internet cafés in China and the Philippines, research on private groups or lists that I joined as a researcher/member, and research on a public online news discussion group. Each of the Internet-related dimensions of my work revealed different facets of the wider virtual community, a community that includes others besides the couples involved in intercultural relationships. I turn first to Internet cafés and introduction agencies, then to my experiences as a member and participant-observer on several private lists whose members were at first mainly western men married to, engaged to, or corresponding with Filipinas or Chinese women. Next, I examine an online news article published by a Philippine-based Internet newspaper, and the reader comments and discussion that ensued. As a member of sorts in this wider virtual community, I could observe firsthand the way in which the boundaries between the local, the national, and the global are challenged, resulting in a community that at once "feels" local but is in fact highly global, and intimately intertwined with state boundaries and the policies that permit a degree of permeability.

INTRODUCTION AGENCIES AND CYBER-CAFÉS

Since the 1980s, patterns of international correspondence courtship and marriage have broadened greatly in scope. Filipino-Australian marriages are among the best known examples, but other marriage flows have included Filipinas who have married men from rural Japan and from northern and western Europe and North America.[16] Although printed catalogs still circulate, the field has seen a huge expansion in the 1990s with the rise of Internet-based agencies that rapidly and efficiently introduce women from Asia, Eastern Europe, the former Soviet Union, and Latin America to men in other parts of the world.[17] Women listed on Internet web sites come from all parts of Asia, but most are from the Philippines and a growing number are from the PRC.[18]

Research on correspondence courtship and marriage led me to explore some of the several hundred Internet introduction agencies designed to introduce "marriage-minded" foreign women to western men. There are many types of introduction services, some geared explicitly toward men and women who hope to find a marriage partner, while others (like that which introduced Netty and Len) are oriented more toward dating, escort, and sexual services.[19] Scholes suggests that as of mid-March 1998 there were 153 listings for international introduction services on goodwife.com and by early May of the same year, 202.[20] As of August 2000, I found 350 listed. Under the category "Asian," the number had increased from 55 in May 1998 to 89 in August 2000. The "Soviet" category had increased from 105 in May 1998 to 164 in August 2000. The goodwife.com count does not appear to include a number of pen pal clubs, including oneandonly.com, kiss.com, friendfinder.com, and several other popular sites that do not charge women fees, nor does it include individually run personal web sites that aim to introduce men and women. My estimate of 350 agencies is therefore conservative.

Some of the online agencies I examined included kiss.com, Oceanbridge, and China Bride. Listings at these agencies are available to anyone who logs onto the site. Most allow nonmembers or nonsubscribers access to photographs of women (and sometimes men) and to women's autobiographical statements. As described in chapter 1, this material typically includes a woman's name, age, occupation, education, religion, height and weight, marital status, and a few comments about her interests or hobbies. What is not available, except to members or subscribers, is the identifying information that allows a person to correspond. The mailing or e-mail address, additional photographs, and sometimes further biographical information are available only when a subscriber pays the required fee. Some agencies require women to pay to be listed. Although this fee is usually less than what men pay for membership and access to addresses, it may be expensive for women in China or the Philippines. A number of women I met selected an agency on the basis of cost. More expensive Chinese agencies that required women to pay membership fees provided access to a translator at additional cost. The rate at one Beijing agency was 400 RMB (U.S.$50) a year for a woman to post her listing, and 20 RMB ($2.50) to send a one-page letter (about 400 Chinese characters) via the Internet, including the cost of translation from Chinese to English. English to Chinese translation cost 10 RMB ($1.25).[21] Most agencies required men to pay to receive women's addresses and did not charge the women. This was often the case with agencies that dealt more exclusively with Filipinas. Several Chinese women who had good English skills used introduction sites such as asianfriendfinder, love@aol, singlesonline, Americansingles, and oneandonly.com, most of which allow a person to be listed free, but require them to pay to obtain an address. One drawback with free agencies is that they may not select for "marriage-minded" individuals to the same extent as those explicitly promoted as facilitating marriage.

Of the men I encountered, many subscribed to only one introduction service, and only a few listed themselves. About three-quarters of the men initiated contact with women. Some women who received letters from men but already had a steady pen pal passed the man's name and address on to a friend, who then initiated correspondence. This seemed especially common among Filipinas, perhaps because writing to pen pals was a common practice. In China, I never heard of women trading names; and several women were embarrassed or hesitant to let their family and friends know of this private activity.[22] Some men joined a second agency if they found the first unsatisfactory, or if a friend, acquaintance, or someone from an Internet list criticized the agency for its financial operations, for listing women whose information was out of date, or for not being "reputable" or oriented toward serious "lifetime partners."

A variation on the formal agencies that require fees is the smaller, individual web site—often owned by a Filipino-American couple—that lists the names and contact information of the woman's friends or relatives in the Philippines. These usually require no fees and can be located with links to other web sites that are of interest to people pursuing cross-cultural relationships. Another variation, in which a couple initially corresponds by mail or Internet, includes men and women who are introduced by a friend or co-worker to a pen pal abroad as a potential spouse. Lisa and Ted (chapter 4) were introduced by Lisa's sister, who lived in the United States with her Filipino American husband whom she had met through correspondence. When Lisa arrived in the United States, she and Ted arranged an introduction of Lisa's next youngest sister to a man Ted had befriended via an Internet group. Some Internet groups also provide names of prospective pen pals but give out their addresses only after a period of screening the men who want to write to them. Since the women are often members' sisters-in-law, or a close friend or relative of a member's wife, men are often protective of them and carefully scrutinize prospective suitors. As mentioned above, especially in the Philippines, letters from men are passed on to friends and relatives, as in the case of Faith and Bob. I met several men who corresponded with the friend or sister of the woman they originally wrote to, and observed Filipinas in Hong Kong poring over letters and photographs of men, saying, "Let me have this one to write to," or, "I don't like this one, do you want it?" thus objectifying the men at a mediated distance.

After a few months of exploring different types of introduction agencies, I selected a few to join. Fees ranged from $40 to $150 for six months to a year of membership. Payment could be made over the Internet, by telephone, or by check or money order. Although my name was included with my e-mail address, agencies addressed me as "Mr. Constable" and took for granted that I must be a man. I received a password and then was allowed access to women's addresses. One large international agency listed women from many parts of the world, including Latin America, Russia and the former Soviet Union, Eastern Europe, and many parts of Asia. Women could be located using a special search instrument indicating nationality, location, or age. I selected "women of any age" from China and the Philippines.

At first I wrote to women who had either e-mail or postal addresses, and later limited my attention to only those who had e-mail addresses, and who resided in or near Hong Kong, Shenzhen, Beijing, and in the Philippines in Manila, Cebu, or Butuan. I wrote to approximately forty women by mail (in Hong Kong and the Philippines) and to another forty via the Internet (in China and the Philippines). The rates of response were far better via the Internet. As with Moira (chapter 1), I sent the same letter by mail and e-mail, explaining who I was, what I was doing, and expressing hope to meet them in person.

Although I included Philippine airmail postage stamps with the letters I sent to the Philippines, I received only about six responses, and most arrived far too late for me to meet them in person. Several envelopes were returned months later marked "no longer at this address" or "addressee unknown." It is important to note that the agency from which I obtained most of the postal mailing addresses in Hong Kong and the Philippines was a small, inexpensive one that sent a quarterly black-and-white photocopied catalog. The time lag between the publication of the catalog and the time it took for letters to reach the women in Hong Kong and the Philippines made it extremely difficult to establish communication. By comparing the birth dates and current ages of the women in the catalog, it was clear that a delay of up to two years contributed to the problem. Especially for Filipinas who worked in Hong Kong on two-year contracts, this mode of introduction was not ideal.

My attempts to contact women via e-mail were much more successful, especially with women in the PRC. I heard back from about three-quarters of all the women I wrote to via e-mail, and met with almost all of the ones I had written to in China. Two women in China, including Moira, and one in the Philippines automatically sent me a form letter that was designed for a male pen pal interested in meeting a potential spouse. One factor influencing my success in China is that international matchmaking there is very much an urban phenomenon, and that computers are readily available in towns and cities. Although some of the Chinese women I knew best were more privileged (their English-speaking ability was an indication of this), communicating with pen pals via e-mail is not strictly indicative of elite class status among Chinese women. I knew of factory workers and women with very low wages who paid to have their messages translated and sent, or for e-mail access.

Most of the women I corresponded with in the Philippines (including many whom I initially met there) did not own computers or have access to them at work, but used Internet cafés. Although few had originally met their pen pals through the Internet, it became a means of maintaining communication.[23] Sitting in Internet cafés in Manila, Cebu, and Butuan in 1999 and 2000 allowed me to strike up conversations with a number of women who went there to write to their pen pals. The cost was around twenty-five pesos (fifty cents) an hour.[24] The slow Internet connections in the only Internet café in Butuan provided an ideal context in which to meet women.

People would often strike up conversations as they waited (sometimes over an hour before giving up entirely) for an Internet connection. Few women seemed in a hurry, and the technological failure was taken in stride As we waited, women asked where I was from and if I knew her boyfriend abroad. Mention of my research often led to an introduction to someone else at a nearby computer terminal. In contrast to Butuan, Cebu City had numerous cyber-cafés, including many in upscale malls and shopping areas. Most of the machines there worked well and the Internet connections were fast, which made it more difficult to strike up impromptu conversations. In 2000 I had far greater success in Cebu than the previous year. A Filipina friend had opened a coffee shop just outside an Internet business, appropriately named Global Village. She introduced me to many of her customers, including numerous U.S.-Filipino couples she had befriended as they stopped by on their way to or from Global Village.

In contrast, I did not meet any women with pen pals in Internet cafés in China. This was partly because writing to foreign pen pals was much less common in China, and also because Internet cafés functioned more efficiently and are used for many purposes. The Chinese women I met often had Internet access at work, at home, through an agency, or through a friend, and did not use the large, public cyber-cafés unless their home or work computer was out of order. In 2000, use of the Internet at one of the popular cyber-cafés in Beijing cost about 10 RMB ($1.25) an hour, and most women I spoke to considered this expensive and inconvenient.[25] Less formal access to the Internet through a friend or personal contacts, at a university, or in one case through a small photocopying store, was far less expensive. Moira and Lu had free e-mail access at work in 1999, but no longer had this privilege in 2000. Both set up their own Internet connections at home rather than paying the requisite fee at work. Meili and Anna depended mostly on their friend Hong, an English teacher, to help translate and respond to their messages from her home computer. Several others, including some who lacked English language skills, communicated via Jen's agency, where the staff would call when a message arrived and translate it over the telephone.

I ended up writing to some women only twice before we met in person. Many sent a short note conveying their willingness to meet. Others, like Yanyi, wrote numerous times before we finally met in person. As men and women wrote of their experiences with pen pals, some quickly emerged as more outgoing and communicative and others as more reserved. This, of course, had much to do with their English ability. A woman's English ability, like her access to the Internet or, alternatively, her ability to pay for translation of her letters served somewhat as a class filter for Chinese women corresponding with U.S. men. As mentioned above, I knew Chinese factory workers and shop clerks who wrote to U.S. men, sometimes by regular mail, but by and large, the poorest Chinese women, including rural and less educated women, had little opportunity to learn English and usually lacked the funds needed for translation and Internet communication.

My identity as a western woman was sometimes a disadvantage in establishing initial rapport with U.S. men, but it was an advantage among Chinese women, who were interested and curious about the West and very comfortable talking to a married western woman close to their age and status.[26] As a foreigner, I was assumed to be more "open-minded" about relationships and sexuality, or at least someone who would be less easily shocked by their efforts to correspond with foreign men. Women like Ping (see chapter 6) insisted on meeting me alone to discuss certain aspects of their relationships with U.S. men, confirming my sense that they could speak to me more openly about sexuality and other concerns than to their Chinese friends and relatives. Especially in China, I was put in the interesting but often awkward position of culture broker. Several Chinese women expressed their surprise (and pleasure) at meeting a western woman. Around forty at the time, I was over ten years older than most Filipinas I met, but most Chinese women were within five years of my age in one direction or the other. Many Chinese women, even if they had little or no college education, had white-collar occupations. These "middle-class" working women seemed comfortable with me and approached me as a resource for learning about life in the United States, testing their stereotypes about foreigners, and telling me of their doubts and concerns regarding their pen pals.[27]

Filipinas—especially those I met through personal contacts—were often eager to meet me and struck up conversations with me in cyber-cafés, but it took longer to break the ice, and I rarely felt as though I was regarded as a peer or an equal. The age difference was one factor since Filipinas were in their twenties.[28] Most Filipinas came from rural areas, and some were not college educated, but even college-educated women pointed to a disparity in our social status, and like Rosie insisted on maintaining a degree of formality and respect, addressing me as "ma'am" or "Nicole ma'am." This surprised me, since Filipinas in Hong Kong—perhaps because of their more cosmopolitan experience—were often happy to call me "*ate*," or sister. Several of my Filipina pen pals belonged to a lower socioeconomic class than the Chinese women. Among the Chinese women I knew were teachers, office managers, librarians, translators, and secretaries. Filipinas I interviewed included a nursery-school teacher, shop clerks, hotel clerks, domestic helpers, factory workers, waitresses, and college students. Filipinas from wealthier middle-class families, those in businesses where they had more exposure to foreigners (banks, travel agencies, hotels, restaurants, or those who had worked abroad), or those from poor families but who were already married to U.S. men seemed friendlier, more accessible, and more communicative. Greater access to American culture, through work, spouses, or friends who had married foreigners, and to large networks of friends and relations abroad, may have made it easier for some Filipinas to communicate with me, but it may also have meant that I was less of a novelty or a resource than in China.[29] While Chinese women may have seen me as a culture broker or a resource, they were not intimidated by my role as a researcher and seemed to regard us as status equals. Women I met in the Philippines appeared more concerned about fitting me, a white U.S. academic, into a social structure of status differences.

A number of Chinese women showed me photographs of their pen pals and letters they had received. They asked, for example, why a fifty-year-old man would flex his muscles for a photograph, what it meant for a man to be "semi-retired" or to have a "career in transportation," and whether Americans considered it odd for a fifty-five-year-old man to never have married and still live with his mother. In contrast to many Filipinas who preferred meeting men who had never been married, Chinese women preferred men who were divorced to those over forty who were never married. Chinese women showed me photographs of themselves, and asked which would most likely to appeal to western men. Filipinas had their own sources of knowledge about America.

At her Beijing agency, Jen showed me and a Chinese American male friend an array of photographs of Chinese women and western men on the Internet and asked us which we expected to be most popular. We were much better at predicting women's popularity than Jen and her office staff. In some cases they were surprised that a woman they considered attractive by Chinese standards had received few responses and in other cases women they considered fat, plain, or whose faces were too flat or wide had received a number of letters. Jen concluded that Americans like thin women with narrow faces. Asked to recommend alternative photographs of the less popular women, my friend and I chose those with more natural poses, rather than elaborate portrait studio shots of made-up women in hoop skirts or fur coats with miniature well-coifed dyed dogs against false backdrops. Jen pointed out the images of the most popular western men. These were inevitably men in suits, often ties, and with clean-shaven, often boyish, clean-cut appearances.

As we have seen, Internet agencies provide the initial information that allows women and men to gain access to prospective partners with whom they can imagine sharing a future. It also provided me, as an ethnographer, with a natural entrée into the community, one that in many ways paralleled U.S. men's initiation of communication with foreign partners. Like other forms of communication, Internet introduction and communication allow men and women from different parts of the world to meet, communicate, and sometimes marry and emigrate. The time-speed compression of Internet communication is part of what makes it different from printed catalogs and letters that are sent by mail. The social interactions that sometimes result from the places people go to have access to computers distinguishes it as well. One Filipina I met in Butuan, for example, had met her American fiancé when he had come to use a computer at the cyber-café. Cyber-cafés (and their surrounds), introduction bureaus, and the apartments of friends with computers can facilitate communication not only between international couples, but also among women who share common goals or experiences. As such, simply being in such contexts provided unexpected contacts and insight into the correspondence community.

JOINING PRIVATE LISTS

My decision to meet women who were in the early stages of correspondence with foreign men, and even some who were contemplating correspondence, was motivated by the difficulties that other researchers reported in meeting men and women who were part of the correspondence courtship and marriage community.[30] Men in the United States are often wary and critical of the way in which they have been negatively portrayed by the media and by people who label their relationships "mail-order marriages." As a result, many men refuse to speak to researchers or to journalists, and advise their wives or fiancées to do the same. Most couples prefer to live their lives in private, not under the critical eye of those who portray them as social rejects who have failed in the U.S. marriage market due to physical or emotional unattractiveness and their foreign brides as young and beautiful, unable to speak English, and desperate to leave their native countries.

Given the difficulty of meeting couples in the United States, I depended partly on personal networks. Ben introduced me to other Filipino-American couples, told me about many others, and described an Internet list he belonged to for men involved with Filipinas. Ben encouraged me to join Filipino-American Family (FAF). At the time, the membership numbered over four hundred, mostly men who were engaged, married, or intended to become involved with Filipinas. Some men had met their partners in the United States or while traveling abroad, but most had met or carried out much of their courtship through correspondence. This group, which saw itself as an extended family and a close-knit community, defined itself not in terms of how they met their partners, but on the basis that their partners were in or from the Philippines. They shared advice and information about agencies and the process of getting to know someone by correspondence, but their main tie revolved around their experiences in a cross-cultural relationship, and the trials and tribulations of the process of immigration and settling in the United States. These men related to one another as part of an intercultural couple, not on the basis of how they met or from any externally imposed idea of being involved in a mail-order marriage. The challenges such couples face in their courtships and marriages are based on their involvement in a U.S.-Filipino intercultural relationship. Once the couple begins corresponding, there is little to distinguish those who met in person while traveling abroad from those who were introduced by a family member or friend, or who met through a published or Internet catalog.

While in the Philippines in 1999, I witnessed firsthand how men and women who belonged to FAF and other groups maintained contact. Ted regularly logged on to FAF from his Manila hotel room and Ben made a point of visiting an Internet café every day so he could sift through the messages that had accumulated in the last twenty-four hours—often over one hundred messages a day from the list. While Ben updated the list about his experiences in Manila and arranged to meet other list members, it was an ideal time for me to meet with Rosie.

As a member of several lists, I was on the receiving end of messages sent by men who were visiting pen pals and fiancées abroad, sharing success stories ("She has her visa, we'll be home next week!"), frustrations ("The INS turned down the visa and said we are missing some paperwork"), requests for last-minute advice ("Where do we get the police clearance?" "How early should we get in line for the INS interview?"), or suggestions ("What was the name of the good, cheap restaurant near the Embassy?" "What's the best way to send overweight baggage?" "What was the new calling card someone mentioned?").

In the course of my research I belonged to four different Internet lists. FAF was an offshoot of an older list that had broken up a few years earlier "because of poor management," I was told. As described below, I only belonged to FAF for a few days. The second group, U.S.-Filipino Group (UFG), was a small offshoot from FAF with about forty members in late 2000, most of whom initially belonged to FAF or to another large group. Daniel, the moderator of UFG, started the list with the explicit purpose of helping me with my research. By 2001, as my involvement waned and I mostly lurked, the character of UFG changed considerably. It had grown to over 200 members, with several active women members, including fiancées in the Philippines, Filipina wives in the United States, and their friends abroad who were involved with U.S. pen pals. The third list, U.S.-Chinese Relations (UCR), which involved issues facing U.S-Chinese couples, had close to 150 members by late 2000.[31] I was introduced to the moderator of this list by the moderator of UCR. By early 2001, UCR had grown and split into two different groups to which I belonged.[32]

OBSERVER OBSERVED

Ben and Ted talked for hours about couples they had read about and whose photographs they had seen on FAF, and about the importance and value of this community. At Ben's urging, I sought to join. I read all the material on the FAF web pages that was not restricted to members. This included detailed information about visas, the immigration process, INS interview questions, agencies, hotels in the Philippines, and even a public chat or bulletin board on which nonmembers could post questions and answers. The site included two private lists for members only. The main list included mainly men, and the second was explicitly for women only, and its members included Filipina partners of men from the wider list. I wrote to the moderators of both lists, explaining who I was and the nature of my research, and submitting a request to join. I mentioned Ben and Ted's names, suggesting that they might vouch for me, if necessary. I never received a response from the women's list, but shortly after submitting my message I received an automatic response from the FAF main list notifying me that it was closed and they were not currently accepting new members.

A few hours later, I received a message from one of the moderators saying they had discussed my request and would allow me to join. The moderator suggested that I lurk for a while before introducing myself. He said that the moderators did not want to be accused of admitting a researcher without the members' knowledge. He warned me that some members would not be pleased to have me on the list, that they had had "bad experiences in the past," and that I might be "flamed."

For less than two days I observed and wondered—first of all—how I could possibly keep up with the traffic, which came to over a hundred messages a day. As I was later advised, many members simply delete messages based on the subject lines. Others access the messages on the Internet, rather than through e-mail, or have them sent in digest mode in clusters of about twenty-five messages at a time. After lurking for less than two days, I introduced myself. Within just a few hours, a number of members had responded and I had become the latest hot topic.

There were three main responses to my presence: friendly, challenging, and hostile. At first most were very friendly. Many members welcomed me as they do all new members and encouraged me to participate. Some expressed enthusiasm, and said they hoped I would help to represent the less-known, "positive" side of the picture and help to set the record straight about them and their relationships. These were by far the most common responses to my introduction.

Some other members' responses were more challenging, although not hostile. They explicitly and repeatedly called on me to explain and defend my research goals and methods. Two men cited their own research in a university and a hospital setting, and asked why I was studying their group, and what I hoped to "prove." They asked about my credentials and my research design. Why did I chose a qualitative as opposed to a quantitative approach? Had I received Institutional Review Board approval for the study of human subjects? Had I read the latest INS report on the topic? Defending my research to these educated locals was more of a challenge than any dissertation defense or peer review process I have experienced, and certainly far more than was required of me when I conducted my earlier research abroad. From their perspective, for me to simply "observe" and design my research in response to what I learned was not reassuring. They wanted to know in advance exactly what I was looking for and precisely how it would be used.

When I checked my e-mail a few hours later, there were many more messages, including several that were far more hostile. These came from four members, two of whom were especially outspoken and angry. One compared my presence on the list to having a stranger in his home, listening in on all his private conversations and making him feel defensive. The moderators, from his perspective, had betrayed the family by allowing a stranger in their midst. One man objected to being treated like a "lab rat" regardless of any reassurances I might give. These four critics agreed that they would not participate in any discussions while I was there, and they warned the other members of the risks and dangers of a researcher who would observe their interactions, twist their words, and use whatever they said against them.

Other members accused the critics of paranoia, noting possible positive outcomes of having a researcher on the list, and observing that other researchers could already be on the list but not have been so honest as to say so. Several pointed out that I was not an "unknown stranger," as several members had already met me in person. Others debated whether the information on the list was in fact "public" and whether my assurances to "do everything possible to protect their identity" (that is, using pseudonyms, avoiding identifiers, and acquiring permission to quote them) were enough. My use of the phrase "everything possible," one man wrote, gave him greater cause for concern than anything said thus far. Members debated whether there was anything "bad" or "harmful" on the list that could be used against them. One man who claimed there was "nothing bad" and that the list had nothing to hide was harshly chastised for his naivete. How could he not know, the critic wrote, that anything could be used out of context to make them look bad? In response, another member said that he had met me in person and that ultimately it came down to trust. He recommended that others read my book about Filipina domestic workers and judge me on that basis. Another wrote that the moderators (with Ben and Ted's input) had decided to trust me, and I should be given a chance.

The four outspoken critics remained adamantly opposed to my presence. Two of them sent me private messages demanding that I leave. Finally, after being a member for only a few days, I announced my decision to unsubscribe. For the better part of forty-eight hours, my research and I had become the main topic of discussion and hundreds of e-mails on the topic were exchanged. As I explained in my final message, I respected the position of those who preferred not to be studied. I had never knowingly forced myself on research subjects before and had no intention to do so now. I did not want it to come down to—as it seemed to—"either she goes or I go." According to men on the list, the topic dominated the discussion long after I had unsubscribed and created some sharp divisions and conflicts among members.

After I sent my final message, I received hundreds of e-mail messages from men and couples who said they were sorry I had left. Many said that they understood and respected my decision, and that I "had no choice." Many expressed "shame" or "regret" that I had been so ruthlessly and bitterly flamed by a few outspoken members. They commented on the fact that there are some people (such as those who opposed my presence) whose messages they often delete without reading. Others thought I did the right thing, but apologized for the flaming. Many offered to help with my research, and about thirty men sent me brief narratives that described their experiences meeting, courting, and marrying a Filipina.

FIELDWORK ETHICS

The flaming I experienced in the course of my brief membership on FAF was unpleasant but informative and ultimately productive. Anthropologists are not often privy to the lively and controversial discussions of community members and leaders about the pros and cons of their presence. How many community leaders have had to convince the community to accept the anthropologist and how many anthropologists have created or exacerbated existing community conflicts with their mere presence?[33] If anthropologists were more aware of the opposition to their presence, possibly only those with the thickest skins would nonetheless insist on conducting research in that environment.

It was also noteworthy that I was admitted to the main list, whose members were mostly men, but not to the women's list. Perhaps it was assumed by the moderators that I would learn more from the men on the list, that they could keep a better eye on me, or like "traditional" anthropologists that my status as a western scholar placed me in a position that was more analogous to that of the men. Regardless of the reason, the overall result was that I had greater contact with the men than the women on FAF.

The men who opposed my presence had good reasons. Although I prefer to think of myself as an honest and responsible researcher, they had little reason to accept me as such. Despite best intentions, researchers often find themselves in a position where some of the most interesting information is that which research subjects are least likely to want publicized. The issue of "betrayal" is encountered in all qualitative research.[34] Moreover, researchers can take information out of context and are not and cannot be, as many recent works suggest, completely objective. As one of my critics on the list wrote, he did not want to be the subject of any book, even if his name was changed and his identity protected. In the end, I left the list because of the anger and disruption I had caused, and also because I did not want to subject myself and my project to further flaming. As is often the case in anthropological research, the ruckus caused by my presence altered their interactions. I reassured myself that there was little information that I could not glean from other sources anyway. As the list members themselves argued, a researcher could easily join their group in the guise of a regular member. This was not an option I considered, but the Internet does create possibilities for researchers to be "invisible," and thus raises serious ethical questions about their right to use the materials gleaned in such a way. On a list I subsequently joined, I sometimes wondered whether one member was in fact a researcher because of the way his questions were framed to provoke response.

Six months after unsubscribing from FAF, I was introduced by the moderator of UFG to the moderator of UCR (U.S.-China Relations), a relatively new list for Chinese-American couples (mostly U.S. men who were married or engaged to Chinese women). UCR had about seventy members when I joined, close to 150 members six months later, and over 200 members in early 2001. I decided to try to join this list because at the time I had less contact with men who were writing to Chinese women. I braced myself for more flaming (and dreaded it) but decided that, regardless of the outcome, it would teach me something about Internet communities. UCR, to my relief, had a very different culture and social structure than FAF. The moderator put the question of my membership to a confidential vote. Although a few members quickly voiced concerns about the presence of a researcher on the list, the moderator rapidly curtailed the discussion and suggested that members air their concerns to him privately.

Sparing me from what I imagined were the inevitable criticisms and objections made it possible for me to remain on the list despite possible votes against me. Even if I were rejected by the group, I imagined that the benefits would outweigh the costs. Meanwhile, even as the votes were collected, I had access to their discussions. This scenario is perhaps more like the anthropologist's experience in a community study. The anthropologist may be aware of opposition to her presence, but she is not forced to listen and may not be fully aware of who or how many people oppose her. Thus, if the anthropologist is ultimately admitted, everyone "saves face" and the research can be conducted with at least a feigned veneer of innocence and goodwill. This is certainly more comfortable for the researcher, but may not be entirely in the best interest of the members of the community. One of the disadvantages of this approach was that, unlike on FAF, members of UCR had little opportunity to communicate many of their legitimate concerns. Ultimately approval was almost unanimously in my favor.

RESEARCHER OR FRIEND?

When I first unsubscribed from FAF, Daniel offered to start up UFG for me and for people who were willing to participate in my research. UFG began with twenty members and quickly grew to forty, ten of whom were most active. At first, since many of the members still participated in FAF and other lists, this smaller list gave me contacts but was not especially vocal. It was useful if I wanted responses to a particular question, but I could not just sit back and observe. During the first few months, I had the impression that Daniel wanted me to play a more active role, but after a while the list took on a life of its own.

In contrast to some of the larger groups, where it is very difficult to keep track of everyone, the members of UFG, especially those who participated regularly, got to know each other well. They shared stories and information, argued, joked, commiserated, complained, debated, and supported and encouraged one another. Mick wrote frequent updates on the status of his visa and on his fiancée's situation in Singapore, where she worked as a domestic worker for a couple who had confiscated her passport. Others responded with advice, support, and encouragement. One member, who had been married several years, wrote of the birth of his second child and about his growing understanding of the meaning of "love," and Charlie wrote skeptically about older men and young women, midlife crises, and how Filipinas change when they come to the United States. Daniel often sent resources—stories, articles, web sites—that might be of interest to the list. Several kept the list updated on their immigration timetables. Others answered questions about airline tickets, phone cards and calling plans, airport customs procedures, gifts, and places to stay. For several weeks the discussion revolved around their views (including criticisms) of *Maid to Order in Hong Kong*. As Charlie observed, my sympathies were clearly with the domestic workers in Hong Kong, not the employers. How did they know the men wouldn't become the equivalent to the employers in my next book? As I explained, in the Hong Kong domestic worker–employer case, the employer's side of the story is well known, but the workers' situation less so. In the case of correspondence relationships, the negative examples and portrayals are common. What are less well known are cases that question the negative and simplistic stereotypes. If my goal were to portray the men in negative terms, I explained, it would not be necessary to communicate with them on the list.

One discussion had to do with a reunion planned by another group, to which several members of UFG belonged. When some members mentioned that they would be getting together, I—half-seriously and with little tact or forethought—raised the possibility of attending. This began a very heated discussion between those who thought, "Of course she should come, she's one of us," and those who felt it would be inappropriate. The discussion eventually boiled down to whether, if I did attend, I would do so as "researcher or friend." Since I was in the Philippines for the duration of this discussion, I did not reply immediately, and the discussion went on uninterrupted for some time. The subject heading at one point became "Nicole, friend or foe?"

Expressing the "friend" position, Mick wrote:

>You guys are killing me. Ok, I've read all the opinions concerning Nicole attending [the] party. Frankly I can hardly believe some of the paranoia that some of you feel. . . . Nicole will not be walking around with a tape recorder hidden in her guacamole dip. The only reason Nicole wants to attend is because she got to know some of us through [UFG]. She likes us, feels comfortable with us and we [UFG] feel the same. . . . [The] party is a "social" event. I would really like to meet this woman. She wants to meet us. Not in her capacity as a researcher, but as a human being with similar interests to us. It's a social gathering. And that's all.

John represented a different position. In response to Mick, he wrote:

> Really? I don't think so! I have been on [UFG] since this subject came up and I have not missed a single post on the issue. I have gone back and flipped through the archives to be certain. . . . According to the archives, I am not wrong on this, I saw nothing to indicate that you have even a clue what Nicole's incentives are for attending the gathering. . . . In fact, the only thing she did say was that if she could not spend much time with [UFG], she could dig up some other people to visit while there, so just having a meal with some subset of the group would be fine with her. To me this indicates that the project will be paying for her trip . . . the same as it is paying for her trip to Cebu.

I do not question the assertion that she likes everyone and would receive some personal enjoyment from meeting everyone beyond the scope of her work. She appears to be interested in the subjects she studies and has stated that this is one of the reasons she is doing this in the first place. But make no mistake about it. Nicole would not be going to [the] gathering if it were not for her job. . . . Nicole, may I ask your motivations for attending the gathering, and would you be there, at least partially, in the capacity of a researcher?

. . . There are people on this list that have had bad experiences with media and or research, or know someone who has. It may have had something to do with their marriage, and maybe not. But it is all too obvious to many of us that a female Social Anthropologist living in the US is NOT necessarily your buddy. I am sure it comes as no surprise to Nicole that some people may wish to determine who she is and what she is about before exposing so much as their name to her.

When I returned from the Philippines, I replied:

>I didn't much like the "friend or foe" dichotomy (I certainly wouldn't consider myself your foe!!), but I do think the researcher/ friend issue is important and interesting. My main motivation for wanting to attend (and wanting to meet you folks at some point, some- where) was/is research, but I've thought about it a lot and the fact is that research and friendship are NOT necessarily incompatible! . . . There are some people whom I met originally through the Internet for my work whom I now consider friends. . . . Also, as I have become friends with people I have worked with in the past, it has created an even stronger sense of responsibility to represent them fairly. (Many people see this issue differently: friendship is incompatible with re- search because it means lack of objectivity and distance.) . . . I think if we [UFG] could have a get together at some point, it would be great. Yes, I'd be there as a researcher, but I am other things as well!!

My response seemed to settle the matter, and I was glad to have a chance to clarify my position.

By the summer of 2001, there was an increase in women's participation on UFG. In the spring, Daniel's wife, Gina, had arrived from the Philippines and, like many other wives, she was unhappy about the amount of time he spent glued to his computer. While Mick's solution was to leave the list, Daniel tried to recruit more Filipina members, including Gina's friends in the Philippines. Men whose partners had previously been too shy or perhaps uninterested in participating became more outspoken, offered men advice, reassurance, and suggestions for a smooth transition to the United States. Similar patterns also took place on UCR and its offshoot, as the founding members' relationships reached a new phase and their wives arrived in the United States.

The membership of different lists often overlapped. Several members of the Filipino and Chinese lists knew each other from other lists specializing in fiancé and spousal visa matters and Asian immigration. I often observed the same names on different parts of the Internet. For example, a man might update his immigration information with a list devoted to tracking couples' immigration progress and timelines, participate in FAF, and record his opin- ion at the end of an Internet news report. The following section describes one such news report and the lively discussion that ensued, illustrating an- other dimension of the breadth and diversity of this virtual community.

NEWSGROUPS AND CHATS

I originally learned about "Pinay Brides—Internet's Hottest Commodi- ties," an Internet news article on "trafficking" of Filipinas, from a member of UFG. Here I focus narrowly on this article and the varied online responses it received from men (and a few women) in the United States and the Philippines. The responses point to several common themes in the competing narratives about marriages between U.S. men and Asian women. Online responses echoed popular media and antitrafficking images of mail-order brides as passive victims of the global economy who are forced to "sell themselves" to foreign men. They also pointed to the image of women as depicted in the media (and by men whose relationships have failed) as active aggressors who marry western men for green cards and material advantages. Situated in relation to both these images were the less familiar counter-narratives of family values and respectability that often emerge from the stories of U.S. men, Chinese women, and Filipinas (see chapter 4). Notably absent from the online responses to the news article I describe were the voices of women who might be labeled "mail-order brides" but rarely define themselves as such.

"Pinay Brides" was published on a Philippine-based news web site called ABS-CBN News, one of the many online sources that the list members scan daily for news relating to China or the Philippines. The article described the activities of an introduction agency run by William McKnight, an American from Montana, and his Filipina wife, who was said to provide "foreigners with the chance to 'purchase' their own Filipina bride on the net."[35] The article described how McKnight's agency managed to introduce prospective spouses under the guise of a travel agency, despite the illegality of mail-order brides in the Philippines. Since Republic Act 6955 was passed in 1990, it is illegal to advertise in the Philippines for prospective brides for foreigners, but employees of the agency apparently visited department stores and approached "sales ladies" in person to ask if they were interested in marrying Americans.[36]

One member of UFG was especially interested in the article for what it said about unsuspecting U.S. men who are taken advantage of by ruthless agencies and deceitful young women. The article centered on Lilian, a Filipina whose sister worked for the agency, and James, a U.S. man who had come to meet her in the Philippines, fallen in love with her, and "married" her in a ceremony sponsored by the agency. James returned to the United States to begin the procedure to apply for Lilian's visa. He also sent her a great deal of money by way of the agency and then learned that she had married another man. It later became clear that Lilian and James's marriage had never been official; the marriage had been "staged" and the agency had never filed the paperwork. After James's return to the United States, Lilian was convinced by her sister to marry another man through the agency. After describing James's pursuit of justice through the Philippine Center on Transnational Crime, the article ends with the following statement, which I cited in the introduction: "The typical Filipina mail order bride believes that marrying a foreigner is her ticket out of poverty. But it may also lead to a descending hell of spousal abuse or white slavery. Yet still the march goes on—of young Filipinas eager to sell body and soul for a way out of the country. As one Filipina succinctly says, better to be a foreigner's whore than a pauper's wife." [37]

The article received a resounding response from both Filipino and American readers in the United States and the Philippines, including responses from members of FAF and UFG. In the four days following its publication, more than 200 readers' comments were posted. The responses were largely, but not entirely, from men. They represented an immense spectrum of positions, some of which I shall briefly describe. Although my characterization risks simplifying complex positions (and their internal contradictions), three broad responses to the article can be characterized as: vocal nationalist critics of neocolonialism, unabashed liberal pragmatists, and American good old boys. While these three positions are important in and of themselves, my objective is also to indicate how—despite their differences—they all constitute and contribute to the vitality of a wider virtual, global, and transnational community. As Anderson points out, the discourse that produces the imagined community of a nation is not devoid of disagreements. [38] Nations are imagined and formed despite the differences in opinion of their members. Similarly, the three patterns of discourse described below constitute both challenges to a community and alliances being forged within and across it.

The first and most immediate response that reverberated off and on throughout the five days was that of the nationalist critics of neocolonialism, most of whom seemed to be, based on their names, Filipino men and a few women. These messages were highly critical of the existence of such introduction agencies as that described in the article, appalled by the shameful existence of "MOBs" (mail-order brides) and of the foreign men who took advantage of Filipinas, and, in many cases, of the U.S.–Philippine history of colonialism and postcolonialism that has helped to perpetuate Philippine economic dependency and government corruption.

The first angry nationalist cry urged calling on "the lovebug wizard" of computer virus fame to destroy the Internet site of the agency for the shame this caused the Philippines. Another message replied that the lovebug wizard "is not the real answer" but that the problem goes far deeper. Some declared this "an embarrassment . . . nothing more than indirect prostitution"; another labeled it "another sad part of Philippine history." Several messages, including one by "bay agmo," berated the men who patronize these agencies, describing them as "losers, degenerates, dom [sic], perverts in their own country." [39]

The responses then moved in several directions: the American men who defended themselves, and the liberal pragmatists, like Visuck Lat, who explicitly turned the blame away from the agencies and the women and into the realm of the state: "It is not the Internet business [who is] to blame but the roots of the poverty, i.e., the government. If RP has a better and well managed govt., I don't think human export will become its major commodities in today's world market. I feel sorry for those who married their foreign husband as a ticket from poverty, but, they may be so smart and very practical in life. Issues like this (the headline) surfaces when a relationship failed and legal issues are attached" (Visuck Lat, June 10, 2000). This pragmatic defense of the women who take this "route out of poverty" was a theme that was repeated many times. "Combat Doc," a Filipino expatriate doctor who, in the course of his various messages, identified himself as a naturalized U.S. citizen who drives a Mercedes and is married to a white woman (thus laying himself wide open to a flood of criticisms from Filipino "compatriots back home" who attacked his patriotism at a distance),[40] wrote that these women are "smart and courageous enough to recognize an opportunity and take it" (June 13, 2000), and that they

> are only doing what is BEST for them and their families. If the Phil. Govt was NOT AS USELESS AND CORRUPT AS IT IS, our women would not feel any need to go abroad to WORK OR MARRY. It is the govt's INEFFECTIVENESS AND USELESSNESS IN PROVIDING FOR ITS OWN PEOPLE that are driving its citizens to go elsewhere. These websites are great for providing a conduit for these SMART AND INTELLIGENT women to find a BETTER FUTURE ELSEWHERE. Their children will be US citizens with rights and opportunities that many can just DREAM ABOUT. They will have access to the best education. . . . They will drive their own cars in HS. . . . These children will have HIGH PAYING JOBS. . . . These children will have a govt that cares about them. (June 11, 2000)

Likewise, Pierre Tierra writes,

> given a choice, a Filipina would rather be with her family in the Philippines IF THE FAMILY'S FINANCIAL SITUATION PERMITS IT. But because 95% of Filipino homes are in a desperate financial situation, the eldest child in the family (this can sometimes be a female) is forced to look for employment overseas as an OCW just to support their family. . . . Don't blame the "Internet Filipina Brides." Blame the

corrupt officials for not putting the Philippine financial house in order. Dante wrote . . . that 'the hottest spot in Hell is reserved for those who did not lift a finger to help their fellow men.' . . . The Bible assures us that the prostitutes, the abandoned, society's 'throw-aways' etc. will enter the Kingdom of Heaven first. . . . Dante Alighieri has already written where the souls of the corrupt and damned public officials will end up. (June 10, 2000)

Representing the U.S. "good old boys" and defending his and other Americans' marriages to Filipinas, Nathan Watts wrote the first and one of the best received of all the U.S. men's responses. As a member of several lists for U.S. men married or engaged to Filipinas, and as someone who had met his wife through correspondence (partly because he thought U.S. women lack the "traditional family values" of Asian women), he criticized the article and many of the responses for not recognizing the sincerity of many men and women and their relationships:

> I have to agree that there are cases where the ladies are abused or treated as sex objects only. I am an American married to a Filipina. I do not smoke or use liquor of any kind nor do I use drugs. But my interest has never put me in situations where I could meet ladies here in the states. So I joined a penpal club. I wrote a letter to my wife's sister and she gave my letter to her sister who I married. I asked my wife the other day what [was] the biggest surprise she had when she met me. Her answer was that I was kind to her and her family. I belong to 3 groups that deal with immigration from the Philippines and between all groups membership is about 700 members. The love that the men have for their ladies is truly amazing. I love my wife and she is not a sex slave or my maid at all and there is a chance we may decide to live in the Philippines. Yes there are cases where there has been abuse or prostitution involved but this is rare. There are also cases where the ladies take advantage of their husbands. . . . One thing for sure I love my wife very much we only have a 15 year age difference and this makes it easier. When we married I agreed to assist her family and this is no problem in my book because I married a very special lady. I have a friend who had been married to his filipina wife for over 27 years and he is also an American. But there will always be a few bad ones in every group. (June 10, 2000)

Many Filipinos applauded Watts's message. Visuck Lat wrote, "Your point is well taken and I admire you for your understanding and support to your extended family. May God bless you and your family. I'll go take on the day" (June 10, 2000). Pilosopo Tasyo responded, "Nathan Watts, you could be one of the gentle 'dolphins' [as opposed to sharks] I refer to above. Thank you so much for your kindness. In greater measure, may you and people like you be rewarded with continued joy, grace, and peace" (June 10, 2000). Likewise, Frank Navarro commented, "Very well said. Good natured people like you will always be successful. Go on brother" (June 11, 2000).

Yet despite the warm and conciliatory responses to Watts's message, a certain hostility toward U.S. men reemerged in several other messages. When Randy Townley took it upon himself to defend William McKnight and the agency described in the article, Red Dev replied,

> Oh give me a break!!! Give it up! You know what you are and what you do! These men aren't looking for virtuous women, they're men who can't cut it with American women, or are looking for a poor soul who would be under their control to use in anyway they want. It's because of their misfortune that this man is making an "honest" living, isn't it? If he really wanted to help, he wouldn't charge a fee, don't you think? You can hide behind words all you want, but you're nothing but WHOREMONGERS AND PIMPS!!! (June 10, 2000)

Townley apologized for his avid defense of McKnight; after further inquiry he learned that he was "incorrect." Red Dev's reply coolly advised Townley of the wisdom of doing his homework next time "before making grand denouncements" (June 10, 2000).

In response to bay agmo's statement that the foreign men who marry Filipinas are "losers, degenerates, dom *[sic]*, perverts in their own country," Two Otap, an American married to a Filipina, wrote, "PINOYS have a REP[utation] as being drunkards, 2 timing, dead beat scumbags who do not deserve to be with a FILIPINA. Think about that before you call western men whom go to the RP to marry a FILIPINA loosers etc. *[sic]*" (June 11, 2000). Surprisingly, the discussion did not escalate into further insults. Filipina Kalidad Sanchez wrote, "I agree! If Filipino men could take better care of their women then she would not be in every part of the world working as a domestic to some other family. It is not the Philippine government we should change—it's our whole mind set. . . . Time for a change . . . what is happening is just a sign of the times. Filipina women are waking up . . . if we do not take better care of them they will certainly go [to] those they perceive will" (June 13, 2000). Bay agmo added, "It is interesting that many of the males are decades older than the female . . . there might be a few success stories but I'm still not buying it" (June 14, 2000). Several other men whose names I recognized from other lists emphasized and elaborated on Watts's points, adding their own narratives, some adding a Christian dimension to their marital commitment.

After five days, messages began to repeat the same patterns: U.S. men criticized the term and the notion of "mail-order brides" and defended their position on the basis of having experienced their own relationships as sincere and loving and based on "traditional" and "old-fashioned" family values. Filipino critics bemoaned the shame and embarrassment of "mailorder brides" and asserted that "Filipinos should not allow anyone to market them as brides. It is better to die of hunger than to be a commodity exposed for wolves to devour. There is our dignity and self respect. Who will respect us if we practice these embarrassing acts?" (Apoca lypse, June 11, 2000).[41] Others put them in their place: "Oh grow up! Embarrassing?? Not to want to marry and slave for some good for nothing husband? For loving and marrying and bearing children? Our mothers made the same choices. Perhaps you should ask them if they have any regrets. Are we racist or what?!" (Sanchez, June 13, 2000). Many continued to question the source of the problem—poverty, government corruption, global inequality—and sought to discover the underlying truth. Visuck Lat ends on a more philosophical and conciliatory note, asking, "Those Amboys are losers? Those girls are opportunist? Or We're jealous? . . . In my opinion its their lives and lets not intervene in their personal matters whether they are losers, opportunist[s] or really in love, its their life, its their choice and I assumed they are all mature enough to make such decisions. We're only human anyway and obviously nothing is perfect in this world" (June 13, 2000).

The views encapsulated in the Internet news forum point to many powerful critiques of neo/postcolonialism. They echo many of the images found in the popular media and among antitrafficking organizations, of passive so-called mail-order brides and women who are said to be "trafficked" by men and introduction agencies, and of women who will (supposedly) do anything for the material benefits marriage to a foreigner will afford her. Yet such stark and all-encompassing representations of women as agents or victims, which are discussed in further detail in the following chapter, often do not mesh with women's own experiences. In the news forum, we encountered the views of some U.S. men who resist the characterization of their marriages as trafficking and their wives as bought or sold. We also heard the voices of Filipinos who decry the shame of such an industry or of "their" women "prostituting" themselves to foreign men. What we did not hear were the voices of women who might be considered mail-order brides.

In the online news discussion, women were spoken of and about by husbands, fathers, compatriots; they were defended and criticized, and they became the "grounds" on which a broader discourse on gender, nationalism, and colonialism is played out, discussed, or argued.[42] Women who are involved in transnational marriages, who might understandably be loath to identify themselves as mail-order brides, are absent from this discussion. Perhaps this is because women rarely identify themselves as mail-order brides, but rather as women, daughters, or wives of Filipinos or foreign men. As Kalidad Sanchez and "Combat Doc" suggested, Filipinas must contend with marriages in the Philippines or abroad and make decisions based on their own and their families' best interests. This they do within the context of ever more readily available (yet nonetheless structurally constrained) global options and opportunities. Regardless of possible material benefits or improvements they hope to gain for themselves or their family members, they reject sterile market analogies and views of themselves as commodities. It is not surprising, therefore, that except in cases where their marriages have failed or in the most blatant cases of abuse, women do not identify themselves as—or with—the notion of "mail-order brides" or women who are "trafficked." Their voices are thus likely to remain dim unless we listen to them in the subject positions they openly embrace: particularly those of immigrant, daughter, wife, and mother.

CONCLUSION

This chapter has focused on the role of the Internet in the production of a new kind of imagined global community and the role of the Internet in my research. I have argued that the Internet is in some ways a more democratic and less exclusive medium than other forms of print publication. It allows for the emergence of a global community that includes U.S. men and men of other nationalities who seek foreign brides, Chinese and Filipina women (and women of many other nationalities as well) who are open to the possibility of marrying men abroad, and many others—including anthropologists—who are part of the wider community as well. Women participate by sending their names to online agencies and corresponding with foreign men; U.S. men form Internet lists to provide a sense of community and support as they navigate the process of correspondence courtship and marriage; Filipinos in the Philippines and in the United States contribute an important critical dimension to the discourse on mail-order brides. Interactions take place in virtual space (online) and face-to-face as couples meet in person, as women chat in cyber-cafés, and as list members arrange get-togethers. Cumulatively, the voices on the Internet comprise a global community of sorts—not one that is homogenous and unified, nor one that is egalitarian or devoid of privilege or exclusions, but one in which different perspectives and viewpoints are aired, and in which different social identities and positions linked to class, race, nationality, and gender are articulated and imagined within a global context.

Like the imagined community of the nation described by Anderson, members of the virtual global community will never meet face-to-face. Just as books and newsprint provided new sources for imagining and studying nations and nationalism, the Internet provides an invaluable resource for creating and understanding global communities. The Internet and its connections to real people and real places provide new multisited research possibilities for ethnographers and new contexts in which to revisit older ethnographic, methodological, and ethical concerns that arise when we imagine ourselves as researchers to be both inside and outside the communities we study and write about. Internet communities create archives, virtual remains, genealogies of virtual communities that await further excavation.

3 Feminism and Myths of "Mail-Order" Marriages

>What angers me most is when researchers (like G&O)
[Glodava and Onizuka] cede that the men tend to be educated
and "above average . . . certainly in their communication
skills" (attributed to Jedlicka), and yet they make two
dimensional caricatures of us and our motivations, and they
belittle our relationships as superficial. The truth is our
motivations are complex and numerous, and men who
use international personals are as diverse as the women
themselves.   —RYAN, 2000

The bodies of Asian women have often been seen as
erotic and exotic in the Western discourse of "the Orient."
Their smallness has been associated with timidity and
subservience, traits that have made them desirable to many
men in Western societies. This perception has even led to
the development of mail-order businesses in which Asian
women are sold to Western male consumers as brides.
       —FRANCES E. MASCIA-LEES AND NANCY JOHNSON BLACK,
                        Gender and Anthropology, 87

In this chapter I critically examine popular and feminist ideas about mail-order brides as "trafficked women" who are "sold" to western men. In lieu of the sorts of homogenizing images that construct women as victims and men as agents, I propose a reconceptualization of correspondence relationships that is attentive to women and men's motivations and experiences, and to subtle and complex renderings of power. I consider how certain "anti-trafficking" discourses are linked to views of women's oppression that were popular in the 1970s, and are thus subject to more recent anthropological and feminist critiques. Although I oppose a simplistic conflation of correspondence brides and prostitutes, my critique of mail-order brides as "trafficked women" owes an intellectual debt to recent feminist interventions on the topic of sex work, as well as to feminist ethnography in general. Like many recent works, this chapter points to the diverse perspectives and experiences of women and to the complex renderings of power that make simple binary oppositions—between men and women, oppressor and oppressed, East and West, agent and victim—naive and obsolete. A secondary purpose of this chapter is to place correspondence relationships within a wider context, alluding to their affinities with other forms of match-making, personal ads, dating services, and picture brides.

FEMINIST PERSPECTIVES OF THE 1970S AND 1980S

Mail-order brides are often depicted as buying into images of their own subservience and marrying out of economic desperation. These views are seriously flawed for their orientalist, essentializing, and universalizing tendencies, which reflect many now-outdated feminist views of the 1970s. Contemporary critics of mail-order brides often presume the existence of universal gender inequality (that is, that in all cultures women are—at least to some degree—subordinate to men).[1] Since the 1970s, however, anthropologists have become increasingly aware of historical, social, and cultural differences between women, of varied cultural constructions of gender categories, of western-biased assumptions about domestic/public and nature/culture dichotomies, and of problems in measuring or assessing gender inequality.[2] Kamala Kempadoo describes the feminist ethnography of the 1980s as reflecting a shift away from "simple hierarchies and dichotomies" to the "problematization of multiple spaces, seemingly contradictory social locations and plural sites of power," and the multiple "experiences, identities, and struggles of women."[3] Lila Abu-Lughod's work exemplifies such concerns. By "writing against culture," she questions homogenizing social and cultural labels that obscure more than they reveal about "women's worlds."[4]

Early feminist assumptions about universal gender inequality underlie many contemporary critiques of mail-order brides as part of a "traffic in women" and examples of women's sexual and economic slavery.[5] Anti-trafficking NGOs often include mail-order brides among the ranks of trafficked women.[6] Definitions of mail-order brides, as discussed below, are often so broad as to become almost meaningless. Lack of specificity in the definition of what constitutes trafficking also contributes to the assumption that Asian women who meet western men through correspondence have been "trafficked." The Philippine Women Centre of British Columbia, Canada (PWC), for example, opposes any "narrow definition" of trafficking that attempts to isolate "abuse and coercion" and condemns such approaches as a "reprehensible position that effectively sentences poor women to permanent modern-day slavery."[7]

The notion of trafficking in women and female sexual and domestic slavery is bolstered by a 1970s feminist view of marriage as a fundamentally exploitative patriarchal institution. While some 1970s feminists proposed rejecting the institution of marriage altogether, others conceived of less exploitative marital and domestic arrangements, including those in which heterosexual or homosexual couples could more equitably allocate household chores, power, and authority.[8] Certain marriages and domestic arrangements were deemed more equal, namely, those that did not replicate the "traditional" western domestic/public division of labor, in which women perform household chores and men work outside of the home. Households in which men contributed to the unpaid reproductive household labor and/or women participated in the paid labor force were considered more enlightened forms of heterosexual marriage.[9]

Against this western, feminist, white, and middle-class vision of gender equality lay the multitude of other forms of heterosexual marriages and household arrangements, which were often deemed exploitative and unequal, regardless of women's own experiences and views. Women were considered victims who were unaware of their own oppression and who could be liberated only by consciousness-raising and rejecting or reforming marriage. Thus marriages that conformed to a domestic/public division of labor, in which men work outside of the home for a wage and women provide unpaid reproductive work, were subject to criticism. The greater the departure from the western feminist notion of a liberated household, the more exploitative the situation was presumed to be. Using this western feminist yardstick, Third World women were often regarded as exploited, subservient "victims" of marriage and patriarchy; mail-order brides were envisioned as contemporary examples of such Third World victims within western societies.[10]

Often lacking in this critique of marriage and gender relations was an appreciation of the variety of ways in which women in different sociocultural contexts might define liberation. To work for a wage might be liberating to a middle-class American woman, but not to a woman who has worked in fields or a factory for subsistence since childhood. As Lugones and Spelman argue, marriage to a man who embraces the role of provider, and the consequent possibility of rejecting wage labor, may constitute "liberation" to an unwed Hispanic mother in the United States, while to a western, middle-class, white feminist, divorce and economic independence may be a preferable alternative.[11] In response to such criticisms, the 1980s and 1990s witnessed further attempts to understand the interconnectedness of gender, class, and race and cultural difference. Polygynous marriages, the epitome of male exploitation from an outside perspective, might be preferred to monogamy by women from certain Islamic cultures.[12] Likewise, arranged marriages and community- and kin-based forms of matchmaking, long the focus of western critique, may have practical advantages from the perspective of the women and men who practice them. They are not necessarily devoid of love or strong emotional ties, and they are used by educated couples utilizing "modern" technology.[13]

"TRADITIONAL" AND "MODERN" MARRIAGES

Culture-bound assumptions about what constitutes a "good" marriage often prevent critics from viewing correspondence as a valid means of meeting a spouse. Criticisms of a gendered division of labor are also linked to criticisms of correspondence relationships. To *some* working women in China and the Philippines, the division of labor in which the man is the primary breadwinner and the woman provides reproductive labor for the nuclear family household is considered a desirable and "modern" arrangement.

For white-collar Chinese working women like Moira and Lu (in chapter 1) who view their marriage options and their work mobility as limited in China, becoming a "housewife" in a middle-class American home, under the right circumstances, constitutes a welcome alternative. For rural or working-class Filipinas whose day-to-day lives involve a combination of hard work in shops, factories, or rice fields combined with domestic chores and responsibilities for an extended household, the idea of working only at home, with the help of time-saving devices, and of being responsible for her own husband and children may constitute an attractive alternative. To some women in Asia and the West at the turn of the millennium, liberation is equated with the freedom to work outside the home and gain a degree of financial independence, but to others it is the freedom *not to* work outside the home.

Western men correspond with Asian women for many different reasons. Among them is often a stated preference for a so-called traditional division of labor, one that is imagined or remembered from parents' or grandparents' generations. As Kathryn Robinson argues in the case of Australian men, the search for "traditional" brides is linked to the "decline of patriarchalism," the erosion of "father rights" that has taken place since the 1970s, and men's ensuing sense of "nostalgia for an imagined perfect world of the past where women are not spoiled 'by exposure to western ways, western lifestyle or women's lib.'"[14] Robinson's logic also applies to

U.S. men who blame the feminist movement and U.S. women for their marital disappointments. These views are linked to what Susan Faludi describes as a growing sense of disappointment among U.S. men in the post–World War II period. Feminism, in other words, is a scapegoat for wider feelings of social and economic displacement and powerlessness, including a diminished sense of male power in relation to assumptions about women's real or imagined social gains.[15]

Looking to Asia and other parts of the world for women who are thought to willingly embrace the role of wife, housewife, and mother follows a certain logic. Ben, Daniel, and many others who experienced failed relationships or marriages with American women have "come to the realization" that they do not want a relationship in which all roles and duties are shared equally, but one in which the roles are more complementary, divided in a "good old-fashioned way." Some men described this situation as "separate but equal," while others used far less egalitarian metaphors. Some referred to a desire for a home in which the man is the "head of the household" or the "king of his castle," where his wife caters to his interests, and where he can view himself as dominant. But while the man may envision himself as "head" or "king," his wife may correspondingly view herself as a "queen" or "princess" who has been "rescued" from the drudgery of work and who is "in charge" of the home (see chapter 4). Men's ideas of power and control, in other words, can coexist with women's notions of their own power and control. Both men and women, meanwhile, are subjected to other forms of power that at once restrict their options and offer new possibilities.

Women do not necessarily experience household duties and responsibilities as punishment, drudgery, or exploitation. Nor do they necessarily associate gender inequality with men's ideas about their own dominance. As one Chinese woman explained, "Even Chinese men may *think* of themselves as the head of the household, but in fact, women are often the ones in charge, even if the men don't know it!" U.S. men I met likewise spoke of their wives' dominance, their wives' ability to "whip [them] into shape," control their diets (many spoke of losing weight or eating healthier food), take charge of the household budget, and save money or earn money in inventive ways. Men commented, generally in a good-natured way, about the inaccurate stereotype of Asian women as passive and subservient. Timothy, an American doctor married to a Filipina for ten years, explained, "I tease Mary and tell her that she's a classic case of false advertising! In our house, she's the boss! But then, most of the Filipina wives I know are that way." The Filipina nurse who worked for Timothy, in an attempt to explain

Mary's assertiveness, pointed out to me that she is "Waray," a member of a Philippine regional group known for their fierce and aggressive disposition. In a conversation with Mary and her friend Lou, also married to a U.S. man, Mary described how neither of them fit the image of the docile and subservient Asian wife. They pamper their husbands but also enjoy a great deal of social freedom. They stay out late with friends several evenings a week, something that their friends married to Filipinos could not do. Mary and Lou also claimed to gently mold their husband's behavior, encouraging changes in the way they dress, their hygiene, occupations, and lifestyles. Men and women both commented on the way Filipinas may appear subservient, pampering men in public, bringing them drinks, or in one case going so far as to tie her husband's shoes for him in the shopping mall. But in private, I was told, it's often "Grrrr! Go get it yourself!"

While some men seek marriage partners abroad because they think western women are "overly liberated" and place their careers ahead of marriage and family, others seek foreign partners because they think western women are materialistic, spoiled, lazy, and unwilling to work in or outside the home. These two images of western women (motivated career woman versus pampered and lazy) are in fact diametrically opposed, although they are sometimes blurred in men's discussions. Men sometimes said that feminists were to blame for women's lack of commitment to the family, overlooking the fact that women who are lazy and spoiled can hardly be considered feminists. Men hoped to meet foreign women who made fewer material demands, were satisfied or appreciative of less, and were willing to contribute, if necessary, to the household income.

As Daniel, a forty-five-year-old man married to a Filipina, explained, his American ex-wife did not want to work outside the home, did not enjoy doing housework, and mainly sat around watching soap operas all day in her bathrobe. He did much of the cooking and cleaning. Eventually he got tired of working all day and coming home to do the housework as well. Like many others, his experience was not that western women are so liberated that they have no time for the home, but that they are lazy, spoiled, have an aggrandized sense of entitlement, and work neither for a wage nor in the home. Thus to him and others the image of Asian women as diligent and not taking comfort for granted was particularly appealing. Women who had worked as "maids" abroad knew how to work hard, and taking care of their own home and children would presumably be easier and far more rewarding. Such women were also assumed to be more "grateful" and appreciative of men's role as providers.

Despite the consensual nature of many relationships that originate with correspondence, and despite complementary perspectives on gender roles, observers are often highly critical and commonly point to women's lack of agency and their victimization. Consent is seen as "buying" and "selling" of brides, and complementarity is read as exploitation. Men's ideas about power and dominance are assumed to preclude women's power or authority. These views reflect little understanding of feminist critiques that question the ability of western middle-class feminists to speak for all women, and thereby argue for a more complex understanding of gender relations and the rendering of power.

BRIDES FOR SALE?

Mail-Order Brides: Women for Sale, by Mila Glodava and Richard Onizuka, is one of only three books that have been published on the topic of mail-order brides in the United States. The other two include a "how to" book for men, and the memoir of a Thai bride.[16] *Mail-Order Brides* deserves attention because it is widely cited, considered authoritative, and referred to as an important source by the USDOJ-INS Report on "Mail Order Brides."[17] The book expresses many of the most common overgeneralizations and misunderstandings about correspondence relationships, many of which are echoed in other popular sources and in antitrafficking literature. A critical examination of *Mail-Order Brides* therefore provides an opportunity to consider correspondence relationships as something other than powerful men who "buy brides" and victimized women who "sell themselves," and to consider the topic in relation to anthropological and feminist critiques.

In their preface, Glodava and Onizuka express hope that their book "will help in addressing the exploitative nature of the 'selling of women'" (xiii). Glodava writes that in the course of her research (1985 to 1994), she "encountered approximately 30 mail-order brides, a majority of whom were in dreadful situations," and the more she learned of "the mail-order bride issue," the more she "realized the inequity presented by this exploitative situation" (xii). Glodava is one of the founders of the Mail-Order Bride Legal Aid Fund, co-founded with the Asian Pacific Development Center, so it is not surprising that she encountered women in difficult situations. Onizuka, former clinical director of the Asian/Pacific Center for Human Development in Denver, writes, "When I first heard about mail-order brides and the industry for them, it was hard to believe. There was something inherently wrong with 'buying,' 'ordering' or whatever metaphor you might choose to use, other people" (xiv).

Glodava and Onizuka define "mail-order brides" very broadly as "women who find their spouses through the mail. The process may be initiated by an introduction service agency, through the use of a catalog, newspaper or magazine advertisements, or a videotape service. It may also be initiated through introductions made by a friend or relative" (2).[18] They thus conflate introductions by friends or relatives with those by formal introduction services. Throughout the book the authors refer to women as "mail-order brides," despite acknowledgment that the women do not recognize themselves as such, and that the term reflects their own biases (33). Most women I encountered in China and the Philippines are unaware of the term "mail-order bride" and think of themselves and those with whom they correspond as "pen pals." As sociologist Cecilia Julag-Ay points out, the term "perpetuates the more sinister side of these relationships." Julag-Ay thus opts not to use it because it is not "value neutral" and it has "many negative connotations." [19]

Glodava and Onizuka explain that the "mail-order bride business" is a multimillion-dollar industry that has received extensive media attention in the United States since the mid 1980s. A program on *Phil Donahue* in 1980 gave the industry a large boost, and when a "front-page story entitled 'American men find Asian brides fill the unliberated bill' (Joseph 1984) appeared in the *Wall Street Journal,* the issue took off like wildfire. This story gave some legitimacy to this little known cottage industry, and it propelled the mail-order bride phenomenon into society's consciousness. Eventually, mail-order brides became regulars on national television and radio talk and news magazine shows including *Oprah, Donahue, Nightline,* and *20/20*" (3).

Glodava and Onizuka support the common assumption that Asian women are economically desperate to come to the United States. They cite journalist John Krich in *Mother Jones,* who writes, "Since there's a perceived shortage of U.S. homemakers willing to shoulder traditional matrimonial tasks, some entrepreneurs are going abroad—where the labor can be bought cheaper and the quality control kept more rigid. . . . On one side of the Pacific, there's a limitless supply of desperately poor females who'll do anything to become U.S. citizens. On the other hand, there's an increasing demand for their services from men who'll do anything to retain their power advantage within family life" (4).

Citing Elaine Kim, Glodava and Onizuka write that these relationships are based on "unequal political and economic relationships between developing and industrialized nations and between the sexes on a worldwide scale" (4). They argue that the inequalities "between the partners in this marital transaction lead to exploitation, especially for the foreign spouses who are seen as the inferior partners in these relationships. The male citizen spouse feels that he has 'bought' the mail-order wife and, therefore, owns her and has power and control over her" (5).[20] The authors rightly point to the larger political economic context in which these relationships transpire and to wider structures of inequality, but they fail to consider how situations vary, and how they do not simply or necessarily translate into a U.S. man's power over his foreign wife.

Glodava and Onizuka applaud the 1990s "global spotlight" placed on "the issue of trafficking in women, specifically mail-order brides" (5). Failure to "fight against this exploitation of women carries heavy societal consequences—the continued degradation of women and oppression of the weak, which can also promote other forms of sexual exploitation such as pornography, pedophilia, white slavery and prostitution" (6). As mentioned above, this conflation of women who meet spouses through correspondence with slavery and prostitution is misleading but not uncommon.[21] The PWC likewise defines mail-order brides as "trafficked women," a category that includes "domestic workers, mail-order brides, prostitutes and other Filipino women who are forced to emigrate as part of globalization" (1).

Although some women are undoubtedly unaware of the risks and become victims even though they act, Glodava and Onizuka fail to consider that women are not necessarily duped or seduced into these relationships. Women I interviewed were usually aware of the larger context of structural inequality and of the risks involved in meeting people through correspondence, but they planned to navigate within this system. They were careful whom they wrote to, what agencies they used, which men they agreed to meet, and in what context. Most critics of correspondence would not likely consider a Filipina doctor who immigrates to the United States for work a dupe of an exploitative capitalist system, nor is she considered part of a larger pattern of trafficking, although her job opportunity is linked to global structures of inequality. Her judgment and decision to emigrate is not called into question by those who claim to better understand the exploitation the situation entails. The situation of many Filipina brides—many of whom are in fact college-educated adults—is treated in a far more patronizing way because of their assumed youth, innocence, lack of education, and presumed class standing. Far from resolving the situation, the reluctance to identify foreign brides as anything other than potential victims serves to reinforce the very image of which Glodava and Onizuka and others are critical. It is important to stress that recognizing and acknowledging women's active roles in this process of courtship is not to romanticize their relationships or to fail to see the difficulties they might face as new brides and as immigrants.

The following sections of this chapter are organized around four of the themes in Glodava and Onizuka's book: agencies and catalogs, men who "buy" brides, women who "sell" themselves, and marriages. In each section, I aim to situate the "antitrafficking" approach to foreign brides within a broader context and critique.

AGENCIES, CATALOGS, DATING CLUBS, AND PERSONAL ADS

What's a "mail-order bride"? *[laughs]* I never heard of that. . . .
I'm not selling myself *[sounds offended]*. No! Of course not.
That would be like a prostitute!

—LI MING, 1999

Glodava and Onizuka conducted their research mainly in the 1980s, before the Internet became ubiquitous in international and domestic introductions. Some of the best-known printed catalogs (for example, Rainbow Ridge, formerly Cherry Blossoms, American Asian Worldwide Services, and Asian Experience) are produced by agencies that are run by couples who met through correspondence (Glodava and Onizuka, 8–11). Glodava and Onizuka point to the objectification of women in the catalogs. They stress that men select from hundreds of women, in contrast to what they view as the limitations and restrictions placed on women. Their excerpts from singles magazines and catalogs include—strangely enough—teenage New Zealanders and young women from Northern Ireland who aim to meet "American Hunks," cases that seem to undermine their assumptions about the extreme social, political, and economic disparity between the men and women.

Glodava and Onizuka use an example of a woman's letter to *Catholic Singles Magazine* in 1982 to illustrate the "naivete of the women" who hope to meet men through correspondence (23). To me, this letter better illustrates women's ability to represent themselves honestly and articulately in a forum that is not geared toward profit or exploitation of women. The young woman writes of her desire to broaden her knowledge of other cultures and possibly meet an "ideal" pen pal "who would match my personality and character. I prefer guys my age who are professionals with stable jobs, responsible, understanding, sincere and most of all he must be Catholic" (23). It is difficult to see how this woman is "naive," unless one assumes that there is something inherently wrong with trying to meet someone through this medium. The woman states her preferences and objectives in a reputable magazine for Catholic singles. Like many young women I met in the Philippines who were Mormon or Seventh Day Adventist and participated in international introduction clubs, and like many professional women and men in the United States who resort to placing personal ads in newspapers or online, or who join matchmaking clubs to meet partners, these can be seen as resourceful alternatives to more traditional local methods of introduction in an era of globalization.

Glodava and Onizuka conclude their discussion of catalogs and agencies as follows: "The women usually sell themselves as attractive, sensitive, and intelligent. Some unabashedly ask for men who are serious about marriage. The catalogs are filled with photos of women who 'would like to meet a humble, kind, sincere and industrious man with marriage in mind.' This probably is the main difference between the old-fashioned versus modern pen pals. While the goal of the former is simply to make friends and to learn about the culture of another through letter-writing, the latter, where participants have marriage in mind, make no such pretenses" (24).

There are several problems with this statement. First, the distinction between "old-fashioned" pen pals who write to make friends and learn about other cultures and the "modern" ones who have marriage in mind is false. That men and women are direct about their interest in finding a marriage partner does not preclude the possibility of friendship and learning about another culture. Many of the western men on the Internet sites devoted to cross-cultural relationships readily shared names of books about Chinese and Filipino culture and history, news sites, Internet resources for learning the language, and a spectrum of cultural information and experiences. A number of men and women developed a serious relationship with one person but continued to write to several "pen friends" or "e-friends" whom they claimed had no romantic expectations. Natalie, a thirty-two-year-old Filipina, had several pen pals when I first met her in 1999. A year later she had a "serious" Filipino boyfriend, but she continued to write to pen pals in Saudi Arabia and Canada. She had no romantic interest in them but found it interesting and rewarding to communicate.

A more serious problem is Glodava and Onizuka's literal use of the word "sell." Women may *represent* themselves as attractive and intelligent, but from their perspective and that of the men who write to them, they do not "sell themselves." Women I spoke to were embarrassed, shocked, or horrified at the idea that looking for pen pals could be interpreted as such. Selling oneself is what prostitutes do, they said, and like most Americans, they attempted to distance courtship and marriage from prostitution.[22] Women may quite literally put their best face forward, but the market metaphor should not be taken literally in this context. A U.S. teenager who dresses up for a prom date would not likely be said to "sell herself." Would this metaphor be applied to western women and men who use dating services or place personals ads, or does it reflect more pejorative assumptions about foreign or Third World women?

Glodava and Onizuka assert that women are literally "bought and sold" like objects through catalogs. Introduction services, especially those that are profit-oriented businesses, do use images of women and men to sell their services, but this is different from selling women. In some cases they sell tours and travel services as well. As Robinson points out, "There is no doubt that this is a commodified process—the middlemen make money from the use of the women's ads and photos in the catalogues of addresses which they sell to subscribers (much in the same way as Asian airlines use the images of the women to sell tickets, or governments use the images of female docility to attract foreign investors, or luxury car manufacturers use women's bodies to sell products)."[23] Yet it is important to distinguish between the broker or introduction agency that presents commodified images of women and the assumption that women *are* objects who "sell themselves." Villapando seems to miss this distinction with reference to mail-order brides when she states categorically: "And commodities they are." Frances Mascia-Lees and Nancy Johnson Black echo this position in a recent textbook on gender and anthropology when they cite Villapando and state that women are literally "sold to Western male consumers as brides."[24] If women are commodified by the way they are marketed, then it is only fair to consider how official introduction agencies also list men, and how men and women may partake in their own commodification in western-oriented singles ads.

Commodified though their images may be, women and men can and do exert choice in submitting their names to an introduction agency and in deciding what to include in their listings. As Robinson observes, there are limits to the market analogy. Unlike "real" commodities—for example, a lawn mower—women like Lu and Moira decided which photograph to submit, which blurb to provide, whether or not to respond to an e-mail message, and whether or not to establish a relationship with a particular man. Commodities have no choice about where they go or to whom they are sold. They have no say in how they are marketed or represented. Even web sites that objectify women to a high degree allow some choice in their own self-representation.

Julag-Ay makes a strong case for considering the way in which agencies and introduction "clubs" that are set up as profit-making businesses "commodify" women—or rather women's images—in their brochures and web sites. Similar to my argument in the case of Filipina domestic workers and the agencies that promote them to prospective Hong Kong employers, Julag-Ay focuses on how profit-oriented introduction services objectify women by highlighting their physical features, having special promotional "sales" of catalogs, referring to the women with numbers or codes, implying that some women are younger, newer, or "better quality" than others and therefore access to their addresses costs more, and presenting letters from the agency's "satisfied customers." In addition, there is an imbalance between the men, who pay for the service, and the women, who play the more passive role of being approached by men.[25] In contrast to domestic workers listed by employment agencies, who often know nothing about their prospective employers and can be pressured by the agency to accept a job regardless of the employer, women who are listed by introduction services can potentially learn as much about their pen pal through letter-writing as the pen pal knows about them. Moreover, I have never heard of a case where a woman was pressured to choose a partner by the agency. In fact, it might be in the agency's economic best interest to maintain as many available women as possible.

The imbalance between men's and women's access to one another's listings has shifted considerably in recent years. Many people who meet through correspondence meet not through commercial agencies, but rather through "friend finder" clubs that do not require a fee. And although free clubs appear to commodify women less, they may have the disadvantage of not filtering out those who are not interested finding a "life partner." Since the 1990s, more opportunities exist for men to be listed and for women to initiate correspondence with men. Stanley, who listed his name with a Taiwan-based Internet agency, was contacted by several Chinese women. Among them was a Hong Kong Chinese woman who is now his wife.

There is an important difference between interpreting the market and associated processes of commodification metaphorically and taking them literally. As Robinson argues, the market metaphor "obscures the agency of women, presenting them as 'dupes' of the brokers who run the web sites and the men who seek to marry them."[26] Many women and men (in the United States and elsewhere) may seem to willingly commodify themselves, in the sense that they "package" themselves in ways that they believe will be more attractive or appealing to others. Men and women involved in correspondence are like other men and women who are metaphorically said to be "on the marriage market." Men and women select photographs that they hope will be attractive and describe themselves in positive terms. This form of "selling" or "marketing" oneself is not literal (no more literal than the description of bars as "meat markets"), and to define it as such when it involves foreign women not only seriously misrepresents the process but also robs women of their ability to act in meaningful ways. Especially noteworthy is that such images of Third World women are also linked to common stereotypes, or what Patricia Hill Collins calls "controlling images," that naturalize racism and sexism.[27] Thus, while aiming to criticize a process that objectifies women, Glodava and Onizuka and other critics' writings can inadvertently reproduce and naturalize images of Asian and Asian American women as passive, subservient, docile, and demeaned.[28]

THE MEN

Glodava and Onizuka represent the men as "buying brides." Their discussion of men draws in part from an oft-cited unpublished report based on a 1988 survey conducted by Davor Jedlicka, a sociologist at the University of Texas at Tyler.[29] Jedlicka's report, the only research of its kind, is based on 260 responses (out of 607 questionnaires) from men who were seeking brides through correspondence. Jedlicka found that 94 percent of the men were white; they were highly educated (50 percent had two or more years of college); 56 percent identified themselves as politically conservative; 91 percent said sex should be between married or live-in partners; the men were generally economically and professionally successful; their median age was thirty-seven; 22 percent came from California; and 84 percent lived in metropolitan areas. Over half had been married at least once and most had divorced after an average of seven years of marriage; a third had at least one child, and three quarters of them hoped to have more children. Roughly half of the men identified themselves as Protestant, about a quarter as Catholic, 15 percent belonged to other religions, and 14 percent had no religious affiliation (Glodava and Onizuka, 25–26). I did not conduct a formal survey of the several hundred men I met on various lists (see chapter 2), but my impression was that they would generally fit this profile. One difference, however, was that men who corresponded with Chinese women seemed less religious and on the whole of slightly higher socioeconomic status than men who wrote to Filipinas.

According to Glodava and Onizuka, Jedlicka concludes that the men "who choose mail-order methods for mate selection appear 'above average . . . certainly in their communication skills,' and 'exceptional in the sense that they are trying cross-cultural marriage to improve their chances for loving and enduring relationships'" (26). Glodava and Onizuka respond that "such conclusions are thin at best and such interpretations from these data are unwarranted. Our experience and the observations of others show that, contrary to responses in questionnaires, *those who have used the mail-order bride route to find a mate have control in mind more than an enduring and loving relationship*" (26; emphasis added).[30]

It is methodologically difficult (if not impossible) to assess whether a man wants a mate he can "control *more than* a loving and enduring relationship" or how love and control are interrelated, but my own research suggests that men did want loving and enduring relationships. As I discuss in the following chapters, men had often experienced failed relationships with U.S. women, and they expressed deep concern for creating "enduring relationships" that were built on common views regarding the permanence of marriage, shared practical concerns, and also love. Glodava and Onizuka support their claim based on examples of men who supposedly want to "control" their wives. Such examples may not be "typical," nor do they preclude a desire for loving and enduring relationships. Glodava and Onizuka cite a number of uncontextualized quotations from men in journalistic interviews, comments from "experts," and Glodava's own experience among thirty mail-order brides. Quotations from newspaper articles cite men who say they want someone "who'll be there every night" or "who won't cheat, and who I can trust to do right by me" (26). Such statements resemble those I heard as well, but do not necessarily preclude love or a desire for enduring relationships or reflect a need for "control"; nor are they likely to be unique to men with foreign partners.

The authors also cite the age difference between men and women to support their assertion.[31] Glodava's sample of women included only two who were married to men with a four- to six-year age difference: "The other 28 average between 20 to 50 years difference in age. Older men want women 'they can mold' and therefore do not want ones who are too educated" (27).[32] Although older men may want women whom they "can mold" (as might younger men), this does not preclude loving and enduring relationships. That some men want to meet women who are "not too educated" may not be linked so much to "control" as to an expectation that less educated women are more "traditional," have fewer ambitions about work and career, and may therefore derive greater satisfaction from household work.

If men are interested in meeting women who will be satisfied in a domestic role, then their chances may be greater among less educated women.

Glodava and Onizuka's observations about women's low level of education is not supported by other sources. A CFO survey suggests that overall the educational level of Filipinos and their foreign fiancés/spouses is roughly equal.[33] The PWC study in Canada found that 79 percent of the participants in their study had a university degree, 16 percent were vocational college graduates, and 5 percent were high-school graduates (40).[34] Of the men I knew, many had pen pals, wives, or fiancées with college or university degrees. Some women were considerably better educated than the men. Several men expressed pride and pleasure that such educated or intelligent women would be interested in them. Some were attracted to highly educated Chinese women, and others who had married Filipinas encouraged them to attend college in the United States, further their professional training, or pursue a job or career. Unfortunately, when women have less education than men, the automatic assumption is that the men are taking advantage of them. When women have more education than the men, it is often assumed that either the woman is taking advantage of him or that the man wants a woman to support him; in either case, this falls into what Yen Le Espiritu describes as the "dichotomous stereotypes of the Asian woman" as either "the cunning Dragon Lady or the servile Lotus Blossom Baby."[35] The men are also subject to dichotomous and reductionist stereotypes as either the omnipotent, controlling, white/western oppressor, or the reject and loser who becomes an unwitting victim of the "dragon lady." Just as most women do not recognize themselves in these stereotypes, neither do the men.

Glodava and Onizuka cite a women's rights advocate to support certain negative impressions of the men. With no background or context for the quotation, the advocate is quoted as saying: "I consider this an international sex ring, the men who apply, basically they're losers. They cannot make it in this country so they go out and look for women who can be their total slaves" (27–28). The authors also cite men's letters to agencies expressing their pleasure at the success of their relationships, and comments of other "observers" to support the conclusion that men want control, not enduring and loving relationships. Lisa Belkin, a journalist cited in *Mail-Order Brides*, writes that men often prefer "*what they see as* the old fashioned submissiveness of Asian women to the aggressive independence of their western counterparts" (Glodava and Onizuka, 27; emphasis added). As described earlier, this is a common viewpoint among men, yet it is important to point out—as Belkin does and as Glodava and Onizuka seem to overlook—that what some men "perceive" or speak of as old-fashioned submissiveness is not necessarily the same thing as male control, nor does it mean that men do not also see and articulate the limits of such stereotypes of Asian women in the course of developing friendships and romantic relationships with "real women."

Numerous quotations can be found on the Internet, in the popular media, or in published sources that suggest that men want wives they can control and who will fulfill their every need.[36] Glodava and Onizuka are no doubt correct that there are men who meet their wives through correspondence (as well as other means) who are guilty of spousal abuse. But they overlook the possibility that these men and women are a highly diverse group, and that there are also men who are critical of such sexist and chauvinistic behavior and intentions. Many men who are involved in correspondence relationships readily criticize those who depict Filipinas or Chinese women as passive and subservient. They "warn" men that if what they want is a subservient, docile, and subordinate wife, then they should not expect to find this among Asian women. As some men point out, based on their own experiences, Asian women may express their wants, desires, and dissatisfactions in different ways, and their methods may sometimes be less direct and aggressive than American women, but they manage to express their perspectives nonetheless. In several Internet conversations, men and women pointed out that some Filipinas do not argue or shout if they are unhappy, while others insist that they do. Many men and women claimed that Filipinas may be reluctant to express their anger verbally and directly, but they may well bang the pots and pans, burn dinner, sulk, and give the silent treatment until a compromise has been reached.

As we have seen, Glodava and Onizuka cite sources that describe men as "losers" who aim to control foreign women because they have been rejected by American women (29). An Australian journalist likewise suggests that men who "have little currency in their own domestic currency markets," who are "rejected, unrequited casualties of Australia's dating scene" can be "transformed into internationally desirable commodities."[37] Although women are statistically more likely to file for divorce than men in the United States and this may well be linked to women's gains in economic independence in recent years, men may nonetheless "reject" western women. Whether they reject or are rejected, however, this still does not support the claim that these men do not want loving and enduring relationships. As I have argued, men may want to be the "head of the household," but that does not mean, as Glodava and Onizuka assert, that their position will be "enforced with fists" or that women are necessarily "grateful for their new found lifestyle" whether they "are in happy or abusive situations" (30–31). Such statements reinforce stereotypical notions of male dominance and dichotomous conceptions of power. To represent correspondence relationships as the result of men's desire to dominate women who are weaker by virtue of race, class, or nationality is to overlook the question of how various forms of power (including that of the state, capital, popular culture, discourses and ideologies of masculinity and privilege, and foreign and local women) act on men and render their alleged dominance, as members of the western male "elite," problematic.

THE WOMEN

In their chapter on women who "sell themselves," Glodava and Onizuka briefly discuss the topic of early-twentieth-century Japanese "picture brides" and compare them to so-called mail-order brides of today. They point to the fact that picture brides married men from the same cultural background as themselves, "whereas mail-order brides are often involved in interracial marriages" (33). Correspondence marriages that take place within ethnic communities, such as Chinese American marriages to Chinese women and South Asians who marry women from their place of origin, are largely excluded from their discussion. Yet such marriages share much in common with those that involve white men and Asian women and are also subject to similar problems and concerns.[38] The false assumption that mail-order marriages are interracial, risks further reinforcing a simple gender-race dichotomy between white men and Asian women.

Comparisons with Japanese picture brides are nonetheless provocative. Julag-Ay suggests that a key difference was that Japanese picture brides and grooms were matched through family and friends or extended kin networks, whereas many couples who court via correspondence often meet through commercial ventures, agencies, or pen pal clubs.[39] Because early-twentieth-century immigration laws prohibited the entry of unmarried Japanese women, women were often married in Japan by proxy before coming to the United States to meet their husbands. As Glodava and Onizuka point out, these marriages were often difficult and disappointing for the women.[40] It is important to note that familial involvement in arranging a marriage does not necessarily mean it will be a "better match." In cases I encountered, familial involvement was accompanied by a woman's greater sense of pressure from and obligation to her family. In contrast, the impersonal role of the introduction agency can enhance a woman's ability to decide whether or not to reject prospective partners.

In their chapter on "the women," Glodava and Onizuka look at popular media images of Asian women in the United States, ideas about widow-burning *(sati)* in India and foot-binding in China as topics that capture the western imagination and reinforce images of Asian women's role as "one of bearing and rearing of children and giving men pleasure" and of "Asian ancient religions teach[ing] women to honor and accept a subordinate role in a highly patriarchal society such as those of Asia" (40). Glodava and Onizuka accurately stress how such ideas influence western orientalist notions of Asia and Asian women. Yet their discussion quickly shifts from an analysis of inaccurate stereotypical ideas about Asia to an assumption that these views reflect reality and are internalized by women. They write, "In fact, this subordinate role is not only entrenched in the minds of men, it is also accepted by women as their lot in life. Women even make sacrifices for the men in their lives such as suffering concubinage or the ultimate sacrifice, dying for and with them in sati" (40). They thus fail to question women's acceptance of these terms and fail to recognize that these ideas are partly western representations that are essentialized in a timeless way and used strategically, but not grounded in "facts." As scholars have argued, negative stereotypes may be partially internalized, but they are also actively resisted, rejected, questioned, and criticized.[41]

Edward Said defines "Orientalism" as a western representation of the Orient that says more about the West than about the other it purports to represent. Aihwa Ong extends Said's view of orientalism and effectively illustrates how Asians can appropriate certain orientalist characterizations for their own benefit.[42] State-promoted images of Southeast Asian women as docile, hard workers with nimble fingers, for example, serve to promote foreign investments in Asian production and manufacturing sites. Ong's discussion of Asian acceptance of certain orientalist assumptions differs from that of Glodava and Onizuka; Ong is aware of how such images can be used as a conscious strategy with potential benefits. In an insightful analysis of images of Asian women as docile workers and sexual objects, Laura Hyun Yi Kang goes a step further to show how writings about Asian "factory girls" and "hospitality girls" reinforce "the myth of their intellectual inferiority and docility, and . . . further disqualifies them from the model of the self-possessed adult individual, the normative Western subject."[43] Western feminist critics of the objectification of Asian women workers, moreover, uncritically "put the denuded Asian female body on display" (429) and "run the risk of reifying sexist and racist stereotypes in their own figurations" (425).

Women who have internalized religious and cultural views of themselves as inferior and subordinate may be described as victims. Yet women (and men) do not simply accept notions of their own subordination, but express resistance, agency, and choice.[44] Introduction agencies and the women themselves may deploy images of feminine, obedient, and traditional women, but the use of such images may represent a degree of agency and self-determination, not simply an unquestioned acceptance of a subservient role. In an advice book for women, for example, Jullie Daza, a Filipino journalist and television personality, encourages Filipinas to use the "silent treatment"—a practice that men and women associate with Asian women and that is often juxtaposed to the behavior of U.S. women—with their partners. The silent treatment, she writes, "may lower the temperature to freezing point all around, but at least it's a noiseless, bloodless form of warfare. It does not cost anything like shattered crystal, so it's cost-effective. What's more, men can't stand the silent treatment. They prefer you screaming and arguing, your face red and your throat about to burst. But when you clam up, they don't know what to do. When they don't know what to do, they're ready to throw in the towel."[45]

In her memoir, *Confessions of a Thai Mail Order Bride,* Wanwadee Larsen writes of her subtle and gentle manipulations of her husband:

> I am in no position, and of no disposition, to put my foot down: it is not the Oriental way, nor is it *my* way. . . . Paradoxically, only by not pressing time into the issue will I eventually have time on my side. It is perhaps difficult for American women to see my point, to understand why in Thailand we nudge instead of push, especially when there is so much at stake. . . . Some of it has to do with tradition. . . . Some has to do with views of what, in the long run, makes for true marital stability. And some more has to do with our differing concepts of exactly what a woman is and how she is supposed to react to, to cope with, not only males but all the varying circumstances of life.[46]

Although Larsen's "gentle" manipulations of her husband adhere to certain stereotypes of subservient "Oriental women," they also allow us to see how Larsen's "Oriental way" is empowering and enables her to eventually get her way.

Glodava and Onizuka cite numerous studies that generalize about the subordinate role of Asian women and their commitment to their families. They cite journalistic representations of female infanticide and women's low status that reflect widely accepted "truths" about Asia without context or qualification. They cite a journalistic account by Robert Elegant, who writes, in traditional China, a woman was subject to her father before she was married and then to her husband. As a widow she obeyed the new head of the family, usually her own son. . . . For obvious reasons women did not initiate divorce. Social pressures kept families intact. A well-to-do husband would take a second wife—as well as quasi wives known as concubines. . . . No matter how it hurt, wives would put up with other wives and concubines, rather than become unpersons through divorce.[47]

Glodava and Onizuka fail to recognize that the Confucian "three obediences" Elegant describes, refer to ideals of an idealized Chinese *past* that were criticized during most of the twentieth century. They overlook distinctions between ideals, past history, and actual lived experience. As Margery Wolf and others have pointed out, this representation of women is largely a male view of how things *should* work, as opposed to how they actually do or did; women had their own ideas about family structure and their own access to power and authority.[48]

Glodava and Onizuka overlook the vast cultural, educational, and class differences within Asian countries. Their depiction of Chinese, Japanese, and Indian culture promotes dehistoricized, essentialized images of submissive and obedient Asian women and reinforces the assumption of Asian women as victims. They uncritically accept generalizations about "culture." As Abu-Lughod has argued, it is important to "write against culture," to show how cultural over-generalizations objectify whole categories of people and do not adequately represent lived experiences.[49] Glodava and Onizuka reproduce superficial constructions of "Asian culture" without historical contextualization. By essentializing Asian, Chinese, or Indian women, they are predisposed to miss cases in which women reject such "ideals," escape unwanted marriages, form supportive female communities, maintain contact with their natal families, and exert control over their husbands, sons, and daughters-in-law. By representing all correspondence marriages as "trafficking" or "buying and selling," they essentially reduce all such relationships to a cultural stereotype of international, interracial marriages, robbing them of heterogeneity and humanity.

Glodava and Onizuka at times reinforce the notion that the subordination of Asian women is enduring, fixed, and therefore natural. Referring to Japan, they write, "What are the chances for change in this modern age? In reality, very little because 'old prejudices and folk beliefs are too powerful.'" (42). They ignore phenomenal efforts toward social, cultural, and economic change, such as in China following the Communist Revolution of 1949. Their discussion shifts back and forth between Japan, China, India, and other parts of Asia, producing a seamless image of Asia and "Asian women." They write that "in most Asian countries, women are expected to work only if necessary for the family's well being" (43). The Philippines is cited as an exception, as "a more egalitarian society" in which women often work outside the home and can achieve high positions in business and politics. They overlook the phenomenal role of women in the public work force in post-1949 China when women's work was considered central to the advancement of the socialist state and key to the emancipation of women.[50] Such changes belie the notion that "old prejudices and folk beliefs" are so powerful anywhere in Asia as to preclude change.

Glodava and Onizuka also cite political and economic factors to help explain why women "sell" themselves. The sending countries "are often mired in poverty, and they have deteriorating economic conditions and experience feelings of powerlessness. . . . For many women, *the main reason* for leaving is the poverty stricken nature or the political unrest in their homelands" (47, emphasis added). Their prime example is the Philippines, "an important and still growing source of more than 50 percent of the mail-order brides worldwide" (47).

Despite the fact that many women I met in China lived a comfortable, urban, middle-class lifestyle, and some whom I met in the Philippines were from upwardly mobile middle-class families, living in households that could afford servants or "helpers," most were well aware of the high standard of living in the West, and in the United States in particular. I agree that the wider global context against which these relationships are formed is extremely important, but Glodava and Onizuka's claim that economic or political conditions constitute "the main reason" for women's departures from their homelands overlooks many other salient factors (see chapter 5).

As many of the sketches in this book suggest, women often prefer *not to* leave their homelands, given the choice, and women do not accept just any offer of marriage in order to emigrate. Were "getting out" their main objective, then women would not express a high degree of selectivity and choice. Politics and economics—as well as ideas about "modernity"—and imagined geographies of wealth and poverty constitute an important context in which these relationships take place, but they do not provide enough of a reason for men and women to marry a foreigner. Women's chances to marry (in the Philippines) or remarry (in China) were key factors. Their age, marital status, and whether or not they had children could influence their local marriage prospects. Women cited love, attraction, "chemistry," respect, and practical and individual considerations that colored their motivation to meet and sometimes marry foreign men. As I argue in the following chapters, political economy is important for the way that it is linked to the cultural logics of love and desire, but material motives alone are not the only or the primary factor in these relationships.

Glodava and Onizuka describe their interview with Bruce Beardsley, U.S. Consul General in Manila in 1992. In 1991, the Embassy granted 7,678 visas to spouses of Americans. When asked if the office ever denied visas, he answered, "We may delay in some cases, but generally visas are issued because there is no legitimate reason not to" (57). Beardsley cited a case in which a physically handicapped man "petitioned for a young Filipina. It was very obvious to embassy representatives that the only reason he wanted her was for him to have a nursemaid. After they warned the woman about the situation, she still decided to go through with the marriage. 'We had no other choice but to give her the visa.' He added 'the women are reasonably aware of the pitfalls of the (mail-order) marriage. They are not ignorant'" (57). Rather than view this as an example of a woman who has made an informed decision (as Beardsley appears to), Glodava and Onizuka portray this woman as a victim of mail-order marriage.

Citing Elegant, Glodava and Onizuka suggest that "Filipinas are eager to marry foreigners regardless of age, temperament, appearance, or comparative penury. They are desperate to leave the country where their best prospects are unpaid drudgery as rural or slum wives—or the evanescent glitter of the red-light districts" (57).[51] This overlooks the possibility of educated women, whose options go well beyond becoming slum wives or "hospitality girls" in red-light districts. Filipinas I interviewed who corresponded with foreign men had college degrees and were trained as teachers, lawyers, nurses, office workers of various sorts, and clerks. Although they were often underemployed, only one woman had previously worked in the entertainment industry. Elegant's statement gives the impression of only three choices: slum or rural marriage, red-light districts, or marrying foreigners. Rosie (see chapter 4) illustrates the way in which even young rural women with a high-school education may have a number of choices. Her options included remaining single and working as a shop clerk, marrying a local Chinese businessman, or marrying her American fiancé. Like other women she knew, she could have gone abroad to work as a domestic worker, but she preferred to remain in the Philippines. Lee, a beautiful and educated Filipina in her thirties from an elite family, worked in a bank. Several local men had expressed an interest in courting her, but she preferred to wait and consider different options. Maria, a devout Mormon, worked as a school teacher and wrote to several men abroad. None of her pen pals captured her romantic interests, but in 2000 she informed me that she had met a very nice local Filipino. Not all women are as desperate, limited in their options, or as uninformed as some imagine.

Mail-Order Brides, like the feminist studies that Mohanty critic. zes for representing Third World women as victims of patriarchal familial structures, religion, and development, creates the impression of Asia as a breeding ground for women who, blind to their own oppression, must be rescued by enlightened feminists. As Mohanty has written, this amounts to "discursive colonization," in which the singular Third World woman becomes the fuel and fodder for constructions of more liberated and enlightened western feminists.[52]

MARRIAGES

Colored by their assumption that marrying a foreigner is a "ticket out of hell," yet acknowledging that "for women who long for a better life, becoming a mail-order bride is an alternative" (60), Glodava and Onizuka assert that the media depict mail-order marriages in positive terms. In contrast, like Julag-Ay, I have found that media reports present mainly "negative" examples. "In almost all correspondence marriages discussed in the media, the examples that are presented are the extreme examples of abuse . . . although these abuses do occur, the various media do not counter their articles with examples of more mundane, even prosperous marriages. . . . Much that is reported is sensationalized using the more graphic abuse cases" (Julag-Ay, 63). Yet, oddly enough, Glodava and Onizuka claim that "there are more mail-order bride success stories reported than those of failed marriages" (63).

Well-known "success stories" include the marriages of several couples who have founded match-making agencies and who use their own positive experiences to promote their business. Glodava and Onizuka attribute the supposed lack of negative media representations to women's feelings of shame about private marital problems and their unwillingness to report abuse to authorities and social workers. They are no doubt correct about many women's feelings about maintaining their privacy, but this does not explain the dominance of negative representations in the media. The difference may be attributed in part to the time when Glodava and Onizuka did their research. In the 1990s, it was difficult to find representations of correspondence courtship and marriage that did not begin with critical or sensationalist assumptions. Many journalistic accounts cited by Glodava and Onizuka would also seem to support this point. Men and women are very reluctant to talk to representatives of the media because of the negative ways they have been (mis)represented, not necessarily because they feel they have something to hide. One interesting example is the case of Jeffrey and Emelda Hollis, who met through correspondence and agreed to appear on television on *The Maury Povich Show*. As Jeffrey Hollis explains, he felt that the program was designed and edited in such a way as to portray him and his wife and the other couples in the worst possible light.[53]

At least since the highly publicized case of Timothy Blackwell, the U.S. man who shot and killed his estranged, pregnant Filipina wife, Susana Blackwell, and two of her friends in the Seattle courthouse where they waited to testify for the couple's annulment hearing, the mainstream media has clearly chosen to "sell" the more sensationalist and violent side of the topic.[54] Couples are therefore hesitant to publicize how they met and are often defensive toward journalists and researchers who they think will depict them in a negative light. Many reports are based on women who will talk, that is, those who come for marital counseling or who are living in shelters for victims of domestic abuse, which no doubt skews the image of these marriages. Cases that are reported in the popular media often portray such marriages in sensationalist terms.

Glodava and Onizuka describe both well-publicized cases of failed marriages and four "case stories." These cases of difficult or abusive marriages are sad and troubling. But what is interesting is the extent to which the four women have made decisions to court, marry, and either leave the husband (in three cases) or remain with him despite the difficulties. The three women who left their husbands became U.S. citizens or permanent residents. The cases also illustrate how each of the women had other options and opportunities abroad but chose to marry and come to the United States. It is difficult to see them as women who "sold themselves." Although we are not told of one woman's prior occupation, the other three women had good jobs (as a teacher, in public relations, and as a chemist). All three were presumably educated. "Chita," a school teacher, opted to meet and marry an American because at forty-five she was considered too old to find a husband in the Philippines. "Amor" was also forty-two and working for a "prestigious pharmaceutical company in Manila" when she met and corresponded with her husband, a U.S. corporate lawyer. When her husband brought his mistress to live with them, she decided to leave him. "Catherine" was an unwed mother from Malaysia with a "very good job in advertising" who also left her abusive husband when he brought his mistress home.[55]

Glodava and Onizuka end their chapter on "marriages" with three supposedly "positive comments" from magazines and newspapers:

"It's not subservient, but she'll lay down her life for me," says quadri-
plegic professor John Letcham of his spouse Gertrude Estapia (*People*
1985). Sue Cormick, on the other hand, on her marriage to Jim, "Here
I am appreciated. And here I have many appliances" (*USA Today* 1986).
Don Springer (46) says in an article in *The Denver Post* (1987), "The
Philippines are loaded with homemakers. A man like me is not going
to find a woman like this (his 26 year-old wife) here." (73–74)

These "positive" statements reflect what Glodava and Onizuka have already defined as negative issues: in the first case the woman will presumably lay down her life for her husband. The implication, from what Glodava
and Onizuka have written, is that she will do so out of appreciation or subservience, not out of love or devotion. To do so illustrates her victim status
or her husband's delusions about the extent of her devotion. Similar to the
sections of the Maury Povich interview that were edited out, Glodava and
Onizuka do not include Gertrudes Estapia's full statement, which reads,
"Everyone said that I just wanted to marry an American . . . but I was
thinking that I love this man." [56] In the second case, the woman's sense of
appreciation juxtaposed with her own appreciation for appliances with no
further contextualization makes her look like someone who was attracted
and satisfied solely by material considerations. The third quotation is also
difficult to see as "positive," as it plays into assumptions about the superfi-
ciality of a man's interest in his young homemaker wife. Ironically there is
more of what is "positive" to be gleaned from Glodava and Onizuka's "negative" case studies, where we at least gain a sense of women's specific reasons for leaving their homelands and eventually their husbands.

RETHINKING "MAIL-ORDER BRIDES"

This chapter has criticized popular representations of correspondence marriages that depict these relationships as the literal buying and selling of
brides, with men who are motivated solely by a desire for control and
women who accept their own subservience and marry out of economic
desperation. The perspective that is expressed by Glodava and Onizuka and
others, I have argued, reflects a highly problematic orientalist, essentialist,
and universalizing feminist approach and makes false assumptions about
the determining role of material factors and political economy. In such literature, as we have seen, foreign brides are often conflated with prostitutes.

Contemporary feminist studies of the discourse on prostitution and
sex work provide innovative interventions that are relevant to a critical
rethinking of current representations of mail-order brides.[57] Although

mail-order brides and prostitutes are both said to "sell" themselves, it is more accurate to say that a sex worker sells her/his sexual labor and is cognizant of the fact, whereas a foreign bride (like any other bride) contributes some form of reproductive labor, but does not usually consider sex a commodity. In fact, the lines may appear to be more blurred when sex workers conceive of clients as "boyfriends" and payments as "gifts," and marriages can be seen as a contractual agreement that involves the exchange of reproductive labor, sexual services, and material support.[58] The notion that sex workers get paid to have sex, whereas a wife does so for "free" is—regardless of possible arguments to the contrary—likely to be accepted as "true" by most spouses and sex workers.

As in the case of mail-order brides, Kamala Kempadoo observes that Third World prostitutes are most commonly described by terms such as "*slaves, trafficked,* and *victims,* all of which evoke images of helpless, ignorant, dependent women and girls."[59] Third World prostitution is often described as "sexual slavery, as violence to women, or as the ultimate expression of female oppression," despite the fact that "many women who work in the sex trade in Third World and other non-Western countries, including Asia, propose that we understand prostitution in a very different light: as work within a clearly defined industry, as a survival strategy, or as a way of making do when other options are limited or closed" (225). "Despite the marginality and vulnerability of Third World and non-Western sex workers," Kempadoo observes that "the notion of 'victim' is rejected by many who are currently working in the sex trade or researching it from the prostitutes' perspectives"(232). Given women's perspectives, Kempadoo asks whether we are thus to read sex workers' views as representing women's "false consciousness," or as a simple adoption of western discourses on prostitutes' rights, or whether there are other ways to conceptualize the issue.

Kempadoo calls for greater attention to expressions of prostitutes' agency: "Through recognizing sex worker agency it becomes possible to uncover resistances to, and contestations of, oppressive and exploitative structures and regimes as well as the visions and ideologies inscribed in women's practices. Thus this recognition is an attempt to position sex workers as actors in the global arena, as persons capable of making choices and decisions that lead to transformations of consciousness and to changes in everyday life" (233). Kempadoo calls for listening and learning from sex workers themselves and for rethinking and reconceptualizing Third World prostitution at a time when "increasingly, analyses have shifted from simple hierarchies and dichotomies to the problematization of multiple spaces, seemingly contradictory social locations and plural sites of power, [the] experiences, identities, and struggles of women in the global sex trade cannot be neglected" (234). As I argue, a similar move is necessary for understanding foreign brides. Kempadoo identifies Third World sex work as "one of the last sites of gender relations to be interrogated through a critical feminist lens that assumes that women are both active subjects and subjects of domination" (234), but correspondence marriage is among the sites that require a similar reenvisioning through a contemporary critical feminist lens.

Like sex workers, mail-order brides are commonly depicted as victims of patriarchy and the ultimate symbol of female oppression. And like those who "fight for changes within the sex industry—and not for its abolition," those who attempt to represent a different perspective are subject to the charge of "false consciousness" (Kempadoo, 234). The PWC criticizes any "narrow definition" of trafficking that seeks to isolate issues of abuse and coercion, a view that they say is being "peddled by feminists, especially those from the North, who seek to legalize prostitution as a legitimate form of 'work'" as a "reprehensible position" (PWC, 1). Yet it is important to stress that attention to women's "agency" does not imply that they will live happily ever after, or that they are not subject to wider forms of gender discipline and inequality. Instead, it allows us to see how women assert dignity, express strength, and in so doing resist and transform the role and image of passive sex object and submissive wife.

Ironically, the orientalist images of Asia and Asian women that Glodava and Onizuka and other writers uncritically reinscribe are similar to some of the most derogatory images of Asia and Asian women depicted on the web sites of many introduction agencies and espoused by some men. Such images are not "true" by virtue of their patterned repetition and uncritical acceptance. Yet the uncritical reproduction of such images further inscribes the very problem that Glodava and Onizuka seek to eradicate. Assuming that Asian women are objects who are bought and sold, that their culture is traditional and unchanging, teaching them to be submissive, self-sacrificing, and obedient wives is not only a bad feminist argument, but it is one that fits with the most demeaning and essentializing images of mail-order brides. Such images rob women of their ability to express intelligence, resistance, creativity, independence, dignity, and strength. The following chapters further problematize such misassumptions and point to the role of political economy in relation to cultural logics of love and desire.

4   Fairy Tales, Family Values, and the Global Politics of Romance

You called me your "little princess" . . . if I am your little
princess . . . then you are my "Majesty King." It is like a
fairy tale.

—LISA, 1999

In her chapter "Alien Romance," Anna Tsing briefly refers to "mail-order
bride catalogs," drawing on the work of Ara Wilson and Venny Villapando.
The women are presented in the catalogs, Tsing writes, as "sexy and selfless—a pleasant alternative to selfish American women. The words ex-
cerpted from the women's letters confirm this image: their hobbies are child-
ish; their English is broken. The catalogs, like so much scholarship, create
a gaze in which we victimize and homogenize even as we learn 'a woman's
story.'" Yet we must ask whether the women are in fact "presented" as "sexy
and selfless" or whether they are read or assumed to be that way. Tsing ac-
knowledges that there is another way to read the catalogs. "The photographs and letters that American men interpret as signs of sexy selflessness
are, for the women who choose to send them in, features of a search for self-
actualization. The women's intentions contradict the catalog's assumptions,
refusing to be totally absorbed."[1] Tsing's observation helps open up an
arena for other interpretations. There are other ways to read these catalogs,
not only from the perspective of the women who send in their listings, but
also from the viewpoints of men. Scholars and critics often read "sexiness"
into women's clean-cut, morally conservative, and highly respectable representations of themselves. That men also claim to look for and to see "respectability" in these images must also be recognized.

In this chapter I first describe some of the discourse about Asian women
from catalogs, web sites, and scholarly studies. I then turn to Ben and Rosie
and Lisa and Ted, two couples I got to know in the Philippines in the summer of 1999. Set against the backdrop of U.S.-Philippine colonial history
and contemporary conservative family politics in the United States, Ben
and Rosie and Lisa and Ted serve as the primary ethnographic focus of this
chapter. Their words and stories are used to support two main points. One

point is to provide a reading of marriage introduction catalogs in which sexuality is recognized as an important issue but is not given center stage and in which "real experiences" and ethnographic examples are considered. Despite the claim that ethnographic research on correspondence relationships is difficult to do, it is not impossible,[2] and it can serve as an important critique of more exclusively textual and discursive feminist or cultural studies that overemphasize the sexual dimensions of correspondence courtship and largely overlook the possibility of women's agency.[3] The second point relates to my critical analysis of the analogy of the "fairy tale" and the narrative of a young woman who is rescued by a prince, a theme that repeatedly appears in the letters, stories, and words of men and women. Men and women often speak of their relationships as being "like a fairy tale," but as folklorists point out, a fairy tale's meaning depends on the particular historical, political, and personal context in which it is told. As I argue, a critical reading of the "fairy tale" of correspondence relationships reveals internal tensions surrounding gender, class, marriage, and global and national politics.

Correspondence marriages raise questions about where and why the interests of U.S. men and Asian women converge and how their relationships are linked to fairy tales of family values. Unlike the radical and subversive Asian American cultural productions that Lisa Lowe describes as creating "countersites to U.S. national memory and national culture," the men and women I knew (like many first-generation immigrants) often consciously or inadvertently allied themselves with conservative core values at the center of U.S. national culture.[4] A strictly gendered domestic-public division of labor within the nuclear family and "appropriate" sexuality restricted and contained within heterosexual marriages are often espoused by these couples and reinforced by government policies. These perspectives point us toward the "center," not the margins, of U.S. national culture.[5] The center, or the conservative right—depending on one's vantage point—is not incompatible with these immigrants' perspectives. Men's ideals often resemble conservative family-values advocates' notions of heterosexual, married, male-headed nuclear families as the "foundation" of U.S. society and the basis of the future well-being of the nation.[6] Given such views, it becomes clear why immigrant women, as prospective "colonized nationals" married to U.S. citizens, must pass the test of ideal wife and mother before they can immigrate and qualify to become permanent residents.

This chapter builds on Chandra Mohanty's critique of studies that depict Third World women as victims and thus discursively colonize their subjects.[7] As described earlier, I am critical of depictions of mail-order brides as passive victims and sex slaves. But I am also wary of romanticizing resistance and critical of depictions of mail-order brides or immigrant wives on the other end of the spectrum as hyperagents and calculating opportunists who seduce and take advantage of naive and unsuspecting western men. Within both of these images are embedded well known but highly problematic stereotypes of Asian women—the innocent sex slave and the manipulative seductress or whore, the "lotus blossom" and the "dragon lady."[8] For different reasons, both these images of mail-order brides fuel arguments for stronger policing of U.S. borders, adding further justification to keep certain immigrants out. Particularly interesting in the case of correspondence relationships is that the state must balance the interests of a nation that problematizes and opposes the inclusion of immigrant racial others against the interests of western men—citizens who often support conservative family values and expect their rights to extend to their noncitizen wives and fiancées.[9]

WEB SITES AND CATALOGS

As mentioned in chapter 2, there are over 350 web sites whose stated aim is to introduce marriage-minded western men to foreign women. As of 1998, about 70 percent of the women listed were from the Philippines.[10] The United States is considered an attractive destination by many Filipinos. As Lowe points out, "For Filipino immigrants, modes of capitalist incorporation and acculturation into American life begin not at the moment of immigration, but rather in the 'homeland' already deeply affected by U.S. influences and modes of social organization."[11] Despite ambivalent and varied attitudes toward America, for many Filipinos the United States is a fantasy. As Fenella Cannell writes, rural Filipinos from Bicol are "extremely interested in thinking about the Philippines with reference to somewhere else. Usually that somewhere else is America, and usually the comparisons stress that the 'outside' or distant place—the imagined America—is a place of power, wealth, cleanliness, glamor, and enjoyment. Opinions differ on whether it is a more moral place than the Philippines."[12] The United States represents to some a place with modern amenities, modern government freer of corruption, and modern values and attitudes toward marriage and gender relations in contrast to the imagined shortcomings of the homeland. Although women are often attracted to the United States in part for its promise of modernity, U.S. men are often drawn to women from the Philippines and other parts of Asia for the promise of so-called traditional family values and gender roles.[13]

According to Internet introduction agencies, Filipinas are popular because they are more familiar with the English language and American culture than other Asians; their appearance (more rounded eyes and wavy hair) is considered more European, and yet they are untainted by feminism and other western values.[14] By the late 1970s, printed marriage introduction catalogs became more popular in the United States, but were still less well known than in Australia.[15] At that time, U.S. men mainly came into contact with Filipinas while in the military. Even with the closing of the last U.S. military bases in the Philippines in 1992 and the transformation of former bases into tourist areas and sites for foreign investment, the image of Filipinas as more receptive to American culture has persisted.[16] Yet men who seek wives in the Philippines are often concerned that they be good, "traditional" women, untainted by negative western values. Thus the values and morals of women who have had contact with the (former) bases—working as "hospitality girls," waitresses, and entertainers, or simply residing in the region—are often suspect. The avoidance of women with possible "base contacts" is part of a conscious effort on the part of many men to distance themselves from overt references to women's sexuality. Often this effort is couched in terms of pious Christianity. As we shall see in the following chapter, most of the men I knew wanted to meet good "traditional" women.

The web sites I examined all had the stated objective of introducing "marriage-minded" people looking for "lifetime partners" and they focused mainly on introducing women in China and the Philippines to men in the United States. Although a number of individuals—for example, Filipinas who have recently married a foreigner and come to the United States, and some men belonging to chat groups—use their personal web sites as a means of introducing women abroad to men in the United States, most introduction web sites are run as businesses. In many cases they are run by Filipino-American couples who originally met through correspondence.[17]

FAIRY TALES AND FAMILY VALUES

Studies of printed representations of women from catalogs and Internet web sites have paid a great deal of attention to western male racialized sexual fantasies that reflect orientalist views and objectify women's bodies, but some have not fully appreciated the way in which these images often are not explicitly sexual but rather are overtly associated with ideas of love, "family values," and "traditional" gender roles.[18] Roland Tolentino's analysis of representations of mail-order brides, for example, focuses largely on the issue of sexuality as it comes into play with a "nuclear-family fantasy" and "colonialist fantasy" of racial conquest and rescue.[19] His analysis also blurs important distinctions between Filipinos who work as "oppressed victims of labor regimes," as "exploited domestic workers," as "abused entertainers and prostitutes," and "mail-order brides," much like Glodava and Onizuka's book described in the previous chapter. Blurring foreign brides with other categories of people who are exploited, abused, or oppressed obscures crucial differences and denies many possible degrees of choice and self-determination in any particular woman's decision to correspond with foreign men.

Ara Wilson is one of a few scholars who acknowledge that the catalog images of women are not explicitly erotic or sensually alluring. She suggests that their appeal derives in part from ideas about "how tradition or culture make these women so different from American women and, therefore, such good wives."[20] This idea is graphically illustrated by the logo for China Bride/Heart of Asia agency: a heart within which is printed "China Bride," framed by the phrase "Traditional Women" above, and "Family Values" below.[21]

As scholars have argued is the case in the Disney version of the tale of Cinderella, a fairy tale notion of "love" serves to bring family values and sex together without ever having to explicitly allude to sex.[22] Likewise, the Internet and introduction-catalog discourse on foreign brides often refers only implicitly to sexuality under the screen of a much more conservative and pervasive discourse about family values, love, and marriage. It would be difficult to argue that images of Asian women are not linked in certain ways to ideas about sexuality. Yet a heightened focus on sexuality reads more than is warranted into these representations and risks overshadowing the more prevalent and overt representation of Asian women as ideal partners, traditional wives and mothers who fit into a nuclea-family ideal.

Photographs of Filipinas on the Internet and in published catalogs are usually strikingly prudish and conservative, especially in contrast to images of Russian and Eastern European women, who often appear scantily dressed and in full body shots in seductive poses. As Wilson notes, "Some of the photographs [of Filipinas] actually are passport photos, but most strongly resemble American high school yearbook pictures."[23] Certainly American men may read "signs of sexy selflessness"[24] into the respectable-looking photographs of Asian women, but in the case of Filipinas (and also Chinese women) sexuality is in the eye of the beholder. On the whole these images reflect a much more conservative moral tenor than many scholars acknowledge. Visual and printed representations of Filipinas are more in keeping with the Disney version of *Cinderella*, which refers to sexuality only in the most highly veiled terms, with assumptions of sexual innocence.[25] Just as Cathy Preston argues that Cinderella's classical body— fully clothed and attempting no explicit allusion to sexuality or lower body processes—is essential for the story to function as an American bourgeois fantasy, so, I would argue, does the fantasy of a Filipina marriage partner generally depend on a representation of her innocence and perceived respectability as opposed to an overt sexuality.[26] Like the Disney Cinderella, prospective Filipina brides are often represented as poor, innocent young women who deserve to be rescued from menial labor and shabby clothes by way of marriage to a western hero prince.

To the men who seek them out, Asian women are models of tradition, respectability, morality, and religious piety. Their bodies are objectified, but these images are very different from the bodies of women presented in ads for "sex tours" or "Victoria's Secret lingerie," which some scholars argue constitute part of a common objectifying male gaze and therefore an extension of the same phenomenon.[27]

In a section entitled "Why Choose Women from Asia," China Bride lists a number of typical views about "Asian Women" solicited from men who have successfully found a partner. The Asian woman is "upstanding and gentle." She "shares your beliefs and values tradition, home, family and fidelity." As Wilson writes, "when references to the erotic aspects of Asian women appear, they seem almost an afterthought."[28] Sexuality is clearly implied, but it is not the central focus of China Bride: "Women from Asia are feminine. They are normally petite and slender with delicate bone structure," and in a statement that gets closest to the material body, "They typically have smooth, silky, hairless skin." Making a common turn, the text then implicitly contrasts Asian women and western women, raising the issue of appropriate feminine decorum:

> They don't bust your chops when you come home a little late or forget an anniversary. They let you know if they are unhappy with your behavior, but this is typically done in [a] warm, friendly way. . . . Women from Asia appreciate a gentleman . . . do not scold you and call you a male chauvinist when you hold a door open for them. . . . Women from Asia value marriage. They do not believe in divorce. They marry for life. . . . Women from Asia value family. Family is all important. Husband, children, parents, relatives come first. Husband and children never take second place to her career.

As the web site's home page states, these Asian women "are not spoiled by exposure to western ways, western lifestyle or women's lib. They remain pure, protected by their traditions, their culture and by their families."

Similarly, World Class Service asks visitors to the site, "Had your fill of feminists, gold-diggers, air heads, unfaithful partners and party girls? Too busy to find the right woman? This is your best opportunity in the world to find a beautiful and well educated woman of traditional values who is dedicated to marriage as a lifelong commitment."[29] The motifs of traditional values, faithfulness, and dedication to marriage appear repeatedly. The rampant sexuality of western women and "party girls" is presented in stark contrast to the marital fidelity and sexual purity of prospective Asian wives.

Some sites attempt to distinguish Filipinas from other Asian women. Filipina Brides notes that "the Filipina is, by nature and culture, very devoted, caring, old fashioned, loving and unselfish." According to Love Match International, the Philippines is the best place from which to select a pen pal because Filipinas are "attractive, [E]nglish speaking, sincere." They are the "prettiest women in the world"; "raised with traditional values they make faithful, loving wives." Filipino values are contrasted to U.S. values:

> With divorce rates continuing to climb and exceeding 50% in North America many men are now seeking more traditional wives. Wives that are faithful, attractive, loving, and who will make them a good wife, and in return make them a better person. Tired of the bar scene . . . Tired of women here who have attitudes . . . Who are spoiled . . . Well try *something new . . . something different . . . something exciting. . . .* a penpal from the Philippines. (emphasis added)[30]

The something "new and different" is the women's culture and race, and as Tolentino notes, "race is positioned as a surrogate ideal, a concession of in-betweens" for men who feel they have been emasculated by white women.[31] Race and sexuality are clearly important factors in the appeal of Asian women and white women from the former Soviet bloc. Touted by some as "superior" because of their Caucasian appearance, women from Eastern Europe and the former Soviet Union have experienced unprecedented popularity since the end of the Cold War.[32] Yet these women are often represented, according to Robinson, as women who are "good mothers," who seek a better future for their children. As Uma Narayan has aptly observed, "the 'mail-order bride' phenomenon illuminates interesting details about the nexus between race and gender stereotypes prevalent in the United States." Women from African countries "are not in demand as wives. Submissiveness and deference do not seem to be stereotypical qualities attributed to women of African descent."[33]

Ladies of the Philippines states that Filipinas listed on their site "are mostly looking for marriage. They are warm, caring, understanding, honest, loving and believe marriage is a lifetime commitment. They are the most loyal and faithful females in the world. They are beautiful and can speak English. They are very conservative and are taught the values that they are supposed to take care of their husband and family. They are more concerned about what is inside a man than his looks or age." Although women often list their religion, Filipina Penpal is one of the few sites that explicitly mentions religion in its general statement. They state that Filipinas are especially "sincere, educated, religious, caring, and humble ladies. . . . Due to their upbringing, filipinas [sic] have strong devotion towards family and religion."[34]

One can easily locate comments on public Internet chat forums by men who compare Filipinas to women of other nationalities. After watching a television program on A&E about "Russian mail order brides," "Robert" expressed disgust at Russian women who take men "for a 90 day shopping spree in the States and then return home," and also at the men who "exploited" and "seduced [these] women" by showing off their financial holdings. In contrast, he writes, "It makes you appreciate Filipina women that much more for their family values and spiritual integrity . . . I am sure that most . . . men feel secure in their courtships with Filipina fiancees. It is a good sign of sincerity when they [women] insist on marrying in PI [the Philippines] first despite the legal redtape it creates." Another man responds, "I agree with you that one is more likely to find a faithful partner and have a trusting relationship with a Filipina than with many other nationalities. Be aware, though, that in the Philippines, as anywhere else, there are scams to fleece foreign bride seekers."[35]

I now turn to Lisa and Ted and Ben and Rosie to show how detailed ethnographic studies can offer a critique of oversimplified and limited characterizations of men and women involved in correspondence relationships. Rather than reinscribe two-dimensional images of women as commodified objects of sexual desire in catalogs and on web sites, and images of men as simple consumers of these images, ethnographic research points to complex motivations on the part of men and women, and the marked yet often overlooked individual agency of women as they negotiate their decisions to correspond with, court, and marry U.S. men. These cases point to disparate threads of conservatism and contestation that emerge and intersect in some unexpected locations and to the intersection of private politics with national culture. Ethnographic research is not the only possible source of alternative readings, and it can of course produce its own "partial truths,"[36] but it can also reveal aspects of correspondence courtship and marriage that are not evident from analyses based solely on textual analyses of marriage introduction catalogs or from politically motivated studies that reduce them to simply "buying brides" or "trafficking in women."

TWO COUPLES

I first met Lisa and Ted in Manila in July 1999 through Rosie and Ben. Both couples had met and courted via correspondence. Ben (see Introduction) was a fifty-five-year-old university professor I had met in the United States. Ben had not yet met his "virtual friend" Ted in person, but knew him from the large network of men from FAF who were linked by their connections to partners in the Philippines, by the trials and tribulations of long-distance courtship and cross-cultural (mis)communication, and by tangles of INS red tape. I had been in e-mail contact with Rosie, Ben's twenty-seven-year-old fiancée, but had only recently met her in person. Manila was still new to Rosie, who had lived in a rural part of the southern island of Mindanao, and she was clearly awed by Ted and Lisa's five-star hotel room in the ritziest part of Makati and shocked by the prices at the restaurant where we ate. Ben and Rosie were engaged, but Ben had taken a detour in his career to come to Manila and work for a year for a large firm. Since divorce is illegal in the Philippines, he and Rosie were waiting out the long, tense, and expensive process of attaining legal annulment of Rosie's previous marriage. Until then, they stood no hope of getting married or of securing a fiancée (K1) visa for Rosie to come to the United States. So it was with some degree of envious anticipation and hopefulness that they listened to Ted and Lisa rehearse for their INS interview scheduled for the next day.

I met Ted and Lisa several times. On one occasion, they gave me a pile of their year-long correspondences to read. The last time I saw them was with Ben and Rosie as we celebrated their successful attainment of a visa just before their departure to the United States. Meanwhile, Ben and Rosie traveled with me to Rosie's hometown in Mindanao for a short holiday and family reunion before moving into a house in an exclusive gated community on the outskirts of Manila. There they moved with Paul, Rosie's eight-year-old son, and a few members of Rosie's extended family who would help with household chores and child care while Ben went to the office and Rosie attended a nearby college. This move represented a significant change from

Rosie's *barangay* (village) with no indoor plumbing, where the neighbors all shared one faucet, and where she had lived with her son in a two-room thatched nipa hut, built with Ben's remittances, next door to her extended family. Both Ben and Rosie expressed excitement and concern about the move and the changes it signified. Rosie expressed ambivalence about moving to an unfamiliar city far from family and friends, and Ben about the two-hour commute, about living and working outside the United States, and about Rosie and Paul's ability to adjust to life in Manila.

TED AND LISA

Ted was an athletic, good-looking white man of thirty-four who worked as a systems analyst. At one time he had run his own business, but he had financial problems and opted for the greater security of working for a well-known U.S. West Coast company. Raised in a Protestant fundamentalist household, Ted no longer considered himself religious, but respected Lisa's Roman Catholic religious views, especially her desire to be married in a church. He and Lisa had reconciled their views regarding contraception, since they did not want children in the immediate future. Ted had been married to an American woman for several years, and as he explained bitterly, "Western women are great for sex, but not for a meaningful relationship, for communication and companionship." He married his ex-wife, he said, for "all the wrong reasons." Although he would not expound on the reasons, he said that she was too controlling and the breakup was bitter. He was reluctant to say more, concerned that it would sound like the "same old story" that is told by many men who prefer foreign women and are critical of western ones. Lisa elaborated a bit: "He says that western women are lazy and drink a lot." Then she gently teased, "How do you know I won't get fat and lazy when I go to the U.S.?"

To be "fat and lazy" can carry different implications for U.S. men and Filipinas. For men, a common derogatory image of western women is that they are lazy, unwilling to work (in or outside the home), and thus entirely dependent on men. Being "fat" is associated with a lack of sexual appeal or concern about their appearance. Filipinas, by contrast, are assumed by U.S. men to be "naturally" petite and to "appreciate" hard work. Men sometimes remarked about women's tendency to put on weight when they came to the United States. For Filipinas, by contrast, being "fat" (or chubby) can be associated with well-being and prosperity, and few seemed critical of their partner's extra weight. In my earlier research, I found that Filipina domestic workers in Hong Kong often considered weight gain a sign that their employers were good and kind. Photographs of themselves looking "fat" were sent as evidence to their families that they were happy and prosperous. Weight loss was often associated with having an uncaring or cruel employer.[37] Although many urban and cosmopolitan Filipinos have adopted "modern" ideas about the health risks of excess weight and current associations of slimness with beauty, such views come into conflict with older ideas about the privilege, prestige, and beauty associated with looking "chubby." While Lisa understood that this was undesirable to Ted, she also seemed amused that to be fat and lazy would necessarily be a bad thing. To many prospective immigrants, to be fat and lazy is part of the American dream.

According to Ted, he decided to look for a wife abroad because he was tired of American feminists and of women like his ex-wife. Like many men, he lamented the difficulties of dating and the high demands and unrealistic expectations of western women, and he described himself as someone who "is not good on dates." He wanted a wife who would stay at home with the kids, but preferred to wait to have children. In the meantime Lisa could work, he said, "if she finds something that's not too demeaning." "I really want to be a waitress!" Lisa teased, knowing how to push Ted's buttons. Ben commented later on, somewhat cynically, that Ted's comments about wanting "communication and companionship" in a relationship was the sort of comment men include for the benefit of outsiders. Ben's impression was that many men want "an obedient wife." He was amused that Lisa had developed a joking response to Ted's demands.

A few years ago, recently divorced and before he met Lisa, Ted had dated a Filipino American woman he had met through a West Coast dating service. She was close to his age, had a son, but was "a psychological mess." Ted wrote to a number of Russian women he met through an introduction agency. He found them especially attractive, he said, because he had a close childhood friend from Russia, and because "Russian women are often highly educated" and he likes "a good intellectual conversation." Meanwhile, a friend's Korean wife recommended "Asian women." She talked to a Filipina with whom she worked, and Consuela agreed to introduce Ted to her sister Lisa in the Philippines. Ted became acquainted with Consuela and her husband (they had also met as pen pals). He found Consuela's appearnce, personality, and attitude attractive, so although he was initially reluctant to become involved with someone so young (she was nineteen at the time, over ten years his junior), he agreed to write. Lisa had recently submitted her name and photograph to a correspondence agency but had not yet received a reply.

Lisa was twenty-two when I met her. From northern Luzon, she was lovely, slim, and graceful, with a bubbly personality and a quick but gentle wit. She grew up doing farm work and studying. Her favorite aunt (who had helped to raise her) and her older sister had both married men in the United States and she had, ever since elementary school, harbored the hope that she would go there too. Her aunt had told her, "It is difficult in the U.S., but a different kind of difficult than in the Philippines." She did not want to dwell on the difficulties, but they included the food (you can't eat fish and rice every day there); the cold, short, dark days of winter; and the loneliness (in the winter you just stay inside and see very few people); difficulties that I would hear repeated many times by other women. She was working in the rice fields when Ted's letter arrived, and she clearly recalled her excitement. Their correspondence developed from photographs and notes on Hallmark cards to innocent but sentimental letters, all of which were kept in a bundle to show to the immigration officer at the visa interview, and thus available for me to read as well. Unaware that her barangay had no phone, at first Ted had misunderstood Lisa's reluctance to communicate by telephone.

Lisa lived a sheltered childhood, and Ted was her first (and only) boyfriend. She attended a Catholic girl's college, where she recently graduated with a degree in elementary education. Ted came to visit and attended her graduation ceremony. As Lisa described, she was so innocent she was embarrassed by Ted's letter before his first visit quizzing her about her views on sex and contraception. In the letter Ted recounted a story of an Italian man who wanted to marry a Japanese woman. The woman was eager to marry him because she had heard Italian men were very romantic and had strong sexual appetites. The man, on the other hand, wanted to meet a woman who wasn't Italian because he didn't have a strong sex drive and didn't want a wife who expected one. Both were seriously disappointed. Lisa blushed when the matter of sex was raised. Although she and Ted slept in the same bed at the hotel in Manila, they were offended by Lisa's "strict aunties" who disapproved of them staying together, despite their insistence that Lisa was still a virgin and that they had "saved themselves" for sex after marriage.

Lisa and Ted both characterized their relationship as "like a fairy tale." In one letter to him during the first year of their courtship she responded: "You called me your 'little princess' . . . if I am your little princess . . . then you are my 'Majesty King.' It is like a fairy tale." Their Internet photographs of the wedding in the United States again refer to Lisa as a princess and, as with many other such couples, the notion of a "fairy tale ending" is commonly expressed.

In Lisa and Ted's hotel room, Ben and Ted exchanged well-known stories of animosity toward the INS as Rosie, Lisa, and I listened intently. They recounted tales of the difficulties and unfairness of the immigration process: of couples who were turned away because the required number of copies of various notarized statements were not available, or because regulations had recently been changed; couples whose visas were denied for seemingly ridiculous or unknown reasons; immigration officers' suspicion of women being prostitutes or simply out to take advantage of the men; women whose friends and families in remote provinces were visited by immigration staff presumably looking for evidence of "other boyfriends" or "marriage fraud." Their attitude was not appreciation for the paternalistic role of the state in protecting them from fraudulent marriages or from predatory, insincere women with children and physical ailments. Instead they took offense at the fact that adults, American citizens, taxpayers, and in many cases men who had served their time and risked their lives in the U.S. military could not simply receive visas to bring their wives or fiancées "home." As Ted and Lisa explained, they were optimistic about obtaining Lisa's visa.

The U.S. visa procedures specify that the fiancé(e) must demonstrate having a "legitimate" relationship with the petitioner. Those ineligible for a visa include "applicants who have a communicable disease, or have a dangerous physical or mental disorder; are drug addicts; have committed serious criminal acts, including crimes involving moral turpitude, drug trafficking, and prostitution; are likely to become a public charge; have used fraud or other illegal means to enter the United States; or are ineligible for citizenship."[38] The process for applying for a K1 nonimmigrant fiancé visa—which allows a fiancée to enter the country but requires her to marry and complete the immigration procedure within ninety days or return home—is similar to the procedure for applying for a spousal visa (I-130), but usually requires less time.[39] For fiancées from the Philippines, the K1 visa sometimes takes over a year to obtain, but for most couples I knew it took around six to nine months. The K1 visa requires that the petitioner (a U.S. citizen) file an I-129F form, a petition on behalf of his or her fiancé(e).[40] This part of the process takes about three months before the process of applying for a K1 visa can begin (see chapter 7). The K1 visa requires that the couple has met at least once within two years of filing the forms, although exceptions are sometimes granted in cases of extreme hardship or religious/cultural prohibitions. Both must provide proof that they are eligible to marry. The K1 visa requires an Affidavit of Support (I-134), which includes information about the U.S. citizen's work, finances, taxes, and bank balance. The foreign fiancée is required to submit a medical report from an embassy-approved doctor, along with proof of having had the ten or more required inoculations; she also needs a passport, visa photos, a birth certificate (or the equivalent), and records of various types of clearance.[41] For women who are unfamiliar with Manila, where the U.S. embassy is located, or with the specialized language on the various forms, or who do not have the time and money readily available for photographs, transportation, and time away from work, this process can constitute a serious hardship. Lines for those who wait to submit visa applications at the Manila office are notoriously long and slow. Once the fiancée has been approved for a visa interview, if she passes the interview, the wait for a visa is normally just a few days.[42]

Ted and Lisa had waited almost nine months when their names came up. Lisa had passed her physical examination and their paperwork was in order. Ted made the trip to the Philippines (his third) to accompany her to the interview because he had heard it would help convince the immigration officer of their sincerity. The women who have to worry, Ted explained, are those who have worked in or near military bases, in bars or nightclubs, or who are or have been prostitutes or have children, older women who are assumed to be married, and "gold diggers." Since Lisa was young, had never married and had not had prior romantic relationships, and since they had records of their correspondences and photographs from previous visits, they expected things to go smoothly. They rehearsed facts about each other. Lisa recounted Ted's siblings' names, his birthday, the brand of toothpaste he used. Typical questions are said to include "How did you meet?" "What made you fall in love with him?" "How many times have you met?" "Has he met your parents?"

As they described the experience, Lisa was asked to enter the interview booth, and Ted was told to wait outside. "I showed my face," he recounted, "my job was done." Lisa was asked if it was Ted who was with her. Then she was asked her age, the duration of Ted's first marriage, and why she wanted to marry him. "Because I love him very, very much" she answered. "The officer smiled. He was very cute and seemed to like my answer. It was all over within a few minutes." They were instructed to return in two days for her visa.

Before turning to Ben and Rosie, it is important to highlight the way in which the immigration process serves to police marriages and to define which women (and men) are eligible to marry U.S. citizens, a point I return to again in chapter 7. As I interviewed other couples at the INS office in Manila, I talked to many who were far less well prepared, well informed, and successful in their attempts to secure visas. Some women had their applications denied, and their fiancés sought to find out why. Some were told they had not sufficiently documented the authenticity of their relationships. Men complained about the bureaucratic red tape and the length of time the process required. Many men were quick to express frustration and anger at a system that should be "our government working for us." As one immigration enforcement officer explained to me as an aside, their main objective is to protect the men as well as the women. They have to determine whether or not the relationship is "real." The danger, he said, echoing views discussed in chapter 3, is that the women are taking advantage of the men or, alternatively, that they risk being sold into prostitution or slave labor by unscrupulous men. Lisa was in many ways an ideal candidate to become a wife and mother. She was neither too old or too young, and had never worked at a bar or nightclub. Likewise, Ted was a white-collar professional.

BEN AND ROSIE

Ben and Rosie and their respective social situations were quite different from Ted and Lisa's. Like Lisa, Rosie was from a rural part of the Philippines, but she had a child and was once married, although she was not aware at the time that the marriage was official. As a teenager, she had worked as a domestic "helper" for a wealthy Filipino family and had become involved with her employer's son. She became pregnant, and was required by the young man's mother to sign a marriage agreement. The man's mother was fond of Rosie, and hoped that the marriage would encourage her son to settle down. Yet his affairs continued and Rosie returned to Mindanao. Her mother looked after Paul while Rosie stayed in town and worked in a small shop, contributing most of her earnings to her mother and stepfather's household. On a whim, at the suggestion of a friend, she submitted her name to an introduction service. She received many letters besides Ben's. After several months of corresponding by mail and a few telephone conversations, Ben told her he was coming to visit.

Ben had been married twice before, once as a very young man for a short period of time, and ten years later for a decade. The second marriage dissolved in the mid 1990s, a few years before he began writing to Rosie.

His second marriage, to an American he had met through the singles column of a U.S. newspaper, ended because, as he put it, he and his wife could not reconcile their ideas about children. She was a successful career woman who did not want children. He had hoped she would change her mind, but she did not. Later, when he described his relationship with Rosie, he feared that his friends and family might not regard her as his intellectual equal. His ex-wife was someone, he thought, who was unable to deal with his intellect and his increasingly successful career. When they split up, she advised him to "marry a Filipina" if what he wanted was a family. A Filipina friend had recommended the same thing, but in a much less flippant tone. Ben was not a "partier" or a drinker and he found it difficult to meet women. Like Ted, he considered his dating experiences unsatisfactory. He tried placing an ad in the personals section of a local newspaper, but most of the women who responded were not young enough to bear children, and those who were, were not interested in a man his age. He met one woman he liked who wanted to have a child with him, but she did not want to get married. To him this would have been "a failure."

Ben finally decided to "widen the pool" and correspond with foreign women. For several weeks he let the catalog sit in a dresser drawer. Finally, he pulled it out and wrote to women of various nationalities in the hope of meeting some who were receptive to marriage and family. As a university professor, he could have dated students, but he considered this inappropriate "because of the power imbalance." Only much later did he recognize the contradiction between his position regarding women students and foreign women of vastly different socioeconomic status. Initially, he had not intended to restrict his correspondences to Filipinas, but having been raised as a Roman Catholic, he was attracted to that aspect of Philippine culture, and to the fact that Filipinas speak some English.

After a few months of correspondence with several women, he decided to go and meet two pen pals. It was his first time outside of the United States. Rosie was the second woman he visited, but she soon became his favorite. She seemed bright, and he was particularly taken with her relationship with her son. Having once experienced a weight problem, he was attracted to very slim women like Rosie. When he arrived in the small rural community where she lived, he was impressed by the seriousness of her relatives and the elders of the barangay, who immediately demanded to know whether his intentions were serious. Warned by friends and family in the United States about predatory foreign women, he was suddenly struck by the fact that she too was vulnerable. Chaperoned by Rosie's younger brother, they agreed early in the course of Ben's visit to become engaged. Over the following year, Ben visited again and set up a telephone and a computer so he and Rosie and Paul could correspond by e-mail on a daily basis. He sent money and invested himself emotionally and financially in her life. Rosie, meanwhile, alternated between joy and anxiety, finding it difficult to believe that Ben would fulfill his promises to her and her son.

After their first visit, it became clear that Rosie's marital situation was more complicated than she had suspected. Her mother-in-law had indeed filed the marriage papers, and since divorce is illegal in the Philippines, they had to secure an annulment before Rosie could qualify for a visa.[43] The annulment required that they hire lawyers, pay a number of "unofficial" fees (bribes), change to a municipality with a more receptive judge, and attain the support of a local government official when it became clear that a corrupt lawyer intended to stall the process indefinitely. It took over a year to schedule the hearing, and another six months before the judge finally granted the annulment. Meanwhile, rather than spend another year or more apart while awaiting the ruling, Ben accepted a one-year position in a large international firm in Manila.

Rosie said she originally corresponded with western men simply on a whim, in the hope of "making friends" rather than out of a serious desire to get to the United States. A number of local men were interested in her, including a local Chinese man. Like many other women, she thought it would be fun to have pen pals, but she hardly dared to invest the idea with serious expectations. About forty men wrote to her, and she corresponded by mail with nineteen of them. The process was slow and it sometimes took several weeks for a letter to arrive. She preferred to write to Americans rather than men of other nationalities, because they spoke English. At first she was reluctant to correspond with men who were divorced or had children. She would not write to men who did not want children, and at fifty-five, Ben was at the upper age limit she had set. One German man had come to visit, and another from the United States planned to come as well.

Since she met Ben, she said, "Life is just like a fairy tale, and I can't imagine how happy and lucky I am that I found my real happiness in life at last." Likewise, Ben had told me early on that their relationship was — to her — much like a fairy tale and he was the knight in shining armor who had come to her rescue. It thus came as a bit of a surprise to him later on that Rosie's preference was not to go to the United States, but to remain in the Philippines, or even for them to spend long periods of time apart, he in Manila and she in the provinces with her family. Long separations, it should be noted, are not necessarily an indication of lack of marital commitment, but a way of life for many Filipino couples among whom one of the partners works abroad.[44] Rosie recounted that at first some of her friends said, "You must be crazy to agree to marry someone you don't know," but her family and most of her friends later said she is "one of the very lucky women." Filipinas are "proud" when they are seen with foreign men, she said, because other women envy them. The envy is linked in part, she explained, to the differences between Pinoys (Filipino men) and western men. Pinoys only want women who are "beautiful and sexy," whereas U.S. men "are mostly looking for someone who is very sincere and loving and caring. . . . Foreigners are not just chasing beautiful Filipinas. They like Filipinas because they are nice women, honest and loving." Western men, to Rosie and her friends, have a more "modern" and enlightened perspective than local men.

When I first met her, Rosie was shy, but she later approached me as someone who was "like a mother," to whom she could turn for advice. I was struck that she chose this analogy rather the more egalitarian notion of "sisters" or the more common Filipino notion of *ate*, or older sister, as many domestic workers had addressed me in Hong Kong. Despite the fact that we were less than fifteen years apart in age and that our sons were the same age, she still considered me "like a mother." Her mother was in fact only a few years older than me, and she also had a son Paul's age. Later, when I urged her to call me "Nicole," not "Nicole ma'am," she said that if I was a Filipina professor, she would do so out of respect and in recognition of my status, no matter how close our friendship.[45]

During and after my visit, Rosie expressed concern to me about Ben's former wives and "girl friends." She wondered if he was a "playboy," as anyone who has had two wives and women friends would appear in the Philippines. Although he insisted these were platonic friendships, she found it difficult to believe that men could have nonsexual heterosocial relationships. She was not sure she trusted him or the married women friends who had accompanied him to movies in the United States. The fact that Ben had taken a major detour in his career to live with her in the Philippines did not assuage her concerns about his faithfulness or commitment. She wanted to marry him, she told me, but she was afraid of coming to the United States, where the divorce rate is so high and people take marital commitment so lightly.

The triumphant return to the United States with their wives is a common theme in men's rescue narratives of correspondence courtship and marriage.[46] This is similar but not identical to the stories of "salvage and redemption" that Ann Anagnost describes in the context of the adoption of

Chinese children by U.S. parents.[47] Given the assumed poverty and difficulties associated with women's lives in the Philippines, the prevalent belief
among westerners that Filipinas look for any opportunity to leave and that
foreign women would "do anything for a green card," it sometimes comes
as a shock to men that their partners prefer to remain there. Rosie preferred to stay with Ben in the Philippines, where she had a better understanding and more control of their situation. A church marriage there, she
believed, would be more meaningful than one in the United States. Settling
with a foreign husband in the Philippines was Rosie's idea of a fairy tale
ending, but not Ben's. Nor was settling abroad the ending that most U.S.
men imagined, although some, including some who are retired, who spent
time there while in the military, or who work over the Internet prefer it
because there they can afford a higher standard of living. A modest U.S.
retirement pension can allow a more comfortable lifestyle—and even servants—in the rural Philippines. At one point, unsure of what would happen regarding Rosie's annulment, Ben contemplated remaining abroad. After the annulment was approved in early 2000, she and Ben were married.
Shortly after, Ben found a job in the United States, so in the summer of
2000 they came with Paul to the United States. Rosie reluctantly agreed to
give life in the United States a try, and Ben expressed some willingness to
reconsider returning to the Philippines.

CONTRASTS

Unlike Lisa, Rosie had a son. Although that made her a less ideal candidate
for a visa, Ben's reputation as an employee at a prestigious firm and his
membership in the Chamber of Commerce attested to his position as an
upright member of society, the kind of citizen whose wife should be granted
a visa. Their cohabitation in the Philippines supported the view that theirs
was a legitimate relationship. After the annulment was approved, a Chamber of Commerce connection helped smooth the process. Most couples who
marry before attaining a U.S. visa experience a longer wait, but since Ben
was working in the Philippines, it took less time.

Like many of the men I spoke with, Ben and Ted were attracted to Filipinas partly for their image as ideal, traditional wives and mothers. Both
were cautious to avoid potential "gold diggers"—women (like Cinderella's
"ugly stepsisters") whose intentions were not sincere, who were interested
in material wealth and social mobility rather than love. They both followed
the popular advice of meeting women from more remote rural areas of the

provinces rather than risk becoming involved with more cosmopolitan and sophisticated, worldly and less innocent women from Manila or Hong Kong. As "Paul," who was married to a Filipina, advised another man who was looking into pen pal relationships on a public Internet chat site:

> Girls from the provinces and small barangays will be more traditional in all respects and a great deal less likely to bug out on you for any reason. Remember that the typical Filipino husband doesn't treat his wife all that well—one of the reasons a Filipina looks to marry a foreigner. . . . It's a lot more likely divorce will happen if you get a Filipina from Manila or Cebu (but Cebu is much better than Manila). . . . That isn't to say you aren't going to find good girls in Manila, just that you have to be careful because you will find many more girls who have abandoned the more traditional views and live a more Americanized lifestyle, with accompanying attitudes.[48]

Unlike men who would not correspond with women who already had children, or with women who were married, since in most cases that would preclude ever obtaining a visa, Ben was pleased that Rosie had a son and looked forward to having "a ready-made family." Were it not for his position and network in Manila and the financial resources at his disposal, it is unlikely that Rosie would have successfully obtained an annulment (a process that took altogether close to two years) or a visa. Likewise, some women preferred not to correspond with men who were divorced or who already had children.

At one point, both Ted and Ben sent Lisa and Rosie monthly checks, but both quickly reconsidered. Ted was concerned that the money he sent was simply absorbed into the family budget but made little difference to their way of life. Like many others, he was frustrated that the check simply meant that certain family members could work less or live in leisure rather than "improving their way of life" in any way he deemed significant. Likewise, Ben tried to devise ways of ensuring that his financial contributions would not become just a substitute for work. He paid for one of Rosie's brothers' advanced schooling, for example, with the understanding that he would later support his younger brother. He invested in a motorized three-wheeler that Rosie's stepfather could rent from her for a minimal daily rate. The plan was that he could earn a better living with the three-wheeler than with the bicycle trishaw he had previously used. Although Ben intended to contribute to the wider family's welfare, and also to provide Rosie with more authority within the household and with some income while he was in the United States, he had not realized that the household power structure would not change so easily. Each time Ben returned to the United States,

Rosie was reestablished in her "normal" position near the bottom of the household hierarchy. As a single mother who had been largely dependent on her mother and stepfather, but who had long contributed to the household income, Rosie found it difficult, if not impossible, to reverse existing and ingrained patterns of authority. Instead of driving the three-wheeler himself, her stepfather stopped working and rented it out. Eventually, the demands of Rosie's family, friends, and neighbors led her to distance herself from them. Although Ben seemed not to mind most of their requests, Rosie became increasingly concerned that family, friends, and neighbors were taking advantage of Ben, and she began to establish limits on their contributions.

CINDERELLA'S AGENCY AND
THE POLICING OF BOUNDARIES

Lisa and Ted and Ben and Rosie's experiences show that sexual orientalist fantasies are but one of the factors that shape correspondence courtship and marriage. These relationships are linked—as discussed in further detail in chapter 5—to a wider political economy, to personal circumstances, cultural notions, and global imaginings, all of which contribute to the politics of romance. Men's decisions to correspond with Filipinas are linked to ideas about race, sexuality, colonialism, and also to ideas about gender and family roles. Women's decisions to correspond with U.S. men are colored by their personal situations and their ideas about the promise of a better life in the United States. Both men and women may be drawn to the narrative of rescue and romance. These cases also begin to suggest ways in which the immigration process helps to police national boundaries and the marriages of its citizens. The experience of immigration can alienate both U.S. men—as citizens whose status is put to the test—and immigrant women, whose prospective citizenship is under question. These cases also illustrate the way in which such relationships support national constructions of good wives and good women, as both men and women aim to construct relationships that they deem "respectable."

These encounters raise more subtle gender issues as well. Filipinas expressed curiosity about western women and strong views about local men. To Rosie it seemed at first very logical that western men would look for wives abroad since western women (like Ben's ex-wife) did not take marriage, husband, and children seriously enough, and since Filipinas are honest, caring, and sincere about familial relationships. Yet with time, she began to worry that western men were subject to such weaknesses and she feared that outside of the Philippines, or in her absence, Ben might exhibit traits of other Americans. (After two weeks in the United States, her mother asked her anxiously on the phone whether Ben had "changed.") For her it was perhaps more difficult than for Lisa, since Ben did not criticize or demonize his ex-wives. Instead he tried to convey his lack of animosity and his respect for them. To Lisa, the hostile and negative images of western women, embodied in Ted's characterization of his ex-wife, seemed somewhat amusing, but also somewhat suspect. ("They can't all be that bad, can they?" she teased. "Look at Nicole, she doesn't drink much and she's not fat!") Both women seemed quite curious about me and about my family. Like many others I met in the Philippines and in China, they were surprised that I was their size, that I did not resemble the American women on *Baywatch*, and that I drank little and did not smoke. Photographs of my husband and children spurred discussions of how lucky I was to be married and have two children, and the comment that "at least some western women do have families."

Pinoys can be as romantic and as handsome as westerners, especially, I was told, men who have Spanish blood and western features. Some also commented that Pinoys are often spoiled, and tend to be unfaithful.[49] Women suggested that western men were in large part—and in contradiction to Rosie's personal concerns to the contrary—more serious about marriage. Western men often expressed their own sense of superiority over Filipinos. One of the more extreme expressions of this view came from a red-faced, overweight, white man who struck up a conversation with me at the Hong Kong airport. As he burst out angrily, "I'm married to a Filipina, and of course they prefer western men because Filipinos are bastards! They get them pregnant, drink and gamble the money away, and then leave them for another woman."

The two Filipino-American couples described in this chapter allow us to consider the cluster and flow of ideas that often accompany the movement of Asian women and U.S. men across international borders. Of particular interest are the complex exchanges, contradictions, and paradoxes that are inflected in the discourse about love and marriage, a discourse that is also about gender, sexuality, nationality, race and culture, colonialism, tradition and modernity, and more explicitly about work, motherhood, and family values. The flow of ideas I refer to do not simply replicate, reinforce, and reproduce orientalist or occidentalist views, or ideas of women as victims or hyperagents. They are, I argue, far more nuanced, and are potentially transformed and transformative as they come into contact with men and women's real life experiences and practice. In contrast to many popular stereotypes and representations, women and men both exert a multitude of choices, compromises, and negotiations. This is hinted at when Lisa contends with Ted's biased and rigid views, when Ted realizes that Lisa is criticizing him, when Rosie confronts the realities of relocating, and when Ben faces the unforeseen hurdles associated with Rosie's annulment.

Orientalist sexual fantasies — the focal point of many studies of mail-order catalogs — seem to have relatively little importance in the day-to-day lives and actual relationships of these couples. As I have argued, much of the writing on mail-order brides overemphasizes sexuality at the expense of other issues. According to Wilson, despite the "dearth of sensuality and sexuality in the photographs and the descriptions" the catalogs nonetheless point to "the latent eroticism of these women." To Tolentino, the catalogs are prefigured as erotic and objectifying. Although the possibility of what Wilson calls the viewer's "private fantasy" cannot be denied, it is important to note that discursive analyses that depict women as orientalist objects of fantasy and men as viewers who are caught up in private sexual fantasies ultimately say very little about the actual lives and mundane experiences of men and women.[50]

Popular and academic views often posit, as Tolentino does, that "bride and groom bind themselves in a contract of marriage without physically seeing each other," or that the "First World groom and Third World bride will most likely meet for the first time a few days before their marriage." Tajima writes that American men "order Asian brides from picture catalogues, just as you might buy an imported cheese slicer from Spiegel's," and Delia Aguilar compares them to Sears Roebuck catalogs.[51] Rosie and Ben and Lisa and Ted are fairly typical of the couples I have encountered in the sense that they corresponded for more than a year, sometimes on a daily basis by e-mail, and met in person (often several times) before deciding or agreeing to get married. In contrast to Tolentino's idea that the catalog's "description provides ample information on women's lives and bodies [for men] to pass judgement," I have yet to meet anyone who considered such information adequate.[52] Such representations simply contribute to the notion of women as commodities, dupes, or victims, serve to mask their ability to think and act in reasoned ways, and deny the complexity of women's and men's motives.

Yet a tension clearly exists between the stated existence of agency and the way in which this agency is enacted within larger structures of power. As Lila Abu-Lughod and Sherry Ortner remind us, to simply identify agency or resistance is to risk romanticizing it.[53] Certainly it should be possible to identify agency without reifying it and without denying the way in which it can also be used by individuals to assert their position within a system of inequality. Returning briefly to the fairy tale analogy, many scholars have noted that the Disney version of *Cinderella* (as opposed to some earlier versions of the tale) portrays a female character who is largely devoid of agency, unable to act of her own accord.[54] She is dependent for her deliverance on the fairy godmother (for a temporary transformation) and on the prince (for a permanent one). But this should not prevent us from asking what pleasure and satisfaction the princess derives from the situation, and how power is linked to pleasure.[55] Her marriage to the prince can potentially bring her greater material wealth, social status, and respectability. Unlike Disney's Cinderella, foreign women can and often do exert initiative and power in ways that I have enumerated: by submitting their names, representing themselves in particular ways, carefully selecting whether and which men deserve responses, and ultimately in deciding whether or not to marry them.

Yet women who buy into the shared fantasy of their rescue by the prince, or what Delia Aguilar describes as "dreams of blonde princes in castles glittering with gold," also locate themselves within a larger scheme of historically constituted gender roles and gender hierarchy. Like Cinderella, their roles as wives and mothers require an acceptance of the gendered premises of the fairy tale. In the fairy tale, "happily ever after" assumes that the prince and princess will remain married. According to "Filipino tradition" the weight of making the marriage work rests unequally on a woman's shoulders. As Aguilar points out, "Marriage is not like hot rice which may be spat out if it burns the mouth"; it is up to the wife to make the marriage work. Romantic dreams of "betrothal to a tall, light-skinned man across the seas" are—like the "dream of rescue by G.I. Joe"—fueled by "centuries of colonially-induced self disparagement."[56] The fairy tale neglects not only the wider colonial history, but also the sometimes harsh and difficult realities of everyday life, the hard work of making a marriage work, not to mention the residential and marital requirements necessary for permanent residence in the United States.[57]

Women may aim for "modern marriages" and to escape certain confines of the Philippine patriarchal family, only to discover that their U.S. husbands want "traditional wives." When Lisa jokingly teased Ted about becoming "fat and lazy" in America and about his overgeneralizations about U.S. women, we sense her ability to see beyond a simple fairy tale to some of the nuances of her husband and his (mis)perceptions about women. We also gain a sense of the way in which Asian women are often drawn into a discourse in which they are understood to stand in opposition to western women, who are depicted as having failed the test of family and marriage, and against other Third World women who are less befitting of the role, even before they enter the country.

If, as conservative U.S. family-values scholars and advocates argue, "Nothing is more important for our children or for our future as a nation" than heterosexual married parents in nuclear families,[58] and that "economically independent families headed by men . . . represent the historic foundation of liberal society,"[59] then it becomes clear why immigration laws and policies appear to be designed to gauge the suitability of foreign women as prospective wives and mothers of citizens. Yet this chapter also hints at the fact that, although men are often politically conservative and often support "family values" discourses, they are often highly ambivalent about the U.S. government's ability to interfere with the perceived "right" of the wife or fiancée of a U.S. citizen to emigrate to the United States.

Like U.S. government and INS regulations that create further red tape and bureaucratic procedures or place foreign women under ever-closer scrutiny, feminist critiques and opposition to correspondence relationships on the grounds that they are equivalent to selling bodies, forced prostitution, and traffic in women also contribute to policing of the borders. Like INS regulations, critics often claim to be protecting the rights of women, but their arguments may in fact serve to curtail women's (and men's) opportunities to shape the direction of their own lives as they see fit. It seems ironic that borders are policed not only by the INS but also indirectly by some women's organizations, academics, and middle-class professional Filipinos in the United States and abroad. Such groups seem intent on protecting rural Filipino women from becoming victims of their own decisions.

5 Political Economy and Cultural Logics of Desire

> An anthropology of the present should analyze people's everyday actions as a form of cultural politics embedded in specific power contexts.
>
> —AIHWA ONG, *Flexible Citizenship*, 5

> Desire, sexual or otherwise, is not a constant or a given, but is shaped in crucial ways by the very manner in which we think and speak about it.
>
> —GREGORY PFLUGFELDER, *Cartographies of Desire*, 3

> I had an acquaintance once whose brother told him, "Only hang around rich girls, then you can marry for love, but she'll be rich!" No kidding, this was a real person. Maybe not so different from the rationale for meeting people of a cultural "type" which fits your desires.
>
> —SIMON, 2000

POLITICS AND CONJUGAL LOVE

Filipinas and Chinese women rarely objected to the idea that their relationships with U.S. men were related in part to political relations and the global flow of capital. U.S. men, by contrast, often objected strongly. Most men considered it distasteful to connect politics and market forces with personal lives and intimate relationships, or to propose that love might not be the single or most essential ingredient of a marriage. Women from China and the Philippines often articulated the importance of love, but were not so resistant to the idea that marriage involves personal and political considerations.

U.S. men's aversion to connecting political economy and marriage is linked to a common western notion of a domestic-public split, wherein the home and family provide refuge from the impersonal forces of capitalism and politics. Popular American views of the family cast it as "the antithesis of the market relations of capitalism; it is also sacralized . . . as the last stronghold against the state, as the symbolic refuge from the intrusion of the public domain that consistently threatens our sense of privacy and self-determination."[1] Of course, families and personal relationships are not immune from the state or the economy. Studies of international adoption and foreign spouses clearly illustrate that this is the case.[2] Yet certain ideologies serve to bolster the claim that family exists separately from—and in opposition to—impersonal political-economic forces.

U.S. men were often defensive when friends and relatives asked how they knew their partner was not looking for a "free lunch" or a "ticket to the U.S.," or when critics suggested that the men really want "a maid and a sex slave." Like adoptive parents who respond defensively to the question of how much an Asian adoptee "costs" or how much a surrogate mother "charges," thus threatening to reduce what is conceived of as an intimate familial affair into a blatant market transaction,[3] U.S. men are defensive about the pragmatic aspects of their relationships and about the market analogy that underlies the very notion of a mail-order bride. They defend their marriages as part of a "modern western ideal of the conjugal union, founded on intimacy and romantic love,"[4] in contrast to critics who see correspondence marriages as precisely the opposite. The idea that marriage should be based on conjugal love is not universal. Anthony Giddens claims that "passionate love" is "more or less universal," but that "romantic love" is "much more culturally specific."[5] Giddens suggests that romantic love as the foundation of marriage is a relatively recent idea that emerged in western Europe in the late eighteenth century with notions of individualism arising from capitalism, but others such as Jack Goody have argued that "conjugal love is more widely distributed 'both in time and space.'"[6] According to Kathryn Robinson, Giddens's historical model runs counter to the way in which global technology has facilitated new types of marriage opportunities, such as brokered marriages, in which romantic love is presumed to be absent.[7] As this chapter shows, however, many men and women in correspondence relationships valorize romantic love as the basis of the intimate bond of marriage, and defend themselves against contrary claims, while simultaneously expressing practical and pragmatic considerations that they associate with "older" or less "modern" forms of marriage.

This chapter builds on the previous one but grapples more closely with the cultural logics of love and desire. My aim is to point to the link between political economy and cultural logics of desire in Filipina- or Chinese-U.S. relationships; to illustrate the way in which men and women involved in correspondence relationships articulate a discourse on romantic love and its importance to their relationships; and to consider the limitations of perspectives that highlight the material and practical aspects of these relationships, view them foremost as a migration strategy for women, or express skepticism about the possibility of love. Overall, I argue against privileging or prematurely dismissing a notion of romantic love, and against categorically opposing practical and material desires to emotional ones.

I argue that correspondence relationships are often based on ideals of romantic love or, at the very least, reflect attempts to define them in such terms. They are thus sorely misrepresented if boiled down to crude materialist motives. But it is also important to consider how and why love, romance, and marriage are linked—despite a strong American cultural reluctance to burst the fairy tale bubble and see it this way—to money, class, and power, as represented by and embodied in nationality, race, gender, and place at a particular time. In the previous chapter, I began to suggest some ways that political economy is linked to correspondence relationships. Here I ask how political economy can further our understanding of personal relationships without simply reducing men and women to opportunistic actors or eliding the issue of love and emotion.

POLITICAL ECONOMY AND EVERYDAY LIVES

In her ground-breaking study of "flexible citizenship" and the transnational strategies of Chinese global capitalists, Aihwa Ong argues that it is insufficient to treat political economy as a backdrop for human relationships. She recommends that we consider the "*transnational practices and imaginings* of the nomadic subject and the social conditions that allow his flexibility."[8] The social and geographical flexibility of Chinese global capitalists is "an effect of novel articulations between regimes of the family, the state, and capital" (3). Ong avoids reducing her argument to economics or creating a model that views the local as cultural, the global as political-economic, with the former subsumed within or subordinate to the latter (4). She is concerned with "human agency and its production and negotiation of cultural meanings" (3) and with the "cultural logics" that make certain actions on the part of Chinese global capitalists "thinkable, practicable, and desirable" (5). In other words, she aims to bridge the common divide between practice and structure.

Since Ong's study deals with Chinese global capitalists, it makes sense to merge cultural and political-economic analysis in discussions of their lives, residences, investments, families, and citizenships. But is the same move warranted when discussing individuals whose sense of personhood does not so explicitly revolve around markets and finances? What is the role of political economy in shaping values and desires when women and men's motives are not primarily or explicitly economic?

In a section entitled "Working Women's Dreams of Traveling Romance," Ong describes working-class women in Shenzhen and other booming regions of South China and their attraction to overseas Chinese men "in charge of mobility" (153). She notes that the Chinese men from Hong Kong and elsewhere are perceived as "good catches" and as "a vision of capitalist autonomy and a source of new 'network capital'" (154). Network capital, in contrast to Pierre Bourdieu's notion of symbolic capital, alludes to the importance of *guanxi*, or potentially advantageous "connections," which are especially important in the Chinese context in the reform period.[9] Because of their potential to improve the circumstances of the woman and her family, "road-trip Romeos from Hong Kong can be an irresistible catch because he literally and figuratively embodies the guanxi (ideally through marriage) that will lead to the dazzling world of overseas-Chinese capitalism. Marriage to a traveling man enables one to expand one's accumulation of network capital and can also benefit the members of one's family, who eventually may migrate to the capitalist world, where their desires for wealth and personal freedom can be met" (Ong, 155–56). Ong writes that "mobility, wealth, and an imagined metropolitan future, *rather than love* or class solidarity, account for the lure of family romances" (156; emphasis added). The "romance of mobile capitalism," Ong argues, "conjures up a felicitous brew of imagined personal freedom and wealth, a heady mix that young women imagine traveling men can provide the passports to" (156).

Although Ong's main interest lies with overseas Chinese capitalists, her observations are more broadly applicable and her analysis raises a number of questions that are pertinent to correspondence relationships between U.S. men and Asian women. Are these relationships best understood as providing a "passport" to personal freedom and wealth, a bridge to the West for kin, or are there other salient issues that such an emphasis tends to eclipse? Ong's description of women's interests in "road-trip Romeos" highlights material or practical forms of desire and familial strategies of migration but downplays other more emotional dimensions of desire and dismisses out of hand the possibility of love.

My own analysis points to a more subtle rendering of—as Ong suggests in her own introduction—the cultural logics of desire in relation to wider political and economic factors. In contrast to Ong's broad notion of "family romance," which takes little notice of love and emotion, I ask how love and emotion are intertwined with political economy through cultural logics of desire. Political-economic approaches that neglect the possibility of emotion risk reducing an individual's life-altering decisions to seemingly "rational" calculations that fail to recognize the humanity and sentiment of even the most ruthless and seemingly pragmatic acts.[10] To separate politics from intimacy further reifies the western illusion of a divide between the personal and the political.[11] Given a western tendency to stereotype Asians as cold and calculating, it is important to consider emotions alongside pragmatics.

Network capital, a possible "bridge to America," and the potential for greater wealth and freedom are certainly attractive to many Chinese and Filipinas and to their kin in Asia. But do these attractions preclude romantic love—or other deep emotions—as Glodava and Onizuka and other critical representatives of international marriages as "trafficking in women" suggest?[12] Following Ong, we might posit that Filipina and Chinese women's understandings of U.S. men and of the imagined America they represent are *part of* the cultural notions of desire that are made thinkable, desirable, and practicable by a wider political economy. In contrast to Glodava and Onizuka's interpretation of men's pragmatic motives as excluding the possibility of loving and enduring relationships (see chapter 3), I argue that love can be no less of an integral concern in correspondence marriages than in any other marriages. What is distinctive is not that these relationships involve pragmatic and practical concerns (all marriages do), but that they allow the apparent contradictions and paradoxes to become apparent. Those involved in correspondence relationships are often defensive about romantic love because observers assume its absence, whereas in most other U.S. marriages, its presence may be taken for granted. Correspondence marriages thus threaten to reveal tensions that other marriages more easily ignore or mystify.

The following sections turn to U.S.-Philippine and U.S.-Chinese relations. I briefly highlight some socioeconomical, political, and historical aspects of China-U.S. and Philippine-U.S. relations that help to situate correspondence relationships. This discussion stresses how the local and the global are intertwined, and indicates ways that political economy and cultural logics of desire are jointly constituted.

PHILIPPINE-U.S. RELATIONS

As suggested in the previous chapter, Philippine-U.S. relations are informed by the colonial history of the Philippines, including the period of Spanish colonization, which lasted from the middle of the sixteenth century until 1898. Spaniards introduced Catholicism to the Philippines, now considered the only "Christian country" in Asia. Catholicism still bears a strong influence today. It underlies the legal ban on divorce and the country's pro-natal policies. Although divorce is not legally permitted, annulments on the grounds of "psychological incapacity" serve as a practical alternative for those—like Ben and Rosie—who have the financial resources and knowledge to avail themselves of it.[13]

In 1898, Filipinos fought for independence, the United States declared war on Spain, and following the Spanish-American War and intense debate in U.S. Congress, the United States assumed colonial rule of the Philippines. Several years of bloody resistance and brutal pacification ensued.[14] U.S.-style education and English as the language of instruction were introduced. Citing Filipino historian Renato Constantino, Yen Le Espiritu writes, "With the use of U.S. textbooks, 'young Filipinos began learning not only a new language but a new culture. Education became miseducation because it began to de-Filipinize the youth, taught them to regard American culture as superior to any other.'" (3).

U.S. sovereignty continued until 1946, when, following Japanese occupation, the war-torn territory was granted political independence, only to enter a new period of neocolonial dependency that continues today. After a brief period of economic development in the 1950s and 1960s, little growth took place in the 1970s. Rebellions and internal conflicts threatened stability, and the United States provided military and economic aid to fend off the perceived threat of communism. Ferdinand Marcos established martial law and received U.S. backing until he was toppled by the People Power movement in the 1980s.

The economic difficulties of the 1970s and 1980s set the scene for Marcos's labor export policy, marking the third massive wave of migration from the Philippines. Hundreds of thousands of Filipinos sought temporary jobs abroad as seamen, construction workers, domestic workers, and other types of contract laborers. By the 1990s, one in five Filipinos was supported partly by economic remittances from abroad. Thus migrant labor grew from a "stop-gap measure" to a "vital lifeline for the nation," and overseas contract workers were hailed as the nation's "new economic heroes."[15]

Marriage to a foreigner constitutes another important pattern of migration. By 1999, 2.5 million Filipinos made their permanent homes abroad.[16] In the 1990s, an average of 17,000 Filipinos went abroad annually as spouses or fiancé(e)s of foreigners. About 92 percent of these fiancés/ spouses were women, and the largest number, 70,828 (almost 40 percent), were married or engaged to U.S. nationals.[17] The Philippine government's Commission on Filipinos Overseas (CFO) was established in the 1980s to protect and promote the welfare of Filipinos overseas and to "strengthen and sustain ties" among overseas Filipinos and between them and their country. A major CFO objective is to promote the economic role of Filipinos overseas in "national development," including investment in and remittances to the Philippines.[18]

Women's decisions to write to U.S. men reflect a certain cultural logic. The prestige, status, and assumed wealth associated with U.S. residence, light skin, western features, or a U.S. accent—reinforced by U.S. popular culture—help fuel such desires. In the summer of 2000, a Filipina friend gave me a copy of *Metro*, a popular glossy Filipino magazine that had run a main feature in 1998 on "the expat world in Manila." The magazine introduced readers to the "most eligible expat bachelors," described where they party, their relationships with Filipinas, and their impressions of the Philippines. Such articles blatantly promote white men as "prize catches" and leave little doubt about the existence of power relations that are inextricably linked to gender, race, class, and nationality.[19] For Filipinas, who often consider people with fairer skin and western features "more attractive," or to women who associate white men with imperialistic or paternalistic power, political economy clearly promotes certain "cartographies of desire."[20]

As mentioned in chapter 4, western notions of the Philippines as an ex-colony, as "Third World," or as "underdeveloped" contribute to the belief that Filipinas are more traditional, less modern, less influenced by feminism and other ills of western culture, and therefore more devoted to marriage and family than western women. For U.S. men, a rescue narrative juxtaposed with Asian images of sexuality and innocence, images from their own military experiences in the Philippines, or images of the nurturing Filipino doctor or nurse may feed into the attraction of Filipinas as prospective spouses. Men who write to Filipinas (often but not always Christian themselves) are often attracted to their Catholic and Christian values, a legacy of the Spanish era. They are also attracted to women's English language ability and their assumed "familiarity" or receptivity to western culture, legacies of the American colonial era. American popular cultural images of Asian women as beautiful, exotic, sexy, and submissive are also influential.[21] Such an observation is not to reduce these relationships to artifacts of political economy, to rob them of their authenticity, or to question individuals' complex motives, but rather to consider how love and desire are constructed within a wider historical context of power relations.[22]

CHINESE-U.S. RELATIONS

Relationships between U.S. men and Chinese women must also be viewed within a historical and political-economic framework. Unlike the Philippines, China was never officially colonized (with the exception of Hong Kong and Macao). Yet China experienced imperialism during the nineteenth and early twentieth centuries as foreign powers established rights to Chinese treaty ports and markets through the "unequal treaties" following China's defeat in the Opium Wars. The United States maintained good relations with the Republic of China (ROC) during the first half of the twentieth century, under the leadership of the Nationalist Party (KMT) led by Dr. Sun Yatsen and Chiang Kai-shek. This ended when the Chinese Communist Party (CCP) came to power and allied the People's Republic (PRC) with the Soviet Union. The United States and the PRC were further alienated when the United States established official ties with Taiwan, where the KMT established itself as China's rightful leadership. The establishment of the PRC in 1949 was followed by several decades of Cold War between China and the West and the maintenance of a rigid "closed door" policy.

Were it not for the death of Mao in 1976 and the subsequent era of economic reform, it is unlikely that U.S.-Chinese correspondence relationships would exist today. With the "post-socialist" open door policies came a thaw in U.S.-China relations. The establishment of Special Economic Zones in the 1980s created new possibilities for economic relations between China and the West. Foreign investments and joint ventures, and new cultural and academic exchanges, also facilitated closer ties. Although Chinese officials still resist labeling the economic changes as "capitalist," they clearly veered away from communist ideals of state ownership and communalism. Many westerners found such changes positive and reassuring. Burgeoning private enterprises, incentive systems, and international investment led to a phenomenal increase in the standard of living of many urban Chinese. Rural-urban migration increased as a result of urban employment opportunities and decreased controls on internal migration. The loosening of state control over popular culture and the arts alongside growth of consumer opportunities led to phenomenal changes over the past two decades, including far greater exposure to the West.

The United States is considered a desirable destination for many Chinese. The most common routes through which Chinese citizens legally come to the United States are by way of student visas, relatives' sponsorship (including spouses), and fiancé(e) visas. The opening up of China has meant greater visibility, communication, and interest between two countries whose citizens are no longer so apprehensive or suspicious of the labels "capitalist," "communist," or "socialist." For many Chinese women, the United States is imagined—as Ong notes—as a place for freedom and opportunity. At the same time as U.S. men "discovered" China as a source of "more traditional wives," so did overseas Chinese men from Taiwan, Hong Kong, and Singapore.[23]

Unlike many U.S. men involved with Filipinas, men's interest in Chinese women was not so directly influenced by military experiences. None mentioned friends or acquaintances married to Chinese women before they had established their own relationships. One commented that all he knew about China was from eating at Chinese restaurants in the United States. A few men cited their experiences as tourists in China, acquaintance with someone who taught English there, participation in an academic exchange program, or business trips to China as factors that prompted their interest in China and made marriage across cultural borders more imaginable. Most men I knew had never been to China before they wrote to Chinese women. Many mentioned—as did those who wrote to Filipinas—that they had "always been attracted to Asian women." Several men had written to women of different nationalities and eventually decided to write to a Chinese woman. A few men who were attracted to Chinese women did not distinguish between women from Taiwan, Hong Kong, and mainland China, or women from rural or urban regions, but assumed that they were all "traditional." The recent popularity of Chinese films in the United States did not motivate men to look for Chinese spouses, although many men became interested in Chinese films, praised and admired the actress Gong Li, for example, and paid close attention to U.S. films with Chinese themes after they had established a relationship with a Chinese woman.

The infrastructural framework for introducing mainland Chinese women to U.S. men has had less longevity and is less commercially developed than the networks for introducing Filipinas to American men. Almost all the men I met who corresponded with Chinese women had met them over the Internet (including informal chat groups), whereas most men involved with Filipinas had met through printed publications and initially communicated through the postal service.[24]

A few men said they had not selected prospective pen pals by nationality, but were attracted to the fact that the Chinese had "no religion," and a few mentioned Buddhism or "spirituality." Several mentioned their attraction to Chinese women, whom they considered especially bright, educated, and devoted to the family, or because of their "feminine qualities." Men's descriptions of Chinese pen pals, wives, or fiancées often reflected respect for women's willingness to work hard, their high educational attainment, their "go-getter" attitudes—features of the Asian "model minority" image in the United States. Several men expressed pride in their wife or girlfriend's Chinese patriotism, even when they had differing views regarding, for example, the Chinese Embassy bombing in Belgrade in 1999, or the detained U.S. spy plane in 2001. I was surprised when one very outspoken man equated his wife's family's strong military and Chinese Communist Party background with his own family's military and Republican Party involvement in the United States. Rather than view such backgrounds as a source of conflict, they considered their strong political convictions a common bond and a provocative source of lively discussion and debate. Many men reported "falling in love" with China when they visited. They raved about the food and the warm welcome from their fiancée's relatives, and they reportedly missed China when they left. Men who wrote to Filipinas, in contrast, often described Filipinas' Christianity or Catholicism, simple way of life, or conservative family values (including virginity and opposition to divorce) as attractive features. Many men complained about their difficulties with transportation (or their sense of danger from the speed and traffic) in both China and the Philippines. Men who had traveled in the Philippines complained about the food, weather, and bureaucratic red tape; when they left, they missed their wives or girlfriends, but few spoke of "falling in love" with the place.

SIMON AND XIAOLI

Simon is a fifty-year-old investment banker from Florida, who began a new career in education and moved to the Midwest because his Chinese wife had friends there. When I first met him over the Internet, he had been married to Xiaoli, a forty-three-year-old high-school teacher from northeastern China, for just under a year. Simon had previously been married for fifteen years, then divorced for ten, when he decided a few years ago that he would like to remarry if he met "the right person." Xiaoli had been married for fifteen years and had been divorced for three when they met. She had a nineteen-year-old daughter in China, and Simon had grown children in the United States. Simon's description of meeting Xiaoli illustrates the blending of emotional and practical considerations into a relationship that is thinkable and attainable. It is also noteworthy for Simon's ideas about Xiaoli's Chinese femininity, and for the way in which Simon envisions "love" fitting in.

When asked why he decided to look for a partner through correspondence, Simon explained,

> I can only speak for our own case, of course. My own choice to find
> a foreign woman started with practical considerations of the cultural
> type. In other words, I knew if I fell in love with someone who tended
> to view a husband as "competition" or "an obstacle to success," we'd
> have big problems. I was once in love with someone [an American] . . .
> who had an ingrained belief (or feeling) that she was a victim and all
> men were basically perpetrators. I actually tried to marry her, but just
> couldn't take being the "bad guy" 24 hours a day. So, my decision was
> to find a woman who would be really good for me, and let me be good
> for her, even if it were someone I had to "learn" to love.

At first, Simon took a pragmatic approach to meeting women. "I originally wanted to collect 4 or 5 'prospects,' based on what I could tell of their personality and character, then choose the one with whom I had the best interpersonal 'chemistry.' That plan didn't come to pass because [Xiaoli] bowled me over completely after our first meeting." Commenting further on his early motivation to meet women abroad, Simon noted that "our culture has some barriers to successful relationships. I wasn't meeting anyone I was interested in here, so I decided to look abroad, via the Internet. After corresponding with several people from different countries, I decided that, in general, women from China had an outlook and upbringing that seemed more supportive of happy long term relationships, so I focused on China about 2 years ago." Simon looked at listings of women of various nationalities, but quickly developed a preference for Chinese women. "The first difference I noted about Chinese women showed up in the way they write their classified ads! When describing their characteristics, they overwhelmingly noted 'devoted to family,' 'soft,' 'kind,' 'virtuous,' and so on . . . old-fashioned 'feminine' virtues which don't get as much prominence in ads from other countries. Also, they were seeking men with the virtues of 'kindness' and 'good habits' more than anything else such as wealth, age, ambition and so on." He corresponded with "some really nice women, but most of them were almost twenty years younger than me." Then he got "sidetracked by a local girlfriend" and lost track of most of the women he had written to. He resumed his "search" and

> wrote a letter to one woman who was older and not as gorgeous as the
> rest, but whose face seemed to have a lot of character. That did it! One
> of [Xiaoli's] . . . students had posted a 'net ad for her on a dinky local
> service with not-so-hot photos, but once we got into an e-mail corre-
> spondence, the relationship took off. We started calling, and I went to
> see her [five months later]. . . . We hit it off even better in person, and

started to plan for the K-1 visa process. There were a few snags, and I went to China again this [spring] to help her with paperwork and family matters, and finally got her through the interview at the Consulate, and flew back to America with her [early in the summer].

Early in the process, Simon thought he might meet someone whom he would "learn" to love. Recalling his earliest encounter with Xiaoli, however, he felt "very lucky that I didn't have to learn to love anyone, we just jelled right away, and she happens to have the strongest character of any of the women I corresponded with." It is worth noting that Simon's description of how he and Xiaoli "jelled right away"—and his sense of the inevitability of their relationship ("that did it!" "the relationship took off")—is in keeping with Giddens's description of marriage and romantic love. As Giddens describes it, romantic love involves an "intuitive grasp of qualities of the other. It is a process of attraction to someone who can make one's life, as it is said, 'complete.'"[25]

According to Simon, Xiaoli was "seeking an American man not so much for the economic opportunity (she's pretty well-off herself), but because they have a reputation for being romantic, democratic husbands, and because as a divorced [woman in her forties], her chances of a remarriage in China were pretty slim. So far, it looks like we both made the right decision, cultural bumps and all." Simon stressed the importance of love (even as he approached it with a practical attitude), alongside other considerations that he associated with "Chinese culture." As Simon explained, "I hope I made myself clear: I wouldn't marry someone I couldn't love, but this time around I wanted very much to do my first 'screening' based on the practical aspects of a long-term relationship . . . could I respect her in every way, is she tender and respectful to her mate, do we agree on the purpose of a marriage, is 'a happy home' the top priority, and so on. The Chinese idea of marriage is much like the America of 50 years ago, and I like it." Returning to the tension between "pragmatic" arrangements and love marriages, Simon concluded, "I've also heard that arranged marriages work out better than we in America would expect . . . something about the older folks having more sense about who's good for each other than the young ones in the throes of heat." His reference to young people "in the throes of heat" is reminiscent of Giddens's distinction between passionate love, "which may lead the individual, or both individuals, to ignore their obligations" and which is "religious in its fervor" and can be seen as a deterrent to marriage, and "romantic love," which is more closely associated with virtue, less with sexual passion, and more compatible with marriage.[26]

TRUE LOVE?

It would be impossible to "prove" whether love is present in these relationships. Even when the individuals claim "it is there," the skeptic can assume someone is pretending. There is no question, however, that a discourse about romantic love is often present among couples involved in correspondence relationships. Simon's account is one of many that seem to contradict the claim that men who meet women through correspondence do not want enduring and loving relationships. Like many women I met, Xiaoli had a successful career, a high income, and a good standard of living in China. Although we do not hear it in her own words, she does not appear to support the assumption that "mobility, wealth, and an imagined metropolitan future, *rather than love*" account for Chinese working women's attraction to overseas Chinese or foreign men.[27]

Both scholarly and popular representations of correspondence relationships often express doubt about the existence of love or seek to separate cases of "true love" from those that are motivated primarily by material, pragmatic, or practical considerations. This attempt to polarize love and pragmatics and to represent them as discontinuous represents a particularly western perspective and bias. Underlying such a dichotomy is the idea that "true love" is somehow selfless and "pure," and not only incompatible with but also diametrically opposed to pragmatic or practical concerns.

Practical considerations and opportunism (the idea that a person can benefit from such a match materially, for example) can call true love into question and imply that it is false, impure, or legally constitutive of marriage fraud. Western critics of arranged marriage have implicitly or explicitly based their moral claim to superiority on the idea that a "love match" is superior, more "modern," or more genuine. This dichotomy implies first and foremost that love is or should be a required ingredient of all marriages. It also implies that love is somehow antithetical to arranged marriages, that love is either present or not from the beginning, rather than viewing it as an emotion that may take different forms and that has the potential to grow and develop after marriage. It also assumes that love is measured and expressed by universal rather than different cultural standards.

As Ellen, the Chinese manager of ChinaMiss introduction service, explains to prospective clients, expressions of love may vary cross-culturally:[28]

> Chinese seldom use the word "love," and we never use it as casually as people in the U.S. seem to. To us, love is not demonstrated by a word, but rather by how we treat our spouse, our family and each other. Usually, you will wait a long time before you hear a Chinese girl say, "I

love you!" This has nothing to do with how she feels, or whether she truly cares for you. It's a cultural difference.

In China, *(yuen)* the concept of "romantic love" is thought of more as "devoted commitment." . . . When "yuen" is present between you and a Chinese girl, you will know that she loves you by the way she treats you. And likewise, she will judge how much you care for her not by what you say, but by what you do. There is an old saying that goes: "It's easy for someone to move their lips, but keep your eyes on their feet." In other words, actions speak louder than words.

Men often cited the 50 percent divorce rate in the United States as a factor in the decision to look for a marriage partner from abroad. The desire for "enduring relationships" was thus one of the primary reasons U.S. men cited for their interest in women they believed placed a strong value on marital commitment. Ricky, a forty-year-old man, told me of his divorce four years earlier from his American wife of six years:

> I thought we had a good marriage. We were happy and we had two great kids. But we ran into a rough spot—I won't get into that—but to make a long story short, she left. Just walked out. She didn't want to work things out. If it was up to me we'd still be married. I thought I'd never marry again. But later, I started thinking I want to get married, but to someone who is as committed to marriage, someone who believes in their vows, and thinks marriage is sacred. . . . I had a co-worker who had been happily married to a lady from the Philippines for ten years. So I got the idea of joining a pen pal club and started writing to some ladies there.

Many men felt they had "failed at love," and many blamed this on feminism and the "unrealistic demands" or "lack of commitment" of western women. Love American style did not bring the long-term and stable marital relationships these men desired, and underlying their desire to meet Asian women was often an expressed pragmatic and emotional concern for relationships "that will last." One forty-five-year-old, twice-divorced man, who described himself as a politically conservative born-again Christian, was attracted by an ad in a singles publication that described Filipinas as "Women who believe in the Ten Commandments every day of the week, not just on Sunday." Mick, twice-divorced and insecure about relationships with western women, engaged to a Filipina who had worked as a domestic worker in Singapore, explained, "My understanding was that Filipinas held to a higher standard, traditional family and marriage values. I was correct. Also, I have always been physically attracted to Asian women." Jimmy, after five years of marriage to his American wife, came to the sudden realization that she "didn't want kids and would have made a bad mother anyway." Like Ben (chapter 4), he decided that his chances of finding someone who shared his family goal would be better among Asian women.

When I sent an e-mail message to members of UFG asking, "How [do] different people see 'love' fitting in? How important is it? Where and when do/did you start to see it? Is love a necessary ingredient in your relationship?" I received a variety of responses. Mick, a lively and good-spirited member of the group, replied, "I found that last question objectionable. I'm not offended really, but I am surprised that you asked if 'love was necessary.' To me, that implies that a Fil-Am relationship does not require 'love' to succeed. . . . Is that what you meant? I can't speak for anyone else but love is of primary importance to me. Without love, there is really is no relationship." JJ also commented at length about the importance of love in correspondence relationships and marriages. The absence of direct discussion of the issue, he said, may be misleading.

> I hope that the attitude I display when I write to fellows regarding issues with courting a Filipina does not mislead you. I talk about a lot of issues, but I don't talk about love much. It is not that I consider it off topic, in fact the bottom line is that this is really the number one topic. I write with the attitude that of course they love the women so I don't need to question that. Love . . . is a topic all of it's own and could generate a whole lot more traffic than the INS does. :) Also, I consider that my understanding of love at the time that I asked my wife to marry me was only mediocre, so who am I to talk.

The only exception to his silence regarding love, JJ wrote, based on his experience on two lists with several hundred members, "is when someone has displayed some sort of 'ugly male syndrome' and it is obvious that they have bit into the 'Mail Order Maid You Can Have Sex With' scenario. Or something along those lines. Thankfully that does not come along often, only twice that I have come across." Yet hinting at the "pressure" that men may exert on one another to conform to the idea that "love" is the single key ingredient, JJ also points to the way in which the list discourages discussion of blatant pragmatic or practical concerns.

> How often it [the "ugly male syndrome"] really happens I have no idea because if someone joins the list and reads for a while before posting it will quickly become apparent to them that their attitudes would not make them a favorite if they open up honestly. Of the two that spoke up, one was stupid enough to just assume we were all the same. . . . The other did not realize what he was like until we all took great care to point it out to him. But I don't think most people are that unconscious so I'm sure we have missed a few more, probably helped them on their

nasty way by giving them lots of good info and helping them to refine their masks.

Especially interesting in JJ's statement is the idea that men put pressure on one another to treat love (as opposed to sex) as the primary basis of their relationships: "I can't say that others dance around the love subject on the list for a similar reason that I do, but it seems most avoid direct discussion until their relationships have flowered to the point that they can confidently proclaim that they do love the woman, and that she loves him."

Kevin, whose Chinese wife spoke little English and who had initially communicated with her largely through translators, was the most openly pragmatic man I met. He explained his decision to correspond with Chinese women and the relevance of "love" as follows:

> Each marriage is different so it will be hard to say what motivates a person to marry and to marry outside their normal social structure. As for myself I think I am a little more practical than a lot of people when it comes to love and marriage. Even tho my wife and I had very little time together when we started this process we both believed that a marriage can work without the pheromones running wild.
>
> Our letters showed some desires in what we were looking for in a mate and there was no illusion created by raging hormones. We both talked about this and were honest that we both were looking for a strong friendship first and tolerance for each other. Since I have been married before under the guise of Love both fell apart because of our strong physical attraction instead of the deeper person. I hope you are able to understand what I am saying, sometimes it is hard to put our feelings into words. My grandfather put it best when he told about marriage and what we need to look at to make it work. He had said that marriage was like a bowl of oatmeal and that love was like sugar on the cereal which made it sweeter and more desirable but without the oatmeal it would have no nutritional value. I guess that is the way I look at my marriage now that when it started it was just the oatmeal but as we get to know each other it adds the sugar to it.

Kevin wrote to me again the next day, expressing concern that perhaps he had overemphasized "oatmeal" at the expense of "sugar." "After writing to you I wondered if my rational side was the only side that showed in my response or if I was able to express that like sugar emotional bonds make it do much better and there were some there even after knowing each other for such a short time . . . what I am saying is that I was looking for more oatmeal than sugar. I then flew to China where I met my wife to be and found the oatmeal with a little sugar." Reflecting on his and his wife's motivations, he wrote:

I think we were both looking for someone to share a more settled life with the occasional adventure. I think that we both wanted to find someone that understood the hardship of making a good marriage and would deal with the good times as well as the bad times. I personally was looking for someone that would accept me for who I am and not for what they can get out of me and that was another reason I looked for someone closer to my age. She understood that because of my heart that I was unable to work and for us to live together with her daughter that she would have to work some since my income was not that great and little chance of it becoming larger.

Charlie voiced another dissident view on the U.S.-Filipino list. He anticipated that his post would be unpopular, and indeed many wrote back to express their disagreement:

I might be in trouble with other members here but i've got to say it. i'm wondering how much is love and how much is infatuation among age difference men ladies. if a man is 40+ he proably is going through mid life crisis. we start thinking of death. most of our life is over. then some 20 year old filipno lady comes into our life well man oh man who wouldn't jump at the chance to marry and say your in love with someone that nothing sags on? couldn't that be infatuation? or a second childhood for an old fart? my wife and I know and have admitted we didn't really love each other when we married. I liked and was infatuated wit her. I talk about old verses young here but I would proably marry a kid too. but what happens when the man gets hard of hearing or some cancer etc? proably all of us know some filipino lady who divorced or had extra marital affairs etc. they are people with the same desires etc as any other woman. if there's big age difference they will someday maybe hate the aged husband. love or infatuation? ticket to the usa? a better job for the family back home? who knows the answers? [29]

Despite his seemingly cynical outlook, Charlie still expressed love for his wife. Responding to the questions about whether he and his wife were now in love, their age difference, and how they met, Charlie answered:

i'm sure we are in love more now than ever before. i'm 43 she's 42. we met through our churches singles. pen pal type. we've had enough problems though. she is a former maid and independent before we were married. she is stubborn and so am I. before we were married she wrote to me that filipinas never divorce but there's a reason for that they have a law against it. my wife last year filed for divorce. after I pleaded etc we called it off. I never felt worse in my life thinking i'd lost her. we still have our problems what with women in the phillipines running the home and money I had probelems with her trying to handle all the money. but hay she's pretty good at it. we've been married 13 years . . . I love her. I hope we can work out diffences. i've got to learn to let her take charge or at least let her think she's in charge. we have 2 kids and they need us both.

Many men mentioned their physical attraction to Asian women. As I argued in the previous chapter, sexuality is an important issue, but it should not be overemphasized at the expense of other issues. Men, and many introduction agencies, emphasized women's "family values," modesty, purity, and innocence rather than their sexuality or sexual availability. Women's "feminine qualities," as Simon put it, often refer more explicitly to their prospective roles as wives and mothers than as lovers. JJ wrote of one of his wife's Filipina friends who was getting divorced, "They were about the same age, the man was looking for some wild Asian sex and married a very proper girl who is not very adventurous in bed." Images of Asian women's sexual attractiveness no doubt play a role in the cultural logic of their desirability. Even more than love, however, there is often an absence of overt discussion of sexuality on the chat groups. Sex is often explicitly "off limits" as a topic mainly because its mere mention threatens to undermine a concerted effort to represent and construct such relationships as respectable and based on conjugal love and to raise the specter of what JJ called the "ugly male syndrome."

THE PRAGMATICS OF DESIRE

For the women, meeting a foreign man was desirable for a number of practical reasons, but this did not necessarily preclude feelings of love. Although Chinese women are often quite pragmatic about the appeal of foreign men and the desire to live abroad or to provide an opportunity for their children to go abroad, they seemed unwilling to sacrifice themselves for "just any" foreign men, nor were they willing to forego the possibility of love, caring, and affective ties to their prospective partners. Some Chinese women said they had first considered writing to overseas Chinese who would share more of their culture and background. A number of them came to the conclusion that overseas Chinese are often pickier ("they want women who are very young, very beautiful and have never been married before") and more controlling ("they want a very obedient and traditional wife"), so that non-Chinese men might be preferable.

While the promise of life abroad appealed to some women, some Chinese women and even more Filipinas expressed a preference to remain "at home" (in China or the Philippines) with a foreign husband. Some considered going abroad as a means to escape or loosen family controls and decrease their obligations, rather than as a way to mobilize resources as "network capital" for the good of the family. Examples of women who wanted to marry foreigners and "stay at home" varied. Most Chinese women assumed that, if they married a foreigner, they would have little choice but to go and live abroad. One Chinese woman, a young Communist Party member in Shenzhen, said she hoped to meet a foreign man who would stay in China and love her country as much as she does. Several other Chinese women expressed a desire to meet an overseas Chinese or a foreign man who worked in China or was at least familiar with the language or culture so they could both feel at home in both locations. As noted, the vast majority of Chinese women believed foreign men would be more understanding and respectful of the fact that they were divorced. Divorced women, and also women in their thirties who had never been married, spoke of western men as more open-minded and less controlling than Chinese husbands. Most thought foreigners were more romantic, open, and expressive, and knew how to treat women "like ladies." Some spoke of western men as better educated, more cultured, and more intellectual than Chinese men (see chapter 6).

Far more Filipinas than Chinese women I spoke with hoped to settle with their husbands in the Philippines, perhaps because they were familiar with such cases; many expressed ambivalence about the difficulties (e.g., loneliness, isolation, food, climate) of life in the United States. They were less attracted to the green card or to American citizenship than to a way of life that marriage to a foreigner in the Philippines could afford. I met several Filipinas who had experienced married life in the United States and had opted to return to the Philippines with their husband and children because there they could hire household help.

Filipinas most often referred to foreign men as handsome and kind men who know how to "take care of" their wives. Foreign men (often treated as a homogenous group) are thought to be romantic not only at the beginning of a relationship, but also after marriage. I was told that American men are less likely than Filipinos to have mistresses. Marriage to a foreigner can mean greater social freedom for his wife than many Filipino husbands allow. As Rosie explained, a foreign husband in the Philippines meant that many women envy you, but it also meant that other women would be interested in your husband because of his assumed wealth.

DISCERNING LOVE

The possible association of foreign partners with wealth and symbolic and "network capital" does not preclude the possibility of love. Indeed, the perceived "attractiveness" and desirability of foreign partners may be, or may become, the basis of love. The association of foreign men, regardless of their actual socioeconomic standing, with wealth and personal freedom, or the simple fact of a man's light skin (in the Philippines) or his passport (in China) may be the initial basis of interest and attraction, but this does not rule out, and indeed may provide the basis for, real or imagined feelings of love, affection, and devotion.

Men writing to Filipinas sometimes expressed concern about a specific woman's sincerity and love. In an e-mail message to the group, Roland wrote of his concerns about his Filipina fiancée. "The big thing with me was I was not sure if she was sincere about being in love with me. As long as I know she does love me I am willing to be patient and understanding. I told her from the beginning that we would have problems, everyone does, but if we loved each other and were honest with each other we could work anything out."

JJ replied, "And it is so difficult to find out if she does love you. I don't know about your fiancée but asking did not fill me with warmth and security. :) Has she told you she does much? I have heard from many that it is part of the culture not to say 'I love You.' . . . But [my wife] has become accustomed to it in our house, in this culture and she kind of likes it. :) . . . But while we were courting all I could ever get out of her was a very low spoken, sheepish verbal admission." Roland responded, "[my fiancée] is a lot better at telling me she loves me but she does the same as your wife. She just whispers it over the phone. That took a couple of months. But she does tell me a bunch of times in letters."

Filipinas and Chinese women sometimes seemed to avoid the topic of love, but both (especially Filipinas) often spoke openly of their love for their partners. Both gave me piles of letters to read in which they and their fiancés wrote of love. Some women's letters and messages to me were even signed "love." Although verbal and other *expressions* of love may be learned in the process of correspondence and marriage, the concept of love and romance is not foreign to China or the Philippines. Inexpensive paperback romance novels are extremely popular among Filipinas in the Philippines and abroad, and like women's own narratives, they often stress the importance of individual freedom and personal choice of a marriage partner.[30]

Malou was one Filipina who responded passionately to Charlie's assertion (above) that many pen pal relationships are based on infatuation but not love. She used her own story to oppose his more cynical view. Malou had met her husband four years earlier, had written to him for two years, had been married for two years, and had been living with him in the United

States for less than a year. Her excerpts of Charlie's comments are indicated by italics and her own responses follow.

> *i'm wondering how much is love and how much is infatuation among age difference men ladies.*

For D (I ask him) in a rate, [how much] he loves me 8 out of 10. (not enough for me). As for me . . . I don't know maybe more than your mind can reach. It's a little bet different between us. Because I just turn 18 when we started. Excuse myself for saying this. But at that time I was very competent in school . . . I was in the top 10 of teachers list of student who will make great career in the future . . . I was busy in high school but when D came into my life everything change. It changes to suit "his" taste. This is a fact!

> *if a man is 40+ he proably is going through mid life crisis. . . . who wouldn't jump at the chance to marry and say your in love with someone that nothing sags on?*

This I don't know. You know [better] yourself. Don't get me wrong you could be right. In all Fil-Am marriages but on a man's view of point only.

> *couldn't that be infatuation?*

This made me laugh!!! . . . the first picture D sent me was with his daughter, he got a mustache and he is not that kind of American you can see in Guess jeans commercial. It's just a total "eeeeeeehhhhhh" (looks like a maniac). But when I read his letter it runs through my veins. I know there is something to this man right away.

> *or a second childhood for an old fart?*

Yap this is a fact. What else do you expect a man trying to put off his gray hair by coloring it (D does this) to make sure he still looks cute with a darker hair. Telling silly things. Chewing straws to get my attention. Maybe he was thinking I have to do this. Young people do this habits. Old people don't.

> *but what happens when the man gets hard of hearing or some cancer etc?*

Put him in a nursing home!!!LOL This is just something couples like we are . . . should be ready for by now. This is something you have to be prepared of before taking the plunge. Which I think D is lucky with me. I already thought about this before we got married. . . .

> *proably all of us know some filipino lady who divorced or had extra marital affairs etc. they are people with the same desires etc as any other woman. if there's big age difference they will someday maybe hate the aged husband.*

This is true. "WE" (Filipina) are just woman too. We think of men
(just as you guys think of women), we like that "night in shining armor type" a suit and tie type, sporty, and "prince charming" type. But
the thing about it is we are already MARRIED. The best we can do is
"I am just appreciating the beauty I saw" that's bout it. For myself it's
rooted in my mind "love" is something you feel only once and when
you feel it you don't know that it is called love." . . . But the thing is if
it take me almost 2 years to know A LITTLE BIT of my husband and
still wonder if he really loves me. How long will it take to trust and
know this new person??? I have locked my mind in beleiving that it
take's lifetime to really know a person, and if that's the case one man
is enough to spend my life with getting to know him. With this theory
in mind you will never hate an "aged husband"

> *love or infatuation?*

Infatuation turn to a real love!

> *ticket to the usa?*

Most cases true! Goes both ways. A 40 year old man marry a 20 year
old virgin Filipina bring her to the US let her work for the two of them.
She has the right to help her family. She dammed work hard It's part of
the culture. You know that beforehand. A sadist and abuser husband.
He deserved to be cheated!!!

> *a better job for the family back home?*

True! that way when your husband treat you bad you have a family
to come home to. . . .

As Malou concludes her response, she stresses a lack of disjuncture between
love and material/practical considerations. Love in her view is linked to—
but not subsumed by—issues of race, work opportunities, and possibilities
of familial migration:

tell you what . . . I marry my husband because I love him, marrying
him means beautiful kids, moving to the US is not that bad compared
to having a career in the Philippines (But I didn't realized it is too until i started working at Mc Donalds part time), petitioning family to
moved to the US (if this is what you want to hear), why not, life is a lot
better in here than·in there when it comes to material things. But when
it comes to relationship, morals family relationship, parent children relationship. It [the United States] has nothing to be proud off. That's
why most choose to marry a Filipina because, you guys know after examining [them] there is nothing wrong with "our" intentions of coming over here instead of convincing you to move to the Philippines.

Rosie provided another interesting discussion about love and opportunity. I had sent Rosie and Ben an early draft of chapter 4. In her e-mail response, Rosie wrote "Our Love Story" in the subject line. Her message conveyed her reaction to my retelling of her "love story." Her English is not perfect, but conveys her ability to communicate complex feelings despite her lack of fluency.

Hello ma'am Nicole,

. . . I love talking to you. . . . By the way, we received the stories that you wrote on the last few weeks. And I spent few hours to read all in all. Oh, boy super terrifec that was nice your a good writer. That time when I was reading I can't understand what really I felt full of excitement, funny and very suspend.

My story that you wrote it sounds like a diary. I recalled the sadness and happiness that happened from the past. I cannot stopped laughing when I read this story about "Ben and Rosie" we are the foolish people. Until now it's hard me to believed and I began to asked myself, how is that happened? [Rosie] are you okey? Are you dreaming? I can't believe it was true.

How fool I am can you imagined after three days we met from his first visit I was engage right away. We both knows that we are not know each other well and beside I am not his girl friend. But we have unusual feelings we felt the same way. Our closeness sounds long years to me with no holding back. It's amazing and it turned to a serious relationship being a husband and wife.

Now, finally I was married and happy to found him in my life inspite of my homesickness. I think that's it what I can say for now.
Love, Rosie

Rosie's sense that "we have unusual feelings" and that she and Ben "feel the same way," as well as her sense that it was as though they had known each other "long years" and that theirs is a "love story" with the proverbial happy ending (despite her homesickness), fits with Giddens's notion of the connection between romantic love as linked to personal narrative and the telling of a story.

Romantic love introduced the idea of narrative into an individual's life—a formula which radically extended the reflexivity of sublime love. The telling of a story is one of the meanings of "romance," but this story now became individualised, inserting self and other into a personal narrative which had no particular reference to wider social processes. . . . The complex of ideas associated with romantic love for the first time associated love with freedom, both being seen as normatively desirable states.[31]

Similarly, the wider social processes that made such a relationship possible are sublimated to the romantic nature—the feeling that the two individuals share about the inevitability of their relationships. Ben and Rosie, moreover, both viewed their relationship as one that had been entered into "freely," in contrast to "arranged" marriages, in which one or both partners feel they have little choice. Although in fact social pressures can come into play (sometimes from the woman's family to marry and from the man's family not to), the overall sense that is that the relationship was entered into freely. Rosie's impression that there was no choice but that they be together reflected a sense that this was "fate" or somehow meant to be. Insofar as it involves "instantaneous attraction," Giddens suggests that romantic love has to be "separated quite sharply from the sexual/erotic compulsions of passionate love. The 'first glance' is a communicative gesture, an intuitive grasp of qualities of the other. It is a process of attraction to someone who can make one's life, it is said, 'complete.'" Romantic love, moreover, is related to ideas of "cosmic fate." Romance was no longer "an unreal conjuring of possibilities in a realm of fiction" but "a potential avenue for controlling the future."[32] Each of these elements—choice, love at first sight (but not uncontrolled passion), fate, and narrative completion—are expressed and negotiated in men's and women's discussions of their relationships.

ROGER AND CARLITA'S LOVE STORY

As I argued at the beginning of this chapter, for political economy to prove useful in cultural analyses of correspondence relationships, it must allow for the possibility of emotional motives in addition to practical and material ones. The following cases point to elements of this argument and simultaneously illustrate the difficulty of disentangling romantic love and personal narratives, political economy, and everyday lives. Each of the elements Giddens describes, choice, love at first sight (but not uncontrolled passion), fate, and narrative completion, are expressed and negotiated in Carlita and Roger's story.

Carlita, a twenty-one-year-old Filipina from the Visayas, met Johnny, a fifty-year-old American from Houston, Texas, through an Internet introduction service in the late 1990s, when she was in her teens. After corresponding for three years, he suddenly wrote to break things off because he was marrying Fran, another Filipina pen pal who had been working as a domestic worker in Hong Kong. Carlita did not know that Johnny had another pen pal, and she was devastated. As she explained in 2000, he had declared his love and devotion to her, and she had assumed they were exclusive. He had gone to visit Fran first and told Carlita he decided to marry her because she was in her mid-thirties and closer to him in age. In his final letter, Johnny mentioned Roger, his good friend and the best man at his wedding, who was planning to go to the Philippines, and he gave her Roger's address.[33]

Tears resurfaced as Carlita recounted the ordeal. She was young and innocent, she explained, and had made the fatal error of trusting Johnny and "falling in love with him" by mail. They had never met in person, but she had felt as if she knew him from years of correspondence. She trusted him, cared for him, and had believed his expressions of love and devotion. As a staunch Catholic who regularly attended mass, Carlita prayed that God would help her.

In 2000, Carlita had recently graduated from a Catholic college and was the top student in her class. While recounting the story of how she and Roger met, she pulled out a photo album and punctuated her story with photographs. She pointed out her family (and her protective father), her graduation ceremony (in which she was valedictorian), and various college functions that illustrated her popularity and academic success. For three years while she had corresponded with Johnny, she had turned down advances from male classmates and had never had a boyfriend because she considered herself already attached. At the time she "still thought" foreigners made better husbands and that they were more "trustworthy" than Filipinos.

Three months after she received Johnny's final letter, she wrote to Roger. She was cautious and had no expectations, but she wrote and told him that Johnny had broken her heart. She politely offered to meet him when he came to the Philippines, and said she would be happy to help him make arrangements for his trip. Since he was about to leave the United States, Roger had time to write only one letter (which I read), in which he told her he looked forward to meeting her and he hoped they might become friends. He thanked her for her offer to help and said he would contact her upon his arrival. At the time, Carlita did not know that Roger had read all her letters to Johnny, and that he thought of her "as a kind and lovely person."

Roger was in his mid-forties when I met him. As he explained over coffee, he had been divorced for almost twenty years and had no children. He described his twenties and thirties as a period of "hard living and lapsed Christianity." In his early thirties, he had an accident that radically changed his life. As a result of the accident, which caused brain damage and affected his short-term memory, he was unable to work, and lived on a disability pension of ten thousand dollars a year. Even before he met Carlita, he had planned to live abroad, where his limited income would go further. Since his accident, he had dated a number of women in the United States, but on the first date he "could always see the beginning, the middle and the end of the relationship." By this he meant that the women he dated had little interest in a long-term relationship with someone whose economic resources would always be extremely limited. "But here it's different, and my income can stretch a long way," he said. After serious "research" and talking to acquaintances who had been there, he decided to move to the Philippines.

In keeping with the inevitability of romantic narratives, Carlita described meeting Roger as her fate. To their mutual surprise and pleasure, they felt an immediate attraction and "love at first sight." Carlita told herself not to trust Roger, and her parents warned her too. But she thought that he was a kind and religious person and that they were meant to be together. Six months after they met and despite her father's opposition, Carlita and Roger were married. When she met me, she was still sad and bitter about Johnny, but said she had married the "best man," and seemed sure that this was God's plan.

When I met them, Carlita and Roger lived in a small but new and comfortable one-bedroom apartment. For just over two hundred dollars a month, their rent included twice-weekly maid service, use of a car and driver (shared with five other apartments), laundry service, cable television, and local telephone calls. Shortly after they were married, Carlita finished her college degree and worked for a short time in a restaurant frequented by local Filipino-American couples and managed by an American man, but the hours were long and late and the pay was low (about three dollars a day), so she quit. She and Roger continued to go to the restaurant to socialize with other Filipino-American couples, and they took me there to meet their friends.

Like many other Filipinas, Carlita contributed to their income by serving as a small-scale money-lender to friends and acquaintances at a 10 percent interest rate monthly. Her goal was to save money to buy a house and property of their own. So far, she could not afford to go back to school, but she hoped to eventually do so. Roger, meanwhile, spent time visiting friends, writing home from the local Internet café, and watching television. They shared the cooking, some of the housework, and attended church together regularly. As he explained, he is happy and very satisfied with his new life. A decade ago he almost died. That prompted him to "clean up my act," and he stopped drinking, taking drugs, smoking, and other vices. Although he only mentioned religion when I asked, he said that religion had become important to him. His sense of good fortune at having found Carlita was evident. In a few years, he and Carlita planned to try to have a child. Meanwhile, they hoped to enjoy their time together. Carlita expressed satisfaction over the direction her life had taken.

CONCLUSION

When I described Frank, a heavy-set, retired state trooper in his mid-fifties, and Angel, his lovely twenty-two-year-old fiancée, to Filipino friends, one woman asked, "She never finished college? Girls like that are only interested in him because of his money." "Many Filipinas are pretty desperate," said another. "Have you seen the women in the mall hanging around waiting to meet any old foreign men? They think foreign men are rich or can help get them to the U.S." Yet two young women were more empathetic: "Filipinas can fall in love very easily, it's true." "If he pampers her and treats her well, she can convince herself she loves him. And maybe she really does." Questioning my characterization of the couple, one woman asked, "Why is it so hard for you to believe that she loves him, Nicole? So what if he's ugly, as long as he treats her well!"

U.S. men often assumed that the women they wrote to in China or the Philippines would be happy to hear from Americans because they assumed (often mistakenly) that the women are in difficult, dire, or desperate financial situations. Men claim that "foreign women care less about age," "don't care if you aren't handsome," "don't care if you aren't rich." They are often aware that their wife's family (especially rural families in the Philippines) appreciates their financial contributions. Yet when it comes to their own relationships, they are reluctant to believe that financial factors might be a factor. Men depict their relationships in terms of love and romance. Only a few men (like Charlie and Kevin) suggested a different balance wherein love was neither the premise nor necessarily the ultimate goal.

Many women were very skeptical about *other* women's motives, but they also believed that their own relationships were "solid and sincere," not based on "money." Although men often considered love in a vacuum, for most Filipinas and many Chinese women, love is inseparable from the view of a man who provides or treats her well. Frank's masculinity is embodied in his ability to provide for Angel, or at least to potentially improve her circumstances. Old age, poor health, or a large physique does not necessarily make men unattractive, as long as they have the ability to care and provide. Whether it be through their own financial resources or their ability to offer potentially improved circumstances in the United States, men were flattered and attracted to the idea that women would truly value them "for themselves"—as American men and for the privileges their gender and nationality represent.

Men's circumstances of course vary enormously (a large business owner's circumstances differ from those of a factory worker). Chinese women and Filipinas demonstrated different degrees of understanding of men's actual financial and social standings. Yet what these men share is their gender and (in most cases) their nationality. The two are in many ways intertwined. For many Filipinos, despite overt critiques of western imperialism and colonialism, an (ambivalent) admiration of western food, styles, light skin, and "modern way of life" persists. Filipinos with more western or "Spanish" features are often considered more attractive, and western features come to represent western culture, wealth, and modernity, regardless of the particular circumstances of the individual.

Men's initial attraction to the idea of "Asian women's family values" may later become a source of conflict. As Julag-Ay suggests, commitments to her natal kin can cause marital conflict if men feel the woman's family draws resources away from his own nuclear household.[34] Another problem is that men may look to China and the Philippines for "traditional wives," but women may look to the West for "modern" lives and husbands and for a way to escape the constraints of familial obligations. Just as there are differences between U.S. men, so are there differences between the aims and desires of Asian women.

To connect the minutiae of everyday life with wider patterns of power and culture without reducing them to some rigid mold or draining them of their life, flexibility, and uniqueness is one of the challenges posed to scholars of transnationalism. Men's assumptions about Asian women's commitment to marriage and their assumed appreciation and attraction to western men are linked to actual historical connections among the United States, China, and the Philippines.

In this chapter, I have argued that political economy should not be viewed as simply a "macro" backdrop for anthropological studies that deal with power on the "micro" or local level, but rather that political economy is implicated in the production and reproduction of desire and is implicated in even the most minute and intimate levels of interaction. The historical relations between China, the Philippines, and the United States are intertwined with cultural logics of love and desire, which are themselves rooted in complex and subtle renderings of power. Modern and rapid forms of communication and transportation and relationships between nation-states make marriages between U.S. men and Asian women more practical and more imaginable than ever. Women may desire wealth, opportunity, freedom, citizenship, marriage, or a better way of life conceived of in an almost infinite variety of ways. Men's desires are also complex and varied, involving visions of domestic order, enduring relationships, modesty, femininity, sexuality, and an "old-fashioned division of labor." Such complementary desires may form the basis upon which meaningful relationships are imagined and realized across borders. At the same time they (re)produce and (re)inscribe certain structures of gendered power and inequality.

6 Women's Agency and the Gendered Geography of Marriage

> Different social groups and different individuals are placed in very distinct ways in relation to these flows and interconnections [of time-space compression]. This point concerns not merely the issue of who moves and who doesn't, although that is an important element of it; it is also about power in relation *to* the flows and the movement.
>
> —DOREEN MASSEY, *Space, Place, and Gender,* 149

> Sally: >Ok, guys, I wanna know what's up the lack of asia men/western women??? I think i'm the only one in the group!
> Jim: >About the lack of Asia men/Western women, I guess you could blame it on this saying that's been going around since approximately the beginning of the "women's movement": "Heaven is an American salary, an English country home, a Japanese chef, and a Chinese wife. Hell is a Chinese salary, an English chef, a Japanese home, and an American wife."
>
> —Internet discussion, 2000

> Why do all of the very best Chinese women, the most beautiful and educated, leave to marry foreign men?
>
> —FENG, 1999

As described in the previous chapter, the opening up of China has led to new social as well as economic relationships with the West. Alongside foreign investment and joint ventures, marriages between U.S. men and Chinese women who meet and correspond via the Internet have become increasingly common. Based mainly on interviews I conducted in 1999 and 2000, this chapter introduces five urban Chinese women and their views and experiences regarding correspondence and the suitability of western men as potential spouses. These sketches reinforce the point that personal circumstances, class backgrounds, and marital prospects in China are key features that underlie their interest in western men. Material concerns, as suggested in the previous chapter, are popularly assumed to be central to women's motivations, but are only one of many factors that influence women's decisions. Despite the larger social structures within which their choices are framed, Chinese women often exert a high degree of selectivity and choice in their dealings with and negotiations of relationships with U.S. men. As Yanyi and Ping's experiences illustrate, whether to write, meet, or marry, and how to negotiate cultural and personal differences in attitudes toward marriage, sex, and money point to the existence of—and also the limits on—women's agency, selectivity, and choice.

Besides questioning women's agency, this chapter also problematizes the widespread assumption that Asian women who marry Americans are "marrying up," in a pattern that I refer to as global hypergamy. Hypergamy refers to an expectation that women will marry up and out of their own social or economic group.[1] The cases of Lacey, Anna, and Meili suggest that some Chinese women imagine marrying a man from the United States as "marrying up in the world," but they do not consider western men their social superiors, nor do they "settle" for just any western man. Women did not always clearly articulate what they meant by a "suitable" marriage partner, but men who were deemed suitable were commonly said to share a woman's interests, her ideas about married life (e.g., fidelity and commitment to family), and to respect her.

The final section of this chapter turns to images of romantic relationships involving Asian men and white women, and the importance of the "global imagination." Images of Asian man–western woman couples often appear incongruous to many in China and the West, and thus serve as a topic of joking that reflects paradoxes of global hypergamy. The humor that surrounds the prospect of correspondence relationships between Asian men and western women reflects power imbalances of gender, nationality, race, and geography.

YANYI'S MISADVENTURE

In 1999, I interviewed six women in Shenzhen, in the region of Guangdong Province that adjoins the Special Administrative Region of Hong Kong. All of them—like the vast majority of the population of the booming southern Special Economic Zones (SEZ)—had moved to Shenzhen from the north or from smaller towns and villages to the west. As one of the first SEZs set up to attract foreign investment and joint capital ventures to the PRC, Shenzhen's growth has been phenomenal. Where in the 1980s stood rice and vegetable fields and a smattering of small villages, by the 1990s were miles of high-rise buildings and urban sprawl reminiscent of neighboring Hong Kong.

As a result of this rapid growth, Shenzhen attracted Chinese men and women seeking "modern" lives, better job opportunities, and often greater freedom from their families and natal communities. Shenzhen, in Constance Clark's words, "became a magnet for youth from across China" where it was believed that "jobs were plentiful and people made their fortunes overnight."[2] To many northern Chinese, Shenzhen, even more than other parts of Guangdong province, had a reputation for being wild and loose. Shenzhen, I was told, is where all the beautiful women from all over China go with no family to watch over them. Here they have ready access to Hong Kong's Pearl and Star television and to foreign popular culture, which is not so readily available elsewhere in China. Women with failed relationships or failed marriages, a past to escape, or dreams of a bright future are often drawn to Shenzhen, a gateway to the rest of the world. Visions of life in Shenzhen, as Clark describes them, "center on making money and experiencing adventure, love, and freedom" (106). Yanyi, like many others, was drawn there by a desire for adventure and opportunity, and for the chance to work for a foreign firm.

Yanyi's story relates to the key themes of women's agency and hypergamy. Agency, or a person's ability to make choices and act upon them within the structural confines that simultaneously limit one's choices, can be seen at various stages of Yanyi's correspondence relationship with Russ. Yanyi's account explains why she initiated correspondence, her ideas about who to write to, who to reply to, and her attempts (not always successful) at negotiating with Russ. Despite the fact that she is bright and educated and had experience in the United States, Yanyi's relationship with Russ was difficult and ended badly. Her narrative illustrates the danger of romanticizing agency, and how an ability to express agency does not mean that a person necessarily acts in her own best interest.

Yanyi is unusually outgoing and bright, committed to her family in northern China, yet also independent, stubborn, and adventuresome. After she finished her degree in English from a reputable Chinese university in the early 1990s, she spent several months in the United States on an internship. Before returning to China, she used her savings to rent a car, and drove across the country alone, sleeping in the back seat at truck stops, so she could see Yellowstone, Yosemite, San Francisco, and other famous sites. One of the few members of her group who returned to China (many of the others overstayed their visas and became illegal immigrants), she planned to return to the United States again.

When I met her in 1999, Yanyi had worked for several years as a manager for a foreign consulting firm. With excellent skills in diplomacy and

English, Yanyi was highly valued. She earned a good salary (about $700 a month) by Chinese standards. Because she was in her early thirties and still unmarried, however, Yanyi was considered unusual and somewhat of a social problem. Although the legal minimum marriage age is twenty for women and twenty-two for men, most urban men and women in China marry in their mid-twenties.[3] As Yanyi explained, remaining unmarried is not considered a good option, and by thirty a woman's marriage prospects diminish.[4] Her age was one reason why she decided to write to foreign men.

While living in Shenzhen with her brother, his wife, and their pet dogs in a new apartment complex, Yanyi submitted her name to an Internet correspondence agency in the hope of meeting a foreign man. She had two friends with "happy ending stories" who had met their partners this way. She hoped to meet an American and imagined a bright future abroad. She was not interested in local men, many of whom were too transient and not serious. She had had a Chinese boyfriend in Shenzhen, but he had returned to his hometown to marry a local woman, following his parents' wishes. During two different time periods, Yanyi had received over 250 responses to her Internet listing. She wrote to ten men for a while, but soon decided to write only to Russ, an Australian. He sent her love poems and very moving letters, and she liked that he had been to China and other parts of Asia. Although he was not American, he shared her attraction to the United States and she was drawn to him.

When I first contacted Yanyi through the Internet introduction agency in 1999, she expressed more than the usual interest in meeting. From her first e-mail message it was clear that she had a gift for communication. She had a story to tell, she said, and we were both eager to meet in person. The morning after my Friday night "date" with Netty and Len in Hong Kong, I boarded a ferry to Shekou, a port town adjoining Shenzhen, and met Yanyi on a hot and humid Saturday, early in the afternoon. She was dressed in simple black pants, wore little if any make-up, and looked casual yet elegant. We had lunch at a small northern Chinese restaurant, then proceeded to her office for an interview. Yanyi spoke so openly that it felt as though we were old friends. Her story was extremely moving, and the honesty and emotion with which she told it was like few other interviews I have experienced. Afterwards she lent me piles of e-mail correspondences—a foot high, single-spaced and double-sided—to read so I could better understand and convey to others her feelings and experiences. She viewed her story as a cautionary tale of youthful trust and naivete, of survival and recovery.

Russ was in his mid-forties and had once been married to a Chinese woman. Because of a serious accident, he was receiving a government pension. Via e-mail, he wrote to Yanyi of his dreams and aspirations: of recovering from his injuries, opening a business, and raising a family. At first he wrote of his familiarity with and respect for Chinese culture. Yanyi's responses were open and warm; she expressed enthusiasm, imagined sharing his life and helping him to realize his ambitions. Their correspondences became more intimate. He called her his "darling wife," sent her poems and declarations of love. In the course of their letters, Yanyi "fell in love with him" and came to believe in their future together.

Yet at times she had nagging doubts. Sometimes his communications would cease for a day or two, and he would later explain that he had been ill. Other times he lashed out at her for not writing often enough. He seemed very jealous and sometimes extremely critical of his former wife. His admiration for "Chinese culture" was interspersed with racist generalizations about "Chinese people" and threats to end their relationship. Yanyi patiently explained that she was not the same as his ex-wife, and that he should treat her and China with more respect. Her patience seemed endless, but she also pointed out—gently but firmly—what she considered disrespectful or wrong about his views. He responded at first with anger and later with heartfelt apologies, appreciating her patience and understanding. He begged her pardon and said that he would understand if she could not forgive him since he had treated her so badly. Each time, he promised to try harder. His illness and depression, and a fear that they might never be together, he said, prompted his irrational responses.

Over a period of six months, their correspondences became increasingly personal, emotional, sexually intimate, and melodramatic. He continued to complain of pains and illnesses, but said that since meeting Yanyi, he had lost weight and become stronger, healthier, and happier. His doctor was pleased with his progress and urged him to continue with a new medication. Russ expressed optimism at what "the love of the right woman" could do. Yet Yanyi was concerned and wrote asking exactly what ailed him. Among his problems were anxiety, depression, bronchitis, diabetes, posttraumatic stress disorder, and high blood pressure. But he insisted that their relationship made him stronger and healthier; when they were finally together everything would be fine.

In one message, Russ fantasized about their first long and lingering passionate kiss when they would finally meet in person at the train station. Yanyi responded that she would "turn purple with embarrassment" should that happen. He answered that if she didn't kiss him, he would turn around and go back. Her reply was circumspect: "You know, maybe its our cultural shortcoming—we [Chinese] don't address sweetly, hug, kiss, or touch so much to show our feelings or intimacy as people do in Western cultures. (That's why I don't know if I can give you a long deep kiss as the first hello right in the public.)" Again, he threatened to end it all, then later apologized and begged her forgiveness. The fact that they had weathered their difficulties, Russ wrote, meant that their relationship would be stronger. Their difficulties were a test of their faith and commitment; he loved her all the more for her honesty. Yanyi was moved and reassured by his response.

After six months of almost twice-daily correspondence, they made plans to meet in person. Russ would sell his car to secure the necessary funds for the trip, but when the time came he did not have enough money to pay for his ticket. Yanyi sent him several hundred dollars—a significant portion of her savings—to cover the balance. He arrived in Shenzhen and stayed with her in the flat she shared with her brother and his wife. Virtually penniless, yet awaiting his government check, Russ was entirely dependent on Yanyi's support for three months. She took him to Chinese doctors, and initially his health—especially his back injury—improved significantly. Yanyi soon realized, however, that while she was at work he spent the day drinking, and when she came home at lunch and in the evening he was drunk. When she confronted him, he complained and made excuses: he was lonely and bored, she didn't spend enough time with him, her brother didn't like him. Yanyi grew more concerned about his health and about the economic imbalance in their relationship, but when she raised the topic of money, he accused her of pettiness and angrily assured her that he would pay her back.

As the situation got worse, Yanyi did not speak to her family and friends about it for fear of betraying Russ's trust, losing face, and making the situation worse. Yet her family was concerned, and her parents came from the north to visit. Although they were outwardly polite, they disapproved of Russ. He sensed their disapproval and felt Yanyi did not sufficiently side with him. She felt torn. Emotionally invested in their relationship, she could not easily admit that things were bad and he should leave. The situation reached a climax when an argument between Russ and Yanyi's brother turned into a violent confrontation. Soon after, Russ's government check arrived. He bought a ticket to the United States and promised he would make a success of himself, send for her, and prove her family wrong. When he left, she gradually felt a growing sense of relief. She admitted that their relationship was over and she wrote and told him so.

Six months later, by the time we met, Yanyi had half-heartedly resumed her attempt to meet pen pals. She thought that correspondence was risky, but she was cautious. Her parents urged her to focus on her education. She wrote to several men, and one came for a brief visit, though nothing came of it. She began to explore the possibility of going to graduate school abroad. Later in 1999, she began to correspond with a U.S. businessman whom she had met very briefly while he was visiting Shenzhen for work. Meanwhile, her student visa was approved and she came to the United States to study. This, she explained, would allow her to get to know her pen pal in person—slowly and with less pressure—while she earned a master's degree.

Had Yanyi initially met Russ in person rather than through the Internet, she speculated that things might have turned out differently and that she might have seen his faults more clearly, in time to back away from a serious relationship. Despite her sense of helplessness upon Russ's arrival, their problems were not solely or centrally linked to the way they met or to Yanyi's "inferior" structural position. Despite her emotional dependency on him, she was Russ's social and economic superior, and he was economically dependent on her. Yet she found it difficult to call on the support of family and friends and to put an end to an increasingly unpleasant relationship.

PING'S CONCERNS

Ping, a fifty-year-old divorcee from Beijing, is married to Elvin, a sixty-five-year-old artist from northern California, with a law degree and experience in political activism. Elvin had always been attracted to socialist politics and to what he saw as the "spiritual side" of Chinese culture. As he told Ping, he was attracted to Chinese philosophy and "the lack of materialism" that he associated with China's communist history. He expected Chinese women to be "less materialistic and more committed to marriage" than western ones. He also had a friend, a western intellectual, who appeared to have a good relationship with his Chinese wife. Elvin was divorced, with grown children. He had hoped to remarry but had little in the way of financial assets. He hoped that his appreciation for Buddhism, atheism, tai chi, and a simple lifestyle would appeal to a Chinese woman. He began to write to Ping over the Internet. They corresponded via e-mail and through Internet chat for over a year, then met in person when he came for a two-week visit.

I met Ping in the summer of 2000, after Elvin's visit and while she was considering whether to accept his marriage proposal. Two of her co-workers invited us to join them for lunch. They introduced her to me as a "success story"—a woman who had met a wonderful man and who was on her way to the United States—and they thought she would be a good example for my research. Ping did not appear to share their enthusiasm. As she explained, there were "some problems to iron out." Unlike her co-workers, Ping referred to Elvin as her "friend," not her "fiancé." Her friends urged her to discuss her relationship with me. She would like to, she said, but only in private, and she hoped that they would not feel offended.

After lunch Ping invited me to the large, western-style flat where she lived with her college-aged son in a fast-growing part of northeastern Beijing. In clear view from the dining room table where we sat was a very large television screen, a video player, and many other amenities that seemed to be an integral part of the boom in materialism in China over recent years. I looked over her flat as she described Elvin's notion of the Chinese lack of materialism. "Do you think he's right?" I asked. She laughed and said, "You know much more about Chinese than he does!" I asked whether, after his visit, he still thought Chinese people were less materialistic. Answering indirectly, she laughed again and said that he had promised to buy a television set if she agreed to come to the United States. The fact that he was attracted to what he considered the "spiritual" and "communist" aspects of Chinese culture bothered her less than some of his other attitudes.

Just as Ping was about to embark on her "problem," her son came home. My heart sank, as I assumed the conversation would shift to more innocuous topics. To my surprise, after introducing us, she proceeded to discuss her main concern in his presence. One was that Elvin lived in a nudist colony. If she went to live with him, how could her friends—much less her son—come to visit? How could she tell people where she lived? She wanted me to tell her how common nudism was in the United States. Elvin had asked her to come to the United States on a ninety-day (K1) fiancée visa so that she could see for herself that there was nothing wrong, indecent, or unethical about nudity. She was considering this option. She cared for Elvin; she had a lot of respect for his work and his intellect, and her son had also liked him.

Ping had other concerns about sexuality that she did not discuss in front of her son. Like several women I had met, she was curious about western ideas about sexuality. Some women had opted out of correspondence because the man seemed "too forward" about sex or to be a "sex maniac"— advancing to sexual topics after only two or three correspondences. Ping was concerned about Elvin's ideas about nudity, just as Yanyi was concerned about Russ's expectations of a kiss upon first meeting in person. One forty-five-year-old woman expressed concern (and distaste) for her pen pal's interest in oral sex ("Chinese of my generation," she said, "are not comfortable with this idea as Americans are"). Dr. Wu, an attractive woman doctor in her late thirties who had never been married, met a pen pal who was also a doctor from the United States. He had said that "sleeping together allows a couple to get to know one another's physical condition ahead of time." From a medical perspective, Dr. Wu agreed, but she nonetheless opted against getting to know his "physical condition" because she was not interested in pursuing their relationship.

One friend of Ping's anticipated meeting a man from Arkansas. She was uncomfortable with his assumption that he could either stay with her at her flat or that they would stay together at a hotel. One day Ping's friend asked me point blank whether most western men expected them to sleep together when they first met. She explained that for women her age this was a source of concern, yet the men who planned to visit seemed to expect to "get to know one another physically" before making a commitment to marriage. In many cases, Chinese women seemed less concerned with actually sleeping with the man than with having a commitment from him first. Unsure of how to answer the question, uncomfortable with the responsibility of serving as cultural broker, I said I thought most couples in the United States sleep together before marriage, but that most did not agree to do so before they had met in person; nor were most couples, I speculated, likely to go to bed together after knowing each other for only a day or two. I also noted that people who sleep together may not necessarily have plans to marry.

Ping's friends were not entirely satisfied with my highly qualified answer, which contrasted so much with their impression of American culture. Based mainly on what they had heard or seen on television, they assumed that all Americans hop into bed at the drop of a hat. I suggested that I post their question on one of the Internet lists of western men. Briefly describing the situation, I wrote that several Chinese women had asked me whether western men expected to sleep with their pen pals before making a commitment. I received a variety of responses. Most men from UFG answered that they were attracted to Filipinas partly for their sexual purity, morality, Christianity, and their "traditional" values, and that they therefore had greater respect for women who protected their virginity and refused to have sex before marriage. Several of them advised women to "dump" any man who insists on sleeping with her if she is at all reluctant or unwilling. "There are plenty of other good guys out there," one man with a Chinese fiancée wrote, "so they [the women] shouldn't waste their

time with the jerks who only want sex or who won't respect their traditional views." Kevin (see chapter 5) described his own situation, admitting
that he and his Chinese wife had slept together during his first two-week
visit, after a year-long correspondence, but that it was a mutual decision to
do so, and they had already become "engaged." "Many men," he wrote
(and he hoped I would not take offense at the analogy), view sex and marriage a bit like buying a car, "and they wouldn't buy a car without test driving it." On the other hand, he was not "defending this attitude." He stressed
that there is no single answer; it depends on the man and the woman.

Since divorce is officially practiced in China (and not in the Philippines),
and since divorced women with children were obviously not virgins, the
situation was different than in the Philippines. Yet Ping's friends and others to whom I forwarded the men's answers were somewhat reassur.ed. As
Jen explained in 2000, women who frequent her agency have come to believe that whether they sleep with the men or not, the men are not going
to marry them. The women are not as concerned with having sex as they
are with the thought that it will not lead to marriage. One of the men on
the list explained that certain agencies have distinct reputations. Some
men are attracted to agencies that seem to advertise a good time (like an
escort service), while others seem much more explicitly directed toward
marriage-minded men and women. He wondered whether Jen's agency
attracted less "marriage-minded" men, those who only wanted what Jen
called a "sexual vacation."

Ultimately Ping's friend did not invite her pen pal to stay at her home,
and she told him she would not stay with him at the hotel, since it is officially illegal in China for unmarried couples to do so. Ping's friend was
aware that this law is not often enforced and that there are ways around it,
but in this case she was pleased to use it as an excuse. Later I heard that her
pen pal had decided to visit anyway, but they "disagreed about everything"
and quickly ended their relationship.

Another of Ping's concerns was that Elvin had said very little about his
financial situation. As she explained, it is quite normal, indeed expected,
among Chinese couples to disclose the precise details of their financial situation before they discuss marriage. Elvin was not well off, of that she was
quite certain, but what worried her was not his poverty but his reluctance
to disclose the details. As Ping and others explained, they see it as their job
to know the household financial situation and to arrange the finances so
as to save money. One woman said any household should save "as much as
a third or half of their overall income." "How can I help him save if I don't
know how much money he has?" was a common complaint.

In striking contrast to Asian women's reputation for "subservience," women in China and the Philippines often control the household budget. Although most women I spoke to agreed with this generalization, they also pointed to subtle distinctions and variations. As Ping explained, husbands will often turn their paychecks over to their wives, but some may hold back a part of it for their own discretionary use. Men may be involved in decisions involving household expenditures, especially large or unusual ones. In some Chinese households where women work, men may shop for food and may even cook, and thus control the budget on a daily basis. In such cases, women may keep part of their incomes for themselves. In households with dual incomes, men and women may pool part of their income for the household budget, yet keep part of their earnings independent.

To most Chinese, questions about money are not considered indiscreet, although some realize that money is a more private matter to Americans. U.S. men, moreover, were concerned when women asked "too many questions" about money at the courting stage, raising the spectre of "gold diggers," or women interested only in their money. Women, in turn, might respond by not asking questions about money, despite their concerns. Although they wanted to know about the man's finances, they were put off by men who appeared to flaunt their material wealth or who bragged about their possessions. Ping's friends all had a good laugh about a man who sent his pen pal a five dollar bill and assumed that this would go far in China or would be viewed as a sign of his wealth and generosity. Another man, who sent a photograph of himself next to a fancy sports car in front of a mansion, also drew suspicion. Not only did the photograph suggest that he was a show-off who was too eager to impress a woman and who placed material factors before personality and compatibility, but they also commented that any man could have his photograph taken in front of such a house or car; it did not necessarily mean that it belonged to him.[5] Conspicuous consumption, moreover, was not as highly valued as thrift and the ability to save money.

When I asked men engaged or married to Chinese women whether women's control of the household budget was a source of concern or conflict for them, several pointed out that money is a matter of concern in all marriages. Most men said they did not expect their wives, especially upon arrival in the United States, to manage the household budget alone. Some who were married to Chinese women admired their wives' abilities to budget, economize, and save for major purchases. The following excerpt from an Internet discussion between Charlie, who had been married to a Filipina for over ten years, and Mark, who was engaged and awaiting his fiancée's arrival, illustrates an array of views. Charlie wrote that one major problem is "with women in the phillipines running the home and money i had problems with her trying to handle all the money. but hay she's pretty good at it . . . i love her. i hope we can work out diffences. i've got to learn to let her take charge or at least let her think she's in charge." Mark responded, "This is where you and I differ. I can hardly wait until [my wife] takes over the finances. I intend to hand over my paycheck and have her take charge from there. It wouldn't bother me if I never saw the checkbook again! I'm making assumptions here that she will be good at this sort of thing. I hope I am right."

Two men with Chinese partners wrote that their mothers were single parents who had run the household, so they were unperturbed by the idea of a woman controlling the budget. Another man said his Italian American mother had controlled the budget, so he was comfortable with his wife doing so. Like others, he wanted to introduce her to the system, the methods of paying bills, the lifestyle, before allowing her to completely take charge. Several men expressed pride in their partner's ability to manage their Chinese *yuan* or Philippine *pesos* while they were abroad. Men spoke of women's skills in bargaining, preventing them from "getting ripped off." Others, like Charlie, seemed more comfortable with the idea that financial plans and decisions would be made "jointly." Several men complimented their wives' abilities to devise ways to save money, including working sometimes more than one job. Other men preferred that their wives not work.

In contrast to several Filipinas who were willing to buy things on credit, Thomas described his Chinese wife's opposition to debt. She asked him how much money they would need to save to buy an SUV. He explained that they could buy the car immediately on credit. She then calculated the interest and proceeded to save money to buy it outright. Thomas was thrilled at the money they saved and at his wife's attitude. Although it is beginning to be common for Chinese in urban China to buy apartments on payment plans (often payments in installments to their work units), many prefer to save and buy property outright rather than to buy on credit.[6]

Contrary to what one might expect, given the common assumptions of poverty in Asia and wealth in the West, Chinese women and Filipinas often said they would not mind marrying men with little money. Like Ping, most women were confident that they could "help earn and save money." What disturbed them was men's secrecy about money and their attitude toward saving. Jen described how shocked she and other women were when in the course of conversations, men would say that they had "spent their entire savings" or had "spent their last penny" to visit a pen pal. She and others were amazed that a man would spend all his money in order to marry, rather than save money *for* their marriage and family. "Why can't they save at least $100 a month from every pay check?" I was asked. "Why wouldn't a person just get a cheaper or smaller apartment and save money rather than a big place and save nothing?" That people in the United States increase their standard of living to match (or exceed) their incomes rather than save money was to many Chinese women I spoke to almost unfathomable.[7]

A month or two after I met her in Beijing, Ping received a fiancée visa and agreed to go to California. She could always go back, she said, if things did not work out. She wanted to see where Elvin lived and what his community was like. Upon her arrival, they traveled together, stayed in the nudist community for a while, and then got married. She phoned to tell me the "happy news." She was pleasantly surprised to find that the people at the nudist colony were "nice and respectable," and included families, ministers, judges, and other professionals. There would be difficulties and hard work in store for her and Elvin. She would have to get a work permit, find a job, learn to drive, and go back to school. Elvin's finances were, as she had suspected, not good. She insisted that they prepare a prenuptial agreement to put his children's minds at ease that she was not after the little money he had, but overall she sounded optimistic.

A few weeks later, Ping expressed more concern. The community was isolated, and the nearest city was over an hour's drive away. She was shocked at U.S. prices. As she became aware of taxes, retirement and health insurance costs, and rental prices, she lost confidence in her ability to save money and improve their lives. Her employment opportunities were bleak. The Cultural Revolution had interrupted her education and she had not attended college; there were few prospects of utilizing her Chinese skills to find work. When friends (whom she met at a Chinese church some distance away) offered to visit or pick her up, she felt uncomfortable telling them where she lived. A week later she decided it would be better if she went back to China.

She cared about Elvin and respected him, she said, but could not conceive of living with him in a nudist colony, with little opportunity for work or to improve their circumstances. "The apartment is ideal for him. It's near his grown up children and his ex-wife. But it's no good for me and there's little I can do to help the situation. I can't afford to go to school and can't get a job here. We can't afford to move either." As an artist, she said, he was like many Chinese intellectuals: "spiritually rich but materially poor." His material circumstances bothered her less than the fact that she could not figure out how to make improvements. "If I was younger, it would be different," she explained. Given their ages, she worried about the cost of health care and insurance. She could not adjust to living in a nudist colony. Although she had come to terms with it intellectually, sharing a kitchen with naked strangers made her uncomfortable. Although Elvin would consider renting an apartment in town, they could not afford to do so on his current income, and her attempts to find work had been unsuccessful. Ultimately Ping had been drawn to Elvin's intellectual and artistic side. They got along best, she said, when they went to museums, concerts, and art exhibits, but she was unhappy about their everyday life and her prospects for work: "If I stay, I will have to endure much bitterness," she explained.

Two weeks later she contacted me from the Midwest where she was visiting an old friend from the Cultural Revolution. Her friend, the single mother of three children, had been in the United States for ten years and urged her to stay. Ping had reconsidered and had postponed her plans to return to China. She decided to wait until her son had finished his college examinations and to consult with him before making a decision. Two months later, she was still in the United States. She admitted that "life is hard," but things were better. She and Elvin had moved to an apartment in town. She had found a minimum-wage job and paid half their rent. The possibility of returning to China was still open to her, but life would be difficult for her if she went back because she no longer had her old job. It would be impossible to find a new one, and she was still too young to collect a retirement pension. I asked Ping if she would have come to the United States had she known what it would be like. She expressed doubt and criticized the ninety-day limit on the K1 fiancé visa, which she said did not allow enough time to make a "proper decision." Meanwhile, life was not easy, but Elvin had made some sacrifices for her. She was learning about American life, and she hoped to give her son the opportunity to visit the United States to decide. She still planned to return to Beijing one day, but for now she would remain, learn to drive, save more money, and look for a better paying job.

LACEY: WAITING FOR THE RIGHT MATCH

The following sketches of Lacey, Meili, and Anna raise the question of what women sought in a match. While many critics assume that women want marriages that allow them economic upward mobility, and this is sometimes the case, most sought a "status match" in the sense of a compatible partner and companion based mainly on personal character traits.[8] These sketches also raise the question of whether, and in what multiplicity of ways, women and men marry—or aim to marry—up or down.

Lacey was one of the youngest Chinese women I met through a marriage-oriented Internet introduction agency. Like the men who wrote to Lacey, I originally paid the required fee (approximately $50 for a three-month membership) to join the "club." I then gained access to her e-mail address and wrote to her about my research. We exchanged several messages and arranged to meet in Beijing a few months later, and maintained contact and met again in 2000.

Lacey was an English graduate from a prestigious university. In 1999, she worked for an international firm that utilized her language skills and paid her about $1,000 a month. Although beauty is highly subjective, both westerners and Chinese who saw her photograph considered her very attractive. Despite the fact that she was bright, educated, attractive, and had a good job, Lacey—like Yanyi—caused her family concern because she was close to thirty and unmarried. When she visited her home town, family members and neighbors made rude remarks, asked nosey questions, and offered to make introductions. Unlike her family and friends, Lacey claimed she felt no urgency to marry. As a well-educated, well-employed, and attractive woman, she felt she could wait. She had been introduced to many men, but she wanted to meet someone to love and respect. Although she hoped to go to the United States or Canada one day, like many other young, educated women, she considered graduate school another—possibly more viable—route.

Despite her stated lack of concern, Lacey allowed her older sister (who had married a Chinese classmate and settled in the United States after earning a Ph.D. from an American university) to submit her name and photograph to a U.S.-based online introduction agency. Her photograph depicted her standing on the Great Wall with two long braids and a friendly smile, reminiscent of a pretty young peasant from the Maoist era. Her sister chose the photo, she said, because it made her look young, wholesome, and pretty. Lacey's sister wanted her to meet an overseas Chinese man or, alternatively, a nice white professional. Accordingly, she filtered through the many responses and forwarded to Lacey only the most appropriate and promising ones. As Lacey explained, her sister filtered out anyone deemed inappropriate, including men who were too old (over 38), blue-collar, divorced, neither Chinese nor white, or who were Muslim. Implicit in these decisions about age, marital status, class, race, and religion, which Lacey seemed to accept without question, was a sense that to do otherwise would be to consider someone subordinate or socially inappropriate.

When I met Lacey in 1999, her hair was short and she struck me as much more stylish and sophisticated than her photograph. She had been writing to three men by e-mail on a weekly basis. One was Chinese, originally from Beijing, but studying for a Ph.D. in Canada; the two others were white professionals from the United States. As she explained to them, she wanted to make friends, but she did not believe she could fall in love by e-mail. The men's letters became more intimate. All three expressed a desire for a girlfriend, a commitment, or a willingness to develop a serious and exclusive relationship. Lacey considered it "okay to become friends" and "even share secrets" with pen pals, and she was open to the possibility that more than a friendship might ensue *after* they had met in person. She thought it was fun and interesting to get to know people this way, but she was not convinced that these pen pals were potential spouses. Friends meanwhile introduced her to local men, but no one caught her interest. "In China," she explained, "girls generally have higher qualities than men." It is "difficult for them to meet good men" because there are more women who are "financially independent, intelligent, and good-hearted." In school, she said, the good men were interested in younger students, not their classmates or equals. She hoped to meet at least her social equal.

A year later I met Lacey at the south gate of Beijing University, and we walked to a nearby restaurant. Her hair had grown long and she wore blue jeans and a T-shirt. She filled me in on the latest developments: her Chinese Canadian pen pal had come to Beijing the previous winter, but she had not arranged to meet him. He was too desperate, too pushy and lonely, and as a student, he had financial difficulties. She stopped writing to her other pen pals as well. They complained that she should write more often, but she had had neither the time nor the inclination. Her main news was that she was engaged. Her fiancé was a former classmate, an old friend who was completing his Ph.D. at Beijing University. He had been interested in her for years, but she had only recently noticed him and begun to reciprocate his feelings.

I commented that her parents must be very pleased since he was a graduate of a top university. Her father and her sister were relieved that she was getting married, she said, but her mother was disappointed because she considered the young man neither tall nor handsome enough, and not well established. He was not someone her mother could show off and brag about.[9] Lacey was happy, however, and enthusiastic about their plans to attend graduate and postdoctoral programs in the United States or Canada. Her news took me by surprise, given her earlier lack of concern about marrying before she reached thirty. What I found particularly noteworthy, was that neither she nor Yanyi was desperate enough to pursue a relationship with a pen pal just to get to the United States. Both were concerned with meeting "the right person" and, like Yanyi, Lacey would find other ways to get to the United States. The right person in the end was a Chinese, well-educated man who shared her desire to go abroad.

ANNA AND MEILI

If marriage prospects diminish for attractive and educated young women close to thirty, finding an appropriate partner is of greater concern for women in their late thirties or forties with a child. Meili and Anna (like Moira, described in chapter 1) were both professional women in their forties who were divorced. I got to know them, and they got to know each other, through our mutual friend Hong, a widow in her early fifties who worked as an English teacher in Beijing and who had spent a year teaching Chinese in the United States. With her English skills and her home computer, Hong helped Meili and Anna write to pen pals—sometimes once a week.[10]

When I met her in 1999, Anna was forty-five and worked as a librarian at small college. Her income was very modest. For several years, she and her daughter had slept in an office in the library, but they had recently begun to rent a tiny one-room flat. Meili was forty and lived in a large, modern apartment with her elderly parents. Both women had been divorced for several years. Their friend Hong described them as attractive middle-aged women. Anna's personality and appearance was like a splash of color—the antithesis of the Maoist androgynous woman. She was cheerful and bubbly and exuded warmth. Always carefully made up and stylishly coifed, she was chubby from a Chinese perspective but she had very pale skin, a shapely figure, and shoulder-length wavy black hair. Meili was more serious and less flamboyant than Anna in style and demeanor; she was petite, more made up than most urban Chinese women, and wore conservative designer brand suits and elegant jewelry.[11]

Like several divorced, professional Chinese women I met, Anna and Meili hoped to meet a man from abroad, preferably from the United States, because they thought they might make "more suitable partners and companions." Not only did the stigma of divorce make it difficult for them to meet "good local men" to marry, but their status as professional women (especially for those with a good income) made them attractive to local men for the wrong reasons. Meili, partly because of her high-profile job and high income, had many suitors, but she feared that they were attracted to her money.

Anna's situation provided some insight into the claim that western men might be "more suitable." Because her parents were criticized as intellectuals, she had a bad class label during the Maoist period. In the late 1970s, she married a man who did not share her interests or her intellectual class background. Their marriage, she explained, was based on the practical considerations of the Cultural Revolution era. Anna's father was a well-known artist who had studied western-style painting in his youth. During the Cultural Revolution he had been criticized for not adequately espousing socialist ideology and a socialist realist style in his art. Like Moira, Meili (whose parents were writers), and Hong (the daughter of western-style musicians), Anna had suffered from class labels. To redeem herself perhaps, and because it was expected at the time that marriages reflect political correctness, Anna married a man who did not share her background. Her ex-husband's family had a working-class background and were thus considered most reputable during the Maoist era. Ironically, during that time it could be said that Anna (from an educated and professional family) had married "up"—into the family of a worker. According to Whyte and Parish, such marriages were unusual, as class standing, especially during the Cultural Revolution, tended to be matched, as men and women tried to avoid those with bad class labels.[12]

In 1978, class labels were officially abolished. Music, art, and literature, once condemned for bearing western influence, now reemerged and— despite the sporadic (but short-lived) campaigns against western spiritual pollution—regained much popularity and prestige. Western and foreign taste and culture became a form of symbolic capital that marked social distinctions, if not economic ones.[13] Ideals of romantic love and compatibility in marriage became more widely accepted than before.[14] Divorce, discouraged during most of the Maoist period, became increasingly common, as couples sought legal separations. Divorce in urban China rose dramatically to about 20 percent in the late 1990s, but still remained well below western rates. Over half the divorces were initiated by women.[15]

Meili and Anna's divorces had much to do, in their view, with the fact that they had little in common with their husbands. While having "little in common" may be a way of glossing personal issues they did not want to discuss, many divorced women spoke openly of a husband's infidelity and also stressed a lack of common interests or of basic compatibility. As Anna explained, she married "for the wrong reasons" a man who later seemed incompatible. She described him as lazy, with little sense of familial responsibility; all he wanted to do was watch television, and he had few intellectual interests.

This incompatibility was accentuated by China's opening up since the 1980s. Hong resumed playing the piano, something she had not done since childhood, when her father was criticized. Anna's father was "rehabilitated" and the impressionist style that had brought him earlier criticism now brought him popular acclaim. Anna was not well off by any means, but she had sophisticated and cosmopolitan taste, which alienated her from her husband. Her tiny apartment displayed several of her father's paintings, and housed art books and a phenomenal collection of western music CDs. Anna's daughter took up classical western music, won a top prize at a competition in Eastern Europe, and dreamt of attending Juilliard in the United States. Anna's marriage ultimately ended after over ten years, she explained, because her husband was selfish, showed little responsibility, and was not supportive of their daughter's musical talent. Shortly after their divorce, he married a younger woman.

Men like their ex-husbands, Anna and Meili complained, did not share their interests. The foreigners they hoped to meet would be more "cultured," more introspective, and would share their cultural and spiritual interests. They criticized men and women in China "who just want money and material things." Anna's imagined husband was a responsible family man with refined taste who would share her enthusiasm for museums, music, and fine art. She hoped to meet a man who valued marital fidelity, took good care of his health and hygiene, and enjoyed ballroom dancing. She also hoped he would speak Chinese or be interested in and familiar with Chinese culture.

Anna and her friends were "cultured" in the narrow sense of sharing elite interests and taste. They knew far more about western art, music, literature, and even popular culture than I did. One evening, after a feast of *jiaozi* (dumplings), the conversation moved smoothly from Beethoven and Bach to Elizabeth Taylor's latest marriage, Prince William, the trade accord, the pros and cons of hormone therapy for menopause, and the election of Taiwan's new president. Their cosmopolitan interests provide a striking contrast to stereotypes of mail-order brides.

Meili had many opportunities to meet local men, but did not trust them. Western men, she said (and she included overseas Chinese in this category) are more likely to be direct and straightforward about what they want. "They say what is on their mind." They are also more likely to want an "equal" relationship with women, but here she questioned whether or not to include overseas Chinese. By "equal," she did not seem to mean that both would divide the household work and contribute to the household income. Instead, she alluded to a "balanced" division of labor. Despite her preference to work, she would happily stay at home if her husband could afford to support her. She believed men in the United States seemed more willing to "take care of their wives." Chinese men, in contrast, wanted women they could "boss around and feel superior to," or they wanted to marry women for their money and were intimidated by successful women. Like Anna, Meili spoke little English, and she wanted to meet a Chinese American or a white man who spoke Chinese. Meili preferred to meet a man who is "well educated" with a "white-collar" occupation, whereas Anna was less particular about his occupation as long as he was "cultured." (Anna seemed to skim over the fact that a man with such interests would very likely be middle-class or higher in the United States.) Hong described Meili as "very picky." "She has very high standards, but she can afford to be. She prefers to remain alone than to marry someone who isn't perfect."

Anna and Meili had both submitted their names to introduction agencies in the hope of meeting "suitable" western or overseas Chinese men. They had each received letters or e-mail messages from several men in the course of two years, but both were disappointed. They dismissed out of hand men who bragged of high incomes or sent tacky photographs of themselves in tank tops or exposing hairy chests, those who had been married more than once and those who had never been married, and one who lived with his mother. Each had written to a man whom they considered a good prospect, but both men had stopped writing. Anna's pen pal said that his mother was ill, so he no longer had time to write; Meili's had married his translator.

Yanyi, Ping, Lacey, Anna, and Meili were all looking for a "good match." Although it was difficult to get them to explain exactly what they meant by this, they all wanted to meet "kind," "respectful," "healthy" men who have good "hygiene." They didn't want just anyone; they wanted compatibility. To some this meant sharing interests in "high culture" and appreciating their good taste. They wanted to meet men who would appreciate their status as educated or professional women, but who would not take economic advantage of them. All of them hoped to meet someone to fulfill emotional and practical interests. None of them could be called desperate. They did not include or exclude men on the basis of their income. Although Lacey considered her Chinese Canadian pen pal less appealing because he was "poor," he was no poorer than the Chinese man she eventually married. The fact that her pen pal studied in Canada was not enough to counterbalance her sense that he seemed too "desperate" to find a wife. Each of these women aimed to find a social equal. They did not jump at the first opportunity to create a "bridge" for their families to migrate to the United States. Although Yanyi, Lacey, and Meili expressed a strong desire to go to the United States, none allowed this desire to outweigh other considerations. None was interested in a man just because he was American or solely because of his income. If that were the case, they would all be married and living in the United States today.

HYPERGAMY

Hypergamy refers to "marrying up," most often to the cultural expectation in some societies that women will marry up and out of their own social or economic group.[16] According to Parkin, "the term *hypergamy* is applied to the situation in which a man marries a woman from an affinal group of lower status; *hypogamy* (sometimes called *reverse hypergamy*) to the situation in which a man marries a woman from an affinal group of higher status (with both words the perspective is that of the groom)" (42). North Indian women who marry into a higher *jati* (or subcaste) are a prime example of this type of exogamous marriage in the anthropological literature, as are the Kachin of Burma.[17]

Hypergamy has not been as strictly adhered to in Chinese society as in some others, but it is an important cultural concept. Margery Wolf described the trouble that befell a marriage—and an extended family in Taiwan in the late 1950s—because the patriarch "dismissed the long-accepted custom that wives should be selected from families whose status was the same or slightly inferior to their husband's," and arranged his son's marriage to a woman from a wealthier household. In reference to how marriages in the PRC in the 1990s are influenced by older "cultural frames," William Parish and James Farrer write that the "traditional practice [is] of women marrying up and men marrying down" and that "women [still] complain when this pattern is reversed." Indeed, Chinese women often complained that it is difficult for educated and well-employed women to marry a social equal because men are likely to marry down. By that they meant that men married women who were younger, had less income and less prestigious occupations, and were often their juniors in school.[18]

A *South China Morning Post* report made a similar point. Tan Jun, the general manager of Golden Destiny Valley, the largest dating agency in Beijing, explained in an interview that in China professional women are the most difficult to match. "In theory, city women should . . . enjoy the pick of the bunch. But only, it seems, if they lower their sights." Tan Jun described a woman who was on his books for six years. "She's now 44, not bad looking, got her Ph.D. in America, and came back to be a cadre at the Academy of Sciences. But Chinese men are afraid of women like her." Mr. Tan "prides himself on introducing 18,000 people to wedded bliss over the past seven years. But successful women like the doctor are proving some of the toughest cases to crack." As Tan explains, Chinese men look for women who are "gentle, soft and virtuous. They don't want strong career women, as they fear the pressure and may develop an inferiority complex." Tan advised the woman to "list herself as a masters or graduate student to reduce male anxiety." According to Liu Bohong, sociologist from the All China Women's Federation, "Even in the Internet age, the ancient feudal concepts of male chauvinism still dominate many Chinese men's minds. . . . If a woman makes more money, has a higher degree or social position, the husband may worry that he would lose authority over her."[19]

Studies of marriages during the Maoist period suggest that "status matching"—rather than hypergamy—was the expected norm and that romantic attractions could sometimes undermine family efforts to "'match doors and households' [*mendang hudui*]."[20] Martin Whyte and William Parish state unequivocally, "In pre-1949 China it was generally thought that marriages should involve status matching" (129). In the pre-Mao period couples tended to be matched according to family status and property ownership, while in the Maoist period traits such as "class labels and urban registration" were more significant.[21] This is similar to the European context, where Goody has argued that a strong emphasis was placed until recently on forming a "good match."

According to Goody, a good match involved class endogamy (marriage within one's class). A "match" implied "the pairing of like to like," in which a woman's prospective dowry is matched with a man's prospective inheritance.[22] As Linda Stone explains, "This does not mean that everyone marries an exact class equal. In Europe . . . parents were only too pleased to marry a son or daughter into a slightly wealthier or higher-status family, seeing this achievement as enhancing their own status." Stone claims that the pattern was not so different in Asia. Despite ambitions to marry a daughter up, "throughout Eurasia a general class endogamy was maintained, and wide gaps in the status of husband and wife were rare and usually denounced."[23]

In societies in which marriage is expected to be hypergamous or isogamous (i.e., lateral, or between social equals) women who marry down—or men who marry too far up—are subject to social disapproval. Chinese novels such as Ba Jin's *Family*, set in mainland China in the 1920s, point to social pressure for people to marry a suitable match rather than for love.[24] In cases where a man or a woman refuses to follow the culturally prescribed pattern of marriage within or close to his or her own social class or caste, a widely held assumption is that he or she has gone against expectations and propriety because of passionate love or, alternatively, greed.

One problem with the notion of hypergamy, as it has often been used, is that it fails to ask on any but the broadest level of social and cultural generalization how "up" might be defined differently according to one's social position. In many older social anthropological studies, hypergamy is defined by one broad social variable, such as caste or class. The term is used to refer to group movement rather than to individuals. Beyond broad social categories, no one asked, "up" in what sense(s) and to whom? If a marriage is deemed up for the woman, is it necessarily down for the man? Although a woman who marries into a higher caste is marrying up in terms of caste, is she marrying down in other ways? Has her husband necessarily married down, from his own perspective, that of his mother, and that of his younger sister? Are marriages only up, down, or equal, or are there inconsistencies, contradictions, and discrepancies? Can men and women creatively utilize ambiguous assumptions about "up" and "down" to justify new patterns of marriage?

Another problem with the term "hypergamy," as it has commonly been used, is that it reflects a gender-biased assumption that women are the ones who marry up or are "exchanged." Claude Lévi-Strauss and many others wrote quite unselfconsciously of "wife givers" (or "givers of wives") and "wife takers," but never of husband givers or husband takers. As Parkin aptly observes, the word "hypergamy" refers to the perspective of the groom.[25] It is commonly assumed that women benefit by marrying into a higher status family; the vantage point is thus that of the groom and his family looking down at the bride and her family. From the vantage point of her in-laws, a bride is "acquired," and from the point of view of an older style of anthropology, this male perspective was unproblematic.

GLOBAL HYPERGAMY?

How useful and accurate is the notion that Asian women who marry western men marry "up"? Regardless of the man's actual socioeconomic standing, foreign women who marry U.S. men—men who are citizens or residents of the "world's greatest super power," as the United States is widely viewed from both the inside and the outside, are commonly thought to marry "up" in a global and geographical sense. As in the classic anthropological cases of hypergamy, such marriages are said to benefit not only the woman but also her family and kin. The couple provides a bridge to the west by which family members may later follow.[26]

In the case of international correspondence courtship and marriage, it is assumed that women marry up in terms of social and geographical location. Yet they may be said to marry down in other ways. Some women admitted that their parents would rather they marry someone Asian or Chinese than of a different race; others described parents who "lost" or resisted giving the daughter the family registration book, making it difficult if not impossible for her to apply for a passport. In other cases parents were pleased at the prospect of a foreign son-in-law, especially for a woman over thirty. Views about Chinese-western couples are often ambivalent. As Yanyi explained, when she was seen in Guangzhou with a western man, people stared and made rude remarks. On the one hand, "they are critical or angry because they think Chinese girls should only be with other Chinese." At the same time, "some people are jealous and they envy someone who has a foreign boyfriend. They think foreigners are rich and can take a girl to live in America."

Some couples I encountered involved Chinese women with higher levels of education and higher status professions than their U.S. partners. In one case a woman engineer with a large Beijing firm married a plumber in Seattle. His income was high, but he was doubtful, early in their courtship, that a woman with a Ph.D. could "really" be interested in a man without a college education. Members of the Internet chat group wrote to reassure him. They mentioned cases of successful marriages between blue-collar U.S. men and highly educated Chinese women. Their reassurances also pointed to the wider context of what a U.S. working-class man with a good income could provide to an educated Chinese woman in terms of U.S. opportunities and "freedom." The geographic (upward) mobility, in other words, was said to counterbalance the imbalance of social and economic class.

Today, scholars of China commonly assume, and can readily cite many current examples of, a "shortage of brides" in the rural areas, where men from poorer villages find it difficult to find marriage partners as rural women express a degree of agency in their ability to marry "up" into more prosperous communities and women from more prosperous communities marry out of the countryside into cities.[27] Even within urban China, it is commonly understood that, like the poorest men, the best educated and highest status women will find it difficult to marry. Thus, as Whyte and Parish observe, unlike societies in which "upper class families tend to shelter and restrict their daughters, while working class women have more freedom in picking a mate," in China, "having a good job, a well-off family, parents living elsewhere" seems to give women greater freedom in mate selection (135). Parish and Whyte's statement fits my impression of educated, professional women, especially those who are divorced or in their thirties. As Yanyi explained, "My parents believe it's my choice who I marry. If I'm happy and he's a good man, they don't mind if he's a foreigner. [She laughs.] Since I am in my thirties already, they think my chances may be much better to find a foreigner to marry!"

Criticisms of hypergamy also apply to "global hypergamy." What might appear as a simple scheme of hypergamy and upward mobility—rural to urban, East to West—must be considered alongside other issues. Although western men often assume that Asian women who marry Americans are (as a group) marrying up in a global sense, they are also highly aware of certain differences in status. Blue-collar men who marry college-educated Chinese professionals are aware that they are "marrying up" in terms of education and class. Equally educated and attractive professional U.S. women seem inaccessible. Men often comment that they are amazed that such a beautiful Chinese woman or Filipina is interested. Many Chinese women and Filipinas aspire to a better life in the United States—a place that they imagine as better than China or the Philippines in many ways—but once they come to the United States, like Ping, their views may become more circumspect. Many Chinese women conceive of themselves as marrying down in certain ways—especially in terms of class and education. As mentioned above, some Chinese women consider overseas Chinese or other Asian men preferable to white westerners. U.S. men who marry Chinese women or Filipinas may also, in some ways, conceive of themselves as marrying up.

If the notion of hypergamy is to retain value for today's anthropology, it must be posed as a problem, a question, and a means of producing more complicated and nuanced pictures of social reality. We must ask in what ways and from whose vantage point a marriage can be considered hypergamous. What do assumptions of hypergamy—that women simply marry "up"—fail to consider? And how do the ambiguities that are inherent in local ideas about marrying up allow individuals to maneuver in creative ways?

GENDER INVERSIONS, JOKES, AND INCONGRUITY

In order to highlight the combined importance of gender, race, and nationality in these relationships, it is useful to consider inversions. Women from

the United States rarely, to my knowledge, submit their names to introduction agencies to meet men in China and the Philippines. Nor do Chinese
or Filipino men have much opportunity to meet U.S. women pen pals who
aim to marry Asian men. Chinese women and western men, a fairly common sight in major Chinese cities and tourist areas, I was told are usually
assumed to be a "couple," whereas the reverse is generally not true. I was
told three different anecdotes about Chinese men seen with western women
in which the man was assumed to be the woman's driver or tour guide. Jen
and her staff at the introduction agency laughingly recalled encountering
one Chinese man who offered to pay an unusually high fee if she could find
him a western wife.

U.S. women may place ads in newspapers or join matchmaking services, but these services rarely aim to introduce U.S. women to Asian men
abroad. Although the Internet groups I belonged to included a few western
women who are engaged or married to Chinese men or Filipinos, they constituted only 1 or 2 percent of the members, and only one such couple I
knew had met through the Internet, in this case a non-couples-related chat
group. The others met while one was traveling or working abroad. One response I have encountered in the United States when I raise the possibility
of U.S. women looking for Asian husbands abroad through correspondence
is that this scenario is almost "unimaginable." Why and for whom is it
unimaginable?[28]

The lack of gender symmetry in U.S.-Asian relationships points to several important issues. One is the extent to which the "global imagination"
is not only gendered but also raced. As Brackette Williams has argued, by
virtue of their gender and race, individuals are positioned differently in relation to nationality, citizenship, and notions of respectability.[29] Relationships between U.S. men and Asian women are part of a more common cultural logic, a well-recognized imaginary, in which it is considered more
acceptable for women to marry partrilocally and more acceptable for men
to marry "down" than for women. Another factor is how these imaginings
are structured around assumptions of particular types of upward global
mobility. "Upward mobility" is not only asymmetrically gendered, but it
also involves a particular logic of global geography that can, at times,
negate considerations of class and ethnicity. In other words, marriage of
women in Asia to U.S. men is assumed to be a "logical" or imaginable upward geographic trajectory from "East to West," "Third to First World," or
from assumed poverty, lack of freedom, or lack of opportunity to a place
that is understood or assumed to be more "advanced," "modern," or "developed," at least from a western perspective.[30]

Such logic is also supported by gender stereotypes of western men as more "masculine" than Asian men, and therefore an implicit upward move for Asian women. In Hong Kong in the 1980s, I was told that the most attractive couples in the world involve Cantonese women and western men. Western men were said to be more attractive because of their greater height and stronger build, whereas Cantonese women were said to have the most delicate feminine features.[31] Hong Kong men, more recently, are reported to view mainland Chinese women from the north as more attractive: they are considered prettier, taller, fairer skinned, and larger breasted than Hong Kong women.[32] Ideas about "attractiveness" are linked to assumptions about gender roles—women's passivity and obedience—no matter that such assumptions are contradicted by actual cases. Similar to western men's views of "Asian women" versus western women, Hong Kong men are said to view mainland women as less demanding, gentler, and more caring than Hong Kong women.[33]

It is far more difficult for both westerners and Chinese to imagine situations in which a western woman would want to meet an Asian man and settle in Asia or bring him to the United States because he would make a more suitable husband. From both a Chinese and a western perspective, women "should" marry social equals or should marry up. Issues of race, gender, and nationality combine to define Asian men as social and geographic inferiors from a western as well as a Chinese perspective. That is not to say that such men might not in fact make good husbands, or that western women do not make good wives, but that gender stereotypes that are articulated in the United States and in China often define Chinese men as less desirable and Chinese women as more desirable than their western counterparts. Although stereotypes of weak Asian men and delicate, submissive Asian women originated in the history of western imperialism, which defined Asians and the colonized as inherently weak and effeminized relative to the images of masculine western aggressors, these stereotypes are also voiced by Chinese. Chinese and westerners alike often characterize western men as more virile than Asian ones, and Asian women as more feminine (less masculine) than western ones.[34] In Beijing I was told that western men are hairier and go bald at a younger age than Chinese men because of their greater virility and sexual prowess. Not only are Asian husbands less imaginable from a U.S. vantage point, but western wives are also less imaginable from the perspective of many Asians.[35] The reverse of the western man–Asian woman situation may be considered odd or laughable because like a joke it builds on the notion of incongruity as the source of humor.[36] The incongruity stems in large part from the shared Chinese and western ideas that the proper relationship involves masculine (dominant) men and feminine (submissive) women, a situation that is ideologically reversed in the idea of a marriage between an aggressive western woman and a passive Chinese man.[37]

On several occasions in China and the Philippines, men joked with me about finding a western wife. One married Filipino who knew about my research joked that the situation is "so unfair" because there is little opportunity for Asian men to become "mail-order husbands," and another unmarried Filipino said that he wished he could become a "mail-order husband." Western men who contemplate moving to China or the Philippines occasionally jokingly refer to themselves as "mail-order husbands," which underscores their perceptions of the "normal" gendered geographic mobility of such relationships. One evening in 1999, I was invited to have dinner at Jen's house. After dinner and quite a few drinks, Jen's friend Feng, a very successful entrepreneur in his early forties, began to joke about how unfair it was that Chinese women could find American husbands but that he had no opportunity to find an American wife. When the laughter from the three other Chinese dinner guests subsided, the hostess tried to change the subject. Feng, however, moved closer to me on the couch and insisted that someone take a photograph. At the last instant, Feng put his arm around me in a possessive pose and smiled for the picture. A few more drinks and, as Feng and the hostess drove me home, he continued to mumble about wanting an American wife.

A number of factors may have fueled his interest in this topic. One was the ambiguity of his relationship with Jen, who had ample opportunity to make contact with western men. Another was his impression that—as he and others mentioned in 1999—all the "best Chinese women," those who are "most beautiful and educated," go abroad and marry foreigners. Yet in 2000, he pointed to another side of the issue. He resented the fact that many of Jen's women clients at the agency—some of whom he considered unattractive or undesirable "losers" due to their looks, personality, or past marital experience—managed to find partners abroad. He also thought that some of the western men who had come to meet Jen's clients were condescending toward him. They erroneously assumed that simply because they were from the west that they were economically better off (Feng's income was in fact well over US$100,000 per year).[38] The humor derived at least in part from the lack of symmetry in the perceived "ease" with which western men and Chinese women have access to one another. Although his refrain, "I want an American wife! Why can't I marry an American?" was presented and received as a joke, one made more acceptable by the presence of alcohol, the source of humor lay in the perceived unlikeli-hood and incongruity of the image that his statements evoked—were it less unimaginable to him or his audience, the joke might not have been so funny and sad.[39]

CONCLUSION

Yanyi, Ping, Lacey, Meili, and Anna had various reasons for seeking to meet western men. Although each wanted a marriage that would allow for economic and geographical balance, if not upward mobility, they were si-multaneously looking for a "status match" in the sense of a partner and companion based on personal character traits and compatibility.[40] These sketches suggest that, like hypergamous marriages based on affinal social status, which tend to overlook the finer points of whether a marriage was up, down, or both and from whose perspective, an approach to global hy-pergamy that defines hypergamy in terms of women's mobility from more isolated to less isolated rural Chinese villages, from villages to towns, towns to cities, and from Chinese cities to the United States stresses one important feature of mobility but may overlook the question of in what sense, in what multiplicity of ways, particular women and men are marry-ing up and down.

My main argument in this chapter is that correspondence marriages reflect a number of different contradictory patterns and ideas. U.S. men and Chinese women marry "up" in certain ways, although perhaps not in the expected sense of upward social, class, ethnic, or economic mobility. A con-sideration of class, education, and women's occupations makes it difficult to argue that Chinese women are simply marrying "up" and men "down." Alongside the discussion of global hypergamy, I examined Chinese wom-en's reasons for wanting to marry a foreigner—including the marital pros-pects of women who are divorced or who have passed the optimal age of marriage in China. This discussion points to women's agency, selectivity, and choice, as opposed to popular assertions of passivity or desperation.

The asymmetrical images of relationships between Chinese men and western women, and western men and Chinese women, point to the specific ways in which ideas about global mobility are linked to gender, social and economic class, nationality, and race. Ong has written that "the romance of merchant mandarins and the Confucian family defines men to be in charge of both wealth and mobility, while women are localized in domestic situa-tions or workplaces."[41] This study underscores the fact that only certain men are in charge of mobility. Moreover, although women are "localized in domestic situations" and they emigrate by virtue of their roles as fiancée or wife of U.S. citizens, correspondence courtship and marriage privileges their mobility in ways that it does not privilege mainland Chinese men.

In her study of marriages between PRC women and Japanese or overseas Chinese men, Constance Clark builds on Massey's notion of "power geometry" and the idea that "some people are more in charge of [mobility] than others; some initiate flows and movement, others don't; some are more on the receiving end of it than others." Clark suggests that "Asian men pass through international borders in search of brides" with ease, while Chinese women are "more on the receiving end of mobility."[42] This chapter points to another angle in this "power geometry." PRC men, even wealthy ones like Feng, perceive of marriage to western women as a path of global mobility that is largely closed to them. In this particular power geometry, mainland Chinese men are perhaps the least privileged. Patrilocality, a pattern that was once associated with male privilege, affords women both restrictions and possibilities for mobility through marriage. Women like Ping may in a sense be "on the receiving end" of mobility, but they can nonetheless decide whether or not to be mobile or to return to China. Their desire for western marriage partners, moreover, is connected to a perceived lack of marriage options at home or abroad among overseas Chinese—who are understood to want younger, less educated, and more desirable (never married) Chinese women. Chinese women can thus maneuver within these structures in creative ways. They gain mobility by virtue of gendered familial roles and expectations, and they contemplate relationships with western men as a means to fulfill personal dreams of marriage and mobility.

7 Tales of Waiting: History, Immigration, and the State

> Restrictive immigration tends to be caused by fears that immigrants place a drain on the nation's cohesion, identity, or strength (political, economic, social). Targeting the immigrant women in the mail order bride business is in keeping with the historical pattern of responses to cultural threat: the most vulnerable members are the easiest to blame. —SIMONS, "Mail Order Brides," 133

> We who are waiting are scared that anything could give the government fodder to keep them [our fiancées or wives] out of our waiting arms. . . . Please don't judge us too harshly, we are just scared little boys. The government has put us and our wives/fiancées through so much already.
> —JACOB, 2000

> We got along well when he came to visit, but when I told him how long it would take for me to get a visa to come to the U.S. he seems shocked. Then he says he'll write when he goes home. He wrote to me once and said that he wanted to be married right now and that he couldn't wait six months it would take. Then he never wrote again.
> —XIAOMEI, 1999

TALES OF WAITING AND PATTERNS OF IMMIGRATION

"Tales of waiting" are the most common type of stories told by couples whose courtships span two nation-states and whose relationships often involve long periods of separation. There are several distinct periods of waiting, each marked by increased personal commitment and emotional investment. First is the wait to receive a letter or e-mail message from a prospective partner, then the wait before a couple initially meets in person, and again before they are reunited, when in many cases the man goes to visit for a second or third time. Once the couple has decided to marry, there is the final wait of several months to two years for approval of the visa that allows the foreign partner to legally enter the United States. Several men stressed that people who are not serious about their relationships are not likely to have the patience and commitment necessary to survive the process. Others cited the long wait and the complex process of immigration as "proof" of the love and commitment in their relationships: "Without love to spur us on, I doubt we would survive or stick out this process. At times it's torture." The final wait, the stories surrounding it, and the way in which it is linked to the immigration process and the history of Asian immigration to the United States is the central focus of this chapter.

In the first half of the chapter, I look at the immigration of Chinese and Filipina wives in relation to the much broader history of Chinese and Filipino immigration to the United States. The immigration of Chinese and Filipina wives/fiancées constitutes in some ways a new and unique form of Asian immigration, but it is nonetheless linked to older patterns. Although the most extreme exclusions were abolished decades ago, nativism, xenophobia, and public anxiety over immigration resurface, especially during periods of economic downturn and political threat. Foreign spouses or fiancées from China and the Philippines, so-called mail-order brides, must meet the state's moral, physical, and financial requirements, and are still met with suspicion as to their motives for marrying Americans. These suspicions are linked to older concerns. As Lisa Lowe writes, "A national memory haunts the conception of the Asian American, persisting beyond the repeal of actual laws prohibiting Asians from citizenship."[1] New immigration laws and policies are formulated in the shadow of "national memory" and involve forms of state surveillance and gendered and racialized classification. One point, then, is to consider contemporary concerns and reactions to the entry of Asian women alongside nineteenth- and twentieth-century U.S. fears of the so-called "yellow peril."[2]

In the second half of the chapter, I present tales of waiting as evocative narratives that convey a sense of the unofficial process of immigration and the depths of frustration and aggravation that many men and women experience. Tales of waiting are often romantic, but they fluctuate between being sad, reflecting the difficulty of separation, the loneliness after hearing a loved one's voice on the phone, or the frustration of communicating at a distance, to being hopeful and full of promise, as couples imagine their future together. As they wait, women plan what to pack for the United States, including clothing, which will be too expensive or hard to find in very small sizes, and they spend extra time with family and friends. Some men work on "projects" to prepare the house or apartment; some do intensive cleaning; others dispose of mementos from previous relationships or destroy evidence of their "bachelor days." Some stock up on certain types of Asian food or locate the nearest Asian grocery store. Long separations create feelings of worry, insecurity, or jealousy ("perhaps he/she has met someone else?"), and often—especially for men—generate a sense of frustration and hostility toward the immigration bureaucracy. Women sometimes worry that men are intentionally stalling when the immigration timeline exceeds their expectations. Men in turn worry that women will not understand why the process is slower than for another couple whose immigration process began at the same time. When the process drags out, couples become concerned that their file has been lost or mishandled, or that misinformation may prevent them from ever reaching their ultimate goal of reunification. For some men (like Ted in Chapter 4 or Bob in Chapter 1), the immigration process is (at first) assumed to be fair and predictable, if slow and overly bureaucratic; it is believed to present few obstacles for those who follow the rules and do their homework, and for women who are "low risk." But when the process is delayed too long or lacks transparency, it is seen as pernicious, unreasonable, and discriminatory. In this chapter, we again encounter women whose applications are delayed because of the policing of immigration, and men who question the fairness of the process and their rights as citizens. Tales of waiting are linked to current immigration policies and procedures, popular images and attitudes towards Asian immigrants, and the longer history of Asian immigration to the United States, a history that is gendered and raced in particular ways.[3]

GENDER, RACE, NATIONALITY, AND PRE−WORLD WAR II IMMIGRATION

A growing body of literature focuses on a gendered history of Asian immigration to the United States.[4] Immigration laws and policies reflect, on one level, tensions between the desire for cheap immigrant labor and nativist concerns about the economic and social threat posed by growing numbers of immigrants, especially those who pose a threat to a homogenous image of the nation. Between 1852 and the turn of the century, 50,000 Chinese men set foot in Hawaii (not yet a U.S. territory) to work on sugar plantations on five-year contracts.[5] Men were the desired workers, and by 1896 fewer than 1,500 Chinese females resided on the islands.[6] As a result of the gold rush of the 1850s, more than 20,000 Chinese entered California through San Francisco in 1852 alone, followed by 2,000 to 9,000 per year during the following decade. From 1867 to 1870, another 40,000 Chinese came to work on the U.S. transcontinental railroad.[7] According to Sucheng Chan, "Throughout the latter half of the nineteenth century . . . no more than 5,000 Chinese women were found on the entire U.S. mainland at any one time."[8]

By the end of the nineteenth century, the Chinese population was met with growing hostility, racial prejudice, and fear. U.S. nativism was expressed in many ways, including new legislation, anti-Chinese riots, taxation of Chinese miners, and violent expulsion of Chinese farm workers.[9] The Page Law was passed by Congress in 1875 to prohibit the entry of "Chinese, Japanese, and other 'Oriental' laborers brought to the United States involuntarily, as well as that of women brought for the purpose of prostitution, a provision aimed particularly at Chinese women."[10] The law was unsuccessful in curbing the entry of Chinese men, but effectively controlled the entry of Chinese women who were alleged to be prostitutes, and Chinese women suspected of prostitution were deported.[11]

In 1882, Congress passed the Chinese Exclusion Act. According to Lucy Salyer, this act—which halted the entry of Chinese skilled and unskilled laborers for ten years—was the first to exclude immigrants solely on the basis of race and nationality.[12] The act severely limited the entry of Chinese women, who it was feared would lead to the permanence and growth of the Chinese community. Class and nationality played a mediating role, however, as women born in the United States and the daughters or wives of Chinese merchants, officials, and students were allowed entry.[13] Such legislation created a shortage of Chinese women, which further promoted illegal traffic in Chinese prostitutes and deepened concerns about Chinese morality.[14]

The Immigration Act, or National Origins Act, of 1924 further limited immigration on the basis of nationality, but gender and race were not far below the surface. Immigration of Japanese—who had entered in great numbers following Chinese exclusion—and other Asians was prohibited, whereas immigration from Ireland was limited to 17,853, from Italy to 5,802, and from Poland to 6,524.[15] While the 1924 act allowed European immigrants to return to Europe to bring wives back to the United States (outside the quota), women from China, Japan, Korea, and India were barred from entry since they were classified as "aliens ineligible to citizenship." The Cable Act (passed in 1922, repealed in 1936) stipulated that "female U.S. citizens who married aliens ineligible to citizenship would lose their own citizenship," which meant that Chinese women who were citizens by virtue of their birth in the United States lost their citizenship if they married Chinese immigrants.[16] Chinese men in "immigrant 'bachelor' communities," moreover, were "feminized in relation to white male citizens," as they were pushed into "feminine" occupations such as laundry, restaurants, and other service sector jobs.[17]

Unlike early-twentieth-century Chinese, Japanese, and Korean immigrants, Filipinos came from a U.S. territory and were therefore considered neither citizens nor aliens. Early Filipino immigrants were influenced by the *pensionados*—children of Filipino elites who had been selected to study in U.S. colleges and universities during the first decade of 1900 and who later took up well-paid positions in the Philippines.[18] Filipino immigrants of the 1920s described childhoods in the Philippines where they "saluted the Stars and Stripes," said the "Pledge of Allegiance," looked at "pictures of Washington and Lincoln, studied the Declaration of Independence, and read about the 'home of the free and the brave.'"[19] With high expectations of life in the West, tens of thousands of Filipinos flocked to Hawaii in the early 1900s and to the mainland in the 1920s. Among these immigrants were many young men who came as laborers and as nonsponsored high school and college students.

Early Filipino immigration also showed skewed gender ratios, though not as severely skewed as among Chinese immigrants. In 1930, females represented 16.6 percent of the overall population of 63,052 Filipinos in Hawaii, and only 6.5 percent of the overall Filipino population of 45,208 on the mainland.[20] Ronald Takaki attributes the lower gender imbalance in Hawaii to labor conditions. The Hawaiian Sugar Planters' Association argued that men with families were more stable and productive than those without (citing Japanese workers as an example), and thus encouraged the "importation" of Filipino women. The overall gender imbalance, as in the Chinese case, was also related to beliefs about the impropriety of women traveling without their fathers or husbands. Only 18 percent of the Filipino men on the mainland were married, and most expected to remain only temporarily.[21] As Espiritu describes, by 1930 Filipinos were scattered across the United States, but most settled in California, where only 7 percent were female. Filipino laborers thus "lived and worked within a gender-skewed context. Legally prohibited from marrying white women, most Filipino laborers were lonely bachelors, destined for a harsh life without families."[22]

Unlike Chinese, Filipinos were classified as "wards" or "nationals" of the United States. Since they came from a U.S. territory, they were not subject to the 1924 exclusions. Nativists and exclusionists argued, however, that it was "illogical to have an immigration policy to exclude Japanese and Chinese and permit Filipinos en masse to come into the country."[23] During the Great Depression of the late 1920s and 1930s, white resentment of Filipinos and other Asians intensified. Exclusionists argued that the way to legislate against Filipino immigration was to grant the Philippines independence, thus making Filipinos aliens. The Tydings-McDuffie Act of 1934 resulted partly from a desire to halt Filipino immigration. It established the Philippines as a commonwealth and spelled out the process by which it would receive independence. The act redefined Filipinos as aliens and limited Filipino immigration to a trickle of fifty persons per year.[24] A Supreme Court ruling in 1934 reiterated the position that Filipinos—as non-Caucasians—were ineligible for naturalized citizenship.[25]

Besides illustrating discrimination on the basis of race or nationality, early Filipino and Chinese immigration reflects clearly gendered patterns. Several factors discouraged the entry of women: employers often preferred single male laborers; Chinese and Filipinos were reluctant to send women to live abroad; it was less costly for immigrant men to maintain their families in Asia; and U.S. legislation often discouraged the immigration of women, reflecting concern about the greater likelihood of permanent immigration should Asian laborers' wives be permitted to accompany them.[26] Chan argues that at the very point when Chinese immigrants were likely to have sent for their wives and children, exclusion was imposed. Some Asian women did arrive during the nineteenth century, including the wives and daughters of Chinese merchants, Chinese prostitutes who were smuggled in, and Japanese picture brides.

As Chan explains, the Chinese and Japanese situations differed significantly. Chinese exclusion was imposed earlier and all at once, whereas Japanese exclusion was imposed later and in stages, which allowed for the gradual entry of more women, the birth of more children, and the development of a larger Japanese American community. The Gentleman's Agreement with Japan that went into effect in 1908 allowed married Japanese men to send for their wives and unmarried men to either return to Japan to marry or to arrange for their picture brides to join them. Returning to Japan was expensive and could cause men to lose their deferred military draft status, so many opted to have marriages arranged by relatives in Japan. Picture brides would go through a marriage ceremony in the absence of the groom. Because many Japanese men were old by the time they could afford to arrange a marriage, U.S. law stipulated that the Japanese brides could not be more than thirteen years younger than their husbands. Brides had to pass rigorous medical examinations before departure and upon arrival in the United States. As Japanese family formation proceeded, anti-Japanese groups agitated, and after 1920 no more passports were issued to Japanese picture brides.[27]

Antimiscegenation laws were also applied to Asian immigrants. The first such law was passed in Maryland in 1661 to prevent intermarriage between blacks and whites, and by the nineteenth century the law existed in thirty-eight states.[28] In 1880, California lawmakers expanded antimiscegenation laws to include marriages between a white and a "negro, mulatto, or Mongolian."[29] The term "Mongolian" referred to those belonging to the "Asian race." The law affected relatively few Chinese, Japanese, or Koreans, since, according to Chan, in those days East Asians were "not particularly inclined to marry whites," but they had a great impact on Filipinos, who were of mixed Malay-Polynesian, Spanish, and Chinese descent.[30] In the 1920s, as hysteria over racial "hybridization" gained momentum, anti-Filipino spokespersons "portrayed the largely single Filipino men as sexual threats who sought the company of white and Mexican women at taxi-dance halls."[31] Chan describes clubs where "patrons bought strings of tickets, which the hostesses tore off one at a time as they danced with men. . . . Some couples who got acquainted this way desired to marry. Since the precise racial classification of Filipinos was open to question, some county clerks issued marriage licenses to Filipino men and white women, while others refused to do so."[32] In the 1930s, lawsuits were filed by Filipino-white couples who had been refused marriage permits. Some temporary victories were won in court on the basis that Filipinos should be classified as Malay rather than Mongolian, but following these victories, California added the "Malay race" to the excluded category.[33] Only in 1948—following World War II and Philippine independence—were California's antimiscegenation laws declared unconstitutional, and by 1967, "all such statutes in the United States were removed from the books or lapsed from disuse."[34]

WORLD WAR II AND THE POSTWAR PERIOD

World War II marked a significant turning point for Chinese and Filipino immigration to the United States. Under Chiang Kai-shek's Nationalist rule, China was a U.S. ally against the Japanese. U.S. Chinese went to great lengths to identify themselves as Chinese. Takaki describes a 1941 *Time* magazine article that explains the art of racial profiling, or how to distinguish the Chinese "friend" from the Japanese "enemy" by their appearance and demeanor.[35] Chinese men joined the U.S. military, and some returned to China to fight alongside Chiang Kai-shek. Chinese communities contributed money and labor to the war effort. Partly in response to Japan's appeal to Asians to "unite in a race war against white America,"[36] partly because of pressure from China and the Chinese population in the United

States, and partly as a result of mounting criticism of the racist U.S. domestic policies, the United States rescinded the Chinese exclusion laws in 1943, granted Chinese the right of naturalization, and set a quota of 105 Chinese immigrants per year.[37]

The wartime heroism and courage of Filipinos was widely publicized and earned many U.S. citizenship, which in turn helped rescind exclusion laws and open the way for further immigration. Filipinos responded enthusiastically to the call to arms; 40 percent of California's Filipino population registered for the first draft.[38] According to Espiritu, "Filipino nationals are the only Asians who have served in the U.S. armed forces without holding U.S. citizenship." During the war, the status of Filipino "nationals" was conveniently forgotten as thousands were inducted into the military, and some became citizens through mass naturalization ceremonies.[39] The Nationality Act of 1940 gave Filipinos who had worked in the U.S. military for three or more years the opportunity to apply for U.S. citizenship without fulfilling the residence requirements and without counting against the Tydings-McDuffie Act quotas.[40] In 1946 (several years after the Chinese exclusions were rescinded), "seeking to demonstrate U.S. commitment to democracy," Congress passed the Luce-Celler Bill, which permitted the entry of one hundred Filipinos a year (not including those in the military) and granted Filipinos the right of naturalization.[41]

Following World War II, gendered patterns of immigration changed significantly, more closely approaching the current pattern of Asian-U.S. marriages. Between 1946 and 1965, 33,000 Filipinos immigrated to the United States. "Nearly half of the Filipino immigrants (16,000) between 1946–1965 came as wives of U.S. servicemen," including many Filipino Americans serving in the U.S. military, while others came as wives of Filipinos in the United States, as dependents of U.S. citizens, or as students.[42] Notably, most of the Filipina, Japanese, and Korean wives of servicemen were married to non-Asians and entered as "non-quota immigrants (i.e., spouses of U.S. citizens)," whereas most Chinese women who were admitted under the "War Brides Act" were married to Chinese American men.[43] In the late 1950s, about 1,000 Filipinas immigrated each year as U.S. dependents, an average of 1,500 per year in the 1960s, and over 4,000 per year in the 1970s.

Not coincidentally, the song "Filipino Baby," which I learned of from a southern, white U.S. citizen who had served in the U.S. Navy and who later married a Filipina whom he had met through correspondence, reached number four on the U.S. country music charts in 1946. It was re-recorded and re-released numerous times in subsequent years, gaining popularity during the Korean war, the Vietnam war, and in subsequent decades. Possibly based on a song originally written by Charles K. Harris during the Spanish American War, the 1946 hit was originally sung by Lloyd "Cowboy" Copas and re-recorded by many others.[44] The lyrics to the Copas version begin:

> When the warships left Manila, sailin' proudly o'er the sea, deep blue sea
> All the sailor's hearts were filled with fond regret.
> Looking backward to this island,
> Where they spent those happy hours, happy hours
> Making love to every pretty girl they met.
> When up stepped a little sailor, with his bright eyes all aglow, all aglow
> Said "take a look at my gal's photograph"
> And the sailors gathered round him just to look upon her face . . .
> And he said, "I love my dark faced Filipino."[45]
> [Chorus:] She's my Filipino baby, she's my treasure and my pet
> Her teeth are bright and pearly and her hair is black as jet
> Oh her lips are sweet as honey, and her heart is pure, I know, yes I know
> And he said "I love my dark faced Filipino."

That this song maintains popularity today and has been re-released (especially the Tubb version) in numerous 1990s CD collections attests to the ongoing appeal of the romantic image of U.S.-Filipina relationships and to their link to U.S. military and colonial history. The song encapsulates a gendered, racialized, dehistoricized, and romanticized version of the relationship between American (post)colonizers and Filipino (post)colonial subjects.

POST-1965 CHANGES

Major changes took place following the 1965 U.S. Immigration and Nationality Act. The act eliminated the immigration quota system, removed "national origins" as the basis for immigration legislation, and established a system based mainly on family reunification and occupation, which allowed for a significant increase in Asian women immigrants.[46] Before 1965, immigrants were predominantly European, and most Asian immigrants were men. The unintended consequence of the reforms was a sharp increase in Asian and Latin American immigration. In the twenty years following the 1965 act, about 40 percent of legal immigration came from Asia, with the Philippines the largest source, constituting nearly a fourth of the Asian immigrants.[47] At the turn of the twenty-first century, Mexicans remain the single largest group of immigrants to the United States, followed by Filipinos and Chinese.[48]

In 1965, a Western-Hemisphere immigration ceiling was set at 120,000 per year with no country limits, and an Eastern-Hemisphere limit was set at 170,000 visas per year with country limits of 20,000. Spouses, unmarried minor children, and parents of citizens could enter as non-quota immigrants with no numerical limit. The seven quota preferences for Eastern-Hemisphere immigrants included: (1) unmarried adult children of U.S. citizens; (2) spouses and unmarried children of legal permanent residents; (3) professionals, scientists, and artists of "exceptional ability"; (4) married children over 21 of U.S. citizens; (5) siblings of U.S. citizens; (6) skilled or unskilled workers in occupations for which labor is in short supply in the United States; (7) refugees.[49] Proponents of the 1965 act mistakenly predicted that "European immigration would continue to predominate and that there would be only a slight increase in Asian immigration" because "citizens of Asian ancestry comprised only half of 1 percent of the U.S. population in the mid 1960s," too few to "make wide use of the 'family reunification' provisions of the new law."[50]

Between 1965 and 1984, almost 665,000 Filipinos entered the United States.[51] Since the 1960s, Filipinos have accounted for the largest number of white-collar professionals to enter the United States, mainly medical professionals. Between 1966 and 1985, over 25,000 Filipino nurses (predominantly women) arrived.[52] In the first decade following the 1965 act, Filipinos entered in the employment and reunification categories in roughly equal numbers, but in the mid-1970s the occupational category dropped to about 20 percent of all immigrants, due to stricter entry requirements for professionals.[53] In striking contrast to earlier periods, women immigrants far outnumbered men. Filipino immigration was spurred by a number of factors in the Philippines, including the post–World War II educational boom, political turmoil and corruption, and economic difficulties and severe unemployment, underemployment, and low wages.[54] As Yen Le Espiritu explains, Filipino immigrants' relatives tend to have similar socioeconomic backgrounds as their sponsors, thus Filipino immigrants "represent a continuation of the unskilled and semiskilled Filipino labor that had immigrated before 1995," as relatives of professionals who "originate from the middle and upper social, economic, and educational sectors of Philippine society." These class differences are reflected in geographical, organizational, and social divisions within and between U.S. Filipino communities.[55]

The Chinese population in 1960 was only 237,000; by 1980 it had jumped to 812,200. It shifted from 61 percent U.S. born to 63 percent foreign born.[56] Chinese motives for migration were varied but are said to include a desire "to escape political conflict and instability in China" or to take advantage of economic or educational opportunities abroad.[57] According to Takaki, education was one avenue for immigration. One person would come to the United States for university education, acquire training and a job, and then sponsor his wife and children. Having become U.S. citizens a few years later, they could sponsor parents and siblings, establishing a "chain migration." Most of these early "second wave" immigrants were refugees from the PRC who immigrated via Taiwan or Hong Kong. Since the normalization of relations between the United States and the PRC in 1979, the PRC was allowed its own quota. As among Filipinos, Takaki also points to a class split among Chinese immigrants and a resultant "bi-polar" Chinese community in the United States. One is working class (where women work mainly in the garment industry and men in restaurants), and the other is an entrepreneurial professional class that increasingly settles in new suburban developments.[58]

Aside from the fiancé(e) non-immigrant K1 visa, the immigration category of "family reunification" is of greatest relevance to this study. Family reunification immigration can be broken down into "quota" and "non-quota" categories. People who are considered "immediate relatives" of adult naturalized or natural-born U.S. citizens—including their spouses, minor children (including adopted children), and parents—fall outside of the immigrant quota categories. The number of visas awarded in these categories is unlimited, but can have an impact on the number of visas allocated to other family preference categories. Other categories of family members (including the brothers and sisters of citizens and the spouses and children of permanent residents) fall into the wider "preference" categories.[59] Between 1971 and 1997, spouses constituted 20 to 30 percent of all immigrants. Census and immigration department figures show that, during the 1997 fiscal year, out of 796,000 immigrants over 25 percent were spouses of U.S. citizens (170,226) or legal permanent residents (31,576). Of these spouses, 66 percent (over 132,000) were women.[60]

Beginning in 1970, U.S. citizens had the option of petitioning for a fiancé(e) to enter with a nonimmigrant K visa, instead of petitioning (with I-130) for a wife to enter under the family reunification category. The K1 visa, described in chapter 4, allows the fiancé(e) to enter the United States, but she/he must marry the petitioner or leave the United States within ninety days. According to the 1999 Department of Justice Report to Congress, during the 1980s and 1990s an average of 5,300 people immigrated as spouses of U.S. citizens, and between 1990 and 1997 the yearly average was 6,400, 79 percent of whom were women. Of those who entered with K visas in the 1970s and 1980s, about 1,100 per year did not adjust to permanent resident status, and in the 1990s 2,200 per year.[61] In December 2000, the "LIFE Act" (Legal Immigration Family Equity Act) was passed, creating new K and V visas to allow the spouses of U.S. citizens and legal permanent residents and the spouses' children to enter the United States as non-immigrants to complete the immigration process.[62]

According to the INS Report to Congress, if the estimate of four thousand to six thousand marriages resulting from mail-order agencies per year is correct, then mail-order marriages account for 2.7 to 4.1 percent of all immigration involving female spouses.[63] The proportion entering as fiancées is probably higher. Vermont Service Center data from February 1998 classified 5.5 percent of fiancée visa applications as "definitely or probably mail-order introductions."[64]

Following the 1965 immigration reforms, the INS created the "Marriage Viability Requirement" to ensure that the marriage is "bona fide," but by 1985, "there was enough alarmism in the popular media about marriage fraud and the mail order bride business for the INS to request that Congress grant statutory authority for a limited standard."[65] As a result, Congress passed the Immigration and Marriage Fraud Amendments (IMFA) in 1986, allowing the INS to impose Conditional Permanent Resident (CPR) status. CPR status meant that an immigrant spouse could be deported if she left the marriage before two years elapsed.[66] As Lisa Simons argues, the IMFA were passed "by vilifying the aliens believed to be exploiting generous US immigration law by deceitfully marrying unsuspecting US citizens" (133). Although immigration laws are theoretically gender neutral, legal scholars have argued that the IMFA were fueled by publicity surrounding the issue of mail-order brides, and that the disproportionate impact on foreign women may have been intentional (Simons, 134). In response to criticisms of CPR status as disadvantaging women immigrants and serving as a "warranty" for husbands because it tells immigrant wives "they may be deported unless they give their consumer husbands their money's worth," the Immigration Act of 1990 and the subsequent Violent Crime Control and Law Enforcement Act of 1994 were legislated.[67] Designed to waive conditional status in cases of battery or extreme cruelty, critics have argued that the level of proof required by the 1990 act was impossibly high and that it focused on women's "mental state rather than on that of the abuser." The 1994 amendment was also criticized for placing the burden of proof on the foreign spouse.[68]

So far I have outlined some of the ways in which gender, race, nationality, and class are reflected in or intertwined with the history of Chinese and Filipino immigration to the United States. As Lowe characterizes it, the nineteenth century involved the "racialized and gendered formation of Chinese male immigrants as laborers"; the post-1965 Asian immigrant group is "still racialized and exploited yet complicated by class and gender stratification"; and since the 1980s we have seen "increased proletarianization of Asian immigrant women's labor."[69] In the post-1965 period, greater numbers of Filipinas entered the United States as professionals, independent from family connections or familial bases for immigration. The number of women entering under the family non-quota category has continued to grow, as has the number of Chinese and Filipina women married to U.S. citizens of non-Asian descent. Whereas earlier patterns of spousal immigration rarely crossed ethnic/racial lines, with the notable exception of postwar Filipino, Korean, or Japanese military wives, the current pattern of correspondence marriages often does. As the marriage fraud legislation and government inquiries into mail order marriages suggest, this pattern makes foreign partners even more suspect and recalls what Lowe describes as a "national memory" of wars in Asia, which sustains an image of Asian immigrants as the "foreigner-within."[70]

In popular sources, government reports, and legislation, mail order relationships reflect a high degree of social anxiety.[71] Simons writes that "the story [of mail-order brides], as told by the popular press, fits a script repeated throughout history. Different immigrant groups are singled out according to various politically motivating factors ranging from foreign policy concerns to national immigration advocacy lobbies. The fear is that the incoming group threatens the US by draining resources and/or constituting a threat to citizens' jobs, health or morality."[72] Correspondence relationships are not only the focus of new legislation and policies, but they also receive close scrutiny from those who administer the immigration process.[73] Relationships that cross ethnic/racial lines are more visible (as are significant age differences) and can raise more "red flags" among those who seek to uncover cases of immigration fraud. Intra-ethnic marriages (though often involving men and women of vastly different class backgrounds) are less visible. Although all immigration is subject to broader anti-immigrant hostility, intra-ethnic marriages may be perceived as an issue for the ethnic (e.g., South Asian or Chinese) community rather than a subject of wider national concerns.[74] By virtue of the fact that they involve interethnic/racial/national relationships, Asian partners of U.S. white men are viewed with suspicion and public anxiety.

The following section shifts to tales of waiting. These tales provide neither advice nor instruction on how to navigate the process of immigration, nor are they necessarily "typical" of the process or of the problems or difficulties couples encountered. They convey the human side of the picture, which is indirectly connected to wider historical patterns, attitudes, and policies regarding Asian women's immigration to the United States.

THE FINAL STAGES OF WAITING

One of the most common Internet list topics among Chinese-U.S. and Filipino-U.S. couples involves experiences, questions, and concerns about the bureaucratic aspects of the immigration process. While the Internet community of couples is—as I have argued in previous chapters—in many ways transnational, the bureaucratic procedures they grapple with are linked to state policies and regulations. One common theme in Internet communications, as well as in face-to-face conversations, is the high level of frustration, often verging on anger, that people experience in the course of their encounters with what appears to be an inefficient, highly variable, and arbitrary process of applying for a visa.

This process also evokes humor, an outlet for otherwise hostile and angry feelings. For example, when I began looking into immigration time lines and experiences, Daniel explained that there are four INS information processing centers, or "Service Centers," in the United States (Vermont, Texas, Nebraska, and California) to which people submit their petitions, depending on their place of residence. "Each has their own processing times some are faster and some slower," he wrote. Mick replied, "Good point [Daniel]. But I would not say 'faster,' I would say some are inexcusably, deplorably, to the point of offending human and constitutional rights slow. And others are worse."

Most cases I knew involved U.S. men and foreign women, yet the few U.S. women I knew who petitioned for foreign spouses expressed many of the same feelings as U.S. men. In the cases I followed, it seemed that the U.S. partner experienced—or at least expressed—a higher degree of anger and frustration regarding the bureaucratic process than the partner abroad. Although this is highly speculative, it appears that men (and women) from the United States focused a great deal of their attention on the weakness and failure of "the system." That is not to say that they did not write about missing their spouses and the emotional pain of separation, but they also wrote in a very heated and emotional way about the aggravations and disappointments of the bureaucratic side of this process. Women I encountered in China and the Philippines spoke or wrote of the process in terms of missing their partners, and most were eager to be reunited, but they did not express such high levels of anxiety, anger, or frustration regarding "the system," its inefficiency, or its bureaucracy as did the men. The process did not, it seems, threaten to rob them of their humanity in the same way. One Filipina fiancée said she was "sad, excited, and nervous" at the idea of coming to the United States. Another viewed the time that she was separated from her husband as she awaited a visa as difficult because she missed him, but also a time to appreciate her family and friends. Women who had emigrated looked back on this time with emotion, but not with anger and frustration. A few women expressed concern about interviews and forms that could potentially delay immigration or cause them to be refused entry to the United States. Many worried about life in the United States. Some men said they thought this was "a much more difficult time for the ladies" because they "know less about the new situation they are headed for" and because they don't have Internet support groups. Yet women did not express the same degree of anger, frustration, or paranoia as their U.S. partners.

There are many possible reasons why Filipinas and Chinese women expressed less frustration about the bureaucratic process. One reason (discussed below) may be that they are simply more used to dealing with inefficient bureaucracies. Another may be a cultural reluctance to complain (especially to a foreign researcher), in contrast to an American cultural approval for "letting off steam." Aside from a reluctance to air personal problems in public, a few women I interviewed stressed the need to always be "polite" to government bureaucrats (be they American, Chinese, or Filipino) because such people have the power to protract a long and difficult process. They could make it difficult to obtain a passport, birth certificate, marriage license, or required travel documents.

Another reason may be that women were simply less involved with the U.S. side of the bureaucratic process. Indeed, some men seemed torn between reassuring their partners that "everything is under control—it just takes time" (even when they were not convinced this was the case) and commiserating with them about the frustrations and complications. Many turned to the list and to the Internet—to others who had "survived the process"—for reassurance, and they tried in turn to reassure their partners. Women's concerns centered less on bureaucracy and more on fears that their partners might be dragging their feet out of indecisiveness or lack of commitment. Instead of placing the blame on the U.S. government, which was sometimes idealized (especially by some Filipinas) as fair and efficient compared to their own, concern was often displaced onto the partner and expressed only to close family members or friends. One Filipina member of the list (whose U.S. partner was not a member) wrote poignantly as a "last resort" of her concern about friends whose processes had been less long. Relatives and friends fueled her anxiety by warning her about fickle U.S. men who play the field. Members of the list reassured her that delays were normal and the fault of the immigration bureaucracy, but one advised her to ask herself why she did not trust her partner.

Even though the U.S. partners often took care of most of the U.S. side of the process, women still had to fill out and sign forms, procure police clearances, birth certificates, and other documents, obtain passports, pass physical examinations, and overcome many other obstacles in China or the Philippines. Some women knew of organizations or individuals that charged exorbitant rates in China to facilitate the process of immigration. Filipinas complained of having to attend the required Philippine government-sponsored predeparture seminars before they could leave the country. Others reported having to pay bribes or give "gifts" to the right people, or having to pay higher official rates in order to smooth the process and obtain required records. Meanwhile, U.S. partners sometimes worried about the unexpected expenses, comparing notes and reassuring themselves that these were "routine" rather than an attempt to milk them for additional funds.

Dale, who was living in China with his wife Ling, described her ability to effectively negotiate the Chinese bureaucracy even if it meant spending a bit more money.

> One thing my wife has found is that anytime you go to any official gov't agency agree to do anything the officials suggest (within reason) and you can make friends with them and get additional information. A perfect example of this would be what my wife did yesterday when she went to the passport office. When she went there, she had them take the pictures for the passport on site (60 RMB), she then also paid them an additional 30 RMB to have the finished passport delivered to us at our house.

As Dale explained, when you do things like this, the officials get more money, are very happy with you, and give you better treatment. Ling

> is also very good at making friends with [officials]. . . . After my wife left the passport office . . . she spoke with another girl that has been trying for two weeks to get the passport office to issue her a passport. When questioned [Ling] told her how easy it was and showed her some of the pictures she had taken. The girl looked at the pictures and said, "hey, I have had the pictures I had taken 3 times and they still won't accept them," she said that she got one set rejected for having a barrette in her hair just like [Ling] was wearing in her picture that was accepted.

The thing is this girl tried to save a few RMB by not paying the passport office the 60 RMB to get the pictures taken. She had them taken cheaper outside the office but they keep finding problems with them. If she would have just had them taken at the passport office they would have been guaranteed to pass with no hassles. As [Ling] says if you let them (the officers), as she puts it "find the money," they will be very happy with you. In any case it ended up costing us a total of 250 RMB for the passport with delivery done to our house. I realize this is probably twice what we could have paid to get it done but it may have taken us 6 weeks the other way with a lot of un-necessary trips back and forth which would have cost for taxi each time (not to mention headaches and the lost time expended). I know it usually goes against everybody's human nature to basically pay what we may consider overcharges in the USA to get things done but with a lot of people and gov't agencies in China it is kind of the normal accepted behavior if you want to get things done fast and easy. I don't even think about it anymore, I just consider it a part of the cost of doing business in China.

It is likely that Filipinas and Chinese women expressed less frustration because they had fewer expectations about the efficiency of government bureaucracy and felt resigned to allow bureaucratic wheels to turn at their own pace. They were accustomed, as Dale described, to the need for "greasing the palm" of officials, and they knew how to work the system. As became especially clear during the 2000 presidential elections in the United States, U.S. men and women expected inefficiency and corruption (including voting fraud) abroad, but not in the United States.

IMMIGRATION TIMELINES

Couples often discuss or compare their "timelines." The timeline refers specifically to the time between the date of receipt (or submission) of the visa application by the INS Service Center to the time when the visa is successfully obtained by the fiancée or spouse. Keven and Yu are one of many couples who have set up a "K1 Visa Page" on the web that includes a detailed timeline.[75] Their timeline is considered a "very good one," normative in terms of the overall procedures but unusually fast and smooth compared to other cases I knew. It took only four months overall from the time Keven submitted the I-129F petition until Yu received a K1 fiancée visa. Keven (who is Chinese American) was introduced to Yu by friends while he was visiting China. The fact that they originally met face to face (not through correspondence), that they are both of Chinese origin (or appear to be), and that there is little age difference between them may have contributed to the speed and efficiency of their timeline. I describe this time-line in order to provide a sense of the process of applying for a K1 fiancé visa when it goes smoothly.

In 1999, when they began the formal immigration process, Yu was liv-ing in northern China and Keven was in Texas. On May 10, Keven sent his I-129F packet to the INS Service Center in Texas. Four days later he re-ceived a first "Notice of Action" (NOA), notifying him that the petition had been received. Almost two months later, on July 9, he received a second no-tice, that the I-129F had been approved. At this stage of the process, respon-sibility shifts from the INS (which is part of the Department of Justice) to the U.S. Consulate (which is part of the Department of State). The INS for-warded their approval of the petition to the appropriate U.S. Consular Of-fice. In this case, because Yu was in China, the approval went to the U.S. Consul General in Guangzhou.

Three days after receiving his notice of INS approval, with the under-standing that this might save time in the process later on, Keven sent a fax to the U.S. Consul General at the embassy in Guangzhou requesting that they open a provisional file for him and his fiancée. He sent them informa-tion about himself and his fiancée and the notification of approval from the INS.[76] The following day he received an e-mail response from the INS of-ficer requesting that he send his fiancée's name and address in Chinese. On July 24, Yu received "Packet #3" from the U.S. Consul General in Guang-zhou. This packet included detailed directions in Chinese and in English and a number of forms for Yu to fill out. The forms included a biographical in-formation form, a form to request the Affidavit of Support (I-134) that would be required from her fiancé, and a checklist of information that she would need before her interview. This included a translated and certified police record indicating that she had no criminal record, certified and trans-lated proof of marital status, birth record, passport, the Affidavit of Sup-port, and any other relevant materials. To obtain a Chinese passport Yu had to provide a reason, which was in this case marriage. She had to show a let-ter of invitation from her fiancé and a photocopy of his passport. Sometimes a copy of the I-134 is also required. She needed approval from her work unit or school and proof of residency from her *hukou* (household registra-tion). On July 25, Yu mailed back the Packet #3 forms via overnight mail.

Two weeks later she received Packet #4. This provided information about the required physical examination, a checklist of the materials to bring to the interview, and information about scheduling the interview. The letter indicated that she could come for the interview fifteen days after the date indicated in the letter, Monday through Thursday in the morning. On August 31 she had her medical examination at the one approved hospital in Beijing. Four days later she received the results in a sealed envelope to present to the Consular officials at her interview. On September 7 at 7 a.m., she reported for her interview at the U.S. Embassy in Guangzhou. The place was already crowded and busy. She turned in the forms and waited. Her interview with the consular officer was brief. She was asked how she and Keven had met and why she wanted to marry him. The officer looked at the photographs she had brought as part of a package of materials to document the authenticity of their relationship, and then he informed her that her visa would be approved and ready the next day. Since she had to return to work, she was allowed to pick it up later that afternoon. Two weeks later she arrived in the United States and within the required ninety-day period she and Keven were married.

Connie and Gary (2001) and Bruce and Cecile (2001) had similar time lines but since Connie and Cecile were from the Philippines—like Lisa and Rosie, described in chapter 4—the second half of the process differed. In contrast to the fifteen days required for INS approval to be forwarded to the U.S. Consulate in Guangzhou and for Yu to receive Packet #3, it took seven weeks before Connie was notified by the U.S. Embassy in Manila that they had received INS approval. At that time (late 1998) she had to go to the embassy in person to pick up Packet #3. Bruce and Cecile also waited seven weeks to hear that their approval had reached Manila. When Cecile went to the embassy to pick up Packet #3, she was told that the policy had changed and that the packet would be mailed to her, which took two more weeks. In contrast to Yu's letter from the Consulate in Guangzhou, Connie and Cecile's Packet #4 letter specified the scheduled interview dates. Connie's letter notified her that her interview was in two and a half months; Cecile's was in less than three weeks.[77] Overall, from filing the petition to receiving the visa took Keven and Yu about four months, Cecile and Bruce a week over five months, and Connie and Gary about six and a half months.[78]

COMPARING TIME LINES

The overall consensus among people involved in correspondence relationships is that the immigration process takes far longer for a spouse than for a fiancée but that both take much longer than is warranted. Another common assumption is that Asian spouses and fiancées are treated with greater suspicion than those from English-speaking countries and that their applications therefore take longer. Based on the limited research described below, this claim seems to have some credibility, especially in the case of spousal visas. Certainly, men who submitted petitions for a wife/fiancée to come from the Philippines expressed more worry and frustration than men whose partners came from China. Spouses/fiancées from the Philippines are still far more numerous than those from China, and the waiting times of Filipino partners are often longer. It is not entirely clear why this is the case, since the initial time for approval of the I-129F petitions is roughly comparable. It is likely that the process is delayed when it reaches the U.S. embassy or consulate abroad due to the workload and staffing of the offices, the local postal and delivery times, or the time it takes for prospective immigrants to obtain required predeparture documentation.

Using material available on the Internet through the Marriage-Based Visas Timelines Project, K1 Timeline Home Page, as of December 2000,[79] I examined over 300 timelines for U.S.-Chinese and U.S.-Filipino couples, and approximately 300 for U.S.-Canadian and U.S.-U.K. couples who submitted an I-129F petition for a K-1 fiancé(e) visa. Despite common assumptions to the contrary, these 600 timelines showed few differences in the time it takes for a petition to be approved within the same INS service center for petitioners with fiancé(e)s of Chinese, Filipino, Canadian, or British nationality. Some individual cases may go through more slowly or quickly than others, but on the whole, the average time is similar regardless of nationality. I only found one significant exception to this general pattern at the Nebraska Service Center, where it took 62 days on average for petitions to be approved, 60 days for those with fiancé(e)s from the Philippines, 69 days for those from China, 66 days for those from Canada, yet only 52 days for those from the United Kingdom.[80]

Once the petition is approved, there is usually a wait of several months. The time period following INS approval often accounts for the longest delays and for the differences between timelines of petitioners with fiancées in China and the Philippines. I closely examined twenty cases of petitioners with Chinese fiancé(e)s (three from Hong Kong) who had completed the entire process of securing a visa. The total time from the submission of the I-129 petition up to the time of the interview at the embassy in Guangzhou (or Hong Kong) and the attainment of the visa averaged just under four months. The two fastest cases went through the Vermont Service Center in less than two weeks and took about two months until the time of the interview at the foreign embassy. The slowest completed case listed at the Marriage-Based Visas Timelines Project went through the Nebraska Service Center. It initially took 45 days for the petition to be approved; the main delay was therefore after the petition was approved. Of the 90 *completed* cases of petitioners with fiancé(e)s in the Philippines, the average time was about five months, with the shortest wait three months, and the longest over eight months.[81] The case that took over eight months took three months for initial approval from the Nebraska Service Center and an additional five months to obtain the K1 visa from the U.S. embassy in Manila.

For couples who had married in China or the Philippines and who petitioned with the I-130 for their wives to come in as immediate relatives, the wait was usually longer than for those who petitioned as fiancées. I located 46 timelines of people who petitioned for their spouses to emigrate to the United States from the Philippines, China, the United Kingdom, or Canada. This included 18 spouses from the Philippines, 7 from China, 11 from the United Kingdom, and 10 from Canada. It normally took over four months for the initial approval of the I-130 petition by the INS, but this ranged from over six months on average at the Texas Service Center to about two months at the Vermont Service Center. The greatest variation based on the nationality of the spouse (as in the case of fiancées described above) was again at the Nebraska Service Center, where the average time for approval of spouses of all nationalities was about 100 days, but the average time for approval of spouses from the United Kingdom was only 43 days.[82] Of the spousal visa cases I examined, only 10 spouses in the Philippines had completed the immigration process by September 2000. Of those, the shortest timeline was five months (for a petitioner whose initial approval took less than two months at the Vermont Service Center). The longest timeline was sixteen months and went through the Texas Service Center. Initial approval in this case took over eight months.

As noted, fiancée timelines of U.S.-Chinese and U.S.-Filipino couples did not differ a lot based on the Marriage-Based Visas Website Project cases.[83] Spousal timelines showed greater variation within each service center, but the numbers of completed timelines were so few that any conclusions are highly speculative. Nonetheless, the most extreme differences based on the spouse's nationality were at the Nebraska Service Center, where, based on Marriage-Based Visas cases, it took almost twice as long for spouses in China and the Philippines than for those in Canada and the United Kingdom to receive visa approval.[84] Further research is necessary to determine if this is typical or the result of a few unrepresentative cases. Nonetheless, the general complaints—regardless of the nationality of the fiancée/spouse—were the same: "If the INS was a business," wrote one U.S. man, "it would be far more efficient." The common assumption that

Asian spouses and relatives are treated with greater suspicion than those from western Europe gains some credibility from these limited cases.

MORE WAITING AND BUREAUCRACY

While waiting for visa approval, women in the Philippines were sometimes warned or teased that their partner had changed his mind. Several women were told that they "know" that the process does not take this long. Anecdotal evidence as well as news reports of INS backlogs suggest that the immigration process takes longer today than it did a decade or more ago. A few men described cases that took three or four months in the mid- or late 1980s, which they claimed now typically take six months or more. It is also clear that some cases pass through the process more quickly than others. Misinformation and misunderstandings about timelines that vary from one service center to another, or that take longer to process by the embassies abroad, create insecurity and tension. The possibility that minor errors or omissions will delay the process are also cause for concern. Men compare notes about the validity of photocopies and notarized forms, about extra copies of birth certificates, marriage certificates, and other materials in duplicate and triplicate, the validity of tax forms that were submitted over the Internet, and additional supporting documentation that "might help." Men and women worry about why their case is taking longer than someone else's. Some fear the worst in terms of delays and lost files.

U.S. men spoke of never having encountered such inefficient bureaucracy. They described the frustration of constant busy signals; finally getting a live operator as opposed to a recording and being put on hold numerous times for hours on end; being transferred, getting disconnected, and dealing with busy fax lines and unpleasant personnel. Some, like Keven and Ted, reported that their timelines were smooth and even under the projected time. They assured others that the process is fine if you are prepared, fill out the forms carefully, and do your homework. Some attributed their success to their conscientiousness. They had "done their homework," advised their fiancée to collect the required paperwork before the petition had been approved, requested a "provisional file," kept files of materials to demonstrate the authenticity of their relationship (phone bills, copies of e-mails, photographs, correspondences), and made extra notarized copies of required documents. They voluntarily sent extra documentation of their financial situation (e.g., extra years of W-2 forms), and they urged others to follow their example. Others, by contrast, experienced serious difficulties and defended themselves as "organized, educated, and of above average intelligence!" Some reached a degree of helplessness and frustration that they thought unimaginable. As the estimated time passed for the receipt of the next stage of paperwork, as they waited in lines for forms and information, as they were kept on hold or given recorded messages at customer hotlines, or were told to resubmit forms they had already sent, their frustration mounted. They wondered if their forms were lost or filled out imprecisely, if they had inadvertently left a blank or written "N/A" when "none" was the appropriate response, and they debated—as a last resort— whether to contact an immigration lawyer, senator, or congressman.

Once spouses and fiancées finally arrive in the United States, the bureaucratic process is far from over. Foreign partners must still deal with their conditional permanent resident status (and adjustment of status if she entered on a fiancée visa), social security, work permits, and eventually naturalization. Some men and women reported being treated with hostility and condescension by overworked staff and workers at government offices. Some men, whose spouses had been in the United States for five years or more and were finally U.S. citizens, still spoke of anger that readily reemerged and blood pressure that still escalated at the very thought of the immigration process.

Underlying the anger and frustration is the central concern that foreign partners might be denied entry. One man, whose wife had a heart defect, was afraid that she would fail the required physical examination. He was reassured by someone who quoted from an INS web site that this was generally not a health condition that warranted denying entry. Another man reported that the medical examiner asked for a bribe in order for his wife to pass her physical exam in China. Without the payment, he threatened to report that she had a "dormant" venereal disease, which would prevent her from obtaining a visa. Further examination proved she had no such disease, but the mere threat caused tension, anxiety, and a time delay for her and her fiancé as they scheduled another physical with a different physician.

The Internet—including, but not limited to, the lists—seeks to disseminate information that is helpful and reassuring to men and women who are going through this process. To a large extent, it does so. I found private web sites written by men and women who had navigated through the process and had "learned the hard way" far more helpful in explaining the process and the "pros and cons" of a fiancé or spousal visa than the official INS web site and directions.[85] At the same time, so much information is available on the web that it can also contribute to a person's confusion and anxiety. While the web gives people information, it can also inadvertently fuel greater concern. For example, most people I knew decided to go the I-129 (K1 fiancée visa) route rather than the I-130 (spousal visa) route because it generally takes less time from start to finish. Yet some men who had already married their spouses abroad (because they mistakenly thought it would be faster or more failsafe, out of a desire to reassure the bride and her family about his intentions, or so the family in China or the Philippines could attend the marriage) often expressed confusion about the required forms because they heard much more about the I-129 process. Had they simply obtained information about the I-130, without having to disentangle which parts of the process apply to their situation and which parts did not, it would have been much simpler. Others read about government requirements that applied to one foreign country but did not realize that they did not apply elsewhere. Because some people who share their tales on the Internet are reluctant to include certain particulars for fear of retribution from the government "powers that be," concerns, complaints, and stories often take on the appearance of hearsay, rumor, or urban legend. Some people were reluctant to mention the name or give out e-mail addresses of helpful congresspersons, senators, or staff at the U.S. Consulate, the U.S. Embassy, or the INS, for fear that their own case would be slowed down if the officials were swamped with more requests. Others worried that complaining about rude and unhelpful people by name could get them singled out for further maltreatment that could delay their petition indefinitely. One common concern, as the case of Freddie illustrates, is that a petition could get lost.

FREDDIE: FALLING BETWEEN THE CRACKS

Freddie expressed his sense of frustration over the process of immigration very articulately in several e-mail messages sent to me and other members of UFG in the course of several months in 2000. One of the problems he encountered was that his petition was lost between the cracks: it had been approved by the INS but had not been received by the embassy in Manila. The petition seemed to have disappeared, and each agency pointed fingers at the other, claiming there was nothing they could do. Freddie's case not only illustrates the frequent frustration and anger that results from bureaucratic inefficiency, but it also shows some of the negative attitudes toward foreigners in general and correspondence relationships in particular that may be encountered among government workers in the course of immigration.

As Freddie explained, he first mailed his I-129 application for a K1 fiancé visa to the Texas Service Center of the INS on May 11, 2000.[86] The return receipt informed him that it had been received five days later. Freddie received a Notice of Action telling him that the file had been opened and processing had begun on May 19. As Freddie explained, "After waiting a few weeks, I couldn't get thru to the TSC [Texas Service Center] to find out the petition's status, [so] I contacted my Senator's office. I don't know if this helped or not, but the petition was approved a few days later." Freddie's notice of initial approval was dated June 30 and was valid for six months, until October 31, 2000. This stage of the process took about a month and a half. As Freddie explained, "Then there was more waiting . . . and after waiting a reasonable amount of time I called the embassy to see if they had received the approved petition. They said they had not . . . so I waited some more . . . and called again . . . and again . . . and again." Freddie then checked one of the timeline web sites on the Internet and learned that several other fiancé petitions that had been filed at the same service center later than his had already arrived at the U.S. Embassy in Manila. He called Manila to check again, but his petition had not been received. The staff member at the embassy advised him to contact the INS. "So I tried and tried, then I called the INS National Customer Service number . . . no help there. After getting some advice I called back, and talked to a INS Information Officer. No help there either. I have called the State Department, and talked to a Visa Information Officer . . . no help there. I am also working with the Senator's office again."

In October, concerned that the six months would expire, Freddie received a letter from his senator's office containing a fax from the Consul General stating that the embassy in Manila had not received the approved petition. The letter said that the Director of Constituent Services would contact the INS with this information. The next working day, Freddie called the INS customer service number. The woman at the service center asked that he fax her a copy of the letter from the embassy. Freddie then spent two days attempting to send the fax, but the number was continuously busy.

What a joke . . . the fax would never go through. After a not so great day at work, I decided to call the customer service number again, and tell them I can never get through to the TSC. After talking to the customer service person and explaining the problem I was passed off to an "Information Officer," yeah right . . . they should change the title to Misinformation Officer. This lady was no help. She checked on her computer and said it had been sent to the Dept. of State to be forwarded to the embassy in Manila. Every time I tried to explain to her that they should have already received it, she would give some explanation as to why it might not be there . . . all very lame excuses. She then went on to explain that . . . and this is what she said: "Well YOU declined state-hood." She then rambled some more nonsense about this being the rea-son visas to the USA are so hard to get for Filipinos. I didn't know I had even been offered statehood! Imagine my surprise! Well I guess she thought I was Filipino or something.

The information officer revealed her dislike for immigrants, her partic-ular prejudice against Filipinos, and her ignorance of Filipino history.[87] From her mistaken perspective, the Philippines had the option of becoming part of the United States but had chosen independence. She implied that, for that reason, Filipinos do not deserve visas to the United States and have greater difficulty obtaining them. When Freddie explained that this was irrelevant, that Filipinos should not be dealt with differently because they had "declined statehood," but that he was in any case not Filipino, she dropped this line of reasoning and referred him elsewhere. She explained that once the service center forwards the petition to the State Department, they no longer have anything to do with it. She gave him two other tele-phone numbers. Freddie explained, "I was so shocked at what she had said I was glad to be off the phone. Too bad I missed out on statehood. I think I would have made a great state. The Great State of [Freddie]."

Freddie then tried the toll-free numbers she gave him. "I had tried this number before, and had no luck. So when the option to get an "agent" came up I hit that number. Haha! It was only an operator, and she said her job was to only give out other numbers, but she asked me what I needed. I told her my story, which she finally understood, and filled out some form, which she said would be given to a research person to try and find out where the petition was. She told me I would be contacted in a couple of days. I felt a little better."

Encouraged, Freddie decided to contact his senator's office again, only to learn that the staff member who had been assisting him had just retired. "I guess I overworked her. I just about went into shock, and the guy on the phone said not to panic. He transferred me to another lady, and I explained my problem to her. She said that my petition had been approved! I tried to remain calm and explained to her that I knew that, and that it had been approved on [June 30]. I went on to explain all the nitty gritty details. Eventually she understood." The staff member, revealing her prejudice, then told Freddie that she had told the senator, that she would not handle "mail-order bride" matters, and that she would have to find someone else to handle them.

I tried to calmly explain that the term 'mail-order brides' wasn't nice, but she cut me off, and made a joke about 'cold showers.' I don't think it was directed at me, but something she told the Senator that she might say if she had to deal with men petitioning for fiancees and wives. I think she is overwhelmed now that the other lady retired. Anyway, I also discovered that my case file had been closed. (Because the INS told them I had been approved.) And that I needed to fax her the letter I received from the Embassy.

Freddie explained that he had already sent it. Her response was that they could not keep copies of everything. Thus Freddie re-sent a copy of the approval and the letter from the Consul General in Manila. Stressing her dislike for what she called "mail-order" marriages, "the lady went on to talk about how some guys want their petitions expedited, and I told her that when I first contacted their office I said I wanted no special treatment, and that I just wanted to make sure nothing had happened to my petition. She said I had a legitimate complaint and would try to discover where the petition was." Freddie faxed the paperwork and called a week later. "And she was in a mood! She said she can't do anything because she is always on the phone or e-mailing people. I told her that I wouldn't call her for two weeks. I kept my word. [Two weeks later] I called her back, and the first thing she said to me was, 'I thought you were taken care of. Your petition was approved.' I explained to her the problem again . . . she said she would e-mail the embassy and the INS."

The next day Freddie called the embassy again. The e-mail message and petition still had not been received. "I e-mailed the lady at the senator's office and told her that I didn't think another e-mail to the embassy or INS would help. I told her that I thought the petition has been lost, and I wanted to find out how to solve this problem. I haven't heard back from her yet. I think I am getting the run around." Freddie's level of stress and anxiety increased and his remarks became more critical.

> After numerous e-mails, phone calls, and faxes, and snail mail letters I still don't know where the approved petition is at. It has been 148 days with no end in sight . . . am I upset? Heck yes. Do I get angry? I try not to . . . but . . . I am only human. You wouldn't believe some of the things I have heard from INS Info Officers. . . . The approved petition is no longer valid, but I have been reassured that this doesn't matter, and the countdown will start once the petition gets to the embassy . . . if that ever happens. This weekend I regroup and try some different tactics. It has been 148 days since the petition was approved.

In his next e-mail message, Freddie wrote: "The senator's office has been no help. If she runs again, I won't vote for her. . . . So here is a question to the list. . . . When is the paperwork officially considered lost? And what do I do about it?"

Others identified with Freddie's frustration. One wrote: "It's my opinion that the INS needs a major overhaul. And everyone who works for them needs brain transplants. I think chimpanzee brains would be an improvement, but I wouldn't want to waste chimps on INS employees . . . actually the chimps could do a better job . . . but I digress." Mick, who had also experienced significant delays and whose fiancée's passport had been temporarily "confiscated" by her employers in Singapore, where she worked as a domestic helper, wrote to commiserate. "When this is all over with, I know that I will harbor resentment for a long time. I am trying to marry a woman legally, following all the rules. I am not trying to import drugs, guns or other contraband. They make it very tough on a law-abiding, tax-paying citizen to 'do the right thing.' I hate this whole process."

Pat responded to Mick's message. He also empathized, but tried to shift the focus to the reason for going through the difficult process in the first place.

> Hi [Mick], This is really a subject that a good many of us could go on and on about forever. You have my sympathy also. Although the circumstances vary from experience to experience, the stigma of resentment towards the process can stay with us for a long time, as [JJ] stated. It is easy to point fingers at the INS, NVC [National Visa Center], and Embassy and 99% of the time it is most likely true [that it's their fault] . . . in my case, it finally came down to "how much mettle do I really have"? Am I in this through thick and thin or am I just on a lark? And like You, I truly felt that I was going to stick with it through thick and thin. After all, it was I not the Government that chose to take this path. . . . The bottom line for me was (and still is) even though it is behind us is that the time, energy, and especially resources could have been put to much better use. The peripheral costs, while the government twiddled it's thumbs with a non-suspicious, honest, willing to do what is right for all concerned—spousal visa were almost devastating. . . . There were a few times I found myself wondering—'Am I crazy'? And is the Government lending credence to that? But then, what about that significant other person? Are we going to let her down in midstream? Hang in there!

Daniel, in contrast to Freddie and Mick, expressed less anger and frustration, and a need to "go with the flow," even though it took almost two years from the time of his marriage in the Philippines until Gina's arrival in the United States. Others reminded him that it is much easier to maintain this position *after* the visa has been approved, as in his case.

Most of you know that I have been very patient through the immigration process. I recall a comment [X, a member of the list] made after I got married that they were going to have to listen to me whine and complain about the process. Well I knew I could not change the system so I just accepted the fact and went with the flow. The hardest part was a year after [Gina] and I married when it really sunk in [that we were still apart]. For the most part it would not have done me much good to complain at all. Now it's just down hill for us. I spoke to [Gina] a few minutes ago and she is getting excited. It's really nice to be able to joke and such with her about her arrival. We do go over important stuff and things like how much money she needs to take when she goes to the airport in Manila. How much she can take out of the ATM at LAX.[88]

Mick, on the other hand, still in the thick of the process, felt differently and stressed his feelings of helplessness. "I know I am not alone in my feelings and frustrations, it's just that I feel helpless. I don't like that feeling. That's probably why I own my own business. :) There are no short cuts and no way to kiss up to these people. They are all covering their butts so they need to play by the book. I understand that . . . I've tried to remain calm about this whole thing, but it seems with every piece of good news, two other things go wrong." JJ recalled going through the process about five years ago. "It took 7 months almost to the day for our spousal process from the day I mailed in the petition until the day [Carmel] was given a visa. That was about average for a petition in 1996. In some ways we had it easier than some of the couples today. Our petition moved through the process without any delay in any particular area. . . . On the other hand, it was still 7 months and that is a very long time."

Knowing of my interest in the topic, JJ had an analogy he thought I might relate to.

Nicole, imagine yourself going overseas for some research then for some reason the US won't let you back in for 7 months keeping you separated from your family. . . . Imagine there is some validity to the reason, possibly you caught some ebola virus or something. Lets say that the circumstances surrounding the issue was something you would not wish to expose your family to anyway and that 30 days is really the reasonable time frame but the US keeps you out for 7 months. OK, now you know how I feel. 30 days would have been plenty for the US to process our immigration request. In fact, if [Carmel] had come from England a few weeks would be all we would have been separated. With over a million illegal immigrants walking across our southern border each year I find keeping legally married couples apart for 7 months or more unconscionable. Since it can be done much more quickly when the foreign spouse is from many other countries it is obvious that this is intentional on the governments part.

JJ's remarks deserve further comment. Like many men, he felt that some waiting period is necessary to protect those at home from the threat of something analogous to a disease, but he also criticizes what he considers the disproportionate amount of time and attention paid to policing "legally married couples." JJ's criticism of INS policies and his resentment of illegal Latin American immigrants is also common. Like many others, JJ prides himself on his open-mindedness regarding "deserving" immigrants, yet he simultaneously expresses resentment of illegal immigrants who disadvantage those with more "legitimate" claims to entry. Criticisms of the INS are thus paired with resentment of other immigrant groups that are considered less worthy of entry than the wives of (white) U.S. citizens and taxpayers.

ANGEL AND FRANK AT THE CFO OFFICE

Besides U.S. immigration procedures, there are numerous bureaucratic procedures required by foreign states. Rather than deal with them comprehensively, I describe one bureaucratic requirement that is specific to the Philippines. This involves obtaining a required stamp from the Commission on Filipinos Overseas (CFO) that certifies that a fiancée or spouse has completed the required predeparture seminar and the guidance counseling. The stamp validates her passport, allowing her to leave the country.

I first met Frank, a retired Michigan state trooper, outside the CFO office in Cebu as he sat in the hallway chatting with an older Australian man. I was there in the hope of attending a predeparture seminar, and Frank and the man sitting next to him were waiting for their fiancées to obtain the certification. Angel, Frank's fiancée, had already completed most of the requirements, and she was at the CFO office to have her passport validated. While sweat collected on his forehead, Frank explained that the travel agent would not let them pick up Angel's airline ticket without the CFO stamp in her passport.

The CFO requirements could only be fulfilled, and the resulting stamp of approval obtained, in the Manila office on the northern island of Luzon, or at the Cebu City office in the central Visayas. Since there were only two offices, women and men often complained about the time, expense, and inconvenience of attending the seminar, especially for women who lived and worked on other islands or in other areas of the Philippines. Frank and Angel were lucky because Angel lived near Cebu and did not have to travel far.

Like several other men, Frank was concerned that the seminar often "scared the girls," making them think "that all foreign men are going to abuse them." (One man referred to the seminar as the "your-husband-will-beat-you-and-turn-you-into-a-maid class." One woman described the fear of Filipino parents that their daughter is marrying "hell spawn" because of all the stories circulating in the Philippines about domestic abuse and murder by western men.) On the other hand, Frank thought the seminar was a "good idea" because some women did not know what they were getting themselves into. His daughter, he explained, had worked for a battered women's shelter in the United States, and as a state trooper he knew some sad stories. But still, he could not quite appreciate the requirements in his own case.

According to the CFO's printed information, and as unofficially explained to me by one of the CFO staff members, the predeparture procedure is required by law. As of August 1989, the Department of Filipino Affairs requires the fiancé/spouse of foreign nationals to attend CFO guidance and counseling as a prerequisite to the issuance of a passport. According to one *Filipino Immigrant Handbook*, counseling services are provided to "Filipinas emigrating as fiancées or spouses of foreign nationals to help them develop informed decisions about intermarriage and life overseas, covering topics such as cultural differences and harmonization, available welfare and support services overseas, and rights and obligations of migrant overseas." [89] Unofficially, I was told that the seminars are designed in part to make women aware of the risks involved in the phenomenon of mail-order brides.

The seminars and guidance counseling are divided up by country or groups of countries. Women going to the United States and Canada attend together; women going to Japan attend a separate one. As part of the predeparture requirements, Filipina fiancées/spouses of foreigners (who comprise 90 percent of all fiancés and spouses from the Philippines) must fill out a number of forms answering detailed questions about their partner. This form, I was told, helps ascertain how well the woman knows her partner and whether she is a mail-order bride. One indication of a mail-order bride, I was told, is "a woman who hardly knows her husband or fiancé." If she doesn't know his occupation, his education, his birthday, for example, then the case is considered suspicious. Women worry that they do not know enough about their future in-laws or spouse's siblings and will "fail" the test.

Frank and Angel had originally met in the Philippines while he was travelling there several years earlier. When they met, Angel worked in a local department store and had completed one year of college. Frank returned to the United States, and they wrote to each other for over a year before he returned and they became engaged. Frank was in his mid-fifties, very heavy set, with a ruddy complexion, balding, with hair dyed brown. Angel was very attractive, twenty-two, and dressed like an American college student in a striped T-shirt and low slung, very baggy jeans. Angel and I talked for a while at a local Jollibee fast food restaurant while Frank went to pick up her airline tickets. She described the seminar as useful and interesting. She and several other women had tears in their eyes, she said, as they watched the video news documentary about six women who married foreigners. Three of the cases were "successful" stories of women who had married Americans. The fourth was of a woman who had married a Dutch man who subjected her to physical abuse and forced her to pose nude in the snow for photographs. A fifth case described a woman married to an American who took her money and then divorced her, and the final case described a woman who was married to a Canadian who physically and verbally assaulted her. When she left him, he immediately petitioned and succeeded in bringing another woman to Canada. Since then he had been placed on an unofficial "blacklist." Should he petition for another wife, she would be counseled and warned about his background.

Angel thought she knew Frank well. These stories upset her, but she said that she loved and trusted him. They had minor problems, she said, but nothing serious. She gets annoyed, for example, when he says "come to Daddy," and she tells him "I'm your wife; don't treat me like a child!" He sometimes wants her to dress in sexy clothes. "But I tell him that isn't what I like, and he is okay." When Frank returned from the travel agency, complaining again about their inefficiency, Angel said, laughing, "Friends always ask why I am with this old, fat man!" Snuggling up to him, she said, "And I tell them, because I love him!" With a smile Frank added, "I've already lost some weight and when we get back to the United States we'll have an exercise routine."

IN THE UNITED STATES

Please delete anything I said or wrote that sounds critical of INS or other government offices. Delete the name of the service center, the congressman's name, and our general location. Even though [X] is here in the U.S. now, we are still in this process for at least another four years until

she becomes a citizen. I wouldn't want anything to mess things up
for us.

—Anonymous, 2000

Bureaucratic requirements do not end when the foreign partner arrives in
the United States. Jianming, for example, arrived from China in the summer
of 2000 with a K1 visa and a ninety-day work permit stamped on her visa.
One week later, she applied for a Social Security card, as she had been encouraged to do by the American consulate in China. When the couple went
to a local Social Security office to apply for her card, the staff looked at the
computer and turned her down, telling her that she was not eligible. The
couple went to another office and were told that "secondary verification"
was required from the INS, that the office would write to the INS, and that
such verification would take two to four weeks rather than the usual two.

Meanwhile, Jianming and her husband had to return to the INS office,
where they were due to pick up Jianming's one-year work permit. Jianming's husband explained to the immigration officer the problem his wife
was having obtaining her Social Security number. He asked the officer if she
could check on the correspondence between the Social Security office and
the INS. The INS officer said that would not be necessary, that they had
only to show the work permit to the Social Security officer. Jianming and
her husband returned to the Social Security office the same day. Upon further inquiry about the status of Jianming's card, the couple was told that
the work permit stamped on the visa was insufficient. The officer explained
that it could have been altered or forged and that they required secondary
confirmation directly from the INS. When they returned to the Social Security office four weeks later, they were told the process was now taking the
INS approximately three months.

Jianming's husband sent a letter to his congressman explaining the situation. The congressman had his office staff intervene and contact the INS.
He had the INS officer fax Jianming's documentation directly to him. He
then in turn faxed the documentation to the Social Security office. The congressman's office then informed Jianming of her Social Security number by
phone and informed her that she could expect the card in the mail in seven
to ten days. Altogether it had taken more than three months for the local
INS to reply to the local Social Security office. From following the news,
Jianming's husband presumed the INS was understaffed and, like JJ, speculated that this might have to do with the "increased funding going to policing of the borders and not to local offices with increased numbers of immigrants seeking legal entry." The following week, nearly four months after

submitting her application, Jianming received her Social Security card in the mail. She could then apply for a job and apply for a learner's permit so she could begin driving lessons. Jianming's case did not seem to be typical of the process of getting a Social Security card, but it is typical of the bureaucracy and frustration experienced at various stages of the process.

CONCLUSION

This chapter has explored the history of Asian immigration to the United States and the tales of waiting as couples experience the process of immigration. Chinese and Filipina correspondence brides fit into the wider history of U.S. immigration, a history that has been punctuated by differences of class, race/nationality, and gender. Like many of their historical predecessors, these women enter the United States by virtue of their identity as wives. But unlike earlier immigrants, their husbands are often white men who are U.S. citizens but who often feel decidedly helpless and powerless in the face of state bureaucracy.

As we have seen, Asian immigrants have often been vilified, suspected of exploiting U.S. resources or taking jobs or benefits away from U.S. natives. Not far below the surface are concerns about population growth, cultural differences, and morality.[90] Foreign brides face similar concerns about economic opportunism and immorality. In response to such concerns, complicated and time-consuming immigration procedures have been devised to ensure that U.S. citizens or permanent residents have the economic means to support their foreign partners so that they will not become a burden to the state, and to ensure that the foreign partner meets the requirements for morality and mental and physical health. Legislation—such as the IMFA— is also designed to ensure that marriages are "bona fide."[91] As we have seen, U.S. men (who are often depicted as the beneficiaries of immigration policies) are often critical and resentful of immigration procedures that are designed to curb and control the entry of foreigners, to distinguish those who are worthy of entry from those who are not, and to "protect" them as U.S. citizens.[92] Many men believe that the spouse of a tax-paying U.S. citizen should be entitled to immigrate. Yet rather than automatically confer this privilege, their identity as white citizens can in fact render their marriages suspect. The comments Freddie encountered about "Filipino statehood," "mail-order brides," and about taking a "cold shower" from INS officials or his senator's office staff are not unique. They recall the older history of discrimination and public anxiety about Asian immigrants and miscegenation. Yet they differ from the older pattern. The cases I have described involve white U.S. men who are experiencing state power, in the form of immigration restrictions, not as a basis of privilege but as a source of impotence and frustration.

While older immigration policies reflected ambivalence about whether it was better to allow Asian women to enter the United States (to reduce the likelihood of relationships between Asian men and white women) or to restrict the immigration of Asian women (for fear of the resulting Asian American population growth), current state policies point to a different tension between restricting the entry of foreign wives (who represent certain dangers) and U.S. men's right to petition for a wife to immigrate. Restrictions and controls placed on the partners of U.S. citizens are theoretically the same regardless of the citizen's ethnic or national origins, and many similar controls are placed on foreign students, workers, and other family members. Yet some issues are specific to correspondence relationships, as suggested by the discussion of Asian adoptees and Asian brides in the next chapter.

8 Conclusion: Marriage, Migration, and Transnational Families

> Throughout the twentieth century, the figure of the
> Asian immigrant has served as a "screen," a phantasmic
> site, on which the nation projects a series of condensed,
> complicated anxieties regarding internal and external threats
> to the mutable coherence of the national body: the invading
> multitude, the lascivious seductress, the servile yet treacherous
> domestic, the automaton whose inhuman efficiency will
> supersede American ingenuity.
> —LISA LOWE, *Immigrant Acts*, 18

> The issue of immigration evokes an implicit comparison
> registered in the relative mobility and immobility of
> differently marked bodies that allow U.S. citizens to cross
> national boundaries to bring their children home.
> —ANN ANAGNOST, "Scenes of Misrecognition," 398

> What's the worst thing Nicole's book could do? People
> already think we're a bunch of perverts and losers.
> —G, 1999

FOREIGN BRIDES AND FOREIGN ADOPTEES

In her analysis of the discourse surrounding Chinese adoptees and white middle-class adoptive parents, Ann Anagnost points to the relative ease with which Chinese adoptees pass through the U.S. immigration process. "China adoption," Anagnost argues, "represents a particularly privileged form of immigration that is facilitated because the right to form families is a consecrated [U.S.] middle-class imperative." Adoption immigration, moreover, "evokes an implicit comparison" with other groups of prospective immigrants who experience relatively greater degrees of difficulty entering the United States.[1] In contrast to foreign children adopted by U.S. parents, who as of early 2001 are automatically granted citizenship,[2] foreign spouses of U.S. citizens, though also privileged in certain ways over other prospective immigrants, are treated more like suspected criminals and often face long delays in immigration and in obtaining citizenship. This inconsistency is reminiscent of nineteenth- and early-twentieth-century laws that recognized the citizenship of Asian infants born in the United States but still denied their Asian parents the rights of naturalization.

Like the adoptive parents of Chinese children, the U.S. men who use international introduction agencies are also largely middle-class professionals.[3] Both processes of immigration, moreover, are designed to distinguish legitimate and deserving cases from those of illegal trafficking. Both adoptive parents and U.S. spouses are sensitive to the more or less subtle critiques of international adoption or international marriage as a form of "buying" a child or spouse. Yet the foreign wife or fiancée is viewed and treated differently than the adoptive child. Even at the web site of the U.S. Embassy in Guangzhou—through which adoptive children and foreign spouses and fiancées obtain visas—a far more welcoming face is presented to those applying for adoptees' visas than to other sorts of immigrants. The web site presents the image of a smiling infant with the caption, "A Happy Client—one of over 4000 babies processed by ACIVU [Adopted Children Immigrant Visa Unit] in 1999."[4] The "non-immigrant section" for those awaiting fiancée or student visas, by contrast, displays a photograph of a crowded line of people waiting to enter the embassy.

Both Chinese adoptees and those applying for fiancée visas are predominantly female, they share the same citizenship and country of origin by birth, and both are being incorporated into (often) white, middle-class families, but they are viewed quite differently. Adoptive parents, it seems, experience little of the uncertainty about the likelihood of the child obtaining immigration rights that the prospective spouses feel. If, as Anagnost suggests, the middle-class identity of the adoptive parent(s) helps allay certain immigration anxieties concerning Asian children, why does the same logic not apply to men who aim to marry foreign women? How do the class identities and lack of presumed childlike innocence of these women impinge on their immigration experiences? If "the right to form a family" is indeed a middle-class imperative in the United States, as Anagnost argues, and if assumptions about white middle-class rights to have a "complete" family are linked to state regulations surrounding international adoption, then why is the right of middle-class, primarily white men to marry foreign spouses not equally recognized and facilitated by U.S. immigration polices?

The citizenship of the adoptee may be less problematic because the child (often less than two years old) is considered innocent. She will, moreover, be raised (usually) by a white middle-class parent (or two). The child may be imagined as part of a "model minority," with all the class implications associated with this image. Furthermore, as Anagnost argues, international adoption is associated with "stories of salvage and redemption, which contain the political effects of adoption within the domain of private heroic acts" (398). In contrast to middle-class adoptive parents, the more private rescue narratives of U.S. men do not participate in the same public fantasy of "salvage and redemption," since the innocence of the women they marry is suspect. In fact, men who adhere to a rescue narrative of those they may imagine to be women from poor places with difficult lives are viewed not as performing "heroic acts," but as taking advantage of unequal power structures.

The cultural and class differences, as well as the sexuality, of the Asian wife are indelibly inscribed on her adult body, in contrast to the young child, who is viewed, in a sense, as a tabula rasa on which American middle-class values and identity can be more easily inscribed. That she is an adult renders her more suspect and less easily molded into the ideal citizen and model Asian minority in the United States than Asian adoptees may be. While the young child's helplessness and lack of agency render her incapable of immigration fraud or of having pragmatic motives to enter the United States, the lack of agency often attributed to "trafficked women" is used to argue against their immigration, or the assumed hyperagency of foreign women renders her suspect of dishonorable motives or marriage fraud. Anagnost rightly points to adoption as a highly privileged form of immigration. Yet that privilege may not stem so much from the middle-class identity of the parents as from their "heroic act" and the prospective model citizenship of the children.

That marriage to a foreign woman is regarded by the state and the U.S. public as more problematic than adoption of a foreign child may be linked to ideas about a presumed scarcity of available (suitable) local children, whereas no such scarcity is assumed in the case of local wives. Adoptive parents are in many cases perceived as unable to produce their own children, which may evoke a sense of sympathy at something that is considered beyond their control. U.S. men who cannot find a wife, on the other hand, are more likely to evoke a sense of blame and to reinforce the popular media notion that they are simply losers on the domestic marriage market. Ideas about "love" may also be a factor. Perhaps the idea of "love at first sight" is more acceptable in the case of a child and prospective parent than in the case of prospective marriage partners. Love may be assumed to appear "naturally" between adoptive parent and child, whereas it is viewed, as we have seen, with far greater skepticism in a conjugal relationship founded on international correspondence. While the trials and tribulations of the adoption process are often viewed as evidence of a labor of love, no such assumption is made by critics of correspondence marriage. The structural inequalities that surround both instances project far more negatively onto readings of international marriages than in the case of international adoption. Both adoptive parents and U.S. partners are highly sensitive to market analogies and critiques that center on commodification. Ultimately, U.S. public sympathy lies with parents who "heroically rescue" children from "poorer countries," not with men who marry foreign women. One final important contrast between adoptees and wives involves their potential role in facilitating the future entry of more immigrants. Most Chinese adoptions are done "blind" in the sense that the child's biological kin are not known. As a result, the adoptee will not sponsor a chain of immigrants for purposes of family unification, whereas a spouse can do so once she becomes an unconditional permanent resident or citizen.

Lisa Lowe has written about the gendered and racialized history of Asian immigration, the formation of "Asian American culture," and the "contradictions" of Asian immigration, which simultaneously place immigrants "'within' the U.S. nation state, its workplaces, and its markets," yet continue to mark them "linguistically, culturally, and racially" as "'foreign' and 'outside' the national polity," even after many generations.[5] Asian wives and adoptees further illustrate such patterns and contradictions, as they are placed within the most intimate spaces of U.S. homes and families. Such wives and adoptees fit well with the "project of imagining the nation," that builds on the orientalist idea of Asians as ultimate foreigners who are "discovered," "welcomed," or "domesticated" by American society.[6] Adoptees are perhaps sympathetically "welcomed," whereas foreign brides are "discovered" as a solution to what some men perceive as a "wife shortage." As Lowe argues, "Stereotypes that construct Asians as the threatening 'yellow peril,' or alternatively, that pose Asians as the domesticated 'model minority,' are each equally indices" of national anxieties about the "mutable coherence of the national body" (18–19). As we have seen, so-called mail-order brides combine elements of the "yellow peril" in the form of the "lascivious seductress" and the "treacherous domestic," while adoptees are constructed as the "model minority" (18). And like Asian Americans who have been in the United States for many generations, they are still likely to be seen—despite their connections to white, middle-class families—as the "foreigner-within" as a result of racialized identities created by the history of legislation, policies, and classifications (5). Asian wives and adoptees represent only two of many possible points of entry for those who may be seen—or may one day identify themselves as—Asian Americans, and who may one day contribute to the rich and insightful cultural productions and national critiques that Lowe describes as generated from the emergence of Asian American culture.

MIGRATION AND TRAFFICKING

This book contributes to a growing literature that critiques the idea of migration as a one-directional flow of people across boundaries, a process through which immigrants become locals, and in the course of a generation or more adopt or fail to adopt local culture.[7] The nineteenth- and early-twentieth-century migration of Filipinos and Chinese to the United States—mistakenly treated as a one-directional flow of people who would to some extent be incorporated into the "melting pot"—made it difficult to foresee the post-1965 boom in chain migrations of sponsored family members and the contacts back and forth between the United States and other homelands over many decades of physical separation. Such an approach also makes it difficult to see the important connections and complex multidirectional flows of ideas, people, and objects between China, the Philippines, and the United States today.

This book has also drawn attention to the issue of "trafficking," which is generally viewed as a type of forced migration. Women and children who are trafficked are often represented as having little or no ability to exert choice in the matter of their migration. As I have argued, scholarly, popular, and government sources often overlook important distinctions between forced prostitution, sex tourism, sex slaves, sex workers, domestic workers, and foreign brides of various kinds, characterizing them all as trafficked. Feminist and activist critiques often overlook key distinctions between different sorts of international introduction agencies, and different types of transnational relationships. Although the lines between different kinds of immigration and different sorts of brokers may form more of a continuum than clearly distinct types, finer distinctions are important. There are situations in which sex workers correspond with foreign men and become international brides,[8] but meeting someone as a result of sex tourism—though perhaps also aided by the Internet and speeded up by globalization—is in important ways very different from meeting someone via a marriage-oriented pen pal introduction service. Analogies between international marriages, sex tourism, and prostitution may be common, but comparisons with computer dating and other forms of introduction may be more apt.

The rhetorical blur between transnational marriages and the traffic in women is a common but often unwarranted leap. Such blurs, I have argued, serve to justify ever-stricter immigration regulations on both sides of the border. The result of such critiques then becomes—intentionally or not—the barring of certain women from making the choice to marry, and this choice then becomes the privilege of women who fit the ideal profile (like Lisa, described in chapter 4), or of women who are already residents or citizens. This position does what feminists have long been wary of: it creates a universal "Third World Woman" who is incapable of making her own decisions. This position further supports the very notion of subservient and docile women of which so many feminists are critical.

Mail-order brides are often included among the concerns of feminist and antitrafficking groups. Others—including the U.S. Department of Justice Report to Congress—use the term "mail-order bride" to refer to all women whose marriages have been "facilitated by international matchmaking organizations," but are more careful to specify that "not all mail-order brides would be considered trafficked."[9] Nonetheless, the report unabashedly uses the term "mail-order brides," despite the derogatory implication that women are like "commodities" who are "bought and sold" (as the notion of "mail-order" implies) and part of a "marriage market." Likewise, critics of immigration policies such as CPR and IMFA (see chapter 7), who rightly point to immigrant women's vulnerability, undermine their argument when they assert that such policies provide "consumer protection for men," or that immigration policies provide a "warranty" to "consumer-husbands."[10] As I have argued, the market metaphor has serious limitations when dealing with the lives and experiences of real people. Such blurs do little to distinguish between those who actively pursue and choose whether or not to become involved with foreign partners and those who have been "trafficked" against their will and knowledge. Such labels help promote a particular critique or political stance, but their value is limited if the goal is to better understand and accurately represent correspondence relationships.

TRANSNATIONALISM

The concept of transnationalism and transnational marriage is far more useful. In contrast to notions of migration and trafficking, which are viewed as geographically one-directional and one-dimensional in terms of power, the recent literature on transnationalism considers multidirectional

flows of desires, people, ideas, and objects across, between, and beyond national boundaries.[11] Transnationalism is highly relevant to the topic of correspondence courtship and marriage between U.S. men and Chinese and
Filipino women. Ideas about western men and Asian women, about gender,
family, and marriage, traverse national boundaries, are reshaped in local
communities, and return to their supposed places of origin in new and
highly hybrid forms that may or may not correspond with reality. Media
images of the sexual revolution in the West, or complacent and docile Asian
women, or wealthy Americans, for example, are transformed into ideas
about real people and places and are linked to what Appadurai has called the
"global imagination."[12] Orientalist images, once thought to be simply
western projections, are now understood to involve more complex appro-
priations and exchanges.[13] Internet agencies and web sites devoted to introducing western men and Asian women at the click of a button and rapid
forms of mass media and communication have created the time-space compression that makes it possible to communicate, imagine, and live lives that
cross borders and cross back again. Ideas about Asia and about the West underlie men's and women's motivations to meet a foreign partner.

In most cases, foreign women cross national boundaries and emigrate to
the United States as wives and fiancées, but theirs is not a single, unidirectional, or final migration. Men also go to visit pen pals and fiancées abroad.
Men generally return to the United States to file paperwork and wait for
anywhere from a few months to well over a year for their wives to join
them. Meanwhile they correspond via the Internet, the telephone, and old-
fashioned letters while their wives and fiancées apply for passports and em-
igration permits and their visa requests are processed. Once settled in the
United States, many men and women return abroad for visits, and some
settle in Asia for part of the year or for part of their lives, or go there to set
up retirement homes, where the cost of living is lower than in the United
States. Relatives come and go and children attend schools abroad and return home for visits and sometimes work. Money, gifts, and communication flow between national boundaries, following traditional patterns of
gift-giving that may also compete and conflict with demands and commitments to the nuclear family.

Patterns of transnationalism are—as indicated by the involvement of
the INS and other state institutions in China and the Philippines—influenced by state regulations and policies. On each side of the border, states
determine whether and when an individual can emigrate, and under what
circumstances. Fees are required, and sometimes legal or political influence,
to navigate what can otherwise become a prohibitively complicated process.

Like other patterns of Asian-U.S. migration, correspondence marriages are linked to wider patterns of political economy, which are tied, I have argued, to ideas of love and desire.

Today's correspondence relationships are notably different from the older historical cases of frontier brides, proxy brides, and picture brides in terms of the technology they utilize. But they are perhaps not so different in the extent to which they are regulated by laws and policies that are in turn influenced by public opinion and racial prejudice. Although nineteenth- and twentieth-century laws regulated the flow, the health, and even the age difference between Japanese picture brides and their Japanese immigrant spouses in the United States—and the waiting time between the initial arrangement of the marriage and bride's arrival in the United States could take years—today's marriages are also regulated in terms of women's health and personal history. Today, perhaps because he is already considered a privileged U.S. citizen or resident, little attention is paid to the background of the U.S. partner other than his economic ability to support a wife. As in the past, the man's ethnicity and nationality determined his right to facilitate the immigration of his wife. A key difference in marriages today is how they cross ethnic/racial and national lines, whereas the older forms of marriages often involved couples whose experiences differed greatly but who were of the same ethnic or national background. This crossing of ethnic/racial lines may not provoke such extreme reactions as in the past era of anti-miscegenation laws, but many couples have learned firsthand that interracial marriages still provoke hostility.

As discussed in the previous chapter, that their partners are U.S. white middle-class men has not automatically meant that their marriages are privileged. But certain changes are on the horizon. In December 2000, President Clinton signed the LIFE Act into law. Among its provisions were the creation of new K and V visas designed so that spouses of legal permanent residents and U.S. citizens could wait out part of the immigration process in the United States.[14] In July 2001, President Bush spoke to a crowd of recently naturalized citizens in New York about his desire to facilitate the immigration process and reduce the INS waiting time for prospective immigrants to six months or less.[15] These moves were applauded by many men with foreign partners, but other proposed changes were not so popular. Criticized as an attempt to court Latino voters, Bush also spoke of allowing illegal Mexican immigrants to apply for legal permanent residence.[16] Many men with Chinese or Filipina partners commented on the unfairness of the situation if it is not applied to Asians as well. Others expressed resentment that illegal immigrants might take precious INS time and energy away from processing legal immigrants. Yet others joked about smuggling partners in through Mexico and delivering them into the waiting arms of their sweethearts in the United States. Although the partners of those who have met through international matchmaking organizations are conservatively estimated at 4,000 to 6,000 per year, and would therefore constitute less than 1 percent of the yearly immigration to the United States, they are nonetheless a rapidly growing group.[17] Their U.S. partners are middle-class professional men, who often considered their encounters with U.S. immigration both eye-opening and disturbing. Many of them agreed with the public criticism of the INS that erupted in April 2002, and applauded the proposed plans for serious restructuring.

DOMESTIC ABUSE

This book has touched only briefly on the issue of abuse, and I have in fact suggested that abuse may take a much larger place in the discourse and popular imagination than is warranted by the actual experiences of couples who have met through correspondence. As the INS report "International Matchmaking" suggests, there is little basis for assuming that the rate of domestic abuse among couples who meet through international matchmaking agencies is higher than among other immigrants. That said, it is not my intention to undermine the important activist work on this issue. As Uma Narayan has argued, and as many of the men and women I met agreed, immigrant women who are less skilled in English, unfamiliar with U.S. laws and customs, and cut off from family and friends may be more vulnerable to domestic abuse than others.[18] Even if the number of women who experience abuse is small, it nonetheless deserves serious attention.

This study has argued that foreign brides and their spouses should not automatically be suspected of having abusive relationships. The negative stereotypes surrounding the issue of so-called mail-order brides, from which many men and women actively and understandably attempt to distance themselves, create further distance and alienation and can cause more harm than good. Promoting images of Asian women as mail-order brides or passive victims who will willingly do anything or marry anyone just to come to the United States not only is inaccurate but also risks attracting further attention from men who are looking for women they can abuse. Therefore, it is important to question and deconstruct inaccurate, totalizing, hegemonic images of mail-order brides, catalogs, and marriages, and to show how international brides are in fact more active and assertive in their choices and actions than is commonly assumed.

It is also important to ask why foreign women are subjected to intense background checks and disqualified from immigration for any sort of criminal record, while criminal records, a history of violence, or police files documenting domestic abuse are considered irrelevant when considering U.S. men's privilege to petition for foreign partners' immigration. Closer scrutiny or examination of prospective brides will not result in preventing trafficking or domestic abuse. Most women who are labeled as "trafficked" or as "slaves" are unaware at the time of their engagement or marriage—like many other victims of domestic abuse in the United States who have met their partners in more conventional ways—of what their future holds. They have made what seems at the time to be an informed and reasonable choice.[19] Stricter controls on U.S. petitioners—or a requirement that women be informed of criminal records or former charges of domestic abuse—might add to the overall processing time, but the overall advantages would outweigh the disadvantages. It might also help improve the men's reputations. Stricter controls placed on women and their qualifications to immigrate will not prevent domestic abuse. Doing away with the two-year waiting period for unconditional permanent residency would, as Simons and others argue, help assure that women who experience abuse do not feel like they must choose between deportation or remaining with abusive husbands.[20] Despite amendments and exceptions to the IMFA, the requirements to self-petition for permanent residency still places an unreasonable burden of proof on married women. That a woman would prefer to remain in the United States rather than face deportation does not mean that her motives were purely instrumental. To assume that women can simply return home is to misunderstand the extent of the social and personal sacrifices, investments, and commitments they have made to come to the United States in the first place. Many women feel that it is impossible to return the Philippines or to China after a marriage has failed. Like women who have worked overseas for an extended period of time, it is difficult, painful, and often impossible to return home in the shadow of a failed marriage, especially given the changes that have been created between those who left and those who stayed behind.[21]

REVEALING IMAGES

According to the article published by ABS-CBN News discussed in chapter 2, "The typical Filipina mail-order bride believes that marrying a foreigner is her ticket out of poverty. But it may also lead to a descending hell of spousal abuse or white slavery. Yet still the march goes on—of young

Filipinas eager to sell body and soul for a way out of the country."[22] In writing this book, it is my hope, if not to have dispelled such images, at least to have presented equally compelling though much less sensationalist images of the women and men who meet and participate in transnational correspondence marriages. My objective has been to present the tamer and more conservative side of the picture—a side that is far more common and prevalent.

In one of the few existing ethnographic studies of women who met their spouses through correspondence, Raquel Ordonez writes,

> The mail-order bride phenomenon can be viewed from several perspectives. It can be seen as a tributary of the ever-widening stream of overseas migration. . . . It can be interpreted as a form of commodification and sexual exploitation. . . . The U.S. Immigration and Naturalization Service (INS) looks at it as a source of marriage fraud and a way for the women to cheat the immigration restrictions. Still, it can be viewed as a natural way for people seeking friends and life partners to get together across national borders."[23]

In this book, I have considered the interconnections and shortcomings of these perspectives and others. Each, I have argued, presents a "partial" picture, in both senses of the word.

Writing ethnography and conducting research is always a selective and interpretive process. The part of the picture I have focused on does not tell the whole story, but it depicts a side that is rarely told and thus in need of telling. I did not encounter any women I would consider to have been trafficked, but I did not search out women in domestic shelters either. Neither did I intentionally search out women who I thought would be less likely to become victims. Other than Yanyi (chapter 6), I did not meet any women who were, who considered themselves, or who admitted to having been physically or emotionally abused by their partners. Yanyi's story points out, however, that high levels of education, economic status, and even U.S. experience are not guarantees against negative experiences and difficult relationships. Although much of the criticism of trafficking, human slavery, and international correspondence marriages is based on an assumption of women's victimization and powerlessness, this is not necessarily so. Women from the United States and elsewhere, including those who are educated and economically well off, still become victims of domestic violence. The problem stems from more insidious forms of inequality that exist in many marriages, not simply those involving foreign brides.

It would have been easy to write a book filled only with offensive remarks from men, by simply citing from various web sites or newspapers.[24]

Yet I have chosen not to do so partly because such examples already abound in the scholarly and popular literature; also because, as I have argued, they are not the only side of the story, nor are they representative of many or most men I have encountered. It would be a truism to say that offensive, sexist, racist, egotistical, and controlling men exist among those involved in correspondence. But unfortunately, because of popular preconceptions about men who seek to meet women through correspondence, such images are too readily accepted as the unquestionable and only "truth." In an effort to problematize such stereotypes, I have intentionally placed the following examples at the end rather than the beginning of this book.

One day in 2001, Daniel wrote to UFG to say that he might have to withdraw because Gina was upset about the amount of time he spent on the Internet. A fairly new member of the list recommended that Gina do what his wife does. When he is on the computer and she feels neglected, she "sits on my lap with just her panties on." This image could easily be used to simply reinforce the stereotype of the sexually available Asian woman, and the U.S. man who is focused on her sexuality. Yet it might also be read in other ways. It points to the woman's ability to use her sexuality to get her way. Her use of her sexuality might be interpreted as a "weapon of the weak," [25] which has enabled her to successfully realize her objective (distracting him from the computer or achieving sexual satisfaction and pleasure of her own). Yet to assume that this is a weapon of the weak or a form of resistance as opposed to a sexual play between equals reveals both assumptions and misassumptions about correspondence relationships. Many assume that mail-order marriages are between social unequals and that the woman is reduced to a sex object or part of a male sexual fantasy. But were a similar example to take place among, say, two college students, or a couple of the same ethnic, class, and social background, the example would likely be unsettling only to the extent that it reflects broader assumptions about sexuality, gender, and power. Although we know fairly little about the situation, it is unwarranted to assume that either the man or the woman has a monopoly on power; nor should it be assumed that either has a monopoly on pleasure.

The advice Daniel received was also interesting because it was not criticized by list members for being a sexual or "off topic" remark. In the course of about two years, three men had been banned from the same list, one because his personal web site contained a link to a travel-related web site that had information about sex tours, even though he claimed to be unaware of it. The second case involved a self-identified body-building fanatic. He wrote to describe the weight training program he arranged for his fiancée in the Philippines, including a personal trainer and an increasingly rigid regime of exercise and diet (including a gradual reduction of her rice intake). He claimed that she felt healthier and happier, and received many compliments about her sexy body from men and women. He said she would have no choice but to become as obsessed with exercise as he is. Despite his assertion that she was enjoying the exercise, men on the list responded immediately to his implications that she would have "no choice" but to continue, calling him a "control freak" who was insensitive to her cultural background (i.e., eating rice). He had supposedly made intentionally inflammatory remarks on another list as well, and was promptly banned within a day of his posting. Although I too was struck by his dictatorial tone, I found it difficult to tell, based on the one e-mail I had read, whether he was indeed a "control freak" who would place unreasonable demands on his wife against her will, or whether she was a willing and consenting participant in his exercise obsession. While his tone was certainly off-putting and he may well be a very unpleasant and controlling man, stereotypes of Asian women (willing to do anything for the green card) and of western men (taking advantage of their vulnerability) again seem far too reductionistic, simplistic, and misleading. The list members later applauded the fact that his fiancée had "dumped him."

The third case was the most disturbing to me, and the one that presents the greatest challenge to my analysis. It is one about which I know relatively little, and what I do know is based solely on what the man posted on his web site. This case appears in many ways to adhere to the worst presumptions about western men's exploitation of young and innocent Asian women. I encountered this case when the man simply listed the URL for his detailed personal web site, and very briefly mentioned past marital problems on the Internet list. It took several days before members actually looked at the web site and began to respond, but when they did he too was severely criticized and quickly banned. His web site included detailed links to what he claimed were transcripts of his correspondence with his Filipina (now ex-) wife and materials pertaining to court cases that resulted in his conviction for forced oral copulation, felony false imprisonment, and spousal battery, for which he had spent several years in prison. Although he had finished serving jail time and was no longer on probation, he was in the process of appealing his convictions on the basis of what he claimed was (among other things) immigration fraud. My objective is not to summarize or to evaluate the extremely complicated series of claims he made. On the surface he appeared to be a truly despicable character, who defied my attempts at fairness. Based on his own telling of the story, he seemed to have taken advantage of a young woman's naivete, lack of English comprehension, and romantic hopes in order to seduce her into marrying him and becoming what he hoped would be one of several wives. It is unclear whether his pen pal understood that he planned to have multiple spouses, although he claimed to have fully informed her in his early correspondence. She had also apparently received a letter from one of his ex-girlfriends warning her of his intentions. At first she wrote him an angry letter breaking off their relationship, but in a subsequent letter she seemed convinced (based on letter transcripts) that the ex-girlfriend had misrepresented the situation. They married in the Philippines and continued to correspond for more than a year as she awaited immigration approval. Before she arrived in the United States, their relationship already seemed to be strained by her financial requests and his growing concern over money. Upon arrival, she was enraged to learn that he was living with another Asian "wife." He insisted that she earn money and encouraged her to date other men. Within a year, their conflicts grew, and eventually several charges were brought against him (including that of bigamy, which was dropped because he had not officially married his second "wife"). Eventually he was charged with the three aforementioned offenses. He claimed that he had been honest with her and that she "knew" what to expect, and that she filed abuse charges against him in order to remain in the United States. Without proof of cruelty or battery, his wife would not have been allowed to remain in the United States, since she had not satisfied the two-year residence requirement for alien spouses. Meanwhile, he wrote to her parents, spelling out his complaints, criticizing her for adulterous behavior, and presenting himself as the victim.

This case is reminiscent of those that made their way into Glodava and Onizuka's book (see chapter 3). And like the "worst cases" they describe, it is necessary (with even the sketchy and partial information presented here) to ask whether additional warning to this young woman (a teenager when they first corresponded) might have altered her decision to marry. Would being formally informed of previous charges of domestic abuse have made a difference, or would she have been convinced of extenuating circumstances, as in the case of his ex-girlfriend's warnings and accusations? While he painted his wife as a hyperagent willing to do anything for a green card (but also accused her of being manipulated by her lawyer and her new partner and of having difficulty with English), the letter transcripts he posted suggest that immigration was not her primary goal or intention, marriage was. Remaining in the United States no doubt became increasingly important to her as the option of returning home—shamed and scandalized for her failed marriage and as her husband's reports of her infidelity circulated—diminished. Although she appears to have been victimized in many ways, she also defies this label. It is important to consider this case through time: she won her case, remained in the United States, and became a permanent resident (perhaps a citizen by now), and she reportedly remarried.

While this story is reminiscent of the worst cases reported in the media, my point has been to argue that they are not the only stories (only the best-known representations), and they cannot be resolved by legislating against recruitment of women's names for introduction services or by closely judging or casting doubts on the sincerity of a woman's motives for marrying a U.S. man. This case also illustrates how—despite the fact that the man was convicted—the two-year conditional residence requirement can make a bad situation worse. While domestic abuse is common among the broader population as well, the issue of residence enables men to claim their innocence in relation to women's desire or need to remain in the United States. Although there are exceptions to the two-year rule, it nonetheless doubly disadvantages women by making them more likely to endure abuse, and also more vulnerable to the charge that their abuse claims are prompted by a desire to remain in the United States. If men's claims that they are falsely accused are true, then they too stand to benefit from abolishing this legal requirement.

As I have argued, many of the negative assumptions and associations regarding correspondence relationships between Asian women and U.S. men are based on a priori assumptions about inequality. Age, ethnicity/ race, and physical size are visual clues that can reinforce assumptions about power, which means that patterns that are in fact far more common and widespread among U.S. men and women are more easily attributed to couples whose appearances resonate with such differences. In the absence of ethnic/racial differences, an older man and younger woman may not be noticed, or they may pass as father and daughter. Visual clues often trigger assumptions about power and inequality. A complementary division of labor in U.S.-Asian couples—because of their visibility and because of assumptions about power—raises more questions than among couples who appear to be of the same ethnic/racial group. That interethnic couples become targets of criticism because of their visibility may help explain the increased popularity of brides from Eastern Europe and the former Soviet Union. In any case, it is important to view correspondence relationships not as unique, but as representative of many of the issues and concerns raised by the institution of marriage in general.

My objective has been to provide a critical rereading of correspondence relationships that illustrates how they are situated in relation to history and political economy, without robbing people of their individuality, emotion, or sense of personhood. Although Bob's unexpected arrival at Faith's house in a chauffeur-driven car (chapter 1) can be read as a kind of American bravado and a statement of his economic standing relative to Faith's family's poverty, the story does not begin or end with an American man marrying a desperate Filipina and thereby rescuing her from her poverty. As Jolly and Manderson argue, desire involves complex and interactive flows.[26] Bob and Faith's jointly narrated story draws on both her attraction to western men and his attraction to Filipinas, both of which are intertwined with history and broader unequal structures of power. The ethnographic challenge is how to take account of structural inequalities and sociocultural factors that circumscribe women and men's options and inspire new opportunities and imaginings, while simultaneously conveying the richness and dignity of their choices without reducing them to calculating instrumentalists or naive romantics.

Notes

INTRODUCTION

1. ABS-CBN News, "Pinay Brides—Internet's Hottest Commodities" (2000), pt. 4, p. 3; available at *http://www.abs-cbnnews.com.*

2. Lisa Anne Simons, "Mail Order Brides: The Legal Framework and Possibilities for Change," in *Gender and Immigration,* ed. Gregory A. Kelson and Debra DeLaet (New York: New York University Press, 1999), 127. See also Kathleen Barry, *Female Sexual Slavery* (Englewood Cliffs, N.J.: Prentice-Hall, 1979); Philippine Women Centre of British Columbia, *Canada: The New Frontier for Filipino Mail-Order Brides* (2000); available at Site of Status of Women Canada, *http://www.swc-cfc.gc.ca/pube.html.*

3. Mila Glodava and Richard Onizuka, *Mail-Order Brides: Women For Sale* (Fort Collins, Colo.: Alaken, 1994), 50.

4. Ibid., 29.

5. See, for example, *Dateline NBC,* "Bought and Sold," Geraldo Rivera, March 18, 2001; *Maury Povich Show,* February 19, 1998.

6. See, for example, Jeffrey Lee Hollis, "Us Versus Maury Povich" (1998); available at *http://www.geocities.com/~hollismeister/mauryp.html.*

7. Mark Brody, Readers' Comments, "Pinay Brides—Internet's Hottest Commodities" (2000), parts 1–4; available at *http://www.abs-cbnnews.com.*

8. Two important studies of correspondence marriages are: Cecilia Julag-Ay, *Correspondence Marriages between Filipinas and United States Men* (Ph.D. diss., University of California, Riverside, 1997); Raquel Z. Ordonez, "Mail-Order Brides: An Emerging Community," in *Filipino Americans: Transformation and Identity,* ed. Maria P. Root (Thousand Oaks, Calif.: Sage Publications, 1997), 121–42.

9. See Michelle J. Anderson, "A License to Abuse: The Impact of Conditional Status on Female Immigrants," *Yale Law Journal* 102, no. 6 (1993): 1401–30; Ko-Lin Chin, "Out-of-Town Brides: International Marriage and Wife Abuse among Chinese Immigrants," *Journal of Comparative Family*

Studies 25, no. 1 (Spring 1994):53–71; Eddy Meng, "Mail-Order Brides: Gilded Prostitution and the Legal Response," *Michigan Journal of Law Reform* 28 (1994): 197–248; Uma Narayan, "'Male-Order' Brides: Immigrant Women, Domestic Violence and Immigration Law," *Hypatia* 10, no. 1 (1995):104–19; Lisa Simons, "Mail Order Brides."

10. Uma Narayan, "'Male-Order' Brides."

11. Arjun Appadurai, *Modernity at Large: Cultural Dimensions of Globalization* (Minneapolis: University of Minnesota Press, 1996).

1: MAKING INTRODUCTIONS

1. Renee Tajima, "Lotus Blossoms Don't Bleed: Images of Asian Women," in *Making Waves: An Anthology of Writings by and about Asian American Women,* ed. Asian Women United of California (Boston: Beacon, 1989), 309. See also Yen Le Espiritu, *Asian American Women and Men: Labor, Laws, and Love* (Thousand Oaks, Calif.: 1997); and Gina Marchetti, *Romance and the Yellow Peril: Race, Sex and Discursive Strategies in Hollywood Fiction* (Berkeley: University of California Press, 1993).

2. Tajima, "Lotus Blossoms," 309. See also Ara Wilson, "American Catalogues of American Brides," in *Anthropology for the Nineties,* ed. Johnetta Cole (New York: Free Press, 1988), 114–25.

3. Mia Consalvo provides an insightful analysis of the dual images of mail-order brides in media representations of Timothy Blackwell's murder of Susana Blackwell and two of her friends in a Seattle courthouse. Mia Consalvo, "'Three Shot Dead in Courthouse': Examing News Coverage of Domestic Violence and Mail-Order Brides," *Women's Studies in Communication* 21, no.2 (1998): 188–211.

4. Wilson, "Catalogues," 122.

5. Venny Villapando, "The Business of Selling Mail-Order Brides," in *Making Waves,* ed. Asian Women United of California (Boston: Beacon Press, 1989), 326.

6. Rona Tamiko Halualani, "The Intersecting Hegemonic Discourses of an Asian Mail-Order Bride Catalog: Pilipina 'Oriental Butterfly' Dolls for Sale," *Women's Studies in Communication* 11, no. 1 (1995), 45.

7. Kathryn Robinson, "Of Mail Order Brides and 'Boys' Own' Tales: Representations of Asian-Australian Marriages," *Feminist Review* 52 (1996), 53; Roland B. Tolentino, "Bodies, Letters, Catalogs: Filipinas in Transnational Space," *Social Text* 48, vol. 14, no. 3 (fall 1996), 49.

8. Wilson, "Catalogues," 124.

9. Kathryn Robinson, "Marriage, Migration, Family Values, and the 'Global Ecumene,'" (paper presented at the Migration and the Globalising World Conference, Singapore, 2001), 3.

10. Elizabeth Holt, "Writing Filipina-Australian Bodies: The Discourse on Filipina Brides," *Philippine Sociological Review* 44 (1996): 58–78; Anna L. Tsing, *In the Realm of the Diamond Queen: Marginality in an Out-of-the-*

Way Place (Princeton, N. J.: Princeton University Press, 1993), 216; Wilson, "Catalogues"; Robinson, "Marriage, Migration."

11. There are few firsthand studies of correspondence marriages. Among the few are Glodava and Onizuka, *Mail-Order Brides*, and Philippine Women Centre of British Columbia, *Canada*, which focus on abuse in the United States and Canada, respectively. Julag-Ay, *Correspondence Marriages between Filipinas and United States Men*, and Ordonez, "Mail Order Brides," present more subtle and nuanced depictions of the experiences of Filipina correspondence brides. As this book was going to press, an excellent dissertation came to my attention: Lisa Anne Simons, *Marriage, Migration, and Markets: International Matchmaking and International Feminism* (Ph.D. diss., University of Denver, 2001).

12. Mao died in 1976. Economic reforms were announced in 1978 and began in the early 1980s.

13. See also Lisa Rofel, *Other Modernities: Gendered Yearnings in China after Socialism* (Berkeley: University of California Press, 1999).

14. Fiancée visas are not meant by the INS to be used in this way. Had she expressed any hesitation regarding her intent to marry in her INS interview at the U.S. Embassy in Guangzhou, her visa might have been denied. Many men I knew were critical of using the visa in this way.

15. Tsing, *Diamond Queen*, 216–17.

16. Ibid., 216.

17. Tattoos gained some popularity in the 1990s among Chinese youth in the southern coastal regions, but people in their thirties or older often negatively associate such body markings with criminals, prisoners, and members of gangs or secret societies. See Michael Dutton, *Streetlife China* (New York: Cambridge University Press, 1999), 181–90.

18. Dating clubs are very different from the agencies that are geared toward marriage and "lifetime partners." I met most women through the latter sort of club.

19. Many Chinese women and Filipinas expressed dislike or "fear" of men with dark skin. Some made "exceptions" for darker-skinned Asians, but most Chinese women I spoke to preferred Chinese men or white men, and most Filipinas said they preferred men with light skin.

20. Chaperones are common in the Philippines among young single women of all classes. Often more than one chaperone (a sibling or friend) goes on the date. I was told that chaperones are less common for women in their thirties, but still required if her family is middle or upper class.

21. Some Filipino-U.S. couples compromise by having a church ceremony in the Philippines in which the union is blessed by a priest and family and friends attend a reception, but not an official marriage. Some Chinese women preferred to marry before emigrating, but many were pragmatic about coming to the United States to see if they liked it before they married.

22. See Benito Vergara, "Betrayal, Class Fantasies, and the Filipino Nation in Daly City," and Tuula Heinonen, "Connecting Family Resilience and Cul-

ture: Recreation and Leisure among Filipino-Canadians," in *Philippine Socio-logical Review* 44 (1996): 79–100, 210–21, on the relative ease of life for middle-class Filipinos in the Philippines as opposed to life abroad without help-ers or maids.

23. Margaret Jolly and Lenore Manderson, "Introduction: Sites of Desire/Economies of Pleasure in Asia and the Pacific" in *Sites of Desire/Economies of Pleasure: Sexualities in Asia and the Pacific*, ed. M. Jolly and L. Manderson (Chicago: University of Chicago Press, 1997), 1–26.

24. Gregory M. Pflugfelder, *Cartographies of Desire: Male-Male Sexuality in Japanese Discourses, 1600–1950* (Berkeley: University of California Press, 1999), 1.

25. See for example, Joseph S. Alter, *Knowing Dil Das: Stories of a Hima-layan Hunter* (Philadelphia: University of Pennsylvania Press, 2000); James Clifford, "Introduction: Partial Truths," in *Writing Culture: Poetics and Poli-tics of Ethnography*, ed. James Clifford and George Marcus (Berkeley: Univer-sity of California Press, 1986); Jean-Paul Dumont, *The Headman and I* (Austin: University of Texas Press,1978); Paul Rabinow, *Reflections on Fieldwork in Morocco* (Berkeley: University of California Press, 1977); Renato Rosaldo, *Culture and Truth: The Remaking of Social Analysis* (Boston: Beacon Press, 1989); Gayatri Spivak, "Can the Subaltern Speak?" in *Marxism and the Inter-pretation of Culture*, ed. G. Nelson and L. Grossberg (Urbana: University of Illinois Press, 1988).

26. See, for example, Lila Abu-Lughod, "The Romance of Resistance: Trac-ing Transformations of Power through Bedouin Women," *American Ethnolo-gist* 17, no.1 (1990): 41–55, and *Writing Women's Worlds: Bedouin Stories* (Berkeley: University of California Press, 1993); Ruth Behar, *Translated Woman* (Boston: Beacon Press, 1993); Ruth Behar and Deborah A. Gordon, eds., *Women Writing Culture* (Berkeley: University of California Press, 1995); Judith Stacey, "Can There Be a Feminist Ethnography?" in *Women's Worlds: The Feminist Practice of Oral History*, ed. S. Gluck and D. Patai (New York: Routledge, 1990), 111–19; Marilyn Strathern, "An Awkward Relationship: The Case of Feminism and Anthropology," *Signs* 12, no. 2 (1987): 276–92; Ka-mala Visweswaran, *Fictions of Feminist Ethnography* (Minneapolis: Univer-sity of Minnesota Press, 1994).

27. Chandra T. Mohanty, "Under Western Eyes: Feminist Scholarship and Colonial Discourses," in *Third World Women and the Politics of Feminism*, ed. C. T. Mohanty, A. Russo, and L. Torres (Bloomington: Indiana University Press, 1991), 51–80; Michelle Rosaldo, "The Use and Abuse of Anthropology: Reflections on Feminism and Cross-Cultural Understanding," *Signs* 5, no. 3 (1980): 389–417.

28. For excellent critiques of this position in relation to prostitution and sex-worker activism, see Kamala Kempadoo and Jo Doezema, eds., *Global Sex Workers: Rights, Resistance, Redefinition* (New York: Routledge,1998); S. Car-ole Vance, "Innocence and Experience: Narratives of Trafficking in the World of Human Rights" (paper presented at the American Ethnological Society

Meeting, Montreal, Canada, 2001); Heather Montgomery, "Children, Prostitution, and Identity," in Kempadoo and Deozema, eds., *Global Sex Workers*, 139–50.

29. Mohanty, "Under Western Eyes."

30. See Ko-lin Chin, "Out-of-Town Brides"; Consalvo, "Three Shot Dead"; Ninotchka Rosca, "The Philippines' Shameful Export (Emigrant Women)," *The Nation* 260 (April 17, 1995) 15: 522–26; Michael Small and Dirk Mathison, "For Men Who Want an Old-fashioned Girl, the Latest Wedding March Is Here Comes the Asian Mail-Order Bride," *People Weekly* (September 16, 1985), 127–29.

31. For an excellent illustration of different women's notions of liberation, see Maria Lugones and Elizabeth Spelman, "Have We Got a Theory for You!" *Women's Studies International Forum* 6, no.6 (1983):573–81.

32. Michel Foucault, *The History of Sexuality, Volume 1: An Introduction*, (New York: Random House, 1978); and *Discipline and Punish: The Birth of the Prison* (New York: Vintage Books, 1979). See also my discussion in *Maid to Order in Hong Kong: Stories of Filipina Workers* (Ithaca, N. Y.: Cornell University Press, 1997), 11–12.

33. Judith Butler, *The Psychic Life of Power: Theories of Subjection* (Stanford, Calif.: Stanford University Press, 1997), 13.

2: ETHNOGRAPHY IN IMAGINED VIRTUAL COMMUNITIES

1. Benedict Anderson, *Imagined Communities: Reflections on the Origin and Spread of Nationalism* (New York: Verso Press, 1983).

2. Appadurai, *Modernity at Large*, 3, 4, 8.

3. Ibid., 4.

4. Aihwa Ong, *Flexible Citizenship: The Cultural Logics of Transnationality* (Durham, N.C.: Duke University Press), 11.

5. Appadurai, *Modernity at Large*, 48.

6. See, for example, Radhika Gajjala, *The SAWnet Refusal: An Interrupted Ethnography* (Ph.D. diss., University of Pittsburgh, 1998); Gajjala, "Cyborg Diaspora and Virtual Imagined Community: Study in SAWnet," *Cybersociology: Magazine for Social-Scientific Researchers of Cyberspace* 6 (1999); available at *http://www.cybersociology.com;* David Jacobson, "Contexts and Cues in Cyberspace: The Pragmatics of Naming in Text-Based Virtual Realities," *Journal of Anthropological Research* 52 (1996): 461–79; David Jacobson, "Doing Research in Cyberspace," *Field Methods* 11, no. 2 (1999):127–45, available at *http://www.unet.brandeis.edu/~jacobson/Doing_Research.html;* David Jacobson, "Impression Formation in Cyberspace: Online Expectations and Offline Experiences in Text-Based Virtual Communities," *Journal of Computer-Mediated Communication* 5, no. 1 (September 1999), available at *http://www .ascusc.org/jcmc/vol5/issue1/jacobson.html#Virtual Communities;* Eriberto Lozada, "What It Means to Be Hakka in Cyberspace: Diasporic Identity on the Internet" (paper presented at the Third Conference on Hakkaology, Singapore,

November 1996), available at *http://blue.butler.edu/~eriberto/papers/cyber-hak/cyberhak1/htm*; Daniel Miller and Don Slater, *The Internet: An Ethnographic Approach* (New York: Berg, 2000); Howard Rheingold, "A Slice of Life in My Virtual Community," Electronic Frontier Foundation Archives, 1992, available at *http://www.eff.org/pub/Net_culture/virtual_community/slice_of_life.article*; Howard Rheingold, *Virtual Reality* (New York: Simon and Schuster, 1992).

7. Compare Julie M. Albright and Tom Coran, "Online Love: Sex, Gender and Relationships in Cyberspace," Electronic Frontier Foundation Archives, 2001; available at *http://www.eff.org/pub/Net_culture/Virtual_community/online_love.article*.

8. Jacobson, "Doing Research in Cyberspace."

9. I take a conservative approach to Internet citations. I quote freely from public Internet spaces that require no password, but use pseudonyms in some cases. I acquired permission to quote materials from web sites that require passwords or membership, including private messages that were sent to me. In all such cases, I use pseudonyms for individual and list names.

10. Many Asian women in the United States used computer-mediated means to communicate with families back home. Among women with families in China, Internet "phone calls" were very popular in 2000, and the rates far lower than long-distance telephone calls.

11. Electronic computer translators were also a popular topic among men who communicated with Chinese women. Several men reported that they or their fiancées used these to facilitate conversations and overcome communication barriers.

12. Miller and Slater, *The Internet*, define "flaming" as "aggressive comments hurled at a member of a newsgroup," and flame wars as "verbal battles within any Internet social setting" (205).

13. See Albright and Coran, "Online Love"; David Crystal, *Language and the Internet* (New York: Cambridge University Press, 2001), 35–38.

14. Several members defended me, saying it was not so different than passing on the name of a good plumber, but the discussion resulted in flaming. Ultimately I was allowed to join the list.

15. Reader reviews and evaluations of books on Amazon.com illustrate this point.

16. On Filipino-Australian marriages, see Desmond Cahill, *Intermarriages in International Contexts: A Study of Filipina Women Married to Australian, Japanese, and Swiss Men* (Quezon City: Scalabini Research Center, 1990); F. M. Cooke, *Australian-Filipino Marriages in the 1980s* (Queensland, Australia: Griffith University Press, 1986); Holt, "Writing Filipina-Australian Bodies"; Robinson, "Of Mail-Order Brides and 'Boys' Own' Tales." On Filipinas who have married men from rural Japan, see Nicola Piper, "International Marriage in Japan: 'Race' and 'Gender' Perspectives," *Gender, Place and Culture* 4, no. 3 (1997): 321–38; T. Sato, *Mura to Kokusai Kekkon* (Tokyo: Nihon Hyoronsha, 1989); Nobue Suzuki, "Between Two Shores: Transnational Proj-

ects and Filipina Wives in/from Japan," *Women's Studies International Forum* 23, no. 4 (2000): 431–44; Nobue Suzuki, "Women Imagined, Women Imaging: Re/presentations of Filipinas in Japan since the 1980s," *U.S.-Japan Women's Journal* 19 (2000): 142–75. On Filipinas who have married men from northern and western Europe and North America, see "The Asian Bride Boom," *Asiaweek*, April 15, 1983, 36–38, 43–45; Cahill, *Intermarriages in International Contexts*; USDOJ-INS (United States Department of Justice–Immigration and Naturalization Service), "International Matchmaking Organizations: A Report to Congress," 1999, available at *http://www.ins.usdoj.gov/graphics/aboutins/repsstudies.Mobrept.htm.*

17. See Richard N. Côté, *Love by Mail: The International Guide to Personal Advertising* (Silver Springs, Md.: Enigma Books, 1992), and Robert Scholes, "The Mail Order Bride Industry and Its Impact on Immigration," appendix A of *International Matchmaking Organizations: A Report to Congress*, 1999; available at *http://www.ins.usdoj.gov/graphics/aboutins/repsstudies.Mobrept_full.pdf.*

18. Scholes, "Mail Order Bride Industry," notes that of the 202 introduction agencies he located in 1998, 70 percent of the women were from the Philippines and less than 1 percent were Chinese. Based on new agencies listing Chinese women, and on the fact that many urban Chinese women have access to the Internet and use free e-mail "pen pal clubs," this estimate is probably too low.

19. The moderator of one list of men involved with Filipinas directed me to a web site he described as "the worst" pen pal business on the Internet. He was appalled at how women were represented in highly sexualized and objectifying terms, and even more appalled to learn that the owner of the site was a Filipina who lived in the United States. Members of the list were loath to believe that women would choose to represent themselves in such terms. Several months later, the moderator banned a member because he discovered a link to "sex tours" on the man's private web page.

20. Scholes, "Mail Order Bride Industry," 2.

21. According to Jen, the manager of a Beijing introduction agency, some agencies charge up to 2,000 RMB per month. Many women thought Jen's agency was expensive (at 400 RMB per year) and preferred the Internet services that made free listings.

22. In the Philippines there is some ambivalence about local women who are seen with foreign men. Although some Filipinas fear they will be assumed to be prostitutes if they are seen with a white man, others thought they would be envied and admired. In China there is greater ambivalence. Chinese women reported more mixed or negative reactions: public hostility or rudeness when a Chinese woman is seen with a foreign partner. Peers and family might consider a Chinese woman with a foreign partner fortunate, but often thought it was "too bad" he was not Chinese.

23. Surveys by the Commission on Filipinos Overseas entitled "Manner of Introduction of Filipinos and Foreign Spouses/Fiances" suggest that be-

tween 1989 and 1999 only three people who petitioned to emigrate to join their foreign partners said they had met through the Internet. In 2000, the number increased to 426 (5 percent). Between 1989 and 2000, 11,085 Filipinos (5.77 percent) reported "ads or pen pal clubs" as their manner of introduction. The highest percentage (38.3 percent) met through personal introductions; 27.6 percent through work, and 27.5 percent through a relative. See CFO, *Statistics* (2001), *http://cfo.gov.ph/*.

24. Exchange rates in 1999 and early 2000 were forty to forty-five pesos to one U.S. dollar.

25. By late 2000, some cafés, such as Starbucks (in the Friendship Store in Beijing), offered free Internet access. In summer 2000, one Internet café near Beijing University offered free use of the computers one morning a week for one hour as a promotion. By the summer of 2002, many of these Internet cafés had been closed because of a crackdown following fatalities due to a fire in an unlicensed Internet café.

26. My experience was strikingly different from Wai-ki Viki Li, *Seeking an Ideal Wife: Why Hong Kong Men Pursue Mainland Chinese Spouses* (master's thesis, Chinese University of Hong Kong, 2001).

27. It is difficult to say whether the women I met through the Internet, in Internet cafés, or through personal networks were "representative" of women who corresponded with U.S. men. They were strikingly different from the image of downtrodden, desperate "victims." This raises the possibility that the women I met were especially privileged or, as discussed in chapter 3, that where others have seen victimization and desperation, I have not. The women I knew best were Chinese women who responded to my e-mail communications and Filipinas and Chinese women whom I met through personal contacts. These women were "self-selected," as opposed to those who might be more singularly focused or desperate to meet foreign men. Although I met Chinese women only in urban areas, some came from rural backgrounds. Filipinas, by contrast, came from more diverse rural and urban settings and communicated by letters and/or by computer. Most Chinese and Filipina women had high school or college educations, and they spanned the range of lower-level clerical or white-collar jobs. A few had doctorate degrees, and some were factory or domestic workers. On the whole, Chinese women had higher levels of occupations than Filipinas. These characteristics are in keeping with the wives, fiancées, and girlfriends of the hundreds of men I encountered in Internet groups, and also with the listings of various online and printed agencies.

28. According to the 2001 CFO Survey, the average age of Filipinas with foreign spouses or fiancés is twenty-nine.

29. Even in large cities like Beijing, where foreigners were quite common by the late 1990s, they are often approached by curious and friendly Chinese people. On numerous occasions, if alone in a restaurant or at an intersection on my bicycle, people would strike up a conversation to ask where I was from or to practice English.

30. See, for example, Julag-Ay, *Correspondence Marriages;* and Tolentino, "Bodies, Letters, Catalogs."

31. The men I met through these Internet groups seemed to fit the overall sociological and demographic profile found in other studies (see chapter 3). Although the men I met through UFG did (at first) self-select from among those who belonged to FAF and were willing to communicate with me, their views were not much different from other men I met in person or on other lists. Comparing UFG communications with archived messages from the other private lists reflects little difference in content or tone of communications. Moreover, although individuals can and do "invent" identities and role-play on the Internet, it would be difficult to maintain such a charade for two or three years, just as it is difficult to do in repeated and prolonged face-to-face fieldwork encounters. See, for example, Michael Lewis, "Faking It: The Internet Revolution Has Nothing to Do with the Nasdaq," *New York Times Magazine*, July 15, 2001, available at *http://www.nytimes.com/2001/07/15/magazine/15INTERNET.html;* and Michael Lewis, "Jonathan Lebed: Stock Manipulator, S.E.C. Nemesis—and 15," *New York Times Magazine*, February 25, 2001, available at *http://www.nytimes.com/2001/02/25/magazine/25STOCK-TRADER.html.* On all the lists, men policed and criticized one another openly. Some moderators explicitly defined "off topics" and banned flamers or those who presented blatantly racist views or what were considered sexual perversions. Although sometimes criticized, sexist statements, disparaging remarks about western women, and discussions of the advantages of Asian spouses were openly voiced. My presence did not appear to promote self-censorship or political correctness.

32. Despite the emphasis of these lists on issues facing U.S.-Asian couples (mainly Asian women and U.S. men), some lists had a few male members who were not American (including Australians, British, and Europeans) and a few men who were of Filipino or Chinese descent.

33. See, for example, Gerald D. Berreman, *Hindus of the Himalayas* (Berkeley: University of California Press, 1972); Jean Briggs, *Never in Anger: Portrait of an Eskimo Family* (Cambridge, Mass.: Harvard University Press, 1970); Paul Rabinow, *Reflections on Fieldwork in Morocco* (Berkeley: University of California Press, 1977).

34. See Stacey, "Can There Be a Feminist Ethnography?"; and Visweswaran, *Fictions of Feminist Ethnography.*

35. ABS-CBN News, "Pinay Brides—Internet's Hottest Commodities," pt. 1, p. 1.

36. Ordonez, "Mail-Order Brides," points out that the 1990 legislation to "ban personal advertising and to penalize local recruiters" has done little to stop the "supply of Filipino women" because women are easily recruited among OCWs and through other means (137).

37. ABS-CBN News, "Pinay Brides," pt. 4, p. 3.

38. Anderson, *Imagined Communities.*

39. ABS-CBN News, "Pinay Brides," user comments, p. 3; June 10, 2000. Hereafter cited in the text by date.

40. See Vergara, "Betrayal, Class Fantasies, and the Filipino Nation in Daly City," on how "departure" may be viewed as "betrayal of the nation."

41. See Filomeno V. Aguilar, Jr., "The Dialectics of Transnational Shame and National Identity," *Philippine Sociological Review* 44 (1996):101–36, on how commodification of Filipino labor is related to nationalism and shame.

42. See Lata Mani, "Contentious Traditions: The Debate on Sati in Colonial India," *Cultural Critique* (Fall 1987): 119–56; Mohanty, "Under Western Eyes"; Partha Chatterjee, *The Nation and Its Fragments: Colonial and Postcolonial Histories* (Princeton, N.J.: Princeton University Press, 1993).

3: FEMINISM AND MYTHS OF "MAIL-ORDER" MARRIAGES

1. Some anthropologists argued that gender inequality was linked to women's association with the domestic sphere and men's with the public sphere (see Michelle Rosaldo, "Woman, Culture, and Society: A Theoretical Overview," in *Woman, Culture, and Society*, ed. Michelle Rosaldo and Louise Lamphere [Stanford, Ca.: Stanford University Press, 1974] , 17–42), or with women's association with nature and men's with culture (see Sherry Ortner, "Is Female to Male as Nature Is to Culture?" in Rosaldo and Lamphere, *Woman, Culture, and Society*, 67–88). Others were influenced by Engels's view that gender inequality increased with the development of private property and the rise of complex stratified societies and states. See Gerda Lerner, *The Creation of Patriarchy* (New York: Oxford University Press, 1986); Naomi Quinn, "Anthropological Studies on Women's Status," *Annual Review of Anthropology* 6 (1977):181–225; Karen Sacks, "Engels Revisited: Women, the Organization of Production, and Private Property," in Rosaldo and Lamphere, *Woman, Culture, and Society*, 207–22; Irene Silverblatt, "Women in States," *Annual Review of Anthropology* 17 (1988): 427–60. Regardless of the particular perspective, second-wave feminism often seemed to support the idea of a "universal woman" or a sisterhood that shared common interests in achieving gender equality and women's liberation; see Henrietta Moore, *Feminism and Anthropology* (Minneapolis: University of Minnesota Press, 1988).

2. See Rosaldo, "The Use and Abuse of Anthropology"; Sherry Ortner, "Introduction: Accounting for Sexual Meanings," in *Sexual Meanings*, ed. S. Ortner and H. Whitehead (Cambridge: Cambridge University Press, 1981) , 1–27; Moore, *Feminism and Anthropology*; Eleanor B. Leacock, ed., *Myths of Male Dominance: Collected Articles on Women Cross-Culturally* (New York: Monthly Review Press, 1981); Marilyn Strathern, "No Nature, No Culture: The Hagen Case," in *Nature, Culture and Gender*, ed. Carol MacCormack and Marilyn Strathern (New York: Cambridge University Press, 1980), 174–222.

3. Kamala Kempadoo, "Slavery or Work? Reconceptualizing Third World Prostitution," *Positions* 7, no. 1 (1999): 234.

4. Abu-Lughod, *Writing Women's Worlds.*

5. See Barry, *Female Sexual Slavery,* and "Sexual Exploitation Violates Human Rights," Coalition Against Trafficking in Women (fall 1992), available at *http://www.uri.edu/artsci/wms/hughes/catw/barry.htm;* Glodava and Onizuka, *Mail-Order Brides,* hereafter cited in the text; and Tolentino, "Bodies, Letters, Catalogs."

6. See Barry, "Sexual Exploitation"; CAST (Coalition to Abolish Slavery and Trafficking), "What Is Trafficking?" (2001), available at *http://www.trafficked-women.org/trafficked.html;* CATW (Coalition Against Trafficking in Women-International), "Philosophy" (2001), available at *http://www.catwinternational.org/philos.htm;* Philippine Women Centre of British Columbia, *Canada.* Some groups are well aware of the difficulty in building consensus on the definition of "trafficking" (see, for example, Stop-traffic, "UN Trafficking Protocol: Lost Opportunity to Protect the Rights of Trafficked Persons" (2000), available at http://www.stop-traffic.org.news.html.

7. Philippine Women Centre of British Columbia, *Canada,* 1.

8. Gayle Rubin, "The Traffic in Women: Notes on the 'Political Economy' of Sex," in *Toward an Anthropology of Women,* ed. Rayna R. Reiter (New York: Monthly Review Press, 1974), 157–210.

9. Rosaldo, "Woman, Culture, and Society," and "Use and Abuse."

10. Esther Ngan-Ling Chow, "Family, Economy, and the State: A Legacy of Struggle for Chinese American Women," in *Origins and Destinies: Immigration, Race, and Ethnicity in America,* ed. Silvia Pedraza and Ruben G. Rumbaut (Boston: Wadsworth Publishing, 1996), 110–24; Mohanty, "Under Western Eyes."

11. Lugones and Spelman, "Have We Got a Theory for You!"

12. See Abu-Lughod, *Writing Women's Worlds;* and Leila Ahmed, "Western Ethnocentrism and Perceptions of the Harem," *Feminist Studies* 8, no. 3 (1982): 521–34.

13. See for example, Eleanor Smith Bowen [Laura Bohannan], *Return to Laughter* (New York: Doubleday, 1954); Elizabeth Warnock Fernea, *Guests of the Sheik: An Ethnography of an Iraqi Village* (Garden City, N.Y.: Doubleday Books, 1965); Martin King Whyte and William L. Parish, *Urban Life in Contemporary China* (Chicago: University of Chicago Press, 1984).

14. Robinson, "Marriage Migration, Family Values, and the 'Global Ecumene.'"

15. See Susan Faludi, *Backlash: The Undeclared War against American Women* (New York: Doubleday, Anchor Books, 1992), and *Stiffed: The Betrayal of the American Man* (New York: William Morrow and Company, 1999).

16. See Gary Clark, *Your Bride Is in the Mail* (Las Vegas, Nev.: Words that Work Publications, 1998); and Wanwadee Larsen, *Confessions of a Mail Order Bride: American Life through Thai Eyes* (Far Hills, N.J.: New Horizon Press, 1989). Julag-Ay, "Correspondence Marriages," makes a very noteworthy contribution to this literature.

17. USDOJ-INS, "International Matchmaking Organizations."

18. The Philippine Women Centre (PWC) provides an even broader definition. They use "mail-order bride" to refer to a "formal transaction between a man and a woman from different countries, usually brokered by an agent, who is part of the mail-order bride industry, via catalogues or the Internet. The term is also applied to situations where men go to the Philippines with the intention of finding a wife. The PWC also uses the term to encompass Filipino women who have been introduced to Canadian husbands through informal networks of family and friends" (1). PWC also includes Filipinas who meet men through computer dating services in Canada, or who marry their employers (49).

19. Julag-Ay, "Correspondence Marriages," 63, 32 n.7. Like Julag-Ay, I rely on more value-neutral terms, such as "correspondence marriage" or "pen pals," except when I refer to peoples' use of the term or to the discourse about "mail-order brides."

20. See also Philippine Women Centre, *Canada*. Hereafter cited in the text as PWC.

21. See Barry, "Sexual Exploitation"; Jane Margold, "Forced Migration or Mobility Strategy? Assessing Transnational Marriages amidst the Global Marketing of Southeast Asian Brides," paper abstracts, Association for Asian Studies Meeting, March 22–25, 2001; Philippine Women Centre, *Canada*; Tolentino, "Bodies, Letters, Catalogs"; USDOJ-INS, "International Matchmaking Organizations."

22. See Anne McClintock, "Sex Workers and Sex Work: Introduction," *Social Text* 37 (winter 1993): 1–10.

23. Robinson, "Marriage Migration," 2.

24. Villapando, "The Business of Selling Mail-Order Brides"; Frances E. Mascia-Lees and Nancy Johnson Black, *Gender and Anthropology* (Prospect Heights, Ill.: Waveland Press, 2000), 87.

25. Julag-Ay, "Correspondence Marriages," 50–55; Constable, *Maid to Order in Hong Kong*, 59–82; see also Wilson, "Catalogues."

26. Robinson, "Marriage Migration," 1.

27. Patricia Hill Collins, *Black Feminist Thought: Knowledge, Consciousness, and the Politics of Empowerment* (New York: Routledge, 1990), 67.

28. The historical basis of such stereotypes of Asian/American women is discussed in chapter 7. See also Espiritu, *Asian American Women and Men*, 93–98; Laura Hyun Yi Kang, "Si(gh)ting Asian/American Women as Transnational Labor," *Positions* 5, no. 2 (1997): 403–37; Villapando, "The Business of Selling Mail-Order Brides."

29. Glodava and Onizuka, *Mail-Order Brides*, 25–26; see also Villapando, "The Business of Selling Mail-Order Brides," 319, 323; Scholes, "The Mail Order Bride Industry."

30. Scholes, "The Mail Order Bride Industry," mistakenly attributes Glodava and Onizuka's criticism to Jedlicka. He writes, "Although Jedlicka states in his conclusions that his research shows that the men who choose the mail-order methods for mate selection appear '. . . above average . . . certainly in their

communication skills,' and 'exceptional in the sense that they are trying cross cultural marriage to improve their chances for loving and enduring relationships,' he cautions that such conclusions are thin at best and such interpretations from his data are not warranted. His experience and the observation of others show that, contrary to the responses of his questionnaires, those who have used the mail-order route have control in mind more than a loving enduring relationship" (4). Glodava and Onizuka consider Jedlicka's conclusions "thin" and claim that men want control rather than enduring relationships.

31. The CFO survey (2001) for 1989–2000 found that Filipinos and their foreign partners of all nationalities average a nine-year age difference. The overall average age of Filipinos was twenty-nine and of foreigners, thirty-eight. The two extremes of the age distribution reveal a gendered imbalance: women made up almost 81 percent of those aged fifteen to twenty-four, and men made up over 88 percent of those fifty and over. The PWC study of Canadian-Filipino marriages found 3 percent with over a twenty-year age difference, 49 percent with ten to twenty years, and 48 percent with less than ten years difference (41).

32. An "average" between twenty and fifty years is unclear.

33. According to the CFO 2001 survey, from 1995 to 2000, the percentage of foreign partners with "no formal education" is .37 and for Filipinos .3; foreigners with only elementary schooling is 2.3 and for Filipinos 5.6. The percentage with high school or vocational school is closely matched, with 40.7 foreigners and 44.4 Filipinos, those with college education 20.9 for foreigners and 19.2 for Filipinos; college or university graduates is 29.5 and for Filipinos 30.5. This includes spouses of all nationalities and does not reveal inequalities of education in particular cases, but it still suggests less discrepancy in education than critics may assume.

34. Educational levels of Filipinas in Canada may be higher than in the United States because of Canadian immigration requirements for women who enter under the Live-In Caregiver Program, many of whom are included in the PWC study.

35. Espiritu, *Asian American Women and Men*, 93.

36. See, for example, Gary Clark, *Your Bride Is in the Mail;* Gary Clark, "Exactly What is a Mail-Order Bride?" (2001), available at *http://pw1.netcom .com/~wtwpubs/whatis.htm;* and "Some Misconceptions and Outright Lies about So-called 'Mail Order Brides'" (2001), available at *http://www.upbeat .com/wtwpubs/miscon.htm.*

37. Cited in Robinson, "Marriage Migration," 3.

38. See Soo-Young Chin, *Doing What Had to Be Done: The Life Narrative of Dora Yum Kim* (Philadelphia: Temple University Press, 1999); Ko-Lin Chin, "Out-of-Town Brides"; Constance D. Clark, "Foreign Marriage, 'Tradition,' and the Politics of Border Crossings," in *China Urban: Ethnographies of Contemporary Culture,* ed. Nancy Chen et al. (Durham, N.C.: Duke University Press, 2001), 104–22; Narayan, "'Male-Order' Brides," 104–19; Aihwa Ong,

"Women Out of China: Traveling Tales and Traveling Theories in Postcolonial Feminism," in *Women Writing Culture,* ed. Ruth Behar and Deborah A. Gordon, 350–72 (Berkeley: University of California Press, 1995); Louisa Schein, "Forged Transnationality and Oppositional Cosmopolitanism," in *Transnationalism from Below,* ed. Michael Peter Smith and Luis Eduardo Guarnizo (New Brunswick, N.J.: Transaction Publishers, 1998), 291–313. Studies of cross-national relationships outside of the United States include: on South Asia, Veena Das, "National Honor and Practical Kinship: Unwanted Women and Children," in *Conceiving the New World Order,* ed. Faye Ginsburg and Rayna Rapp, 212–33 (Berkeley: University of California Press, 1995); on relationships between Japanese men and Filipinas, see Cahill, *Intermarriages in International Contexts;* Piper, "International Marriage in Japan"; Suzuki, "Between Two Shores," and "Women Imagined, Women Imaging." On Chinese Korean women and South Korean men, see Caren Freeman, "What's Love Got to Do with It? Transnational Marriages between China and Korea" (paper presented at the Association for Asian Studies Meeting, March 22–25, 2001, Chicago, Ill.). On mainland Chinese women and overseas Chinese men, see Constance Clark, "Foreign Marriage"; Shu-mei Shih, "Gender and the Geopolitics of Desire: The Seduction of Mainland Women in Taiwan and Hong Kong Media," in *Spaces of Their Own,* ed. Mayfair Mei-hui Yang, 278–307 (Minneapolis: University of Minnesota Press, 1999).

39. Julag-Ay, "Correspondence Marriages," 34.

40. See also Soo-Young Chin, *Doing What Had to Be Done;* Espiritu, *Asian American Women and Men;* Villapando, "The Business of Selling Mail-Order Brides."

41. Espiritu, *Asian American Women and Men,* 98–106; Lisa Lowe, *Immigrant Acts: On Asian American Cultural Politics* (Durham, N.C.: Duke University Press, 1996).

42. Edward Said, *Orientalism* (New York: Vintage Books, 1979); Longxi Zhang, "The Myth of the Other: China in the Eyes of the West," *Critical Inquiry* 15 (autumn 1989): 108–31; Ong, *Flexible Citizenship.*

43. Kang, "Si(gh)ting Asian/American Women," 424.

44. See Constable, *Maid to Order;* Kempadoo, "Slavery or Work?"; Ong, "Women Out of China."

45. Jullie Yap Daza, *Etiquette for Mistresses . . . and What Wives Can Learn from Them* (Philippines: J. Y. Daza, 1994), 119–20. Men expressed concern about what they called the "great Filipina sulk," or an American desire to "talk things out" coming into conflict with the Filipino "silent treatment." Men expressed a desire to "do anything" if their partners would only stop the treatment.

46. Larsen, *Confessions of a Mail Order Bride,* 103–4.

47. Robert Elegant, *Pacific Destiny* (New York: Crown Publishers, 1990), 41.

48. Margery Wolf, *Women and the Family in Rural Taiwan* (Stanford, Ca.:

Stanford University Press, 1972). See Gloria G. Raheja and Ann G. Gold, *Listen to the Heron's Words: Reimagining Gender and Kinship in North India* (Berkeley: University of California Press, 1994), for an excellent study of the way in which women in North India contest dominant male notions of family and gender.

49. Abu-Lughod, *Writing Women's Worlds*, and "Writing against Culture," in *Recapturing Anthropology*, ed. Richard Fox (Santa Fe, N.M.: School of American Research Press, 1991), 137–62.

50. See Rofel, *Other Modernities*; and Mayfair Mei-hui Yang, ed., *Spaces of Their Own: Women's Public Sphere in Transnational China* (Minneapolis, Minn.: University of Minnesota Press, 1999). Chinese women's role in the public work force was accompanied by major improvements to their lives, including laws prohibiting polygyny, concubinage, and child marriage, allowing divorce, and providing access to family planning and greater access to health care. See Norma Diamond, "Building Socialism with Chinese Characteristics," *Women and International Development* 4 (1995): 147–72; and "Collectivization, Kinship, and the Status of Women in Rural China," *Bulletin of Concerned Asian Scholars* 7, no. 1 (1975): 25–32; Christina Gilmartin, "Gender, Politics, and Patriarchy in China: The Experiences of Early Women Communists, 1920–27," in *Promissory Notes: Women in the Transition to Socialism*, ed. Sonia Kruks, Rayna Rapp, and Marilyn Young (New York: Monthly Review Press, 1989), 82–105, and *Engendering the Chinese Revolution: Radical Women, Communist Politics, and Mass Movements in the 1920s* (Berkeley: University of California Press, 1995); Kay Ann Johnson, *Women, the Family, and Peasant Revolution in China* (Chicago: University of Chicago Press, 1983); Judith Stacey, *Patriarchy and Socialist Revolution in China* (Berkeley: University of California Press, 1983).

51. Compare with Suzuki, "Between Two Shores," and "Women Imagined, Women Imaging."

52. Mohanty, "Under Western Eyes," 53, 51.

53. Hollis, "Us Versus Maury Povich."

54. Consalvo, "Three Shot Dead in Courthouse"; Julag-Ay, "Correspondence Marriages," 1–2.

55. By contrast, the case studies presented in the PWC report attempt to show that women are strong, active, and resistant. The women in the PWC study do not appear simply as victims, but the research is nonetheless aimed at demonstrating the difficulties women face.

56. Small and Matheson, "For Men Who Want an Old-fashioned Girl."

57. See, for example, Kang, "Si(gh)ting Asian/American Women"; Kempadoo, "Slavery or Work?"; Eliza Noh, "'Amazing Grace, Come Sit on My Face': Or Christian Ecumenical Representations of the Asian Sex Tour Industry," *Positions* 5, no. 2 (1997): 439–65.

58. See Erik Cohen, "Lovelorn Farangs: The Correspondence between Foreign Men and Thai Girls," *Anthropological Quarterly* 59, no. 3 (1986): 115–

28; Montgomery, "Children, Prostitution, and Identity"; and McClintock, "Sex Workers."

59. Kempadoo, "Slavery or Work," 234; hereafter cited in the text.

4: FAIRY TALES, FAMILY VALUES, AND THE GLOBAL POLITICS OF ROMANCE

1. Tsing, *In the Realm of the Diamond Queen,* 216–17; Wilson, "Catalogues"; Villapando, "The Business of Selling Mail-Order Brides."

2. For example, Ordonez, "Mail-Order Brides"; and Julag-Ay, "Correspondence Marriages."

3. Tolentino, "Bodies, Letters, Catalogs," states that the regime of the "mail-order bride" business prevented him from "working ethnographically with these women," and that despite "a general knowledge of the existence and operations of mail-order brides, the network is poised to conceal this aspect of the women's pasts, thus making ethnography much more difficult to undertake" (51).

4. Lowe, *Immigrant Acts,* 4.

5. See Judith Stacey, *In the Name of the Family: Rethinking Family Values in the Postmodern Age* (Boston: Beacon Press, 1996), and "Dada-ism in the 1990s: Getting Past Baby Talk about Fatherlessness," in *Lost Fathers: The Politics of Fatherlessness in America,* ed. Cynthia R. Daniels, 51–83 (New York: St. Martin's Press, 1998).

6. See David Popenoe, "Life without Father," in *Lost Fathers: The Politics of Fatherlessness in America,* ed. Cynthia R. Daniels, 33–50 (New York: St. Martin's Press, 1998); Robert L. Griswold, "The History and Politics of Fatherlessness," in Daniels, ed., *Lost Fathers: The Politics of Fatherlessness in America,* 11–32.

7. Mohanty, "Under Western Eyes."

8. On romanticizing resistance, see Abu-Lughod, "The Romance of Resistance"; Constable, *Maid to Order in Hong Kong;* and Sherry Ortner, "Resistance and the Problem of Ethnographic Refusal," *Comparative Studies of Society and History* 34, no. 1 (1995): 173–93. For depictions of women as calculating hyperagents, see Gary Clark, *Your Bride Is in the Mail;* and Clive Halliday, "Filipino Girlfriends and Wives," 1999, available at *http://www.mancunian.com.* On stereotypes of Asian women, see Tajima, "Lotus Blossoms."

9. Legal permanent residents (LPRs) can petition to allow a spouse into the United States, but cannot "bring in their fiancé(e)s" as can U.S. citizens. See USDOJ-INS, "International Matchmaking Organizations."

10. Scholes, "The Mail Order Bride Industry."

11. Lowe, *Immigrant Acts,* 8; see also Filomeno V. Aguilar, Jr., ed., "Filipinos as Transnational Migrants," *Philippine Sociological Review* 44 (1996):4–227; and F. V. Aguilar, "The Dialectics of Transnational Shame"; Yen Le Espi-

ritu, *Filipino American Lives* (Philadelphia: Temple University Press, 1995); Vicente L. Rafael, "White Love: Surveillance and Nationalist Resistance in the U.S. Colonization of the Philippines," in *Cultures of United States Imperialism*, ed. Amy Kaplan and Donald Pease (Durham, N.C.: Duke University Press, 1993), 185–218; Ronald Takaki, *Strangers from a Different Shore: A History of Asian Americans*, rev. ed. (New York: Little, Brown and Co., 1998).

12. Fenella Cannell, "The Power of Appearances: Beauty, Mimicry and Transformation in Bico," in *Discrepant Histories: Translocal Essays on Filipino Cultures*, ed. Vicente L. Rafael (Philadelphia: Temple University Press, 1995), 225.

13. See Wilson, "Catalogues."

14. Filipina Brides (1999), available at *http://www.FilipinaBrides.com*; Ladies of the Philippines (1999), available at *http://www.ladiesofthephilippines* .com/main.html; Love Match International (2000), available at *http://dcg.on* .ca/lovematch/intro.html.

15. Cooke, *Australian-Filipino Marriages in the 1980s*; Holt, "Writing Filipina-Australian Bodies"; Robinson, "Of Mail-Order Brides and 'Boys' Own' Tales"; R. Whitta, *Courtships by Correspondence: Filipina Australian Arranged Marriages* (MSPD thesis, University of Queensland, 1988).

16. See F. V. Aguilar, "The Dialectics of Transnational Shame"; Cynthia Enloe, *Bananas, Beaches, and Bases: Making Sense of International Politics* (Berkeley: University of California Press, 1990), and *The Morning After: Sexual Politics at the End of the Cold War* (Berkeley: University of California Press, 1993).

17. Glodava and Onizuka, *Mail-Order Brides*; Wilson, "Catalogues." Scholes, "The Mail Order Bride Industry," distinguishes between two kinds of services that "an American man seeking a foreign bride can avail himself of" (1): first, the "'Mail-order bride' industry" or "international correspondence service," where women are not charged for the service and men pay from two to five dollars for a mailing address; second, "email 'pen pal' clubs," such as one-and-only.com, friendfinder.com, match.com, and kiss.com, which are "generally free of charge" (1). I found, in contrast, that kiss.com does not charge women to be listed, but does charge a "membership fee" to men and women to gain access to addresses or e-mail information.

18. See, for example, Halualani, "The Intersecting Hegemonic Discourses"; Holt, "Writing Filipina-Australian Bodies"; Tolentino, "Bodies, Letters, Catalogs"; Villapando, "The Business of Selling Mail-Order Brides."

19. Tolentino, "Bodies, Letters, Catalogs," 51.

20. Wilson, "Catalogues," 120–21. Ultimately, Wilson's argument is that these innocent images of Asian women are prefigured by the viewer/reader's orientalist fantasies, which render them erotic nonetheless (121–22).

21. China Bride, "Why Choose Women from Asia?" (2000); available at *http://www.chinabride.com/gen/whyasia.html* and *http://www.chinabride* .com/gen/whyhoa.html.

22. See Cathy Lynn Preston, "'Cinderella' as a Dirty Joke: Gender, Multivocality, and the Polysemic Text," *Western Folklore* 53 (June 1994): 27–49; and Jane Yolen, "America's Cinderella," in *Cinderella: A Casebook,* ed. Alan Dundes (New York: Wildman Press, 1982) , 294–306.

23. Wilson, "Catalogues," 117.

24. Tsing, *In the Realm of the Diamond Queen,* 216.

25. These images evoke what Mikhail Bakhtin, *The Dialogic Imagination: Four Essays* (Austin: University of Texas Press, 1981), calls the "classical" body—the properly clothed or adorned upper body—as opposed to the "grotesque" or material body, which refers explicitly to sex and other "lower body processes."

26. Preston, "'Cinderella' as a Dirty Joke," 29–30.

27. Tolentino, "Bodies, Letters, Catalogs," 68.

28. Wilson, "Catalogues," 121.

29. World Class Service (1998); available at *http://www.filipina.com.*

30. Love Match International (2000); available at *http://dcg.on.ca/love match/intro.html.*

31. Tolentino, "Bodies, Letters, Catalogs," 72.

32. See Halliday, "Filipino Girlfriends and Wives" (1999), available at *http://www.mancunian.com.*

33. Robinson, "Marriage Migration, Family Values, and the 'Global Ecumene,'" 5; Narayan, "'Male-Order' Brides."

34. Filipina Penpal (1999); available at *http://www.filipinapenpal.com/About%20this%20Site.htm.*

35. Robert (October 29, 1999); available at *http://network54.com/Hide/Forum/message?forumid = 30510&messageid = 94123764.*

36. See Clifford, "Introduction."

37. See Constable, *Maid to Order,* 100, 168.

38. USDOS (United States Department of State) Bureau of Consular Affairs, "Tips for U.S. Visas: Fiancé(e)s" (1999); available at *http://travel.state.gov/visa;fiancee.html.*

39. Processing time varies depending on the U.S. INS Service Center at which the citizen is required to file his/her petition and the country where the marriage takes place or from which the fiancé(e) comes. A spousal visa generally takes six to twelve months to process, but for many couples who marry in the Philippines it takes longer. Part of the reason the I-130 takes longer is that it includes application for permanent residency, whereas the fiancé(e) applies for permanent residency (adjustment of status) once in the United States. Foreign spouses who have been married for less than two years when they enter the United States, like those who enter on a fiancé(e) visa, are given two years of *conditional* permanent resident status (see chapter 7).

40. The I-129F form requires that the petitioner submit for him/herself and for the prospective spouse evidence of citizenship, a biographical data sheet, a color photograph of the fiancé(e), divorce decrees or evidence of death or an-

nulment of previous marriage(s), and proof of permission to marry if the person is underage.

41. Some forms must be submitted in person, with copies and notarization, and photographs must fit specified dimensions and poses. Forms and information must be submitted in order, with various fees, to specific sections of the immigration representatives at the U.S. embassy.

42. In July 2001, one couple reported that the procedures had been changed and that applicants for K1 visas in the Philippines were no longer required to be interviewed or to pick up their visas in person at the U.S. embassy. The interview was scheduled by telephone and the paperwork sent by mail. The interviewee was required to pay for the toll call and for the registered postage.

43. See Jullie Yap Daza and Katrina Legarda, *A Time to Love, A Time to Leave* (Philippines: Dazzling Inc.), 1998.

44. See Constable, *Maid to Order,* and "At Home but Not at Home: Filipina Narratives of Ambivalent Returns," *Cultural Anthropology* 14, no. 2 (1998): 203–28.

45. See Visweswaran, *Fictions of Feminist Ethnography,* on Marjorie Shostak's use of the term "sister" despite Nisa's choice of a different analogy.

46. See Wilson, "Catalogues," 123.

47. Ann Anagnost, "Scenes of Misrecognition: Maternal Citizenship in the Age of Transnational Adoption," *Positions: East Asia Cultures Critique* 8, no. 2 (2000): 398, 401.

48. Paul (October 29, 1999); available at *http://network54.com/Hide/ Forum/message?forumid = 30510&messageid = 94123764.*

49. See Christine Carlos, "Filipinas Who Fancy Foreigners: Are Pinoy Men Being Left on the Shelf?" *Cosmopolitan* (Philippines) (August 1997): 76–79; Tolentino, "Bodies, Letters, Catalogs," 66.

50. Wilson, "Catalogues," 121; Tolentino, "Bodies, Letters, Catalogs."

51. Tolentino, "Bodies, Letters, Catalogs," 60. See also Glodava and Onizuka, *Mail Order Brides;* Villapando, "The Business of Selling Mail-Order Brides." Tajima, "Lotus Blossoms"; and Delia M. Aguilar, "Women in the Political Economy of the Philippines," *Alternatives* 12 (1987): 516.

52. Tolentino, "Bodies, Letters, Catalogs," 60.

53. See Abu-Lughod, "The Romance of Resistance"; Ortner, "Resistance and the Problem of Ethnographic Refusal."

54. See David Pace, "Beyond Morphology: Lévi-Strauss and the Analysis of Folktales," in *Cinderella: A Casebook,* ed. Alan Dundes (New York: Wildman Press, 1982); Elizabeth Panttaja, "Going Up in the World: Class in 'Cinderella,'" *Western Folklore* 52 (1993): 85–104; Preston, "'Cinderella' as a Dirty Joke"; Yolen, "America's Cinderella"; Jack Zipes, *Fairy Tales and the Arts of Subversion: The Classical Genre for Children and the Process of Civilization* (New York: Routledge, 1983).

55. Butler, *The Psychic Life of Power;* Foucault, *The History of Sexuality,* and *Discipline and Punish.*

56. Delia Aguilar, "Women in the Political Economy," 516–17.

57. See Narayan, "'Male-Order' Brides"; Scholes, "The Mail Order Bride Industry"; USDOJ-INS, "International Matchmaking Organizations."

58. Popenoe, "Life Without Father," 47.

59. Griswold, "The History and Politics of Fatherlessness," 22.

5: POLITICAL ECONOMY AND
CULTURAL LOGICS OF DESIRE

1. Jane Collier, Michelle Rosaldo, and Sylvia Yanagisako, "Is There a Family? New Anthropological Views," in *Rethinking the Family: Some Feminist Questions*, ed. Barrie Thorne and Marilyn Yalom, (New York: Longman, 1982), 25–39, 37.

2. See Anagnost, "Scenes of Misrecognition"; Frayda Cohen, "International Adoption and Asian Transnational Families" (paper presented at Migration and the "Asian Family" in a Globalizing World Conference, Singapore, April 16–18, 2001).

3. See Anagnost, "Scenes of Misrecognition"; Frayda Cohen, "International Adoption"; and Helena Ragoné, "Chasing the Blood Tie: Surrogate Mothers, Adoptive Mothers, and Fathers," in *Situated Lives, Gender and Culture in Everyday Life*, ed. Louise Lamphere, Helena Ragoné, and Patricia Zavella (New York: Routledge Press, 1997), 110–27.

4. Robinson, "Marriage Migration, Family Values, and the 'Global Ecumene,'" 6.

5. Anthony Giddens, *The Transformation of Intimacy: Sexuality, Love and Eroticism in Modern Societies* (Stanford, Ca.: Stanford University Press, 1992), 38; see also Laura Ahearn, *Invitations to Love: Literacy, Love Letters, and Social Change in Nepal* (Ann Arbor: University of Michigan Press, 2001); William Jankowiak, "Introduction," in *Romantic Passion: A Universal Experience?* ed. W. Jankowiak (New York: Columbia University Press, 1995), 1–19; Jankowiak, "Romantic Passion in the People's Republic of China," in *Romantic Passion: A Universal Experience?* ed. W. Jankowiak (New York: Columbia University Press, 1995), 166–83; Jolly and Manderson, "Introduction"; Linda Anne Rebhun, *The Heart Is Unknown Country: Love in the Changing Economy of Northeast Brazil* (Stanford, Ca.: Stanford University Press, 1999); Pflugfelder, *Cartographies of Desire*; William Jankowiak and E. Fischer, "A Cross-Cultural Perspective on Romantic Love," *Ethnology* 31, no. 2 (1992): 149–55.

6. Jack Goody, *The East in the West* (New York: Cambridge University Press, 1996), 186; see also Giddens, *The Transformation of Intimacy*; Giddens, "Family (Washington, D.C.)," *Runaway World*, BBC 1999 Reith Lectures, available at *http://news.bbc.co.uk/hi/english/static/events/reith_99/*; and Jankowiak, "Introduction."

7. Robinson, "Marriage Migration," 8.

8. Ong, *Flexible Citizenship*, 3.

9. Mayfair Mei-hui Yang, *Gifts, Favors, and Banquets: The Arts of Social Relationships in China* (Ithaca, N.Y.: Cornell University Press, 1989).

10. See Smadar Lavie, Kirin Narayan, and Renato Rosaldo, eds., *Creativity/ Anthropology* (Ithaca, N.Y.: Cornell University Press, 1993); Renato Rosaldo, *Culture and Truth;* Victor Turner and Edward Bruner, eds., *Anthropology of Experience* (Urbana, Ill.: University of Illinois Press, 1986).

11. Enloe, *Bananas, Beaches, and Bases,* and *The Morning After.*

12. See Glodava and Onizuka, *Mail-Order Brides.*

13. See Daza and Legarda, *A Time to Love, a Time to Leave.*

14. Espiritu, *Filipino American Lives,* 2; see also Delia Aguilar, "Women in the Political Economy of the Philippines."

15. AMC (Asian Migrant Center), "Philippines: Making the Export of Labor Really Temporary," *Asian Migrant Forum* 6 (1992): 20; Henry S. Rojas, "Filipino Labor Export: A Comprehensive Analysis," in *Asian Labor Migration* (Hong Kong: Christian Conference of Asia, Urban Rural Mission, 1990), appendix 1, p. 10. See also Delia Aguilar, "Women in the Political Economy of the Philippines"; and Patricia Leahy, *Female Migrant Labor in Asia — A Case Study of Filipina Domestic Workers in Hong Kong* (master's thesis, University of Hong Kong, 1990).

16. CFO statistics available at *http://cfo.gov.ph/.*

17. According to the CFO, 2001, from 1989 to 2000, 39.6 percent of Filipino spouses/fiancés had foreign partners from the United States, 30.4 percent from Japan, 8.7 percent from Australia, 4.2 percent from Germany, 3.8 percent from Canada, 1.7 percent from the United Kingdom, and 11.6 percent from other countries. On Filipinos in Japan, see Piper, "International Marriage in Japan"; Suzuki, "Between Two Shores," and "Women Imagined, Women Imaging"; James A. Tyner, "Constructions of Filipina Migrant Entertainers," *Gender, Place and Culture* 3, no. 1 (1996): 77–93, and "Constructing Images, Constructing Policy: The Case of Filipina Migrant Performing Artists," *Gender, Place and Culture* 4, no. 1 (1997): 19–35.

18. CFO, *Filipino Immigrant Handbook* (Manila, Philippines: Department of Foreign Affairs, n.d.), ii, 13. See also CFO, *Handbook for Filipinos Overseas,* 5th ed. (Manila, Philippines: Department of Foreign Affairs, 2000), 13–17.

19. "The Expat Experience," *Metro* 10, no. 10 (October 1998): 66; see also Delia Aguilar, "Women in the Political Economy of the Philippines."

20. Pflugfelder, *Cartographies of Desire.*

21. On popular images, see especially, Marchetti, *Romance and the Yellow Peril;* Tajima, "Lotus Blossoms."

22. Ann Stoler, "Making Empire Respectable: The Politics of Race and Sexual Morality in Twentieth Century Colonial Cultures," *American Ethnologist* 12, no. 4 (1989): 642–58, and "Carnal Knowledge and Imperial Power: Gender, Race, and Morality in Colonial Asia," in *The Gender/Sexuality Reader,* ed. Roger N. Lancaster and Michaela Di Leonardo (London: Routledge, 1997), 13–36.

23. See Constance D. Clark, "Foreign Marriage, 'Tradition,' and the Poli-

tics of Border Crossings"; Li, *Seeking the Ideal Wife;* Shih, "Gender and the Geopolitics of Desire."

24. One Internet chat group for China-U.S. couples ran a poll asking how the American met his (or her) Chinese partner. Out of 150 members, 49 responded. Over half, 54 percent (32), met by a personal advertisement through an Internet agency, magazine, or newspaper. Almost a quarter, 22 percent (13), met through an Internet chat room or bulletin board. Over three-quarters, therefore, met through the Internet or a personal advertisement. Ten percent (6) met though a "chance encounter during a trip"; 8.5 percent (5) were introduced by a friend or third party. One person (1.7 percent) indicated meeting through work, and one (1.7 percent) while a student. One person indicated another, unspecified means of introduction.

25. Giddens, *The Transformation of Intimacy,* 40.

26. Giddens, *The Transformation of Intimacy,* 38–40.

27. Ong, *Flexible Citizenship,* 156.

28. CMI (China Miss International), "Love and Marriage Chinese Style" (2001), available at *http://www.chinamiss.com/loveandmarriage.html.* See also Ahearn, *Invitations to Love;* Jankowiak, "Romantic Passion"; Rebhun, *The Heart Is Unknown Country.*

29. In an effort to preserve the original flavor of these communications, I have not corrected typographical or grammatical errors in this or other e-mail communications.

30. In contrast to Giddens, Jack Goody, *The East in the West,* argues that romantic love is not exclusive to England or western Europe, and that companionate marriage and romantic love could be found in non-European societies. Romantic love, which Goody associates with "complete freedom of choice," historically in a number of Eurasian societies applies more to "relations with mistresses rather than [those with] wives, where 'choice' as distinct from constraint, the internal 'freedom' against the external 'duty,' is all important" (185).

31. Giddens, *Transformation of Intimacy,* 39–40.

32. Giddens, *Transformation of Intimacy,* 40.

33. Roger thought Johnny meant to keep Carlita "hanging on" in case things did not work out with Fran, but he convinced Johnny to tell her he was getting married.

34. Julag-Ay, "Correspondence Marriages."

6: WOMEN'S AGENCY AND THE
GENDERED GEOGRAPHY OF MARRIAGE

1. For definitions of hypergamy, see Ernest L. Schusky, *Manual for Kinship Analysis* (New York: Southern Illinois University Press, 1983), 91; Robert Parkin, *Kinship: An Introduction to Basic Concepts* (Cambridge, Mass.: Blackwell Publishers, 1997), 42; Linda Stone, *Gender and Kinship: An Introduction* (Boulder, Colo.: Westview Press, 1997), 280.

2. Constance D. Clark, "Foreign Marriage, 'Tradition,' and the Politics of Border Crossings," 106.

3. The 1950 marriage law established the minimum marriage age at eighteen for women and twenty for men; ages were set at twenty and twenty-two in 1980. Since the early 1970s, late marriage has been "forcefully advocated. Often in urban areas the demand has been for the female to be at least 25 and the male 27 or 28, or for the ages of both partners to total at least 50" (Whyte and Parish, *Urban Life in Contemporary China*, 111).

4. See Dutton, *Streetlife China;* Emily Honig and Gail Hershatter, *Personal Voices: Chinese Women in the 1980s* (Stanford, Calif.: Stanford University Press, 1988).

5. During my first visit to China in 1980—when private cars were uncommon and associated with government and foreign elites—I watched Chinese pay to have their photographs taken in front of a fancy black automobile, with the Forbidden City as a backdrop.

6. Resistance to buying on credit was not commonly associated with Filipinas. In contrast to people in China, Filipinos are very familiar with interest and credit. Credit—including credit cards—have begun to gain popularity in large Chinese cities in recent years, but are still an unusual idea. (Thomas Rawski, Wenfang Tang, personal communication, September 2000).

7. As of 2000, no federal or state income tax was paid (although a 3 percent tax had been proposed) in the PRC, and many women were amazed that Americans often pay so much of their income in taxes. Investment in private retirement plans was also a foreign concept.

8. Whyte and Parish, *Urban Life in Contemporary China*, 129.

9. When I asked about Lacey's mother's reaction, I was told that "uneducated Chinese often consider it more important that a man have money and looks than education."

10. Hong had toyed with the idea of meeting a pen pal. A widow for two years when I met her, she missed her husband and often spoke of him with great fondness and affection. She doubted she could meet someone she could love as much. They had both come from families with intellectual backgrounds and were a good match. She thought of meeting a friend to accompany her to concerts and other activities, but she did not like the idea of remarriage.

11. Meili's listing described her as "sincere quiet well-educated understanding tolerant easygoing caring healthy type of lady. I look very young to my own age and I keep my body very slim and healthy. I believe I am more beautiful than my picture. I like reading music movies theater arts cooking traveling. I want to find a man who is sincere nice good-hearted, well-educated gentleman, loving family life. The age group from 45 to 55." In person she is self-assured but more modest than her self-description might suggest to a western reader.

12. Whyte and Parish, *Urban Life in Contemporary China*, 126; see also Elisabeth Croll, "Marriage Choice and Status Groups in Contemporary China," in *Class and Social Stratification in Post-Revolution China*, ed. James L. Wat-

son (Cambridge: Cambridge University Press, 1984) , 175–97; Neil Diamant, *Revolutionizing the Family: Politics, Love, and Divorce in Urban and Rural China, 1949–1968* (Berkeley: University of California Press, 2000); William Lavely, "Marriage and Mobility under Rural Collectivism," in *Marriage and Inequality in Chinese Society*, ed. Rubie S. Watson and Patricia Buckley Ebrey (Berkeley: University of California Press, 1991) , 286–312.

13. Piere Bourdieu, *Distinction: A Social Critique of the Judgement of Taste* (Cambridge, Mass.: Harvard University Press, 1984); Louisa Schein, "The Consumption of Color and the Politics of White Skin in Post-Mao China," in *The Gender/Sexuality Reader*, ed. Roger N. Lancaster and Michaela Di Leonardo (London: Routledge, 1997), 473–86.

14. Honig and Hershatter, *Personal Voices*.

15. William L. Parish and James Farrer, "Gender and Family," in *Chinese Urban Life under Reform: The Changing Social Contract*, ed. Wenfang Tang and William L. Parish (New York: Cambridge University Press, 2000), 265; "Up Close, and Practical," *South China Morning Post*, February 4, 2001.

16. See Parkin, *Kinship*, 42; Schusky, *Manual for Kinship Analysis*, 91; Stone, *Gender and Kinship*, 280.

17. Luc De Heusch, *Why Marry Her? Society and Symbolic Structures*, trans. Janet Lloyd (New York: Cambridge University Press, 1981); Louis Dumont, *Affinity as Value: Marriage Alliance in South India with Comparative Essays on Australia* (Chicago: University of Chicago Press, 1983); Edmund Leach, *Political Systems of Highland Burma* (London: G.. Bell, 1954), and *Rethinking Anthropology*, London School of Economics Monographs on Social Anthropology, no. 22 (London: Althone, 1961); Claude Lévi-Strauss, *Elementary Structures of Kinship*, trans. James H. Bell, John R. von Sturmer, and Rodney Needham (Boston: Beacon Press, 1969); Stone, *Gender and Kinship*.

18. Margery Wolf, *The House of Lim: A Study of a Chinese Farm Family* (New York: Prentice Hall, 1968), 123; Parish and Farrer, "Gender and Family," 267. PRC women studying in U.S. universities also complain about the shortage of eligible Chinese men among their classmates. These men, I was told, look for partners in China, where they have greater social capital because of their prospects of settling abroad. Conversely, PRC men students in the United States complain that they *must* seek partners in China because of greater male competition.

19. "Up Close, and Practical," *South China Morning Post* (Feb. 4, 2001).

20. Whyte and Parish, *Urban Life in Contemporary China*, 124.

21. Croll, "Marriage Choice"; Lavely, "Marriage and Mobility"; Rubie S. Watson, "Afterward: Marriage and Gender Inequality," in *Marriage and Inequality in Chinese Society*, ed. Rubie S. Watson and Patricia Buckley Ebrey (Berkeley: University of California Press, 1991), 347–68.

22. Jack Goody, *Production and Reproduction: A Comparative Study of the Domestic Domain* (New York: Cambridge University Press, 1976), 14.

23. See Stone, *Gender and Kinship*, 229. Interestingly, Stone points to the tale of Cinderella as exemplifying the popular theme of hypergamous marriage

in European folklore. Literary scholars have argued, however, that in older versions the tale of Cinderella was not a story of rags to riches and class mobility, but of a young woman who was returned to the status that was her right by birth, a point that better supports Stone's ideas about the prevalence of class endogamy. See also Panttaja, "Going Up in the World."

24. Pa Chin, *Family* (1931; rpt. Prospect Heights, Ill.: Waveland Press, 1972).

25. Lévi-Strauss, *Elementary Structures;* Rubin, "The Traffic in Women"; Parkin, *Kinship*, 42.

26. Ong, *Flexible Citizenship*, 156.

27. Li, *Seeking an Ideal Wife;* Ellen Oxfeld, "The Woman without a Daughter-in-Law: A New Balance of Power Within Rural Chinese Families?" (paper presented at Association for Asian Studies Annual Meeting, Boston, March 1999). Christina Gilmartin and Lin Tan, "Fleeing Poverty: Rural Women, Expanding Marriage Markets, and Strategies for Social Mobility in Contemporary China," in *Transforming Gender and Development in East Asia,* ed. Esther Ngan-ling Chow (New York: Routledge Press, 2002), 203–16; Nicole Constable, *Cross-Border Marriages: Gender and Mobility in Transnational Asia* (Philadelphia: University of Pennsylvania Press, forthcoming).

28. Esther Pan, "Why Asian Guys Are on a Roll," *Newsweek* 138, no. 8 (February 21, 2000), 50–51; and Zhai Liang and Naomi Ito, "Intermarriage of Asian Americans in the New York Region: Contemporary Patterns and Future Prospects," *International Migration Review* 33, no. 4 (1999): 876–900, suggest that Asian American men are now marrying "outside of their group" at a higher rate and are "gaining popularity" among non-Asian women. See Kathleen Erwin, "White Women, Male Desires: A Televisual Fantasy of the Transnational Chinese Family," in *Spaces of Their Own: Women's Public Sphere in Transnational China*, ed. Mayfair Mei-hui Yang (Minneapolis: University of Minnesota Press, 1999) , 232–57, for an excellent analysis of gender, nationalism, and Chinese modernity through the analysis of a Chinese television serial about a PRC husband and white wife.

29. Brackette Williams, "Introduction: Mannish Women and Gender after the Act," in *Women Out of Place: The Gender of Agency and the Race of Nationality,* ed. B. Williams (New York: Routledge University Press, 1996), 1–36.

30. For an insightful analysis of Japanese women's attraction to Western men, see Karen Kelsky, *Women on the Verge: Japanese Women, western Dreams* (Durham, N.C.: Duke University Press, 2001). Kelsky argues that in Japanese "women's narratives of the international, white Western men are idealized for their exemplification of the modern, romanticized for their alleged sensitivity *(yasashisa)*, and fetishized as signifiers of success and gatekeepers of social upward mobility in the world" (8).

31. See also Tajima, "Lotus Blossoms."

32. Li, *Seeking an Ideal Wife*, 79.

33. Ibid., 80.

34. See Erwin, "White Women, Male Desires." In U.S. popular culture,

Asian men are often depicted as effeminate, in contrast to hypermasculine stereotypes of black men. See, for example, Paulette Pierce, "Boudoir Politics and the Birthing of the Nation: Sex, Marriage, and Structural Deflection in the National Black Independent Party," in *Women Out of Place: The Gender of Agency and the Race of Nationality,* ed. Brackette Williams (New York: Routledge, 1996), 216–44; and Williams, "Introduction." Whereas the masculinity of black men is often portrayed as posing a threat to white men (see Eldridge Cleaver, *Soul on Ice* [New York: McGraw Hill, 1968]; and Patricia Turner, *I Heard It Through the Grapevine* [Berkeley: University of California Press, 1993]), this is far less common in popular depictions of Asian men. For exceptions, see Marchetti, *Romance and the Yellow Peril;* and Tajima, "Lotus Blossoms." Recently popular martial arts films also stand in contrast to this image. See Stoler, "Carnal Knowledge and Imperial Power," on gender-race asymmetry in colonial-native relations in the East Indies.

35. See Marie Norman, *Where the Buffalo Speak English: Tourism and Caste Dynamics in Pokhora, Nepal* (Ph.D. diss., University of Pittsburgh, 1999) on marital relationships between Nepalese and foreigners.

36. Elliott Oring, *Jokes and Their Relations* (Lexington: University of Kentucky Press, 1992).

37. But see Erwin, "White Women, Male Desires."

38. Another incongruity may be in desiring a western "wife" as opposed to the more common assumptions about western women as sex objects or as sexually lax. Schein, "The Consumption of Color," describes western women as status symbols in calendars and advertising (1997). By the late 1990s, western men had gained prominence in Chinese advertising as well.

39. Keith H. Basso, *Portraits of "the Whiteman": Linguistic Play and Cultural Symbols Among the Western Apache* (New York: Cambridge University Press, 1979).

40. Whyte and Parish, *Urban Life in Contemporary China,* 129.

41. Ong, *Flexible Citizenship,* 157.

42. Doreen Massey, *Space, Place and Gender* (Minneapolis: University of Minnesota Press, 1994), 149; Constance Clark, "Foreign Marriage," 105.

7: TALES OF WAITING

1. Lowe, *Immigrant Acts,* 5.

2. In the nineteenth century, "the yellow peril" referred to the threat of Asians displacing white European workers (ibid., 4). Marchetti, *Romance and the Yellow Peril,* explores representations of the "yellow peril" in Hollywood films, including the sexual dimensions of this threat.

3. Lowe, *Immigrant Acts;* Massey, *Space, Place and Gender.*

4. For example, Sucheng Chan, *Asian Americans: An Interpretive History* (Boston: Twayne Publishers, 1991); Espiritu, *Filipino American Lives,* and *Asian American Women and Men;* Lowe, *Immigrant Acts;* Takaki,

Strangers from a Different Shore; Judy Yung, *Unbound Feet: A Social History of Chinese Women in San Francisco* (Berkeley: University of California Press, 1995).

5. Chan, *Asian Americans,* 27.

6. Ibid., 105.

7. Ibid., 28.

8. Ibid., 104–5.

9. Ibid., 45–78; Joel S. Fetzer, *Public Attitudes toward Immigration in the United States, France, and Germany* (New York: Cambridge University Press, 2000), 30.

10. Chan, *Asian Americans,* 54; Lucy E. Salyer, *Laws Harsh as Tigers: Chinese Immigrants and the Shaping of Modern Immigration Law* (Chapel Hill, N.C.: University of North Carolina Press, 1995), 5.

11. Chan, *Asian Americans,* 106.

12. Salyer, *Laws Harsh as Tigers,* 17.

13. Esther Ngan-Ling Chow, "Family, Economy, and the State," 115.

14. Salyer, *Laws Harsh as Tigers,* 44; Judy Yung, *Chinese Women in America: A Pictorial History* (Seattle: University of Washington Press, 1986), and *Unbound Feet.* The Chinese Exclusion Act of 1882 was extended in 1892 and 1902, and in 1904 was extended indefinitely and also barred Chinese from immigrating to the newly acquired territories of Hawaii, the Philippines, and Puerto Rico. See Chan, *Asian Americans,* 55.

15. Takaki, *Strangers from a Different Shore,* 14.

16. Chan, *Asian Americans,* 106. The Fourteenth Amendment stipulates that all persons born in the United States are citizens. As Salyer, *Laws Harsh as Tigers,* notes, this "left Asians in a strange situation regarding citizenship. They could gain citizenship by birth, but not by naturalization" (208).

17. Lowe, *Immigrant Acts,* 11–12.

18. Espiritu, *Filipino American Lives,* 3–4.

19. Takaki, *Strangers from a Different Shore,* 57; see also Vincente L. Rafael, *White Love and Other Events in Filipino History* (Durham, N.C.: Duke University Press, 2000).

20. Takaki, *Strangers from a Different Shore,* 51.

21. Ibid., 59.

22. Espiritu, *Filipino American Lives,* 9–10.

23. Takaki, *Strangers from a Different Shore,* 331–32.

24. Chan, *Asian Americans,* 56; Takaki, *Strangers from a Different Shore,* 14. The Tydings-McDuffie Act was in some ways even stricter than the anti-Chinese (1888) and anti-Japanese (1908) immigration laws because it did not even permit the entry of the wives of Filipino merchants (Takaki, 337).

25. Takaki, *Strangers from a Different Shore,* 331.

26. See Chan, *Asian Americans,* 104–5; Chow, "Family, Economy, and the State."

27. Chan, *Asian Americans,* 107–8.

28. Ibid., 59; Takaki, *Strangers from a Different Shore*, 101.

29. Takaki, *Strangers from a Different Shore*, 102.

30. Chan, *Asian Americans*, 60.

31. Espiritu, *Filipino American Lives*, 13.

32. Chan, *Asian Americans*, 60.

33. Takaki, *Strangers from a Different Shore*, 330.

34. Chan, *Asian Americans*, 61. The antimiscegenation laws raise questions about gender. Asian men were clearly perceived as a greater threat than Asian women on the basis of sheer numbers, but it is unclear whether relationships between white men and Asian women were equally problematic.

35. Takaki, *Strangers from a Different Shore*, 370.

36. Ibid., 377.

37. Chan, *Asian Americans*, 122. Only fifty-nine Chinese per year on average came to the United States in the first ten years of the law's operation, and between 1944 and 1958, only 1,428 Chinese were naturalized (Takaki, *Strangers from a Different Shore*, 378).

38. Takaki, *Strangers from a Different Shore*, 359.

39. By 1970 there were more Filipinos in the U.S. Navy than in the Philippine Navy, and by the 1980s, the U.S. military was the second largest employer in the Philippines—following the Philippine government (Espiritu, *Filipino American Lives*, 15).

40. Ibid., 14, 34 n 58.

41. A few years earlier, President Roosevelt had pledged that Filipinos who fought alongside Americans against the Japanese in World War II would be granted citizenship. A federal act in 1946 rescinded that pledge. In 1990, "the U.S. finally restored citizenship rights to veterans who were stymied when Roosevelt's pledge was rescinded" (Ibid., 34 n 70, 17).

42. Ibid., 18.

43. Chan, *Asian Americans*, 140.

44. The Tubb version is credited to Billy Cox and Clarke Van Ness adapted from the Harris version (Cowpie Songs 2001). Harris's autobiography does not mention this song, but his lyrics resemble elements of it. See Charles K. Harris, *After the Ball: Forty Years of Melody: An Autobiography* (New York: Frank-Maurice, 1926). Later recordings include those of Ernest Tubb, T. Texas Tyler, Pearl Harbour, Hank Locklin, Bob Luman, Mitchell Torok, Charlie Moore, Billie Cox, June Oakley, Bob Jones, Joe Reagan, Dave Dudley, and Roy Acuff.

45. In the Tubb version, "I love my dark-faced Filipino" is changed to "I love my Filipino Baby," and in the T. Texas Tyler version to "She's my darlin' little Filipino baby."

46. Chan, *Asian Americans*; Lowe, *Immigrant Acts*; David M. Reimers, *Still the Golden Door: The Third World Comes to America* (New York: Columbia University Press, 1992).

47. Espiritu, *Filipino American Lives*, 19.

48. USDOJ-INS, "Legal Immigration, Fiscal Year 1997," in *Office of Policy and Planning, Statistics Branch, Annual Report, January 1999*, no. 1 (1999):1–13.

49. Chan, *Asian Americans*, 146. In 1995, family preferences were separated from employment preferences.

50. Chan, *Asian Americans*, 145; see also Reimers, *Still the Golden Door.*

51. Takaki, *Strangers from a Different Shore*, 432.

52. Espiritu, *Filipino American Lives*, 21; Espiritu, *Asian American Women and Men.*

53. Chan, *Asian Americans*, 147.

54. Espiritu, *Filipino American Lives*, 19; Takaki, *Strangers from a Different Shore*, 232–36.

55. Espiritu, *Filipino American Lives*, 21–22. See also Ordonez, "Mail-Order Brides."

56. Takaki, *Strangers from a Different Shore*, 421.

57. Ibid., 423.

58. Ibid., 425–27.

59. USDOJ-INS,*Triennial Comprehensive Report on Immigration* (1999); available at *http://www.ins.usdoj.gov*, 30, 12.

60. USDOJ-INS, "Legal Immigration, Fiscal Year 1997," 8–9; US-CB (United States Census Bureau), "Census Brief 2000: From the Mideast to the Pacific: A Profile of the Nation's Asian Foreign-Born Population," U.S. Census Bureau; Department of Commerce, Economics and Statistics (September 2000):1–2

61. USDOJ-INS, "Legal Immigration, Fiscal Year 1997," 10. The report does not indicate how many of these cases involved fraud (with a fiancé(e) remaining illegally in the United States) and how many involved ex-fiancé(e)s who left the United States.

62. USDOJ-INS, "Adjustment of Status under Legal Immigration Family Equity (LIFE) Act Legalization Provision and LIFE Act Amendments Family Unity Provisions, *Federal Register; Rules and Regulations* 66(106) (June 1, 2001): 29661–82; and USDOS (United States Department of State), "The New K and V Visa Categories" (2001); available at *http://travel.state.gov/vvisas/qualifying_for_the_k.html.*

63. USDOJ-INS, "International Matchmaking Organizations."

64. USDOJ-INS, "International Matchmaking Organizations," 13.

65. Simons, "Mail Order Brides," 133.

66. Ibid., 133; see also Michelle Anderson, "A License to Abuse"; Meng, "Mail-Order Brides." CPR status begins after the fiancé(e) marries the U.S. citizen and files for adjustment of status (AOS). For those married abroad less than two years, CPR begins when the foreign partner enters the United States.

67. See Simons, "Mail Order Brides," 136; and Meng, "Mail-Order Brides."

68. It "requires that the CPR still be married and demonstrate (1) that she

is of 'good moral character'; (2) the marriage was entered into 'in good faith'; (3) that she or her child was 'battered by or has been subject to extreme cruelty perpetrated by [her] spouse'; and (4) that she and her child will face 'extreme hardship' if deported" (Simons, "Mail Order Brides," 134–35). Divorced women who seek to change their CPR status, by contrast, must demonstrate battery or good faith or extreme hardship. See Simons for a discussion of CPR status and charges that it violates constitutional rights to privacy, due process, and equal protection.

69. Lowe, *Immigrant Acts*, 16.

70. Ibid., 5.

71. USDOJ-INS, "International Matchmaking."

72. Simons, "Mail Order Brides," 133.

73. Reimers, *Still the Golden Door*, 214–15.

74. Narayan, "'Male-Order' Brides."

75. Keven Chen, K-1 Visa Page (2001); available at *http://129.109.159.93/ keven/k1visa/index_k1.htm (http://www.k1homepages.com)*.

76. By late 2001, most likely because of the growing number of requests, the embassy was no longer willing to open provisional files.

77. As of July 2001, the Manila embassy began to schedule telephone interviews. See chapter 4.

78. Keven and Gary both submitted their I-129F petitions to the Texas Service Center, and Bruce submitted his to the one in Nebraska. Keven's took 60 days for initial approval, Gary's 35 days, and Bruce's 45 days. Although Keven's initial approval took longer, his overall time was over a month less than Bruce's and two and a half months less than Gary's. This points to differences in the Consular Processing times in different overseas locations.

79. Marriage-Based Visas Timelines Project, "Marriage-Based Visas Timelines Project K-1 Timeline" (2000); available at *http://www.wkh.org/k-1visa/ index.shtml*.

80. These figures are based on an analysis of the timelines that couples voluntarily entered on the Marriage-Based Visas Timelines Project, K-1 Timeline Home Page, as of Dec. 7, 2000. As such, they may not be representative of the larger number of cases that go through the INS service centers. Yet these figures are in keeping with other estimates based on compilations of the American Immigration Lawyers Association, which are not broken down by nationality. See Matthew Udall, "Law Office of Matthew Udall Immigration Services" (2000); available at *http://members@aol.com/MUdall/sctimes.htm*. See also Carl Schusterman, "Immigration: A Practical Guide to Immigration to the U.S.: Homepage of Law Offices of Carl Shusterman" (2001); available at *http://www.shusterman.com/family.html*.

81. Several incomplete cases had taken longer than eight months, but here I discuss only those that had been completed. I also spoke to several people whose timelines exceeded a year but did not have all the details of their cases.

82. This is based on cases recorded in the Marriage-Based Visas Timelines Project, "Marriage-Based Visas Timelines Project Timelines for the I-130

Spousal Visa," available at *http://www.wkh.org/visa/I-130/timelines/index .html*, as of September 19, 2000.

83. Marriage-Based Visas Timelines Project, "Marriage-Based Visas Timelines Project K-1 Timeline."

84. Marriage-Based Visas Timelines Project, "Marriage-Based Visas Timelines Project Timelines for the I-130 Spousal Visa." At the Nebraska Service Center, based on the small sample at the Marriage-Based web site, the 5 cases of spouses from the Philippines averaged 113 days for initial approval, 3 cases of spouses from China averaged 155 days, 3 cases of spouses from the U.K. took 43 days, and 4 cases of spouses from Canada took 86 days.

85. Particularly useful were "Alvena's Website" (1999), available at *http:/www2.apex.net/users/thehydes*; Jonathan Kurtz, "Marrying an Alien in Three (Not-So) Short Steps" (2000), available at *http://www.new2usa.com/ showpage.jsp?PageID = legal-112900-01*. Alveena's web site was shut down in 2001 because of a suit filed against her by the Kentucky Bar Association due to a Kentucky law that prohibits laypersons from giving "legal advice." Demonstrating how the Internet can overcome constraints imposed by the state, a new web site was reincarnated from a Texas base. See Doc Steen, "Doc Steen's Marriage Visa Information Pages" (2001), available at *http://www.mindspring .com/~docsteen/visainfo/visainfo.htm*.

86. Names and dates have been changed, but the time frame and service center remain the same.

87. It is difficult to say how widespread such attitudes are among INS employees. One INS officer explained to me that he gets very angry and impatient with immigrants who don't appear to him to adequately appreciate the privilege of becoming a U.S. citizen.

88. Women sometimes expressed a desire to "stay at home" in China or the Philippines for a while after the visa was approved. One Chinese woman waited until after the Spring Festival (Chinese New Year) to spend time with her parents. Gina delayed her departure until after Christmas. Husbands or fiancés were sometimes chided for "allowing" the women to stay longer. Daniel responded to such a comment that Gina might not have Christmas with her family again for a long time. Compared to a lifetime together, what was another three weeks? Plus, this would make Gina happy.

89. CFO, *Filipino Immigrant Handbook*, 42.

90. Leo R. Chavez, *Covering Immigration: Popular Images and the Politics of the Nation* (Berkeley: University of California Press, 2001); Fetzer, *Public Attitudes*; Reimers, *Still the Golden Door*; Ruben Rumbaut, "Origins and Destinies: Immigration, Race, and Ethnicity in Contemporary America," in *Origins and Destinies: Immigration, Race, and Ethnicity in America*, ed. Silvia Pedraza and Ruben G. Rumbaut (Boston: Wadsworth Publishing, 1996), 21–42.

91. Scholes, "The Mail Order Bride Industry"; Simons, "Mail Order Brides."

92. Meng, "Mail-Order Brides"; Simons, "Mail Order Brides."

8: CONCLUSION

1. Anagnost, "Scenes of Misrecognition," 414, 398.

2. Frayda Cohen, "International Adoption."

3. See reference to Davor Jedlicka in Villapando, "The Business of Selling Mail-Order Brides," 323.

4. U.S. Embassy, Guangzhou, China, "Adopted Children Immigrant Visa Unit" (2001); available at *http://www.usembassy-china.org.cn /consulates/ guangzhou /consular/acivu /acivu.htm*.

5. Lowe, *Immigrant Acts*, 8.

6. Lowe, *Immigrant Acts*, 5.

7. Linda Basch, Nina Glick Schiller, and Cristina Szanton Blanc, *Nations Unbound: Transnational Projects, Postcolonial Predicaments, and Deterritorialized Nation-States* (Langhorne, Penn.: Gordon and Breach, 1994).

8. See Erik Cohen, "Lovelorn Farangs."

9. USDOJ-INS, "International Matchmaking Organizations," 1.

10. Simons, "Mail Order Brides," 135–36; Meng, "Mail-Order Brides."

11. For example, Basch, Schiller, and Blanc, *Nations Unbound;* Filomeno V. Aguilar, Jr., ed., "Filipinos as Transnational Migrants"; Michael Kearney, "The Local and the Global: The Anthropology of Globalization and Transnationalism," *Annual Review of Anthropology* 24 (1995): 547–65; Aihwa Ong and Donald Nonini, eds., *Ungrounded Empires: The Cultural Politics of Modern Chinese Transnationalism* (New York: Routledge, 1997); Roger Rouse, "Mexican Migration and the Social Space of Postmodernism," *Diaspora* 1 (1991): 8–23; Michael Peter Smith and Luis Eduardo Guarnizo, eds., *Transnationalism from Below,* Comparative Urban and Community Research, vol. 6 (New Brunswick, N.J.: Transaction Publishers, 1998).

12. Appadurai, *Modernity at Large.*

13. For example, Ong, *Flexible Citizenship*, 130–31.

14. USDOS, "The New K and V Visa Categories"; USDOJ-INS, "Adjustment of Status."

15. Adam Nagourney, "In New York, Bush Visits Site Evocative of His Philosophy," *New York Times,* July 11, 2001, p. 1.

16. Eric Schmitt, "Bush Panel Backs Legalizing Status of Some Immigrants," *New York Times,* July 24, 2001, p. 1.

17. USDOJ-INS, "International Matchmaking," 1; Scholes, "The Mail Order Bride Industry."

18. Narayan, "'Male-Order' Brides." See also Michelle Anderson, "A License to Abuse"; Simons, "Mail Order Brides." See also Simons, "Marriage, Migration, and Markets," for an important and insightful discussion of this issue.

19. See, for example, *Dateline NBC,* "Bought and Sold," Geraldo Rivera, March 18, 2001.

20. Simons, "Mail Order Brides."

21. Constable, "At Home but Not at Home."

22. ABS-CBN News. "Pinay Brides—Internet's Hottest Commodities."

23. Ordonez, "Mail-Order Brides," 127–28.

24. For example, Gary Clark, *Your Bride Is in the Mail;* "Exactly What is a Mail-Order Bride?" and "Some Misconceptions and Outright Lies about so-called 'Mail Order Brides'" (2001), available at *http://www.upbeat.com/wtwpubs/miscon.htm.*

25. James C. Scott, *Weapons of the Weak: Everyday forms of Peasant Resistance* (New Haven, Conn.: Yale University Press, 1985), and *Domination and the Arts of Resistance: Hidden Transcripts* (New Haven, Conn.: Yale University Press, 1990).

26. Jolly and Manderson, "Introduction." See also Kelsky, *Women on the Verge.*

References Cited

ABS-CBN News. "Pinay Brides—Internet's Hottest Commodities." Parts 1–4. 2000. Available at http://www.abs-cbnnews.com.

Abu-Lughod, Lila. "The Romance of Resistance: Tracing Transformations of Power through Bedouin Women." *American Ethnologist* 17, no. 1 (1990): 41–55.

———. "Writing Against Culture." In *Recapturing Anthropology*, ed. Richard Fox, 137–62. Santa Fe, N.M.: School of American Research Press, 1991.

———. *Writing Women's Worlds: Bedouin Stories.* Berkeley: University of California Press, 1993.

Aguilar, Delia M. "Women in the Political Economy of the Philippines." *Alternatives* 12 (1987): 511–26.

Aguilar, Filomeno V. Jr. "The Dialectics of Transnational Shame and National Identity." *Philippine Sociological Review* 44 (1996): 101–36.

———, ed. "Filipinos as Transnational Migrants." *Philippine Sociological Review* 44 (1996): 4–227.

Ahearn, Laura. *Invitations to Love: Literacy, Love Letters, and Social Change in Nepal.* Ann Arbor: University of Michigan Press, 2001.

Ahmed, Leila. "Western Ethnocentrism and Perceptions of the Harem." *Feminist Studies* 8, no. 3 (1982): 521–34.

Albright, Julie M., and Tom Coran. "Online Love: Sex, Gender and Relationships in Cyberspace." Electronic Frontier Foundation Archives, 2001. Available at http://www.eff.org/pub/Net_culture/Virtual_community/online _love.article.

Alter, Joseph S. *Knowing Dil Das: Stories of a Himalayan Hunter.* Philadelphia: University of Pennsylvania Press, 2000.

Anagnost, Ann. "Scenes of Misrecognition: Maternal Citizenship in the Age of Transnational Adoption." *Positions: East Asia Cultures Critique* 8, no. 2 (2000): 389–421.

Anderson, Benedict. *Imagined Communities: Reflections on the Origin and Spread of Nationalism.* New York: Verso Press, 1983.

Anderson, Michelle J. "A License to Abuse: The Impact of Conditional Status on Female Immigrants." *Yale Law Journal* 102, no. 6 (1993): 1401–30.

Appadurai, Arjun. *Modernity at Large: Cultural Dimensions of Globalization.* Minneapolis: University of Minnesota Press, 1996.

"The Asian Bride Boom." *Asiaweek*, April 15, 1983, 36–38, 43–45.

Asian Migrant Center (AMC). "Philippines: Making the Export of Labor Really Temporary." *Asian Migrant Forum* 6 (1992): 19–20.

Bakhtin, Mikhail. *The Dialogic Imagination: Four Essays.* Austin: University of Texas Press, 1981.

Barry, Kathleen. *Female Sexual Slavery.* Englewood Cliffs, N.J.: Prentice-Hall, 1979.

———. "Sexual Exploitation Violates Human Rights." Coalition Against Trafficking in Women. Fall 1992. Available at http://www.uri.edu/artsci/wms/hughes/catw/barry.htm.

Basch, Linda, Nina Glick Schiller, and Cristina Szanton Blanc. *Nations Unbound: Transnational Projects, Postcolonial Predicaments, and Deterritorialized Nation-States.* Langhorne, Penn.: Gordon and Breach, 1994.

Basso, Keith H. *Portraits of "the Whiteman:" Linguistic Play and Cultural Symbols among the Western Apache.* New York: Cambridge University Press, 1979.

Behar, Ruth. *Translated Woman: Crossing the Border with Esperanza's Story.* Boston: Beacon Press, 1993.

Behar, Ruth, and Deborah A. Gordon, eds. *Women Writing Culture.* Berkeley: University of California Press, 1995.

Berreman, Gerald D. *Hindus of the Himalayas.* Berkeley: University of California Press, 1972.

Bourdieu, Pierre. *Distinction: A Social Critique of the Judgement of Taste.* Cambridge, Mass.: Harvard University Press, 1984.

Bowen, Eleanor Smith [Bohannan, Laura]. *Return to Laughter.* New York: Doubleday, 1954.

Briggs, Jean. *Never in Anger: Portrait of an Eskimo Family.* Cambridge, Mass.: Harvard University Press, 1970.

Butler, Judith. *The Psychic Life of Power: Theories of Subjection.* Stanford, Calif.: Stanford University Press, 1997.

Cahill, Desmond. *Intermarriages in International Contexts: A Study of Filipina Women Married to Australian, Japanese, and Swiss Men.* Quezon City: Scalabini Research Center, 1990.

Cannell, Fenella. "The Power of Appearances: Beauty, Mimicry and Transformation in Bicol." In *Discrepant Histories: Translocal Essays on Filipino Cultures,* ed. Vincente L. Rafael, 223–58. Philadelphia: Temple University Press, 1995.

Carlos, Christine. "Filipinas Who Fancy Foreigners: Are Pinoy Men Being Left on the Shelf?" *Cosmopolitan* (Philippines) (August 1997): 76–79.

Chan, Sucheng. *Asian Americans: An Interpretive History.* Boston: Twayne Publishers, 1991.

Chatterjee, Partha. *The Nation and Its Fragments: Colonial and Postcolonial Histories.* Princeton, N.J.: Princeton University Press, 1993.

Chavez, Leo R. *Covering Immigration: Popular Images and the Politics of the Nation.* Berkeley: University of California Press, 2001.

Chin, Ko-Lin. "Out-of-Town Brides: International Marriage and Wife Abuse among Chinese Immigrants." *Journal of Comparative Family Studies* 25, no. 1 (spring 1994): 53–71.

Chin, Soo-Young. *Doing What Had to Be Done: The Life Narrative of Dora Yum Kim.* Philadelphia: Temple University Press, 1999.

Chow, Esther Ngan-Ling. "Family, Economy, and the State: A Legacy of Struggle for Chinese American Women." In *Origins and Destinies: Immigration, Race, and Ethnicity in America,* ed. Silvia Pedraza and Ruben G. Rumbaut, 110–24. Boston: Wadsworth Publishing, 1996.

Chow, Rey. "Violence in the Other Country: China as Crisis, Spectacle, and Woman." In *Third World Women and the Politics of Feminism,* ed. Chandra T. Mohanty, Ann Russo, and Lourdes Torres, 81–100. Bloomington: Indiana University Press, 1991.

Clark, Constance D. "Foreign Marriage 'Tradition' and the Politics of Border Crossings." In *China Urban: Ethnographies of Contemporary Culture,* ed. Nancy Chen et al., 104–22. Durham, N.C.: Duke University Press, 2001.

Clark, Gary. *Your Bride Is in the Mail.* Las Vegas, Nev.: Words that Work Publications, 1998.

Cleaver, Eldridge. *Soul On Ice.* New York: McGraw Hill, 1968.

Clifford, James. "Introduction: Partial Truths." In *Writing Culture: Poetics and Politics of Ethnography,* ed. James Clifford and George Marcus, 1–26. Berkeley: University of California Press, 1986.

Coalition to Abolish Slavery and Trafficking (CAST). "What Is Trafficking?" 2001. Available at http://www.trafficked-women.org/trafficked.html.

Coalition Against Trafficking in Women-International (CATW). "Philosophy." 2001. Available at http://www.catwinternational.org/philos.htm.

Cohen, Erik. "Lovelorn Farangs: The Correspondence between Foreign Men and Thai Girls." *Anthropological Quarterly* 59, no. 3 (1986):115–28.

Cohen, Frayda. "International Adoption and Asian Transnational Families." Paper presented at Migration and the "Asian Family" in a Globalizing World, Singapore, April 16–18, 2001.

Collier, Jane, Michelle Rosaldo, and Sylvia Yanagisako. "Is There a Family? New Anthropological Views." In *Rethinking the Family: Some Feminist Questions,* ed. Barrie Thorne and Marilyn Yalom, 25–39. New York: Longman, 1982.

Collins, Patricia Hill. *Black Feminist Thought: Knowledge, Consciousness, and the Politics of Empowerment.* New York: Routledge, 1990.

Commission on Filipinos Overseas (CFO). *Handbook for Filipinos Overseas.* 5th ed. Department of Foreign Affairs, CFO, Manila, Philippines, 2000.

———. Statistics. 2001. Available at http://cfo.gov.ph/.

————. Filipino Immigrant Handbook. Department of Foreign Affairs, CFO, Manila, Philippines., n.d.

Consalvo, Mia. "'Three Shot Dead in Courthouse': Examining News Coverage of Domestic Violence and Mail-Order Brides." Women's Studies in Communication 21, no. 2 (1998): 188–211.

Constable, Nicole. Maid to Order in Hong Kong: Stories of Filipina Workers. Ithaca, N.Y.: Cornell University Press, 1997.

————. "At Home but Not at Home: Filipina Narratives of Ambivalent Returns." Cultural Anthropology 14, no. 2 (1998): 203–28.

————, ed. Cross-Border Marriages: Gender and Mobility in Transnational Asia. Philadelphia: Pennsylvania University Press, forthcoming.

Cooke, F. M. Australian-Filipino Marriages in the 1980s. Queensland, Australia: Griffith University Press, 1986.

Côté, Richard. Love by Mail: The International Guide to Personal Advertising. Silver Springs, Md.: Enigma Books, 1992.

Croll, Elisabeth. "Marriage Choice and Status Groups in Contemporary China." In Class and Social Stratification in Post-Revolution China, ed. James L. Watson, 175–97. Cambridge: Cambridge University Press, 1984.

Crystal, David. Language and the Internet. New York: Cambridge University Press, 2001.

Das, Veena. "National Honor and Practical Kinship: Unwanted Women and Children." In Conceiving the New World Order, ed. Faye Ginsburg and Rayna Rapp, 212–33. Berkeley: University of California Press, 1995.

Daza, Jullie Yap. Etiquette for Mistresses . . . and What Wives Can Learn from Them. Philippines: J. Y. Daza, 1994.

Daza, Jullie Yap, and Katrina Legarda. A Time to Love, a Time to Leave. Philippines: Dazzling, 1998.

De Heusch, Luc. Why Marry Her? Society and Symbolic Structures. Trans. Janet Lloyd. New York: Cambridge University Press, 1981.

Diamant, Neil. Revolutionizing the Family: Politics, Love, and Divorce in Urban and Rural China, 1949–1968. Berkeley: University of California Press, 2000.

Diamond, Norma. "Collectivization, Kinship, and the Status of Women in Rural China." Bulletin of Concerned Asian Scholars 7, no. 1 (1975): 25–32.

————. "Building Socialism with Chinese Characteristics." Women and International Development 4 (1995): 147–72.

Dumont, Jean-Paul. The Headman and I: Ambiguity and Ambivalence in the Fieldwork Experience. Austin: University of Texas Press, 1978.

Dumont, Louis. Affinity as Value: Marriage Alliance in South India with Comparative Essays on Australia. Chicago: University of Chicago Press, 1983.

Dutton, Michael. Streetlife China. New York: Cambridge University Press, 1999.

Elegant, Robert. Pacific Destiny. New York: Crown Publishers, 1990.

Enloe, Cynthia. Bananas, Beaches, and Bases: Making Sense of International Politics. Berkeley: University of California Press, 1990.

———. *The Morning After: Sexual Politics at the End of the Cold War.* Berkeley: University of California Press, 1993.

Erwin, Kathleen. "White Women, Male Desires: A Televisual Fantasy of the Transnational Chinese Family." In *Spaces of Their Own: Women's Public Sphere in Transnational China,* ed. Mayfair Mei-hui Yang, 232–57. Minneapolis: University of Minnesota Press, 1999.

Espiritu, Yen Le. *Filipino American Lives.* Philadelphia: Temple University Press, 1995.

———. *Asian American Women and Men: Labor, Laws, and Love.* Thousand Oaks, Calif.: Sage, 1997.

Faludi, Susan. *Backlash: The Undeclared War against American Women.* New York: Doubleday, Anchor Books, 1992.

———. *Stiffed: The Betrayal of the American Man.* New York: William Morrow and Company, 1999.

Fernea, Elizabeth Warnock. *Guests of the Sheik: An Ethnography of an Iraqi Village.* Garden City, N.Y.: Doubleday Books, 1965.

Fetzer, Joel S. *Public Attitudes toward Immigration in the United States, France, and Germany.* New York: Cambridge University Press, 2000.

Foucault, Michel. *The History of Sexuality, Volume 1: An Introduction.* New York: Random House, 1978.

———. *Discipline and Punish: The Birth of the Prison.* New York: Vintage Books, 1979.

Freeman, Caren. "What's Love Got to Do with It? Transnational Marriages between China and Korea." Paper presented at the Association for Asian Studies Meeting, March 22–25, 2001, Chicago, Ill.

Gajjala, Radhika. "The SAWnet Refusal: An Interrupted Ethnography." Ph.D. diss., University of Pittsburgh, 1998.

———. "Cyborg Diaspora and Virtual Imagined Community: Study in SAWnet." *Cybersociology: Magazine for Social-Scientific Researchers of Cyberspace* 6 (1999). Available at http://www.cybersociology.com.

Giddens, Anthony. *The Transformation of Intimacy: Sexuality, Love and Eroticism in Modern Societies.* Stanford, Calif.: Stanford University Press, 1992.

———. "Family (Washington, D.C.)." *Runaway World,* BBC 1999 Reith Lectures. Available at http://news.bbc.co.uk/hi/english/static/events/reith_99/.

Gilmartin, Christina. "Gender, Politics, and Patriarchy in China: The Experiences of Early Women Communists, 1920–27." In *Promissory Notes: Women in the Transition to Socialism,* ed. Sonia Kruks, Rayna Rapp, and Marilyn Young, 82–105. New York: Monthly Review Press, 1989.

———. *Engendering the Chinese Revolution: Radical Women, Communist Politics, and Mass Movements in the 1920s.* Berkeley: University of California Press, 1995.

Gilmartin, Christina, and Lin Tan. "Fleeing Poverty: Rural Women, Expanding Marriage Markets, and Strategies for Social Mobility in Contemporary

China." In *Transforming Gender and Development in East Asia*, ed. Esther Ngan-ling Chow, 203–16. London: Routledge Press, 2002.

Glodava, Mila, and Richard Onizuka. *Mail-Order Brides: Women For Sale*. Fort Collins, Colo.: Alaken, 1994.

Goody, Jack. *Production and Reproduction: A Comparative Study of the Domestic Domain*. New York: Cambridge University Press, 1976.

———. *The East in the West*. New York: Cambridge University Press, 1996.

Griswold, Robert L. "The History and Politics of Fatherlessness." In *Lost Fathers: The Politics of Fatherlessness in America*, ed. Cynthia Daniels, 11–32. New York: St. Martin's Press, 1998.

Halualani, Rona Tamiko. "The Intersecting Hegemonic Discourses of an Asian Mail-Order Bride Catalog: Pilipina 'Oriental Butterfly' Dolls for Sale." *Women's Studies in Communication* 118, no. 1 (1995): 45–64.

Harris, Charles K. *After the Ball: Forty Years of Melody. An Autobiography*. New York: Frank-Maurice, 1926.

Heinonin, Tuula. "Connecting Family Resilience and Culture: Recreation and Leisure among Filipino-Canadians." *Philippine Sociological Review* 44 (1996): 210–21.

Holt, Elizabeth M. "Writing Filipina-Australian Bodies: The Discourse on Filipina Brides." *Philippine Sociological Review* 44 (1996): 58–78.

Honig, Emily, and Gail Hershatter. *Personal Voices: Chinese Women in the 1980s*. Stanford, Calif.: Stanford University Press, 1988.

Jacobson, David. "Contexts and Cues in Cyberspace: The Pragmatics of Naming in Text-Based Virtual Realities." *Journal of Anthropological Research* 52 (1996): 461–79.

———. "Doing Research in Cyberspace." *Field Methods* 11, no. 2 (1999): 127–45. Available at http://www.unet.brandeis.edu/~jacobson/Doing _Research.html.

———. "Impression Formation in Cyberspace: Online Expectations and Offline Experiences in Text-Based Virtual Communities." *Journal of Computer-Mediated Communication* 5, no. 1 (September 1999). Available at http://www.ascusc.org/jcmc/vol5/issue1/jacobson.html#Virtual Communities.

Jankowiak, William. "Introduction." In *Romantic Passion: A Universal Experience?* ed. W. Jankowiak, 1–19. New York: Columbia University Press, 1995.

———. "Romantic Passion in the People's Republic of China." In *Romantic Passion: A Universal Experience?* ed. W. Jankowiak, 166–83. New York: Columbia University Press, 1995.

Jankowiak, William, and E. Fischer. "A Cross-Cultural Perspective on Romantic Love." *Ethnology* 31, no. 2 (1992): 149–55.

Jedlicka, Davor. "American Men in Search of Oriental Brides: A Preliminary Survey Released as a Courtesy to the Survey Participants." Unpublished report, 1988.

Johnson, Kay Ann. *Women, the Family, and Peasant Revolution in China*. Chicago: University of Chicago Press, 1983.

Jolly, Margaret, and Lenore Manderson. "Introduction: Sites of Desire/Economies of Pleasure in Asia and the Pacific." In *Sites of Desire/Economies of Pleasure: Sexualities in Asia and the Pacific*, ed. Margaret Jolly and Lenore Manderson, 1–26. Chicago: University of Chicago Press, 1997.

Julag-Ay, Cecilia. "Correspondence Marriages between Filipinas and United States Men." Ph.D. diss., University of California, Riverside, 1997.

Kang, Laura Hyun Yi. "Si(gh)ting Asian/American Women as Transnational Labor." *Positions* 5, no. 2 (1997): 403–37.

Kearney, Michael. "The Local and the Global: The Anthropology of Globalization and Transnationalism." *Annual Review of Anthropology* 24 (1995): 547–65.

Kelsky, Karen. *Women on the Verge: Japanese Women, Western Dreams*. Durham, N.C.: Duke University Press, 2001.

Kempadoo, Kamala. "Slavery or Work? Reconceptualizing Third World Prostitution." *Positions* 7, no. 1 (1999): 225–37.

Kempadoo, Kamala, and Jo Doezema, eds. *Global Sex Workers: Rights, Resistance, Redefinition*. New York: Routledge, 1998.

Larsen, Wanwadee. *Confessions of a Mail Order Bride: American Life through Thai Eyes*. Far Hills, N.J.: New Horizon Press, 1989.

Lavely, William. "Marriage and Mobility under Rural Collectivism." In *Marriage and Inequality in Chinese Society*, ed. Rubie S. Watson and Patricia Buckley Ebrey, 286–312. Berkeley: University of California Press, 1991.

Lavie, Smadar, Kirin Narayan, and Renato Rosaldo, eds. *Creativity/Anthropology*. Ithaca, N.Y.: Cornell University Press, 1993.

Leach, Edmund. *Political Systems of Highland Burma*. London: G. Bell, 1954.

———. *Rethinking Anthropology*. London School of Economics Monographs on Social Anthropology, no. 22. London: Althone, 1961.

Leacock, Eleanor B., ed. *Myths of Male Dominance: Collected Articles on Women Cross-Culturally*. New York: Monthly Review Press, 1981.

Leahy, Patricia. *Female Migrant Labor in Asia—A Case Study of Filipina Domestic Workers in Hong Kong*. M.A. thesis, University of Hong Kong, 1990.

Lerner, Gerda. *The Creation of Patriarchy*. New York: Oxford University Press, 1986.

Lévi-Strauss, Claude. *Elementary Structures of Kinship*. Trans. James H. Bell, John R. von Sturmer, and Rodney Needham. Boston: Beacon Press, 1969.

Li Wai-ki Viki. *Seeking an Ideal Wife: Why Hong Kong Men Pursue Mainland Chinese Spouses*. M.A. thesis, Chinese University of Hong Kong, 2001.

Liang, Zhai, and Naomi Ito. "Intermarriage of Asian Americans in the New York Region: Contemporary Patterns and Future Prospects." *International Migration Review* 33, no. 4 (1999): 876–900.

Lowe, Lisa. *Immigrant Acts: On Asian American Cultural Politics*. Durham, N.C.: Duke University Press, 1996.

Lozada, Eriberto. "What It Means to be Hakka in Cyberspace: Diasporic Identity on the Internet." Paper presented at the Third Conference on Hakkaology, Singapore, November 1996. Available at http://blue.butler.edu/~eriberto/papers/cyberhak/cyberhak1/htm.

Lugones, Maria C., and Elizabeth V. Spelman. "Have We Got a Theory for You!" Women's Studies International Forum 6, no. 6 (1983): 573–81.

Mani, Lata. "Contentious Traditions: The Debate on Sati in Colonial India." Cultural Critique (fall 1987): 119–56.

Marchetti, Gina. Romance and the Yellow Peril: Race, Sex and Discursive Strategies in Hollywood Fiction. Berkeley: University of California Press, 1993.

Margold, Jane. "Forced Migration or Mobility Strategy? Assessing Transnational Marriages amidst the Global Marketing of Southeast Asian Brides." Paper Abstracts, Association for Asian Studies Meeting, 2001.

Mascia-Lees, Frances, and Nancy Johnson Black. Gender and Anthropology. Prospect Heights, Ill.: Waveland Press, 2000.

Massey, Doreen. Space, Place and Gender. Minneapolis: University of Minnesota Press, 1994.

McClintock, Anne. "Sex Workers and Sex Work: Introduction." Social Text 37 (winter 1993): 1-10.

Meng, Eddy. "Mail-Order Brides: Gilded Prostitution and the Legal Response." Michigan Journal of Law Reform 28 (1994): 197–248.

Miller, Daniel, and Don Slater. The Internet: An Ethnographic Approach. New York: Berg, 2000.

Mohanty, Chandra T. "Under Western Eyes: Feminist Scholarship and Colonial Discourses." In Third World Women and the Politics of Feminism, ed. Chandra T. Mohanty, Ann Russo, and Lourdes Torres, 51–80. Bloomington: Indiana University Press, 1991.

Montgomery, Heather. "Children, Prostitution, and Identity: A Case Study from a Tourist Resort in Thailand." In Global Sex Workers, ed. Kamala Kempadoo and Jo Doezema, 139–50. New York: Routledge Press, 1998.

Moore, Henrietta. Feminism and Anthropology. Minneapolis: University of Minnesota Press, 1988.

Narayan, Uma. "'Male-Order' Brides: Immigrant Women, Domestic Violence and Immigration Law." Hypatia 10, no. 1 (1995): 104–19.

Noh, Eliza. "'Amazing Grace, Come Sit on My Face': Or Christian Ecumenical Representations of the Asian Sex Tour Industry." Positions 5, no. 2 (1997): 439–65.

Norman, Marie. "Where the Buffalo Speak English: Tourism and Caste Dynamics in Pokhora, Nepal." Ph.D. diss., University of Pittsburgh, 1999.

Ong, Aihwa. "Women Out of China: Traveling Tales and Traveling Theories in Postcolonial Feminism." In Women Writing Culture, ed. Ruth Behar and Deborah Gordon, 350–72. Berkeley: University of California Press, 1995.

————. *Flexible Citizenship: The Cultural Logics of Transnationality.* Durham, N.C.: Duke University Press, 1999.

Ong, Aihwa, and Donald Nonini, eds. *Ungrounded Empires: The Cultural Politics of Modern Chinese Transnationalism.* New York: Routledge, 1997.

Ordonez, Raquel Z. "Mail-Order Brides: An Emerging Community." In *Filipino Americans: Transformation and Identity,* ed. Maria P. Root, 121–42. Thousand Oaks, Calif.: Sage Publications, 1997.

Oring, Elliott. *Jokes and Their Relations.* Lexington: University of Kentucky Press, 1992.

Ortner, Sherry. "Is Female to Male as Nature Is to Culture?" In *Woman, Culture, and Society,* ed. Michelle Rosaldo and Louise Lamphere, 67–88. Stanford, Calif.: Stanford University Press, 1974.

————. "Introduction: Accounting for Sexual Meanings." In *Sexual Meanings,* ed. S. Ortner and H. Whitehead, 1–27. Cambridge: Cambridge University Press, 1981.

————. "Resistance and the Problem of Ethnographic Refusal." *Comparative Studies of Society and History* 34, no. 1 (1995): 173–93.

Oxfeld, Ellen. "The Woman without a Daughter-in-Law: A New Balance of Power within Rural Chinese Families?" Paper presented at the Association for Asian Studies annual meeting, Boston, March 1999.

Pa Chin. *Family.* Prospect Heights, Ill.: Waveland Press, 1972 (1931).

Pace, David. "Beyond Morphology: Lévi-Strauss and the Analysis of Folktales." In *Cinderella: A Casebook,* ed. Alan Dundes. New York: Wildman Press, 1982.

Pan, Esther. "Why Asian Guys Are on a Roll." *Newsweek* 138, no. 8 (February 21, 2000): 50–51.

Panttaja, Elizabeth. "Going Up in the World: Class in 'Cinderella'" *Western Folklore* 52 (1993): 85–104.

Parish, William L., and James Farrer. "Gender and Family." In *Chinese Urban Life under Reform: The Changing Social Contract,* ed. Wenfang Tang and William L. Parish, 232–72. New York: Cambridge University Press, 1993.

Parkin, Robert. *Kinship: An Introduction to Basic Concepts.* Cambridge, Mass.: Blackwell Publishers, 1997.

Pflugfelder, Gregory M. *Cartographies of Desire: Male-Male Sexuality in Japanese Discourses, 1600–1950.* Berkeley: University of California Press, 1999.

Philippine Women Centre of British Columbia. *Canada: The New Frontier for Filipino Mail-Order Brides.* 2000. Available at web site of Status of Women Canada, http://www.swc-cfc.gc.ca/pube.html.

Pierce, Paulette. "Boudoir Politics and the Birthing of the Nation: Sex, Marriage, and Structural Deflection in the National Black Independent Party." In *Women Out of Place: The Gender of Agency and the Race of Nationality,* ed. Brackette Williams, 216–44. New York: Routledge, 1996.

Piper, Nicola. "International Marriage in Japan: 'Race' and 'Gender' Perspectives." *Gender, Place and Culture* 4, no. 3 (1997): 321–38.

Popenoe, David. "Life without Father." In *Lost Fathers: The Politics of Father-lessness in America*, ed. Cynthia R. Daniels, 33–50. New York: St. Martin's Press, 1998.

Preston, Cathy Lynn. " 'Cinderella' as a Dirty Joke: Gender, Multivocality, and the Polysemic Text." *Western Folklore* 53 (June 1994): 27–49.

Quinn, Naomi. "Anthropological Studies on Women's Status." *Annual Review of Anthropology* 6 (1977): 181–225.

Rabinow, Paul. *Reflections on Fieldwork in Morocco*. Berkeley: University of California Press, 1977.

Rafael, Vicente L. "White Love: Surveillance and Nationalist Resistance in the U.S. Colonization of the Philippines." In *Cultures of United States Imperialism*, ed. Amy Kaplan and Donald Pease, 185–218. Durham, N.C:. Duke University Press, 1993.

————. *White Love and Other Events in Filipino History*. Durham, N.C.: Duke University Press, 2000.

Ragoné, Helena. "Chasing the Blood Tie: Surrogate Mothers, Adoptive Mothers, and Fathers." In *Situated Lives, Gender and Culture in Everyday Life*, ed. Louise Lamphere, Helena Ragoné, and Patricia Zavella, 110–27. New York: Routledge Press, 1997.

Raheja, Gloria G., and Ann G. Gold. *Listen to the Heron's Words: Reimagining Gender and Kinship in North India*. Berkeley: University of California Press, 1994.

Rebhun, Linda Anne. *The Heart Is Unknown Country: Love in the Changing Economy of Northeast Brazil*. Stanford, Calif.: Stanford University Press, 1999.

Reimers, David M. *Still the Golden Door: The Third World Comes to America*. New York: Columbia University Press, 1992.

Rheingold, Howard. *Virtual Reality*. New York: Simon and Schuster, 1992.

————. "A Slice of Life in My Virtual Community." Electronic Frontier Foundation Archives. 1992. Available at http://www.eff.org/pub/Net_c"lture/virtual_community/slice_ of_ life.article.

Robinson, Kathryn. "Of Mail-Order Brides and 'Boys' Own' Tales: Representations of Asian-Australian Marriages." *Feminist Review* 52 (spring 1996): 53–68.

————. "Marriage Migration, Family Values, and the 'Global Ecumene.' " Paper presented at Migration and the "Asian Family" in a Globalizing World, Singapore, April 16–18, 2001.

Rofel, Lisa. *Other Modernities: Gendered Yearnings in China after Socialism*. Berkeley : University of California Press, 1999.

Rojas, Henry S. "Filipino Labor Export: A Comprehensive Analysis." In *Asian Labor Migration*. Appendix 1, 9–22. Hong Kong: Christian Conference of Asia, Urban Rural Mission, 1990.

Rosaldo, Michelle. "Woman, Culture, and Society: A Theoretical Overview." In *Woman, Culture, and Society*, ed. Michelle Rosaldo and Louise Lamphere, 17–42. Stanford, Calif.: Stanford University Press, 1974.

―――. "The Use and Abuse of Anthropology: Reflections on Feminism and Cross-Cultural Understanding." *Signs* 5, no. 3 (1980): 389–417.

Rosaldo, Renato. *Culture and Truth: The Remaking of Social Analysis.* Boston: Beacon Press, 1989.

Rosca, Ninotchka. "The Philippines's Shameful Export (Emigrant Women)." *The Nation* 260, no. 15 (April 17, 1995): 522–26.

Rouse, Roger. "Mexican Migration and the Social Space of Postmodernism." *Diaspora* 1 (1991): 8–23.

Rubin, Gayle. "The Traffic in Women: Notes on the 'Political Economy' of Sex." In *Toward an Anthropology of Women,* ed. Rayna R. Reiter, 157–210. New York: Monthly Review Press, 1974.

Rumbaut, Ruben. "Origins and Destinies: Immigration, Race, and Ethnicity in Contemporary America." In *Origins and Destinies: Immigration, Race, and Ethnicity in America,* ed. Silvia Pedraza and Ruben G. Rumbaut, 21–42. Boston: Wadsworth Publishing, 1996.

Sacks, Karen. "Engels Revisited: Women, the Organization of Production, and Private Property." In *Woman, Culture, and Society,* ed. Michelle Rosaldo and Louise Lamphere, 207–22. Stanford, Calif.: Stanford University Press, 1974.

Said, Edward. *Orientalism.* New York: Vintage Books, 1979.

Salyer, Lucy E. *Laws Harsh as Tigers: Chinese Immigrants and the Shaping of Modern Immigration Law.* Chapel Hill, N.C.: University of North Carolina Press, 1995.

Sato, T. *Mura to Kokusai Kekkon.* Tokyo: Nihon Hyoronsha, 1989.

Schein, Louisa. "The Consumption of Color and the Politics of White Skin in Post-Mao China." In *The Gender/Sexuality Reader,* ed. Roger N. Lancaster and Michaela Di Leonardo, 473–86. London: Routledge, 1997.

―――. "Forged Transnationality and Oppositional Cosmopolitanism." In *Transnationalism from Below,* ed. Michael Peter Smith and Luis Eduardo Guarnizo, 291–313. New Brunswick, N.J.: Transaction Publishers, 1998.

Scholes, Robert. "The Mail Order Bride Industry and Its Impact on Immigration." In *International Matchmaking Organizations: A Report to Congress* (Appendix A). 1999. Available at http://www.ins.usdoj.gov/graphics/aboutins/repsstudies.Mobrept_full.pdf.

Schusky, Ernest L. *Manual for Kinship Analysis.* New York: Southern Illinois University Press, 1983.

Scott, James C. *Weapons of the Weak: Everyday Forms of Peasant Resistance.* New Haven, Conn.: Yale University Press, 1985.

―――. *Domination and the Arts of Resistance: Hidden Transcripts.* New Haven, Conn.: Yale University Press, 1990.

Shih Shu-mei. "Gender and the Geopolitics of Desire: The Seduction of Mainland Women in Taiwan and Hong Kong Media." In *Spaces of Their Own,* ed. Mayfair Mei-hui Yang, 278–307. Minneapolis: University of Minnesota Press, 1999.

Silverblatt, Irene. "Women in States." *Annual Review of Anthropology* 17 (1988): 427–60.

Simons, Lisa Anne. "Mail Order Brides: The Legal Framework and Possibilities for Change." *Gender and Immigration,* ed. Gregory A. Kelson and Debra DeLaet, 127–43. New York: New York University Press, 1999.

———. "Marriage, Migration, and Markets: International Matchmaking and International Feminism." Ph.D. diss., University of Denver, 2001.

Small, Michael, and Dirk Matheson. "For Men Who Want an Old-fashioned Girl, the Latest Wedding March Is Here Comes the Asian Mail-Order Bride." *People Weekly,* September 16, 1985, 127–29.

Smith, Michael Peter, and Luis Eduardo Guarnizo, eds. *Transnationalism from Below.* Comparative Urban and Community Research, vol. 6. New Brunswick, N.J.: Transaction Publishers, 1998.

Spivak, Gayatri C. "Can the Subaltern Speak?" In *Marxism and the Interpretation of Culture,* ed. G. Nelson and L. Grossberg, 271–313. Urbana: University of Illinois Press, 1988.

Stacey, Judith. *Patriarchy and Socialist Revolution in China.* Berkeley: University of California Press, 1983.

———. "Can There Be a Feminist Ethnography?" In *Women's Words: The Feminist Practice of Oral History,* ed. S. B. Gluck and D. Patai, 111–19. New York: Routledge, 1990.

———. *In the Name of the Family: Rethinking Family Values in the Postmodern Age.* Boston: Beacon Press, 1996.

———. "Dada-ism in the 1990s: Getting Past Baby Talk about Fatherlessness." In *Lost Fathers: The Politics of Fatherlessness in America,* ed. Cynthia R. Daniels, 51–83. New York: St. Martin's Press, 1998.

Stoler, Ann. "Making Empire Respectable: The Politics of Race and Sexual Morality in Twentieth Century Colonial Cultures." *American Ethnologist* 12, no. 4 (1989): 642–58.

———. "Carnal Knowledge and Imperial Power: Gender, Race, and Morality in Colonial Asia." In *The Gender/Sexuality Reader,* ed. Roger N. Lancaster and Michaela Di Leonardo, 13–36. London: Routledge, 1997.

Stone, Linda. *Gender and Kinship: An Introduction.* Boulder, Colo.: Westview Press, 1997.

Stop-traffic. "UN Trafficking Protocol: Lost Opportunity to Protect the Rights of Trafficked Persons." 2000. Available at http://www.stop-traffic.org.news .html.

Strathern, Marilyn. "No Nature, No Culture: The Hagen Case." In *Nature, Culture and Gender,* ed. Carol MacCormack and Marilyn Strathern, 174–222. New York: Cambridge University Press, 1980.

———. "An Awkward Relationship: The Case of Feminism and Anthropology." *Signs* 12, no. 2 (1987): 276–92.

Suzuki, Nobue. "Between Two Shores: Transnational Projects and Filipina Wives in/from Japan." *Women's Studies International Forum* 23, no. 4 (2000): 431–44.

———. "Women Imagined, Women Imaging: Re/presentations of Filipinas in Japan Since the 1980s." *U.S.-Japan Women's Journal* 19 (2000): 142–75.

Tajima, Renee E. "Lotus Blossoms Don't Bleed: Images of Asian Women." In *Making Waves: An Anthology of Writings by and about Asian American Women,* ed. Asian Women United of California, 308–17. Boston: Beacon Press, 1989.

Takaki, Ronald. *Strangers from a Different Shore: A History of Asian Americans.* Rev. ed. New York: Little, Brown and Co., 1998.

Tolentino, Roland B. "Bodies, Letters, Catalogs: Filipinas in Transnational Space." *Social Text* 48, vol. 14, no. 3 (1996): 49–76.

Tsing, Anna Lowenhaupt. *In the Realm of the Diamond Queen: Marginality in an Out-of-the-Way Place.* Princeton, N.J.: Princeton University Press, 1993.

Turner, Patricia. *I Heard It through the Grapevine.* Berkeley: University of California Press, 1993.

Turner, Victor, and Edward Bruner, eds. *Anthropology of Experience.* Urbana: University of Illinois Press, 1986.

Tyner, James A. "Constructions of Filipina Migrant Entertainers." *Gender, Place and Culture* 3, no. 1 (1996): 77–93.

———. "Constructing Images, Constructing Policy: The Case of Filipina Migrant Performing Artists." *Gender, Place and Culture* 4, no. 1 (1997): 19–35.

U.S. Census Bureau (US-CB). "Census Brief 2000: From the Mideast to the Pacific: A Profile of the Nation's Asian Foreign-Born Population." U.S. Census Bureau; Department of Commerce, Economics and Statistics. September 2000: 1–2.

U.S. Department of Justice-Immigration and Naturalization Service (USDOJ-INS). "International Matchmaking Organizations: A Report to Congress." 1999. Available at http://www.ins.usdoj.gov/graphics/aboutins/repsstudies .Mobrept.htm.

———. "Legal Immigration, Fiscal Year 1997." In *Office of Policy and Planning, Statistics Branch, Annual Report, January 1999.* No.1 (1999): 1–13.

———. *Triennial Comprehensive Report on Immigration.* 1999. Available at http://www.ins.usdoj.gov.

———. "Adjustment of Status under Legal Immigration Family Equity (LIFE) Act Legalization Provision and LIFE Act Amendments Family Unity Provisions." *Federal Register: Rules and Regulations* 66 (106) (2001): 29661–82. Friday, June 1, 2001.

U.S. Department of State (USDOS), Bureau of Consular Affairs. "Tips for U.S. Visas: Fiancé(e)s." 1999. Available at http://travel.state.gov/visa;fiancee .html.

———. "The New K and V Visa Categories." 2001. Available at http:// travel.state.gov/vvisas/qualifying_for_the_k.html.

U.S. Embassy, Guangzhou, China. "Adopted Children Immigrant Visa Unit." 2001. Available at http://www.usembassy-china.org.cn/consulates/guang zhou/consular/acivu/acivu.htm.

Vance, S. Carole. "Innocence and Experience: Narratives of Trafficking in the World of Human Rights." Paper presented at the American Ethnological Society meetings, May 3–5, 2001, Montreal, Canada.

Vergara, Benito M. "Betrayal, Class Fantasies, and the Filipino Nation in Daly City." *Philippine Sociological Review* 44 (1996): 79–100.

Villapando, Venny. "The Business of Selling Mail-Order Brides." In *Making Waves: An Anthology of Writings by and about Asian American Women*, ed. Asian Women United of California, 318–27. Boston: Beacon Press, 1989.

Visweswaran, Kamala. *Fictions of Feminist Ethnography*. Minneapolis: University of Minnesota Press, 1994.

Watson, Rubie S. "Afterward: Marriage and Gender Inequality." In *Marriage and Inequality in Chinese Society*, ed. Rubie S. Watson and Patricia Buckley Ebrey, 347–68. Berkeley: University of California Press, 1991.

Whitta, R. "Courtships by Correspondence: Filipina Australian Arranged Marriages." M.S.P.D. thesis, University of Queensland, 1988.

Whyte, Martin King, and William L. Parish. *Urban Life in Contemporary China*. Chicago: University of Chicago Press, 1984.

Williams, Brackette. "Introduction: Mannish Women and Gender after the Act." In *Women Out of Place: The Gender of Agency and the Race of Nationality*, ed. Brackette Williams, 1–36. New York: Routledge University Press, 1996.

Wilson, Ara. "American Catalogues of Asian Brides." In *Anthropology for the Nineties*, ed. Johnetta Cole, 114–25. New York: Free Press, 1988.

Wolf, Margery. *The House of Lim: A Study of a Chinese Farm Family*. New York: Prentice Hall, 1968.

———. *Women and the Family in Rural Taiwan*. Stanford, Calif.: Stanford University Press, 1972.

Yang, Mayfair Mei-hui. *Gifts, Favors, and Banquets: The Arts of Social Relationships in China*. Ithaca, N.Y.: Cornell University Press, 1989.

———, ed. *Spaces of Their Own: Women's Public Sphere in Transnational China*. Minneapolis: University of Minnesota Press, 1999.

Yolen, Jane. "America's Cinderella." In *Cinderella: A Casebook*, ed. Alan Dundes, 294–306. New York: Wildman Press, 1982.

Yung, Judy. *Chinese Women in America: A Pictorial History*. Seattle: University of Washington Press, 1986.

———. *Unbound Feet: A Social History of Chinese Women in San Francisco*. Berkeley: University of California Press, 1995.

Zhang Longxi. "The Myth of the Other: China in the Eyes of the West." *Critical Inquiry* 15 (autumn 1989): 108–131.

Zipes, Jack. *Fairy Tales and the Arts of Subversion: The Classical Genre for Children and the Process of Civilization*. New York: Routledge, 1983.

Index

Abu-Lughod, Lila, 64, 83, 113
Abuse. *See* Domestic abuse
Adopted Children Immigrant Visa Unit, 211
Adoption, 117, 209. *See also under* Chinese
African women, 97–98
Age: of Chinese women, 16, 40, 43, 151; differences, 59, 77, 136, 137, 224, 239n31; of Filipinas, 16, 40, 43, 234n28, 239n31; limits, 107, 180; of marriage in China, 148, 159, 161, 249n3; of picture brides, 180; as unimportant, 142
Agency, 5, 9, 11, 30, 82, 89–90, 113–14; of Filipinas, 56; of global capitalists, 118; romanticized, 147; of sex workers, 89–90. *See also under* Women
Aguilar, Delia, 113–14
America. *See* United States
Anagnost, Ann, 108, 210–11, 212
Anderson, Benedict, 31–32
Annulment, 107, 121
Anthropology: critique of, 1. *See also* Ethnographer
Antimiscegenation laws, 181, 254n34
Antitrafficking, 55, 64; criticism of, 89. *See also* Trafficking
Appadurai, Arjun, 11, 32, 216
Appearance, 21–22, 224; of Chinese women, 44, 161, 171; fat, 100; slim-

ness and beauty, 101, 106; tattoos, 229n17; of western men, 22, 44, 136, 142–43, 206. *See also* Skin color
Asia, seamless image of, 83–84
Asian American, 92; citizenship, 176, 253n16; as foreigner within, 187; as model minority, 125, 213; naturalization of, 253n16. *See also* United States immigration
Asian exclusion, 179, 180
Asian men, 146, 171; attractiveness of, 251n28; as effeminate, 251n34
Asian Pacific Development Center, 69
Asian women: essentialized, 83, 96; as feminine, 96; in film, 13; listed by agencies, 38; as sexy, 95, 96, 133; stereotypes of, 13, 78, 90, 93, 96–97, 222; as traditional wives, 58, 78, 81–82, 94, 101, 130. *See also* Agency; Chinese women; Filipinas
Australia: Filipina brides in, 94, 247n17; marriage in, 38, 232n16; men from, 148

Barangay, 100
Belgrade: bombing of Chinese embassy, 125
Betrayal, 9, 50
Blackwell, Susana, 7, 87
Blackwell, Timothy, 6, 7, 87
Body: building, 221–22; types, 100–101. *See also* Appearance

Compositor:	G & S Typesetters, Inc.
Text:	10/13 Aldus
Display:	Aldus